# Aborigines
# in White
# Australia

A documentary history of the changing
attitudes of white Australians towards
Aborigines which covers the period
from convict settlement to the present
day. The documents are drawn from
contemporary newspapers, court
reports, government papers, private
journals and lectures. They illustrate
the whole range of white Australian
attitudes, from fear, contempt and
paternalism to genuine attempts
to help.

# Aborigines in White Australia

A DOCUMENTARY HISTORY OF THE
ATTITUDES AFFECTING OFFICIAL POLICY
AND THE AUSTRALIAN ABORIGINE, 1697-1973

Selected and Edited by
SHARMAN N. STONE

Heinemann Educational Books

Heinemann Educational Australia Pty Ltd
River House, 24 River Street, South Yarra, Victoria, 3141

Heinemann Educational Books Ltd
48 Charles Street, London, WIX 8AH

Printed in Australia at The Griffin Press, Adelaide
Registered in Australia for transmission through the post as a book

# Contents

Acknowledgements    10

The Selection of Extracts    11

**1**    The Sailing Explorers    13
1.1   1697. William Dampier    15
1.2   August 1770. Captain Cook    15

**2**    The First Penal Settlement    17
2.1   23 April 1787. Instructions to Captain Arthur Phillip    19
2.2   15 May 1788. Governor Phillip's first dispatch    19
2.3   9 July 1788. Governor Phillip's opinion of the Aborigines    21
2.4   10 July 1788. Major Ross's criticisms    22
2.5   30 October 1788. Governor Phillip's report on confrontations with Aborigines    22
2.6   18 November 1788. An officer's complaint    23
2.7   13 February 1790. Governor Phillip's dispatch    23
2.8   December 1790. Governor Phillip "makes an example" of ten Aborigines    24
2.9   May 1791. Captain Tench's observations    25

**3**    The Expansion of the Free Settlement    27
3.1   20 June 1797. Governor Hunter's dispatch to the Duke of Portland    31
3.2   2 January 1800. The trial of accused white men    31
3.3   2 January 1800. Accused white men    32
3.4   4 May 1816. Governor Lachlan Macquarie's proclamation to Aboriginals    33
3.5   20 July 1816. A proclamation of Native Outlawry    36
3.6   October 1832. Backhouse and Walker's observations at Flinders Island (1)    38
3.7   October 1832. Backhouse and Walker (2)    39
3.8   3 June 1837. Sir John Jeffcot's first speech    39
3.9   24 June 1837. George A. Robinson's report from Flinders Island    40
3.10   1837. Tasmanian Aboriginal School Students    43

**4**    Beyond the Limits of Location    45
4.1   21 January 1838. The establishment of the Protectorate    49
4.2   8 June 1838. The Memorial    50
4.3   23 June 1838. Sir George Gipps's reply to the Memorialists    51
4.4   25 April 1838-21 July 1838. Sir George Gipps's reply to Lord Glenelg    52
4.5   November 1838. The Myall Creek Massacre    54
4.6   19 December 1838. Sir George Gipps's report on murder trials    56
4.7   21 December 1838. The Principal Gaoler's letter    58
4.8   1838. Captain Maconochie's observations    58
4.9   1838 and 1845. Sir Thomas Mitchell's observations    62
4.10   21 May 1839. Sir George Gipps's notice to the commissioners    63
4.11   1 September 1839-29 February 1840. Assistant Protector Edward Stone Parker's first report    63
4.12   1840. Edward John Eyre's observations    66
4.13   December 1842. A missionary speaks of tribal warfare    67

4.14  14 August 1846. "The Blacks"    68
4.15  22 January 1852. The education of Aborigines    69
4.16  10 May 1854. Edward Stone Parker's lecture    70
4.17  1860. The Lord Bishop of Adelaide examined    75
4.18  9 May 1861. Royal Commission into the Native Police Force    75
4.19  14 May 1861. Royal Commission into the Native Police Force    78
4.20  22 May 1861. Royal Commission into the Native Police Force    80
4.21  27 June 1861. Royal Commission into the Native Police Force    81
4.22  8 July 1861. Royal Commission into the Native Police Force    82
4.23  20 August 1864. "The Distribution of Blankets to the Australian Natives"    84
4.24  12 July 1865. Gideon Lang's lecture    84
4.25  July 1865. A challenge to Mr. Lang's statements    87
4.26  5 August 1865. Mr. Cobham's amendment    88
4.27  15 August 1865. An article condemning the treatment of Queensland Aborigines    88
4.28  1 November 1876. "A skirmish near Creen Creek, Queensland"    89
4.29  24 March 1877. The objections of "A Mistake Creek Man"    89
4.30  24 March 1877. A letter from "Outsider"    90
4.31  1 May 1880. "The Way We Civilise"    93
4.32  15 May 1880. "Sydney Aborigines, Past and Present"    94
4.33  4 September 1880. "Black Vs. White"    95
4.34  15 July 1882. "Deputation of Blackfellows at Parliament House"    98
4.35  26 December. 1884. "Ration Day"    99
4.36  1888. Alexander Sutherland's justification for killing Victorian Aborigines    99
4.37  13 December 1889. A. W. Howitt, on the Aboriginal tribe    101

5    The Aborigines in the Work Force    103
5.1  14 January 1892. Western Australian debate on settler's protection    107
5.2  5 March 1898. Mounted Constable Thorpe's report    110
5.3  1899. Mr. Paul Foelsche's report    114
5.4  21 September 1899. Select Committee inquiry: J. L. Parson's evidence    117
5.5  4 October 1899. Select Committee inquiry: F. J. Gillen's evidence    119
5.6  29 December 1904. Commissioner W. E. Roth's findings    121

6    The Twentieth Century and a New Deal for Aborigines    133
6.1  12 February 1913. W. E. Dalton's comments    135
6.2  20 May 1913. W. Baldwin Spencer's new policy    136
6.3  23 July 1913. E. C. Stirling's comments    146
6.4  1913. South Australian Royal Commission on Aborigines: committee report    148
6.5  6 August 1926. Reverend Gribble's report    149
6.6  1927. Reverend Gribble's suggestions    152
6.7  4 May 1927. "Aborigines. A Dying Race, Grave Charges Laid Against the Whites"    153
6.8  1928. J. W. Bleakley's conclusions    154
6.9  24 January 1935. Commissioner H. D. Moseley's report    166
6.10  22 November 1937. R. R. Brain's report    170
6.11  December 1937. Donald Thomson's recommendations    175
6.12  1937. Ration allowances on Government Settlements in New South Wales    176
6.13  1937. Powers and duties of the Aborigines' Protection Board of New South Wales    177
6.14  1937. Public Service Board's General Policy recommendations    179
6.15  13 July 1938. Citizen's rights of Aborigines    180
6.16  7 December 1939. Politicians discuss the Native Compound at Darwin    181
6.17  30 June 1943. Aboriginal Employment    183
6.18  December 1944. Newsletter from the Ernabella Mission for Aborigines, South Australia    183
6.19  1944. A Certificate of Citizenship    184

**7**   Becoming an Australian Citizen   187

7.1   8 June 1950. Mr. P. Hasluck's speech   191
7.2   18 October 1951. Mr. Hasluck's report on the Native Welfare
       Conference   193
7.3   1961. A Select Committee's recommended changes to the existing law
       regarding the voting rights of Aborigines   197
7.4   1962-1967. South Australian legislation on Aboriginal reserves and
       institutions, treatment of diseases, and employment   200
7.5   12 July 1963. The Policy of Assimilation   201
7.6   1963. Petition of the Yirrkala people   203
7.7   1963. Commonwealth policy on Aboriginal reserves   203
7.8   8 April 1964. Mr. Beazley comments   205
7.9   29 July 1965. "Aborigines on Stations"   207
7.10  29 September 1966. "Aboriginal Settlement at Lake Tyers"   207
7.11  20 June 1967. "Poverty among Aborigines of the Murray Valley"   207
7.12  30 April 1968. A Parliamentary question on "Black Power"   209
7.13  9 August 1968. Mr. P. J. Nixon's statement   209
7.14  13 August 1968. Mr. Whitlam's comments   211
7.15  11 January 1969. An Aborigine attacks white attitudes (1)   214
7.16  27 January 1969. An Aborigine attacks white attitudes (2)   214
7.17  4 March 1969. Mr. Wentworth's reply   215
7.18  April 1969. "What Does the Future Hold?"   216
7.19  1969. Dr. H. C. Coombs' statement   216
7.20  18 September 1969. Mr. Wentworth's statement   217
7.21  18 March 1970. Senator Keeffe's statement   218
7.22  30 June 1970. The Queensland Director of Aborigine and Islander Affairs'
       Annual Report   219
7.23  4 November 1970. Abschol's summary of the Aborigines and Torres Strait
       Islanders' Affairs Act, 1965   219
7.24  4 November 1970. Senator Keeffe's complaint   226
7.25  4 November 1970. Senator Gair's comments   227
7.26  4 November 1970. Dame Annebelle Rankin's motion   229
7.27  1970. "A Letter to the Editor"   229
7.28  18 March 1971. Aborigines' communication to the United Nations   230
7.29  15 September 1971. "The Shaping of a New Aboriginal Policy in South
       Australia"   231
7.30  23 August 1972. No race within a race for Australia   236
7.31  26 October 1972. Racially discriminating legislation   236
7.32  16 May 1973. Plans for an Aboriginal Consultative Council   237
7.33  29 May 1973. Responsibility for Aborigines, Federal Cabinet approved
       Takeover   238

# List of Plates

12      1824. "Sydney waters are occupied by European vessels and Native canoes."
Reference: Voyage De Decouvertes Aux Terres Australes. Historique Atlas par MM. Lesueur et Petit. Seconde edition. Paris, 1824.
*Latrobe Library Collection. State Library of Victoria.*

13      1824. "A Native camp overlooks the English tents at Sydney Town."
Reference: Ibid.

14      1773. A sketch by Sidney Parkinson, a draftsman on Cook's first voyage to Australia, published in 1773 in J. Hawksworth's (ed) *An account of the voyages . . . for making discoveries in the southern hemisphere.*
Reference: *Discoverers of Australia* by Alf and Shirley Sampson, Golden Press.

18      Engraving, drawn and engraved by J. Carmichael. J. Carmichael, *Select Views of Sydney*, Sydney, 1829, plate 6; National Library of Australia, Canberra.
". . . a view of Sydney from the south at the toll gate on the Parramatta road, where are represented a few of the houseless inhabitants of the forest accompanied by their Chief—Bungaree."

26      Mid 1860's. "Victorian Aborigines pose in a studio, displaying their weapons."
Reference: J. W. Lindt Photograph.
*Latrobe Library Collection. State Library of Victoria.*

28      1860's. "Tommy and Biddy, Members of the Molka Tribe, Victoria".
*Latrobe Library Collection. State Library of Victoria.*

29      Mid 1860's. "Three Victorian women and a child pose in a studio with string bags and digging sticks."
Reference: J. W. Lindt Photograph.
*Latrobe Library Collection. State Library of Victoria.*

29      1850's. "The last of the Tasmanian Aborigines, at Oyster Cove."
*Latrobe Library Collection. State Library of Victoria.*

30      1870's. "Residents of the Coranderrk Aboriginal Settlement, Healsville, Victoria."
*Latrobe Library Collection. State Library of Victoria.*

46      1880's. "Native police encampment."
*Latrobe Library Collection. State Library of Victoria.*

47      1864. "Distribution of blankets to the Australian Natives." (Document 4.29).
Reference: The Illustrated Melbourne Post, Adelaide Edition. 20 August 1864.
*Latrobe Library Collection. State Library of Victoria.*

47 1884. "Ration Day". Document 4.35.
Reference: The Illustrated Australian News. 6th December. 1884. p. 210.
*Latrobe Library Collection. State Library of Victoria.*

47 1882. "Deputation of Blackfellows at Parliament House." (Document 4.34).
Reference: Supplement to the Leader, Melbourne, 15 July 1882.
*Latrobe Library Collection. State Library of Victoria.*

48 1880. "Sydney Aboriginals—Past and Present." (Document 4.32).
Reference: The Illustrated Sydney News, and the New South Wales Agriculturist and Grazier, 15 May 1880, p. 23.
*Latrobe Library Collection. State Library of Victoria.*

104 1911. "The Last of the Tribe.—King Brown and Queen—Tewantin."
*Queensland Parliamentary Papers, Vol. 3, 1912.*

105 1911. "King George VI, of Ravensbourne, Cedar Creek, receiving blanket from Protector at Herberton."
*Queensland Parliamentary Papers, Vol. 3, 1912.*

106 1950's. "An Aboriginal stockman from the Northern Territory."
*The Age, Melbourne.*

134 1914. "An elderly Aboriginal outside his shelter at Lake Tyers Aboriginal Settlement, Victoria."
*The Ministry of Aboriginal Affairs, Melbourne.*

134 1950's. "Cooking in the kitchen of a house at Lake Tyers Aboriginal Settlement."
*The Ministry of Aboriginal Affairs, Melbourne.*

186 1966. "An Aboriginal child takes a bath". (Document 7.9).
*The Sun, Melbourne, 28 September 1966, p. 1.*

186 1967. "Aboriginal Settlement at Dareton, New South Wales." (Document 7.11).
*The Sun, Melbourne, 20 June 1967, p. 8.*

188 1965. "King Brumby". (Document 7.8).
*The Sun, Melbourne, 29 July 1965, p. 32.*

188 1971. "A woman at the Yalata Aboriginal Reserve, South Australia, eats kangaroo meat."
*Mrs. I. M. White, Monash University.*

188 1971. "A woman and children at Yalata Aboriginal Reserve, South Australia."
*Mrs. I. M. White, Monash University.*

189 1971. "Pre-school-aged children receiving their daily ration of cereal, milk and vitamins. Yalata Aboriginal Reserve, South Australia."
*Mrs. I. M. White, Monash University.*

189 1967. "Demonstration supporting the Aborigines' Land Rights Claim, Melbourne."
*The Age, Melbourne, 1967.*

190 1972. "Aboriginal school children enjoy an art lesson."
*The Ministry of Aboriginal Affairs, Melbourne.*

# Acknowledgements

Extracts included in this volume were copied from collections in the following institutions; without the invaluable assistance of their various staff members this book would not have been possible. The Melbourne Public Library, especially the Latrobe Public Library and Archives; the Mitchell Library, Sydney, the National Library, Canberra; the David Derham School of Law Library, Monash University; and the Centre for Research into Aboriginal Affairs, Monash University.

Photographs were generously made available by Mrs. I. M. White, Department of Anthropology and Sociology, Monash University, The Ministry of Aboriginal Affairs, The Herald and Weekly Times Ltd, Melbourne, The Age, Melbourne and the historical collection of the Latrobe Public Library, Victoria. I sincerely thank these persons and organisations for their contributions.

SHARMAN STONE

# The Selection of Extracts

The following documents were selected for their ability to represent both the private and official views on aborigines commonly held in Australia since the coming of Europeans. The only pre-requisite for selection was that at the time of statement, the views were made readily available to the reading public. Thus all attitudes, whether expressed by a Queensland Native Policeman or an assigned servant, have at some time previously been presented unashamedly in print.

*Below*
1824. Sydney waters occupied by European vessels and Native canoes.
*Latrobe Collection.*

*Right*
1824. A Native camp overlooks the English tents at Sydney Town.
*Latrobe Collection.*

# 1

# The Sailing Explorers

The British first heard of the inhabitants of Australia from the journals of the sailing explorers.

William Dampier and later James Cook met with the same culture, but their interpretations of what they saw reflect the altered notions of European society as well as their differing personalities.

Dampier reported that the natives, lacking any of the refinements necessary for dignified human existence, were closest to the "brutes". Captain Cook reported instead that their idyllic simplicity and peaceful relationship with the environment left the Aborigines completely content (1.1 and 1.2).

It was Cook's writings, along with those of other expedition members, which largely influenced the British Government when planning the policy to be adopted towards the natives of New South Wales, and the locality of the penal settlement.

1773. A sketch by Sidney Parkinson, a draftsman on Cook's first voyage to Australia, published in 1773 in J. Hawksworth's (ed) *An account of the voyages . . . for making discoveries in the southern hemisphere.*

## 1.1  1697. William Dampier.

(William Dampier, *A New Voyage Round the World*, N. M. Penzer (ed.),
The Argonaut Press, London, 1927. Entry 1688, Chapter xvi, pp 312, 313, 315.)

*Dampier's book was a best seller in the seventeenth and early eighteenth
centuries. It was an often-quoted authority.*

The inhabitants of this country are the miserablest people in the world . . .
(they) have no Houses and skin Garments, no Sheep, Poultry, and Fruits
of the Earth, Ostrich Eggs etc . . . and setting aside the Human Shape they
differ but little from the Brutes . . . they have no Cloathes . . . their only
food is a kind of fish . . . I did not perceive that they did worship anything.
is a piece of wood shaped somewhat like a cutlass. . . .
These poor creatures have a sort of Weapon to protect their Ware . . .
Some of them had wooden Swords, others had a sort of lance. The sword
(As the ship was short of fresh water, Dampier attempted to get the Natives
to carry some for him in return for some proffered clothing.)

But all the signs we could make were to no purpose, for they stood like
Statues, with no motion but grinned like so many monkeys. Staring one upon
the other, for these poor creatures were not accustomed to carry Burthens
. . . so we were forced to carry our water ourselves and they very fairly put
the Cloathes off again as if Cloathes were only to work in.

I did not perceive that they had any great liking to them at first, nor
did they seem to admire anything that we had.

## 1.2  August 1770. Captain Cook.

(W. J. L. Wharton (ed.), "Captain Cook's Journal during the First Voyage
Round the World made in H. M. Bark 'Endeavour', 1768-1771." A literal
transcription of the MSS Elliot Stock, London, 1893. Australian Facsimile
Editions No. 188, Adelaide, Libraries Board of South Australia, 1968, p. 323.)

*The observations of the Australian Aborigines, entered into Captain James
Cook's Journal in August 1770.*

From what I have seen of the Natives of New Holland they may appear to
some to be the most wretched People upon Earth; but in reality they are far
more happier than we Europeans, being wholly unacquainted not only with
the superfluous, but with the necessary Conveniences so much sought after
in Europe; they are happy in not knowing the use of them. They live in a
Tranquility which is not disturbed by the inequality of Condition. The Earth
and Sea of their own accord furnishes them with all things necessary for
Life. They covet not Magnificent Houses, Household stuff, etc; they live in a
Warm and fine Climate, and enjoy every Wholesome Air, so that they seem
to be fully sensible of, for many to whom we gave Cloth, etc, left it carelessly upon the Sea Beach, and in the Woods, as a thing they had no
manner of use for; in short they seemed to set no Value upon anything of
their own nor any one Article we could offer them. This in my opinion
Argues, that they think themselves provided with all the necessarys of Life,
and that they have no Superfluities.

# 2

# The First Penal Settlement

In May 1787 a fleet of English ships sailed for Botany Bay carrying more than a thousand convicts, marines, officers, and their staff. Captain Arthur Phillip was in command, and his orders were to establish a self-supporting prison farm on the shores of the country described by James Cook.

Phillip carried with him instructions from the Royal Commission directing that the natives of the region be treated with the fairness and respect due to all British subjects (2.1). He determined to carry out this policy, and was impressed by the behaviour of the Aborigines who greeted the ships (2.2).

As it became apparent that the settlement was permanent, that bush was being cleared, native animals were being dispersed, and fish caught, misunderstandings and anxiety between the two races grew. Soon theft of hunting equipment, diseases and malnutrition forced the tribes as far inland as their territory permitted (2.3-2.5).

The extreme physical hardships faced by freemen and convicts alike made many doubly afraid and suspicious of the mysterious vanishing natives (2.6). Those who contacted tribesmen in the interior continued to be impressed by their generosity and intelligence (2.9).

After battling for several years in the settlement, Phillip appeared to lose his initial sympathy for and understanding of the Aborigine's plight. Although the murder of his personal gamekeeper was probably deserved, he ordered any ten natives caught to be beheaded (2.8).

Having located the rivers and potential grazing lands Phillip no longer required the friendly co-operation of the local Aborigines. Some of the dispossessed remnants of local tribes came to beg for food and shelter in the town; others continued to fight for their territory at the limits of the settlement.

Engraving, drawn and engraved by J. Carmichael. J. Carmichael, *Select Views of Sydney,* Sydney, 1829. plate 6; National Library of Australia, Canberra.
". . . A view of Sydney from the south at the toll gate on the Parramatta road, where are represented a few of the houseless inhabitants of the forest accompanied by their Chief—Bungaree."

## 2.1  23 April 1787. Instructions to Captain Arthur Phillip.

(G. B. Barton, *History of New South Wales from the Records*, Government Printer, 1889. Vol. 1, p. 485.)

*"Instructions for Our trusty and well beloved Arthur Phillip esquire, our Captain General and Governor in Chief in and over the territory of New South Wales and its dependencies, . . . Given at our Court at St. James the 23rd day of April, 1787, in the 27the year of our reign. George R."*

You are to endeavour by every possible means to open an intercourse with the natives, and to conciliate their affections, enjoining all our subjects to live in amity and kindness with them. And if any of our subjects shall wantonly destroy them, or give them any unnecessary interruption in the exercise of their several occupations, it is our will and pleasure that you do cause such offenders to be brought to punishment according to the degree of the offence. You will endeavour to procure an account of the numbers inhabiting the neighbourhood of the intended settlement, and to report your opinion to our secretaries of State in what manner our intercourse with the people may be turned to the advantage of this colony.

## 2.2  15 May 1788. Governor Phillip's first dispatch.

(*Historical Records of New South Wales*, Government Printer, 1897. Vol. 1, part 2, pp. 128, 129, 131.)

*Four months after his arrival in Botany Bay, Phillip sent his first dispatch to the Home Secretary, Lord Sydney. In it he described the native inhabitants.*

With respect to the natives, it was my determination from my first landing that nothing less than the most absolute necessity should ever make me fire upon them, and tho' persevering in this resolution has at times been rather difficult, I have hitherto been so fortunate that it never has been necessary. Mons. La Perouse, while at Botany Bay, was not so fortunate. He was obliged to fire on them, in consequence of which, with the bad behaviour of some of the transports' boats and some convicts, the natives have lately avoided us, but proper measures are taken to regain their confidence.

When I first landed in Botany Bay the natives appeared on the beach, and were easily persuaded to receive what was offered them, and, tho' they came armed, very readily returned the confidence I placed in them by going to them alone and unarmed, most of them laying down their spears when desired; and while the ships remained in Botany Bay no dispute happened between our people and the natives. They were all naked, but seemed fond of ornaments, putting the beads or red baize that were given them round their heads or necks. Their arms and canoes being described in "Captain Cook's Voyage," I do not trouble your Lordship with any description of them.

When I first went in the boats to Port Jackson the natives appeared armed near the place at which we landed, and were very vociferous, but, like the others, easily persuaded to accept what was offered them, and I persuaded one man, who appeared to be the chief or master of the family, to go with me to that part of the beach where the people were boiling their meat. When he came near the marines, who were drawn up near the place, and saw that by proceeding he should be separated from his companions, who remained with several officers at some distance, he stopped, and with great firmness seemed by words and acting to threaten if they offered to take any advantage of his situation. He then went on with me to examine what was boiling in the pot, and exprest his admiration in a manner that made me believe he intended to profit from what he saw, and which I made him understand he might very easily by the help of some oyster-shells. I believe they know no other way of dressing their food but by broiling, and they are seldom seen without a fire, or a piece of wood on fire, which they carry with them from place to place, and in their canoes, so that I apprehend they find some difficulty in procuring fire by any other means with which they are acquainted. The boats, in passing near a point of land in the harbour, were seen by a number of men, and twenty of them waded into the water unarmed, received what was offered them, and examined the boats with a curiosity that gave me a much higher opinion of them than I had formed from the behaviour of those seen in Captain Cook's voyage, and their confidence and manly behaviour made me give the name of Manly Cove to this place. The same people afterwards joined us where we dined; they were all armed with lances, two with shields and swords—the latter made of wood, the gripe small, and I thought less formidable than a good stick. As their curiosity made them very troublesome when we were preparing our dinner, I made a circle round us. There was little difficulty in making them understand that they were not to come within it, and they then sat down very quiet. . . .

When the south branch of Broken Bay was first visited we had some difficulty in getting round the headland that separates the two branches, having very heavy squalls of wind and rain, and where we attempted to land there was not sufficient water for the boat to approach the rocks, on which were standing an old man and a youth. They had seen us labour hard to get under the land, and after pointing out the deepest water for the boats, brought us fire, and going with two of the officers to a cave at some distance, the old man made use of every means in his power to make them go in with him, but which they declined; and this was rather unfortunate, for it rained hard, and the cave was the next day found to be sufficiently large to have contained us all, and which he certainly took great pains to make them understand. When this old man saw us prepare for sleeping on the ground, and clearing away the bushes, he assisted, and was the next morning rewarded for his friendly behaviour. Here we saw a woman big with child that had not lost the joints of the little finger.

When we returned, two days afterwards, to the spot where the old man had been so friendly he met us with a dance and a song of joy. His son was with him. A hatchet and several presents were made them, and as I intended to return to Port Jackson the next day every possible means were taken to secure his friendship; but when it was dark he stole a spade, and was caught in the fact. I thought it necessary to show that I was displeased with him, and therefore when he came to me, pushed him away, and gave him two or three slight slaps on the shoulder with the open hand, at the same time pointing to the spade. This destroyed our friendship in a moment, and seizing a spear he came close up to me, poised it, and appeared determined to strike; but whether from seeing that his threats were not regarded—for I chose rather to risk the spear than fire on him—or from anything the other natives said who surrounded him, after a few moments he dropped his spear and left us. This circumstance is mentioned to show that they do not want personal courage, for several officers and men were then near me. He returned the next morning with several others, and seemed desirous of being taken notice of; but he was neglected, whilst hatchets and several other articles were given to the others.

## 2.3  9 July 1788. Governor Phillip's opinion of the Aborigines.

(*Ibid.*, Vol. 1, part 2, pp. 146, 148, 150.)

*Although convicts are being killed, Governor Phillip finds the Aborigines trusting and friendly.*

One of the convicts who, in searching for vegetables, had gone a considerable distance from the camp, returned very dangerously wounded in the back by a spear. He denies having given the natives any provocation, and says that he saw them carrying away a man that had gone out for the same purpose, and who they had wounded on the head. A shirt and hat, both pierced with spears, have been since found in one of the natives' huts, but no intelligence can be got of the man, and I have not any doubt but that the natives have killed him, nor have I the least doubt of the convicts being the aggressors. . . .

The 30th of May two men employed collecting thatch at some distance from the camp were found dead; one of them had four spears in him, one of which had passed through his body; the other was found at some distance dead, but without any apparent injury. This was a very unfortunate circumstance, and the more, as it will be impossible to discover the people who committed the murder, and I am still persuaded the natives were not the aggressors. These men had been seen with one of their canoes, but I was not informed of that circumstance for some days. Though I did not mean to punish any of the natives for killing these people, which, it is more than probable, they did in their own defence, or in defending their canoes, I wished to see them, and as they had carried away the rushcutters' tools, I thought they might be found out, and some explanation take place, for which purpose I went out with a small party the next day, and landed where the men were killed; but traversing the country more than twenty miles we got to the north shore of Botany Bay without meeting any of the natives. There we saw about twenty canoes fishing. It was then sunset, and as we made our fires and slept on the beach I did not doubt but some of them would join us, but not one appeared; and the next morning, tho' fifty canoes were drawn up on the beach, we could not find a single person; but on our return, keeping for some time near the sea-coast, we came to a cove where a number of the natives were assembled, I believe more than what belonged to that particular spot. Though we were within ten yards when we first discovered each other, I had barely time to order the party to halt before numbers appeared in arms, and the foremost of them, as he advanced, made signs for us to retire, but upon my going up to him, making signs of friendship, he gave his spear to another, and in less than three minutes we were surrounded by two hundred and twelve men, numbers of women and children were at a small distance, and whether by their superiority of numbers, for we were only twelve, or from their not being accustomed to act with treachery, the moment the friendship I offered was accepted on their side they joined us, most of them laying down their spears and stone hatchets with the greatest confidence, and afterwards brought down some of their women to receive the little articles we had to give them. I saw nothing to induce me to believe these people had been concerned in the murther which had been committed. We parted on friendly terms, and I was now more than ever convinced of the necessity of placing a confidence in these people as the only means of avoiding a dispute. Had I gone up to them with all the party, though only twelve, or hestitated a moment, a lance would have been thrown, and it would have been impossible to have avoided a dispute.

Here we saw the finest stream of fresh water I have seen in this country, but the cove is open to the sea. When the natives saw we were going on towards the next cove, one of them, an old man, made signs to let him go first, and as soon as we were at the top of the hill he called out, holding up both his hands (a sign of friendship) to the people in the next cove, giving them to understand that we were friends; we did not go to that cove, but saw about forty men; so that, unless these people had assembled on some particular occasion, the inhabitants are still more numerous than I had imagined. I have before had the honor of observing to your Lordship that we had traced the natives thirty miles inland, and this morning, in crossing the hills between Botany Bay and Port Jackson, we saw smoke on the top of Landsdowne Hills, so that I think there cannot be any doubt of there being inhabitants fifty miles inland. . . .

A convict who had committed a robbery, and absconded the 5th of June, returned the 24th, almost starved; he found it impossible to subsist in the woods. One of the natives gave him a fish, but then made signs for him to go away. He says he afterwards joined a party of the natives, who would have burned him, but that he got away from them, and that he saw the remains of a human body on the fire. In the woods he saw four of the natives who were dying, and who made signs for food. This man was tried, pleaded guilty, and suffered with another convict. He persisted in the story respecting the natives intending to burn him, and I now believe they find the procuring a subsistence very difficult, for little fish is caught.

## 2.4   10 July 1788. Major Ross's criticisms.

(*Ibid.*, Vol. 1, part 2, p. 171.)

*With the officers and men of the marine corps under his command, Major R. Ross complains bitterly of the harsh, unyielding country, and the work that Phillip required them to do.*

Here, in justice to myself and the detachment under my command, I must observe to their Lordships that the detachment is at this hour without any kind of place of defence to retire to in case of an alarm or surprize, tho' I have, in justice to myself, repeatedly mention'd and urged his Excellency to get something or other errected for that purpose. Indeed, a surprize seems to me, from all I have seen, to be the only danger we have to apprehend. The natives, tho' in number near us, shew no inclination to any kind of inter-course with us, for ever since our arrival there has not one of them come near us on this side, and only two, who had been known at Botany Bay, visited the other side soon after our arrival.

Tho' we have had little or no opportunity of coming at their real disposi-tions and character, yet I am by no means of opinion that they are that harmless, inoffensive race they have in general been represented to be, and my suspicions have in some measure been confirm'd by an event that Captn. Campbell met with a few weeks past. Being out with a party, he met with the bodies of two of the convicts (who had been sent out to cut thatch for covering in the store-house), who had been most barbarously mangled and murther'd by the natives. One of the bodies had no less than seven spears in it, some of which went through and through, and the skulls of both were fractured. What appears very extraordinary is that they took away no part of the provisions or cloths belonging to the unfortunate men, but the whole of their working implements had been carried off.

## 2.5  30 October 1788. Governor Phillip's report on confrontations with Aborigines.

Governor Phillip reports to Lord Sydney. (*Ibid.*, Vol. 1, part 2, p.208.)

*The confrontation between the convicts and Aborigines after ten months in the settlement was growing. Amongst the British, food and other goods were critically short.*

. . . It is still a doubt whether the cattle we lost have been killed by the natives, or if they have strayed into the country. I fear the former, and am sorry to say that the natives now attack any straggler they meet unarmed; and though the strictest orders have been given to keep the convicts within bounds, neither the fear of death or punishment prevents their going out in the night; and one has been killed since the Sirius sailed. The natives, who appear strictly honest amongst themselves, leave their fizgigs, spears, &c., on the beach, or in their huts, when they go a-fishing; these articles have been taken from them by the convicts, and the people belonging to the transports buy them at the risk of being prosecuted as receivers of stolen goods, if discovered. The natives, as I have observed, revenge themselves on any they meet unarmed; it is not possible to punish them without punishing the innocent with the guilty, and our own people have been the aggressors.

The natives still refuse to come amongst us, and those who are supposed to have murthered several of the convicts have removed from Botany Bay, where they have always been more troublesome than in any other part. I now doubt whether it will be possible to get any of these people to remain with us, in order to get their language, without using force; they see no advantage that can arise from us that may make amends for the loss of that part of the harbour in which we occasionally employ the boats in fishing.

## 2.6  18 November 1788. An officer's complaint.

(G. B. Barton, *op. cit.*, p. 505.)

*A disgruntled officer of the Marine Corps writes a long letter to Sir Joseph Banks hoping for some sympathetic consideration. In it he lists the Aborigines as a source of annoyance.*

The natives do not appear numerous but the most wretched of the human race; they are dressed in nature's garb, subsisting chiefly on fish and roots we are unacquainted with; they inhabit chiefly the cavities of rocks and trees; their miserable huts which are few, are constructed of the bark of trees.

They do not wish to cultivate our acquaintance or friendship; they are treacherous, for they have murdered several convicts and one marine besides wounding many more; indeed they attack every person they meet unarmed; this is what induces me to call them treacherous. . . .

We have laboured incessantly since we arrived here to raise all sorts of vegetables, and even at this distant period we can barely supply our tables, his excellency not excepted. This together with the miserable state of the natives and scarcity of animals are convincing proof of the badness of the country. . . . Every gentleman here, two or three excepted concurs with me in opinion, and sincerely wish that the expedition may be recalled.

## 2.7  13 February 1790. Governor Phillip's dispatch.

(*Historical Records of New South Wales, op. cit.,* Vol. 1, part 2, p. 308.)

*In a further dispatch to Lord Sydney, Phillip speaks of his attempts to be-friend the Aborigines, and the high incidence of diseases among them.*

I have always found the natives friendly, and still retain the opinion I first formed of those people. That they do not betray a confidence placed in them I have reason to believe from their never having attempted to take that advantage which they might have done from the confidence which has been frequently placed in them by myself and those who have been with me in the different excursions, and from the confidence some of them have placed in us; nor do I believe they would have ever been hostile but from having been ill-used and robbed, which has been the case, though every precaution that was possible has been taken to prevent it.

In December, 1788, one of the natives was seized for the purpose of learning the language and reconciling them to us (as mentioned in my former letter to your Lordship), none of the natives having for some months come near the settlement. The man who was taken for that purpose appeared to be about twenty-four years of age, and in three months was so well reconciled that he was freed from all restraint, and lived with me perfectly satisfied with his situation.

In the beginning of the following April numbers of the natives were found dead with the small-pox in different parts of the harbour; and an old man and a boy of about eight years of age were brought to the hospital. The man died, but the boy recovered, and now lives with the surgeon. An elderly man and a girl of about ten or eleven years of age were found soon after and brought up; of the man there was no hopes of recovery, and he died the third day, but the girl recovered, and lives with the clergyman's wife. I brought these people up with the hopes that being cured and sent away with the many little necessaries we could give them would be the means of reconciling them to live near us; but unfortunately both the men died, and the children are too young to have weight with the natives with whom since they have frequently conversed, and what was more unfortunate our native caught the disorder and died. It is not possible to determine the number of natives who were carried off by this fatal disorder. It must be great; and judging from the information of the native now living with us, and who had recovered from the disorder before he was taken, one-half of those who inhabit this part of the country died; and as the natives always retired from where the disorder appeared, and which some must have carried with them, it must have been spread to a considerable distance, as well inland as along the coast. We have seen the traces of it wherever we have been.

## 2.8  December 1790. Governor Phillip "makes an example" of ten Aborigines.

(G. B. Barton, *op. cit.,* pp. 127-128.)

*Whilst out hunting a convict named McEntire, Phillip's personal gamekeeper was speared. Captain Watkin Tench, Captain Lieutenant of the Marines, was sent with a party of fifty soldiers to "make a signal example of that tribe". Tench noted down his personal instructions from Phillip.*

. . . That we were if practicable, to bring away two natives and to put to death ten; that no hut was to be burned; that all women and children were to remain uninjured; . . . that our operations were to be directed either by surprise or open force; that after we had made any prisoners all communication even with the natives with whom we were in the habits of intercourse, was to be avoided, and none of them suffered to approach us; that we were to cut off and bring in the heads of the slain, for which purpose hatchets and bags will be furnished. . . .

. . . from the aversion uniformly shown by all natives to this unhappy man (McEntire) he had long been suspected by us as of having, in his excursions shot and injured them.

### 2.9 May 1791. Captain Tench's observations.

(Watkin Tench, *A Complete Account of the Settlement at Port Jackson*, Sydney, 1793, p. 127, in *ibid.*, p. 163.)

*Captain Tench writes of his experiences while exploring on the Hawkesbury.*

During this long trial of their patience and courtesy, in the latter part of which I was entirely in their power from their having possession of our arms, they had manifested no ungenerous sign of taking advantage of the helplessness and dependence of our situation, no rude curiosity to pry into the packages with which they were entrusted, and no sordid desire to possess the contents of them; although among them were articles exposed to view of which it afterwards appeared they knew the use and longed for the benefit of. Let the banks of those rivers "known to song"; let him whose travels have lain among polished nations, produce me a brighter example of disinterested urbanity than was shown by these denizens of a barbarous clime to a set of destitute wanderers on the side of the Hawkesbury.

1860's. Victorian Aborigines pose in a studio, displaying their weapons.
*Latrobe Collection.*

# 3

# The Expansion of the Free Settlement

Following Phillip's retirement in 1792, Governor John Hunter
set about establishing more securely the safety of the settlement's
food supplies. Although armed with the usual directions to "conciliate
and protect" the natives (3.2) he realized that in order to see the
settlement survive he had in fact to protect the settlers from native
attack. His task was made more difficult as freed convicts joined some
bands and directed Aboriginal skirmishes (3.1).

As the numbers of ex-convicts and freemen grew, so too did the
body of independent thinkers who sought to protect their own property.
Murders of white and black became more commonplace, and when
occasionally Europeans were brought to trial, sympathisers in the
jury found their acts legitimate (3.2).

The frontier wars grew more bitter, with the military and private
sector practically immune to the consequences of killing any natives
found within or near their settlements (3.5).

In 1816 Governor Lachlan Macquarie sought to relieve the situation
by forbidding any gathering of Aborigines near the farms. They were
not to carry weapons, nor to punish tribal members who broke
traditional laws. Those obeying these orders were to be fully protected
within the settlement (3.4). Two months later continuing aggression
brought Macquarie to proclaim a number of Aborigines "Outlaws", to
be shot or captured on sight (3.5). At the same time he wished that
some might come to the native school that he hoped to establish (3.4).

In the establishment of the colony of South Australia, similar bitter
campaigns marked the extension of settlement (3.6). In Tasmania,
terrified settlers living in areas far from military protection insisted
that unless the Aborigines be removed they could not remain or
continue to farm. It was judged expedient that in 1830, unless all
natives were collected together and isolated, none could survive.

A military expedition that combed Tasmania failed to capture the
native population. Instead a lone, self-educated Presbyterian
missionary, George Augustus Robinson, convinced many of them to
surrender. Consequently fifty-six Tasmanians were removed to a
granitic outcrop in Bass Strait. After a second move they were brought
to Flinders Island. For the next fifteen years they were taught to
behave as "civilized Christians".

A year after their arrival on Flinders Island the Settlement was visited by some eminent observers, Messrs. Backhouse and Walker. Although the Aborigines had been previously starved and brutalized, the visitors reported that those remaining were apparently happy and alert (3.7, 3.8).

In 1835 Mr. Robinson completed his mission of conciliation and took charge of the Flinders Island Establishment. His report to his Excellency the Lieutenant Governor revealed his degree of success in educating and converting the people. His only complaint was the increasing number of deaths among them (3.9).

In 1847 forty-four natives, including a number of half-castes, remained alive, although two hundred and three natives had lived on the Island. Despite opposition from the colonists, they were returned to Oyster Cove on the mainland. Here the numbers were soon reduced in 1854 to sixteen individuals. In 1865 Billy Lanne, the last Tasmanian man died, and in 1876 Truganini, the last woman, passed away.

*Above right*
1860's. Three Victorian women and a child pose in a studio with string bags and digging sticks.
*Latrobe Collection.*

*Below right*
1850's. The last of the Tasmanian Aborigines, at Oyster Cove.
*Latrobe Collection.*

1860's. Tommy and Biddy, members of the Molka Tribe, Victoria.
*Latrobe Collection.*

1870's. Residents of the Coranderrk Aboriginal Settlement, Healesville, Victoria. *Latrobe Collection.*

## 3.1    20 June 1797. Governor Hunter's dispatch to the Duke of Portland.

(*Historical Records of New South Wales, op. cit.*, Vol. 3, p. 226.)

*In a dispatch sent to the Duke of Portland, Governor Hunter complained of the behaviour of convicts whose sentences had expired. Although the economy had improved considerably, there was still major concern for the following year's crops.*

We have no less than 700 men out of their time and off the public store, and we have many more whose time being nearly expir'd will be discharg'd if they desire it.

Many of them have become a public and very dangerous nuisance; being too idle to work, they have join'd large bodys of the natives, and have taught them how to annoy and distress the settlers, who have many of them been murder'd by them, their houses burnt, and their stocks destroyed. They have threatened to burn and destroy our crops upon the ground, and to kill our cattle wherever they can find them. I am therefore oblig'd to arm the herds, and it distresses me to say that I fear I shall be under the necessity of sending arm'd parties in all directions to scower the country. I have been out myself with a small party of officers, and I shall frequently do so, and prevent, as far as possible, the destruction of many of those people who are led entirely by the villains who have got amongst them. We are much in want of some small arms and some camp equipage, in order to take particular stations for preventing these mischiefs.

## 3.2    2 January 1800. The trial of accused white men.

(*Ibid.*, Vol. 4, p. 2.)

*Governor Hunter's report to the Duke of Portland concerning the trial of white men accused of murdering Aborigines.*

Two native boys have lately been most barbarously murder'd by several of the settlers at the Hawkesbury River, notwithstanding Orders have upon this subject been repeatedly given pointing out in what instances only they were warranted in punishing with such severity. The above two youths had been in the habit of being much with the settlers, but from the manner in which this shocking murder was perpetrated I judg'd it highly necessary to have the murderers taken immediately into custody, and a court was instantly ordered for their trial. The court having unanimously found the prisoners guilty of killing two natives, were divided with respect to the nature of the sentence, as your Grace will discover by the trial, which is herewith sent at the instance of the majority of the court. The manner in which this decision appears to have been come to, I conceive, my Lord, not to have been correct. I am of opinion that a reference to His Majesty's Minister shou'd have been recommended by the court to the Governor, and not from the court directly and independantly of the Commander-in-Chief, because the power either to approve and confirm or to moderate the severity of any criminal sentence is delegated by His Majesty to him.

Those men found guilty of murder are now at large and living upon their farms, as much at their ease as ever. I conceive, from the nature of the Governor's authority, I might have rejected the bail and kept the prisoners under confinement untill the effect of the special reference was known; but I have been unwilling to shew to the colony that any difference is likely to take place between the judicial and executive authoritys, particularly when in the smallest degree inconsistent with lenity. If I am mistaken in my ideas upon the above trial, I hope and request to be instructed.

You will discover, my Lord, what a host of evidence is brought forward from that quarter to prove what numbers of white people have been kill'd by the natives; but cou'd we have brought with equal ease such proofs from the natives as they are capable of affording of the wanton and barbarous manner in which many of them have been destroy'd, and to have confronted them with those of the white inhabitants, we shou'd have found an astonishing difference in the numbers. Every information within my power respecting the light in which the natives of this country were to be held as a people now under the protection of His Majesty's Government was laid before the court. The Order given upon that subject, both before my time and since, was made known to it. I also laid before its members an article in His Majesty's instructions to the Governor, which is strong and expressive, and is as follows:—"You are to endeavour by every possible means to open an intercourse with the natives, and to conciliate their affections, enjoyning all our subjects to live in amity and kindness with them; and if any of our subjects should wantonly destroy them, or give them any unnecessary interruption in the exercise of their several occupations, it is our will and pleasure that you do cause such offenders to be brought to punishment, according to the degree of the offence."

The intentions of His Majesty from this part of the Governor's Instructions are clear and evident. The above cruel act is the second which I have brought before a Court of Criminal Judicature in order to prevent, as far as in my power, this horrid practice of wantonly destroying the natives. Much of that hostile disposition which has occasionally appear'd in those people has been but too often provoked by the treatment which many of them have received from the white inhabitants, and which have scarsely been heard of by those who have the power of bestowing punishment. . . .

The mischiefs which those people can with ease to themselves do to us renders it highly essential to our own comfort and security that we shou'd live on amicable terms with them. Fire in the hands of a body of irritated and hostile natives may with little trouble to them ruin our prospects of an abundant harvest, for that is the very season in which they might spread desolation over our cultivated lands, and reduce us to extreme distress; and they are not ignorant of having that power in their hands, for after the destruction of the above two boys they threaten'd to burn our crops as soon as it cou'd be effected. I caution'd the settlers in consequence that they might be upon their guard. They did not, however, attempt it.

Their violence against the military proceeded from a soldier having in a most shamefull and wanton manner kill'd a native woman and child, a circumstance which had not come to my knowledge untill long after the fact had been committed.

### 3.3   2 January 1800. Accused white men.

(*Ibid.*, Vol. 4, p. 4.)

*The trial of accused white men—Lieutenant Hobby's evidence.*

*Questions by the prisoner Powell.*   What orders did you give to a party of soldiers who went out to bury the body of Thomas Hodgkinson that had been killed by the Natives?
*A.*   My orders to the soldiers were to go out with the men who were sent to bury the bodies of Hodgkinson and Wimbo (who were murdered by the Natives about two months since), and "that if they fell in with any Natives on the road, either going or returning, to fire in upon them."

*By the Court.* What were your reasons for giving such orders, and by what authority did you do so?

*A.* About two months since, or thereabouts, I was informed by different people that it was the intention of the Natives to come down in numbers from the blue Mountains to the Hawkesbury and to murder some of the white people, and particularly some soldiers. . . .

I then waited upon the Governor again and communicated this last information—His Excellency appeared to be much displeased with the conduct of the Natives—as I had been subpoened down to Sydney on a trial, I observed to the Governor that the sooner I returned to the Hawkesbury the better— the Governor was of the same opinion—I then asked his Excellency what was best to be done if the Natives persevered in committing such enormities —the Governor replied that something must be done—on which I signified to the Governor my intention, if the Natives should still continue such violent outrages, to send out a party of the military to kill five or six of them wherever they were to be found—His Excellency directed me to act discretionally against the Natives, leaving it entirely to me—the next morning I left Sydney and returned to the Hawkesbury, where I arrived the second day about ten o'clock; in the evening of the day of my arrival there, Corporal Farrell called upon me with the information that he knew where to take the Natives that had wounded Serjeant Goodall (who was then reported to be dead). . . .

The next morning Corporal Farrell returned, bringing with him a Native named "Charley," which Native I sent down under a guard to the Governor —on the return of the said Guard, Corporal Farrell and a private soldier named Henry Lambe came to me and reported that said native was, according to orders, taken before the Governor, who expressed himself, in the hearing of the guard of soldiers, that he could not take upon himself to punish the Native in cool blood, but that the Commanding Officer at the Hawkesbury should have punished him on the spot where he was taken— The Native was thereupon discharged.

*Q.* Do you know that the Native you sent down to Sydney was concerned in the wounding of Goodall?

*A.* I was informed by Corporal Farrell that the said Native was concerned. I then went to the Native, he denied wounding Goodall, but said he was present, and offered to take me, or any other person that I would send, to the Native that did wound him—that he was known by the appellation of Major White, this I declined, from conjecturing that this offer was merely made to afford him an opportunity to escape.


### 3.4   4 May 1816. Governor Lachlan Macquarie's proclamation to Aboriginals.

(*Historical Records of Australia*, Sydney, Government Printer, 1917. Series 1, Vol. 9, pp. 141-145.)

By His Excellency Lachlan Macquarie, Esquire, &c., &c. WHEREAS the Ab-origines, or Black Natives of this Country, have for the last three Years manifested a strong and sanguinary Spirit of Animosity and Hostility towards the British Inhabitants residing in the Interior and remote Parts of the Territory, and have been recently guilty of most atrocious and wanton Barbarities in indiscriminately murdering Men Women and Children, from whom they had received no Offence or Provocation; and also in killing the Cattle, and plundering and destroying the Grain and Property of every Description, belonging to the Settlers and Persons residing on or near the Banks of the Rivers Nepean, Grose, and Hawkesbury, and South Creek, to the great Terror, Loss and Distress of the suffering Inhabitants.

And whereas, notwithstanding that the Government has heretofore acted with the utmost Lenity and Humanity towards these Natives in forbearing to punish such wanton Cruelties and Depredations with their merited Severity, thereby hoping to reclaim them from their barbarous Practices and to conciliate them to the British Government, by affording them Protection, Assistance and Indulgence, instead of subjecting them to the Retaliation of Injury, which their own wanton Cruelties would have fully justified; yet they have persevered to the present Day in committing every Species of sanguinary Outrage and depredation on the Lives and Properties of the British Inhabitants, after having been repeatedly cautioned to beware of the Consequences that would result to themselves by the continuance of such destructive and barbarous Courses.

And whereas His Excellency the Governor was lately reluctantly compelled to resort to coercive and strong Measures to prevent the Recurrence of such Crimes and Barbarities, and to bring to condign Punishment such of the Perpetrators of them as could be found and apprehended; and with this View sent out a Military Force to drive away these hostile Tribes from the British Settlements in the remote Parts of the Country, and to take as many of them Prisoners as possible; in executing which Service several Natives have been unavoidably killed and wounded, in Consequence of their not having surrendered themselves on being called on so to do, amongst whom, it may be considered fortunate, that some of the most guilty and atrocious of the Natives concerned in the late Murders and Robberies are numbered. And although it is to be apprehended that some few innocent Men, Women, and Children may have fallen in these Conflicts, yet it is earnestly to be hoped that this unavoidable Result, and the Severity which has attended it, will eventually strike Terror amongst the surviving Tribes, and deter them from the further Commission of such sanguinary Outrages and Barbarities.

And whereas the more effectually to prevent a Recurrence of Murders, Robberies, and Depredations by the Natives, as well as to protect the Lives and Properties of His Majesty's British Subjects residing in the several Settlements of this Territory, His Excellency the Governor deems it his indispensible Duty to prescribe certain Rules, Orders, and Regulations to be observed by the Natives, and rigidly enforced and carried into Effect by all Magistrates and Peace Officers in the Colony of New South Wales; and which are as follows:—

*First.* That from and after the Fourth Day of June ensuing, that being the Birth Day of His Most Gracious Majesty King George the Third, no Black Native or Body of Black Natives shall ever appear at or within one Mile of any Town, Village, or Farm, occupied by, or belonging to any British Subject, armed with any warlike or offensive Weapon or Weapons of any Description, such as Spears, Clubs, or Waddies, on Pain of being deemed and considered in a State of Aggression and Hostility, and treated accordingly.

*Second.* That no Number of Natives, exceeding in the Whole Six Persons, being entirely unarmed, shall ever come to lurk or loiter about any Farm in the Interior, on the Pain of being considered Enemies, and treated accordingly.

*Third.* That the Practice, hitherto observed amongst the Native Tribes, of assembling in large Bodies or Parties armed, and of fighting and attacking each other on the Plea of inflicting Punishments on Transgressors of their own Customs and Manners at or near Sydney, and other principal Towns and Settlements in the Colony, shall be henceforth wholly abolished, as a barbarous Custom repugnant to the British Laws, and strongly militating against the Civilization of the Natives, which is an Object of the highest Importance to effect, if possible. Any Armed Body of Natives, therefore, who shall assemble for the foregoing purposes, either at Sydney or any of the other Settlements of this Colony after the said Fourth Day of June next, shall be considered as Disturbers of the Public Peace and shall be apprehended and punished in a summary Manner accordingly. The Black Natives are therefore hereby enjoined and commanded to discontinue this barbarous Custom, not only at and near the British Settlements but also in their own wild and remote Places of Resort.

*Fourth.* That such of the Natives as may wish to be considered under the Protection of the British Government, and disposed to conduct themselves in a peaceful, inoffensive, and honest Manner, shall be furnished with Passports or Certificates to that Effect, signed by the Governor, on their making Application for the same at the Secretary's Office at Sydney, on the First Monday of every succeeding Month; which Certificates they will find will protect them from being injured or molested by any Person, so long as they conduct themselves peaceably, inoffensively, and honestly, and do not carry or use offensive Weapons, contrary to the Tenor of this Proclamation.

The Governor, however, having thus fulfilled an imperious and necessary Public Duty, in prohibiting the Black Natives from carrying or using offensive Weapons, at least in as far as relates to their usual Intercourse with the British Inhabitants of these Settlements, considers it equally a Part of his Public Duty as a Counterbalance for the Restriction of not allowing them to go about the Country armed to afford the Black Natives such Means as are within his Power to enable them to obtain an honest and comfortable Subsistence by their own Labour and Industry. His Excellency therefore hereby proclaims and makes known to them that he shall always be willing and ready to grant small Portions of Land, in suitable and convenient Parts of the Colony, to such of them as are inclined to become regular Settlers, and such occasional Assistance from Government as may enable them to cultivate their Farms:—Namely,

*First.* That they and their Families shall be victualled from the King's Stores for Six Months, from the Time of their going to reside actually on their Farms.

*Secondly.* That they shall be furnished with the necessary Agricultural Tools, and also with Wheat, Maize and Potatoes for Seed, and

*Thirdly.* To each Person of a Family, one Suit of Slops and one Colonial Blanket from the King's Stores shall be given. But these Indulgencies will not be granted to any Native, unless it shall appear that he is really inclined, and fully resolved to become a Settler, and permanently to reside on such Farm as may be assigned to him for the Purpose of cultivating the same for the Support of himself and his Family.

His Excellency the Governor therefore earnestly exhorts, and thus publicly invites the Natives to relinquish their wandering idle and predatory Habits of Life, and to become industrious and useful Members of a Community where they will find Protection and Encouragement. To such as do not like to cultivate Farms of their own, but would prefer working as Labourers for those Persons who may be disposed to employ them, there will always be found Masters among the Settlers who will hire them as Servants of this Description. And the Governor strongly recommends to the Settlers and other Persons, to accept such Services as may be offered by the industrious Natives, desirous of engaging in their Employ. And the Governor desires it to be understood, that he will be happy to grant Lands to the Natives in such Situations as may be agreeable to themselves, and according to their own particular Choice, provided such Lands are disposable, and belong to the Crown.

And Whereas His Excellency the Governor, from an anxious Wish to civilize the Ab-origines of this Country so as to make them useful to themselves and the Community, has established a Seminary or Institution at Parramatta for the Purpose of educating the Male and Female Children of those Natives who might be willing to place them in that Seminary:—His Excellency therefore now earnestly calls upon such Natives as have Children to embrace so desirable and good an Opportunity of providing for their helpless Offspring and of having them brought up, clothed, fed and educated in a Seminary established for such humane and desirable Purposes. And in Furtherance of this Measure, His Excellency deems it expedient to invite a general Friendly Meeting of all the Natives residing in the Colony, to take place at the Town of Parramatta, on Saturday the Twenty-eighth of December next at Twelve o'Clock at Noon, at the Public Market Place there, for the Purpose of more fully explaining and pointing out to them the Objects of the Institution referred to, as well as for Consulting with them on the best Means of improving their present Condition. On this Occasion, and at this public general Meeting of the Natives, the Governor will feel happy to Reward such of them as have given Proofs of Industry, and an Inclination to be civilized.

And the Governor wishing that this General Meeting, or Congress of friendly Natives should in future be held annually, directs that *the Twenty-eighth Day of December*, in every succeeding Year, shall be considered as fixed for this Purpose, excepting when that Day happens to fall on a Sunday, when the following Day is to be considered as fixed for holding the said Congress.

And finally, His Excellency the Governor hereby orders and directs, that on Occasions of any Natives coming armed, or in a hostile Manner without Arms, or in unarmed Parties exceeding Six in Number, to any Farm belonging to or occupied by British Subjects in the Interior, such Natives are first to be desired in a civil Manner to depart from the said Farm, and if they persist in remaining thereon, or attempt to plunder, rob, or commit any kind of Depredation, they are then to be driven away by Force of Arms by the Settlers themselves; and in case they are not able to do so, they are to apply to a Magistrate for aid from the nearest Military Station; and the Troops stationed there are hereby commanded to render their Assistance when so required. The Troops are also to afford aid at the Towns of Sydney, Parramatta, and Windsor respectively, when called on by the Magistrates or Police Officers at those Stations.

> Given under my Hand, at Government House, Sydney, this Fourth Day of May, in the Year of Our Lord One Thousand eight hundred and sixteen.
>
> LACHLAN MACQUARIE.

By command of His Excellency,

J. T. CAMPBELL, Secretary.

God save the King!

## 3.5    20 July 1816. A Proclamation of Native Outlawry.

(*Ibid.*, Series 1. Vol. 9, pp. 362, 363, 364.)

*Issued by Governor Lachlan Macquarie, authorizing the use of arms against Aborigines.*

. . . it has appeared that there are still amongst these People some Individuals far more determinedly hostile and mischievous than the rest, who, by taking the lead, have lately instigated their deluded Followers to commit several further atrocious Acts of Barbarity on the unoffending and unprotected Settlers and their Families;

And whereas, the Ten Natives whose Names are hereunder mentioned are well known to be the principal and most violent Instigators of the late Murders, Namely,

1. Murrah.
2. Myles.
3. Wallah, alias Warren.
4. Carbone Jack, alias Kurringy.
5. Narrang Jack.
6. Bunduck.
7. Kongate.
8. Woottan.
9. Rachel.
10. Yallaman.

Now it is hereby publicly proclaimed and declared that the said Ten Natives abovementioned, and each and every of them, are deemed and considered to be in a State of Outlawry, and open and avowed Enemies to the Peace and good Order of Society, and therefore unworthy to receive any longer the Protection of that Government, which they have so flagrantly revolted against and abused. And all and every of His Majesty's Subjects, whether Free Men, Prisoners of the Crown, or Friendly Natives, are hereby authorised and enjoined to seize upon and secure the said Ten outlawed Natives, or any of them, wheresoever they may be found, and to bring them before and deliver them up to the nearest Magistrate to be dealt with according to Justice. And in Case the said proscribed Ten hostile Natives cannot be apprehended and secured for that Purpose, then such of His Majesty's Subjects, hereinbefore described, are and shall be at Liberty by such Means as may be within their Power to kill and utterly destroy them as Outlaws and Murderers as aforesaid; and with this View, and to encourage His Majesty's said Subjects, whether white Men or Friendly Natives, to seize upon, secure, or destroy the said Outlaws, a Reward of *Ten Pounds Sterling* for each of the Ten proscribed Natives will be paid by Government to any Person or Persons who shall under such Circumstances bring in their Persons, or produce satisfactory Proof of their having killed or destroyed them within the Period of three Months from the Date hereof.

*Provided* always that nothing in this Proclamation contained is to be construed to extend to allow of Government Servants, of any Description, to depart from their Duty or Services without the special Permission of those Persons to whom they may be assigned.

In Furtherance of the Object of this Proclamation and of the Measures to be adopted pursuant thereto, the several District Magistrates are hereby enjoined forthwith to assemble the Settlers and other Persons dwelling within their respective District at some convenient centrical Situation, and to point out to them the Necessity of forming themselves into Associations along the Rivers Hawkesbury and Nepean, so as to be prepared to afford each other mutual Relief and Assistance on Occasions of any Attack or Incursions of the hostile Natives; and in Cases of any Outrages being attempted against them, their Families, or Property, they are to consider themselves authorised to repel such Attacks or Incursions by Force of Arms; at the same Time they are not wantonly or unprovokedly to commence any Aggressions, but only to guard against and resist the Depredations or Attacks of the hostile Natives with a View to their own immediate Defence and Protection.

And the Settlers are further hereby strictly enjoined and commanded, on no Pretence whatever, to receive, harbour, or conceal any of the said outlawed Banditti, or afford them any Countenance or Assistance whatever; nor are they to furnish Aid or Provisions to any of the Friendly Natives who may frequent their Farms, but upon the express Condition of their engaging and promising to use their best Endeavours to secure and bring in the said Ten Outlaws, and deliver them up to the nearest Magistrate, or lodge them in Prison:—And those friendly Natives are to be given to understand, that if they faithfully and earnestly exert themselves in apprehending and bringing in the said Outlaws, every reasonable Indulgence and Encouragement will be afforded them by Government; whilst, on the contrary, until this object is attained, no Peace or Amnesty with the Natives at large in this Territory will be made or conceded.

It being impossible to station Military Detachments as a Protection for every Farm in the disturbed or exposed Districts, the *Governor* is desirous of apprising the Settlers in this public Manner thereof, in Order that they may the more speedily and effectually adopt the best Means in their Power for their future Security. But with a View to overawe the hostile Natives generally in those Parts of the Colony where they have committed the most flagrant and violent Acts of Cruelty and Outrage, three separate Military Detachments will be forthwith stationed at convenient Distances on the Rivers Nepean, Grose and Hawkesbury, to be ready to assist and afford Protection to the Settlers whenever Occasion may require it, when called upon by the nearest Magistrate for that Purpose; each Detachment to be provided with an European and also a native Guide, which the District Magistrates are enjoined to furnish them with, carefully selecting them from the most intelligent and trustworthy Persons within their several Districts.

The Military Parties, stationed at Parramatta, Liverpool, and Bringelly, will receive similar Instructions to those to be given to the three Military Detachments before mentioned.

And the several Magistrates throughout the Territory are hereby directed to give every possible Publicity and Effect to this Proclamation.

Given under my Hand, at Government House, Sydney, this Twentieth Day of July, One thousand eight hundred and sixteen.

LACHLAN MACQUARIE.

By Command of His Excellency,

JOHN THOMAS CAMPBELL, Secretary.

God save the King!

## 3.6    October 1832. Backhouse and Walker's observations at Flinders Island (1).

(James Backhouse Walker, *The Walker Memorial Volume. Early Tasmania.*, Royal Society of Tasmania, Government Printer, 1902, pp. 238, 239, 249.)

*In 1832 Messrs. James Backhouse and George Washington Walker arrived from England to investigate the condition of the prison population in the Australian colonies, and the treatment of the Aborigines. At Flinders Island, they observed the last of the Tasmanians.*

. . . The opportunities we have had of coming at an estimate of the aboriginal character have strongly impressed us with the opinion that they are not a treacherous and ferocious nor vindictive people. . . . The treachery and outrages they have experienced at the hands of the Europeans excited at one time a spirit of revenge, under the influence of which retaliation was made on some of the innocent people of Van Diemen's Land as well as on the guilty, a thing not uncommon even in what are termed "civilised wars". . . . Amongst other traits, we remarked less indisposition to personal exertion than is usually attributed to savages. The willingness and promptitude with which they perform little services for those whom they consider their friends, as in bringing in wood and water for daily use, show that they are not of a sluggish disposition when there is a sufficient inducement to labour. . . . An idea is becoming prevelent among them that they are transformed after death into white men, and that they return under this renewed form to an island in the Straits, where there is abundance of game, and where they have the pleasure of again hunting, and subsisting upon such animals as they killed in the chase during their lifetime; but I am disposed to believe that this has not originated with themselves, particularly as they connect it with some vague idea respecting the deceased visiting England, or at least coming from beyond the seas ere they inhabit the island in question. . . .

This short excursion has given us a further opportunity of estimating the character of the aborigines; and the favourable opinion we had previously formed of their disposition, and especially of their capabilities for improvement, is more than ever confirmed. They require to be treated with much discretion and forbearance. They are more easily led than driven; for, though they are very tractable and accessible to kindness, it is easy to perceive that they consider themselves a free people. If they do service for others, they do it through courtesy. There is nothing that is servile or abject in their character when they are not under the influence of fear. We are perpetually reminded that in their taste for amusement, and in some respects in their capacities, they are children, though more tractable than the generality of children; but, in many things that occur within the range of their knowledge and acquirements, they show a quickness of perception and powers of reflection that prove them to be a race far from deficient in intellect, and highly susceptible of improvement.

### 3.7 October 1832. Backhouse and Walker (2).

(James B. Walker, *Notes on the Aborigines of Tasmania,* in *Ibid.,* p. 239.)

*Backhouse and Walker reported that some success in civilising the Tasmanians had been achieved.*

The tractability of the captive blacks at the settlement was remarkable. They acted like good-natured children, and were as imitative as monkeys. Thus, at a religious service, at which some of them were present, they behaved with great decorum, and during prayer turned their faces to the wall in imitation of the whites. When they were presented with Scotch caps the young men drew themselves up in a line and imitated the manoeuvres of soldiers. They showed a great desire to copy the ways of their white instructors. The men were particularly anxious to be supplied with trousers, but resented the offer of yellow trousers, the usual garb of prisoners. They also wanted to have stools to sit upon, and tables for their meals, and to be supplied with knives and forks, like Europeans.

Some of the women learned to make bread, to wash clothes, and to sew, and to use soap and water daily.

### 3.8 3 June 1837. Sir John Jeffcot's first speech.

(*South Australian Gazette and Colonial Register*, Adelaide, Vol. 1, No. 11, 3 June 1837.)

*This is an extract from the first speech delivered by Sir John Jeffcot, the judge first appointed to South Australia, at the Communal Court Hearings.*

. . . the system, hitherto adopted in the immediate neighbourhood of this province towards the native population, is one at which humanity shudders . . . And when such is the treatment which they have received at the hands of Europeans, when such is the example set by those who call themselves civilised, is it to be wondered at that they have occasionally broken out into acts of violence, or retaliated upon their oppressors?

### 3.9  24 June 1837. George A. Robinson's report from Flinders Island.

(*House of Commons Parliamentary Papers*, London, Vol. 34, 1839, Enclosure 2, in No. 2, "Copies of Extracts of Dispatches Relative to the Massacre of Various Aborigines of Australia in the Year 1838 and Respecting the Trial of Their Murderers.", pp. 6-13.)

*A report sent from Mr. George A. Robinson, Commandant of the Aboriginal Settlement, Flinder's Island, to the Lieutenant Governor of Tasmania.*

Sir,

I HAVE the honour to submit, for the information of his Excellency the Lieutenant-governor, the subjoined particulars relative to this experimental and interesting institution, since the transmission of my previous report of the 8th of September 1836; and I have much satisfaction in stating that this settlement continues as heretofore in a very quiet and tranquil state, and that the same order and regularity is maintained as mentioned on former occasions.

The only thing to be deplored is the mortality that has taken place among them, and which induces me ardently to desire that His Majesty's Government may accede to the removal of the present establishment to the adjacent coast of New Holland. . . .

I have much satisfaction in stating that the wants of the aborigines are amply and abundantly supplied, and that the provisions furnished by the Government are of the best description; and though, notwithstanding, the fatality to which I have heretofore alluded is of painful character, still it must be conceded that the same is quite providential, and might have occurred in their own native districts; for I do not consider the depopulation wholly attributable to their removal, for in my opinion the same causes did exist in their primeval districts, in proof of which abundant evidence might be adduced; and hence, amid the calamity that has happened, it is a pleasing reflection to know that everything has been done which ingenuity could devise or humanity suggest to alleviate their condition, and of which the aborigines themselves have marked their appreciation, and oft repeated their acknowledgements for the solicitude evinced, and the kind intention of the Government towards them.

The advantages to the aborigines by their removal have been manifold, and many of them of the highest order. In their native forests they were without the knowledge of a God, hence but little removed from the brute themselves. Their mode of life was extremely precarious, and to the juveniles distressing in the extreme; and though in their insidious and deadly attacks on the white inhabitants they invariably eluded pursuit, yet they themselves were not without dangers and alarms, and might reasonably be said to exist by excitement alone. The sanguinary tribes had seldom any progeny, and which could only be attributed to their harassed mode of existence. . . .

Anterior to their arrival . . . they knew not who it was that made them; they were in a deplorable state of mental degradation. Such is not now the case: they not only possess the knowledge of a Deity, but are acquainted with the principles of Christianity.

From the time I first took charge of the settlement, now near two years since, religious knowledge has been daily imparted to them, and religious principles inculcated. In this laudable object the whole of the officers and my family have unitedly assisted, a duty in which they have evinced the greatest aptitude and delight; and I myself can testify with what avidity and eagerness they have attended to and sought after religious knowledge, and which the subjoined paper will amply testify.

But whilst in the foregoing I have chiefly confined my observations to the aborigines, and the advantages incident thereupon, still it will be found that these bear no comparison to the advantages that have accrued to the European inhabitants and colony at large, which are beyond calculation.

*Domestic Economy.*

Their time is wholly employed in useful labour, harmless amusements, in their attendance at school, and religious exercises, and not, as heretofore, wandering about the settlement with listless and careless indifference to what was going on; but on the contrary, evince by their general conduct, their prompt attention to instruction, and their persevering industry, that they have an interest in the affairs of the settlement, and which it has ever been my aim on all occasions to bring them to participate. They are no longer idle spectators, but actors and ready agents to assist, as far as strength and ability will permit, in every useful undertaking.

I have already alluded to their proficiency in useful arts, viz. knitting and fancy network, and though from the paucity of their numbers the manufacture cannot be done to any great extent, still in whatever light we view it, whether as a branch of useful industry, or as an amusement, one thing is certain, that it displays a precocity of intellect of no ordinary kind, and proves that those whom civilized men despised as beings without mind, are, like all God's creatures, perfect in every form, and which only requires the adoption of proper means, when the latent intellect of the degraded savage will be made manifest, and be developed.

There are many and numerous incidents that might be cited to mark their improvement in domestic economy; suffice to say, they are not now, as formerly, content to sit upon the ground, but require seats, both as an article of convenience and a preservation from soiling their clothes. Those among them who have knives and forks habitually use them, and which the residue are anxious to possess; they now also confine themselves more closely to their domiciles, and not interchanging or crouching under bushes or rolling about in idleness.

The aborigines are becoming cleanly in their persons; they now perform the necessary ablutions daily, and the greater part of them have shorn beards; they are not now satisfied as heretofore with one garment, *i.e.* a frock coat, but require trousers also, and their raiment is in general kept in clean and proper order.

The females are equally as anxious to possess clothes of an European fashion. Several pieces of print bought on their account, and sold at the market, were purchased with avidity and manufactured into gowns; they likewise wear under garments, which they keep in clean and good order. They now evince great desire for domestic comforts, and which, though amply supplied, can only be attained by industry and good conduct. Their primitive habits are now all but forgotten: the use of ochre and grease, with which they used formerly to bedaub themselves, is now entirely abolished. Their nocturnal orgies, *i.e.* corroberies, which hurt the repose of the settlement and impaired the health of the natives, as adverted to in my previous reports, never occur. Their wild intonations are now superseded by sacred melody, *i.e.* hymns and psalms, in which they greatly excel; but as this will be spoken of under the head of "Sacred Melody," I forbear now to enlarge.

*Aboriginal Police.*

The police of this establishment consists of four special constables, and their two chiefs, to whom the conservation of the aborigines is confided. The constables are chosen *vivâ voce* from each of the two remnant tribes in full assembly, convened for the occasion. They receive for this duty a weekly stipend of 1*s.* (the pay is only nominal) as the office is considered an honorary distinction.

The constables act under the orders of their chiefs; the latter determine all points of disputes, and on several occasions have displayed tact and judgment highly creditable, and in every instance have administered impartial justice. When this police was first established, it was done as an experiment, and solely with a view to assimilate the natives as much as it was possible to the customs and usages of Europeans.

The experiment has now been fairly tried, and found to answer beyond the most sanguine expectation.

The aboriginal police take a general surveillance over the entire of the aborigines. The authority of the constables is acknowledged and respected. Many circumstances might be adduced to show the utility and advantage of this police. The following is a striking instance, and will tend to show the advancement these people have made in the scale of civilization and moral improvement.

In February last one of the convicts absconded from this settlement, and was proceeding on his way to the south end of the island, for the purpose, as he said, of communicating with the sealers, and then eventually to escape from the island; the aboriginal police, aided by others of their own people, were ordered by me to go in quest of him, and on the evening of the same day, they brought him back to the settlement handcuffed, and safely lodged him in the gaol.

*Christian Instruction.*

The work of Christian instruction and civilization, which has taken place under the auspices of the local government at this settlement, has succeeded beyond the most sanguine expectation, and has determined a question hitherto deemed impracticable.

If, as is made evident, so much has been effected for a people said to possess so little intellectual capacity, a people reputed to be but one remove from the brute creation, and of whom it was said they were but a link between the human and brute species; if so much has been done for such a people, how much more might be performed with those of a different character; and I do trust that the time is not far distant when the experiment will be tried among the numerous tribes inhabiting New Holland; for from the appalling accounts received, and from what I myself have witnessed, as well as from information heretofore communicated, there appears a prompt necessity that some efficient protection be extended to those ill-used and persecuted people. Humanity, religion, and justice require that every effort should be made on their behalf.

The primeval occupants of Van Diemen's Land are not deserving of the obloquy which has been heaped upon them. The hostile feeling evinced by them towards the whites, and their attacks upon the lonely settlement of the colony, are only considered as just retaliation for the wrongs done to them and to their progenitors. They are now well disposed and bear no ill-will or animosity to the white inhabitants. They have been grossly misrepresented; but in this respect they are not alone, but suffer in common with all their unfortunate race, who have in all ages been shamefully maligned and cruelly persecuted.

The aborigines of Van Diemen's Land have not only shown an aptitude to acquire knowledge, but have displayed a precocity of intellect, and have exhibited capabilities of no ordinary character, and which the papers annexed to this report will in part sufficiently establish, and at this settlement there are abundant proofs.

The effects that have been produced on the minds of these people will for ever put to silence the cavils of the most sceptical and prejudicially minded; and if (as I understand) in the sister colony the attempts hitherto brought into operation for the amelioration of the aborigines have failed, it can only be attributed to a defect in the system, and not to the people themselves.

## 3.10 1837. Tasmanian Aboriginal School Students.

(*Ibid.*, Vol. 34, p. 15, School Report from G. A. Robinson, Aboriginal Settlement, Flinders Island, 24 June 1837.)

*The examination of Tasmanian Aboriginal School students at the Native Settlement, Flinder's Island.*

PUPILS of the FOURTH CLASS, Hector, Romeo, Buonaparte, and Christopher.
Teacher, Mr. J. Allen.

*Examination of Hector.*
Imperfect in his letters.
Where is God?—In heaven.
Who made all things?—God made everything.
Do you pray to God?—Yes.
This man is well-behaved, is married, and is a good husband, but inattentive and fond of the chase. Is from the east side of the island of Van Diemen's Land.

*Examination of Romeo.*
Imperfect in his letters.
Who made you?—God.
Who made your father?—God made him.
This man is a good husband and a kind father, and is a native of Port Davy, Van Diemen's Land. Is inattentive at his learning. Is a stout, robust, well-made man.

*Examination of Buonaparte.*
Is perfect in his letters, and learning to spell; has a knowledge of numerals to nine.
Who made you?—God.
Who do you pray to?—God.
What do you say to him.?—Our Father which art in heaven, &c. &c.
Who made the white man?—God made him.
Do you like to hear about God?—Yes.
Is a steady, well-conducted, industrious man; well-behaved, and a good husband. Belongs to the Big River tribe, and was the same individual that was apprehended on the occasion of the military operation, *i.e.* the line.

*Examination of Christopher*
Perfect in the alphabet, and learning to spell.
Who made your country?—God.
Who is God?—A Spirit.
Where is God?—In heaven.
What must we do to be saved?—Believe in the Lord Jesus Christ.
Is a quiet, inoffensive man; a good husband, and industrious. Belongs to the Ben Lomond tribe.

PUPILS of the FIFTH CLASS, Alexander, Tippo Saib, and Arthur.

*Teacher, Master H. Robinson.*

*Examination of Alexander.*
Is perfect in the alphabet; learning to spell.
Who made you?—God.
What must we do to be saved?—Believe on the Lord Jesus Christ.
What did Christ do for us?—He died for our sins, according to the Scriptures.
Where will bad people go to when they die?—They will go to hell.
Who made all things?—God made all things.
Do you pray to God?—Yes.
What do you say to him?—Our Father which, &c. &c.
Are all men sinners?—Yes.
Do you like to sing about God?—Yes.
Do you like to tell your countrymen about God?—Yes.
Is a good husband, studious, industrious, and well-behaved. Belongs to the Big River tribe. Is a fine man, tall, and well made.

*Examination of Tippo Saib.*
Perfect in the alphabet.
Who made you?—God.
How many Gods are there?—One God.
Where do good people go to when they die?—To heaven.
Who made the sun, the moon, and the stars?—God made all things.

# 4

# Beyond the Limits of Location

The pastoral industry was organised on the basis of abundantly available supplies of "Unoccupied" land. As long as the squatter had little security of tenure or constraint placed upon him, investment was directed towards bringing more land into use, rather than switching to a more intensive system of production. This policy soon took the pastoralist beyond the previously known limits where confrontation with the native tribes was inevitable. The pattern of race relations was soon established, with settlers having to rely almost exclusively on their own efforts to defend themselves. When memorialists asked that the Governor and Council provide military protection and that a state of war be declared, they were reminded that their enemies were also British subjects, equal in the eyes of the law and deserving protection (4.3).

In 1838 Sir George Gipps, Governor of New South Wales, attempted to demonstrate this equality by ensuring that those previously found innocent of a massacre of Myall Creek Aborigines were retried and put to death. The condemned men's final comments reveal the tenor of the relationship between black and white on the frontiers (4.4-4.7).

Gipps had to answer repeatedly the demands of an English administration some eight months' sailing time away, which was not aware of the realities of the pioneering life. In 1838 Lord Glenelg of the Home Office suggested that Gipps had only to remind Aborigines of their legal rights in order to prevent bloodshed (4.1). In fact this was a constant source of contention between black and white as Aboriginal evidence was not accepted in any court in the colony.

In 1836, realizing that some representative of the Aborigines was required in the newly-settled regions, the House of Commons in London ordered the establishment of a "Protectorate System". This was to be introduced first in the vicinity of the Port Phillip area, but from its ambitious beginnings the project was doomed. It went against the interests of the powerful pastoralists who were rushing to occupy new grazing lands. The social order of the Aboriginal tribes did not lend itself to their confinement on reserves which frequently were located in the territory of some traditional enemy. Tribal wars and revenge killings increased (4.13-4.14).

For most of the newly-arrived English protectors the task was too difficult, and the help and co-operation of black and white inadequate. The reports of one assistant protector, Edward Stone Parker, tell of the problems that each faced (4.9).

The Aborigines' guerilla warfare was most successful in the interior of Queensland. Here the impenetrable bush and vast distances gave tribes cover and protection from pursuit on horseback. The pastoralists' final solution was to engage a Native Police Force like that established in New South Wales and Victoria. This was a mounted body of semi-military trained Aborigines from remote areas who regarded the Queensland natives as traditional tribal enemies. Led by white officers, the force came to the call of any person who claimed interference from Aborigines, and their methods of "dispersal" were either praised by pastoralists or condemned by townsfolk and philanthropists (4.27-4.32).

A royal commission into the workings of the Native Police Force in 1864 revealed the effectiveness of the system of Aborigine eradication. At this same inquiry the attempts to educate Aborigines were discussed (4.19-4.22).

In 1859 Charles Darwin's book *On the Origin of Species* popularized the notion of biological (and therefore social) evolution. Scholars began to discuss civilisation as a unilinear process with races able to ascend or descend a graduated scale. The European was understood to be at the "top", the "fittest to survive", while the Aborigine was seen to be at the "bottom". He was doomed to die out according to a "natural law", like the dodo and the dinosaur. This theory, supported by the facts at hand, continued to be quoted until well into the twentieth century when it was noticed that the dark-skinned race was muliplying. Until that time it could be used to justify neglect and murder.

1880's. Native police encampment.
*Latrobe Collection.*

1864. Distribution of blankets to the Australian Natives. (4.29).
*Latrobe Collection.*

1884. "Ration Day". (4.35).
*Latrobe Collection.*

1882. Deputation of Blackfellows at Parliament House. (4.34).
*Latrobe Collection.*

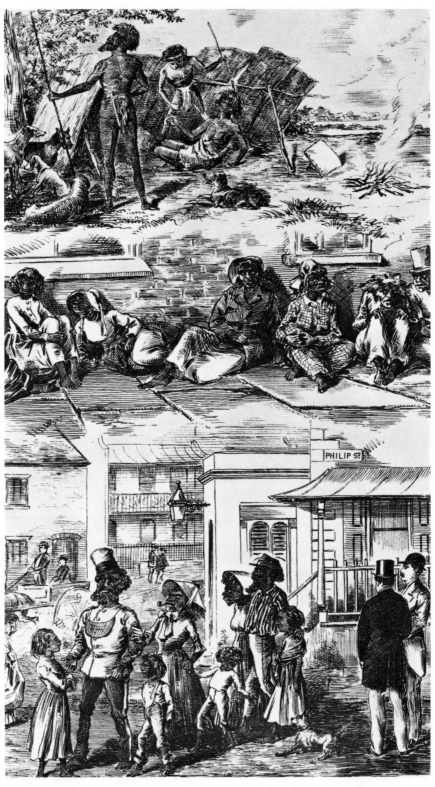

1880. Sydney Aboriginals—Past and Present. (4.32).
*Latrobe Collection.*

**4.1   21 January 1838. The establishment of the Protectorate.**

(*Ibid.*, Vol. 34, paper No. 2, 31 January 1838, p. 4.)

*A dispatch from Lord Glenelg, London, to Governor Gipps, New South Wales, giving details of the protectorate system to be established.*

Sir,                                                          Downing-street, 31 January 1838.

IN transmitting to you a duplicate copy of the last Report of the Select Committee of the House of Commons on Aborigines, I have the honour to communicate to you, that Her Majesty's Government have directed their anxious attention to the adoption of some plan for the better protection and civilization of the native tribes within the limits of your government.

With that view, it has been resolved to appoint at once a small number of persons qualified to fill the office of protectors of aborigines. I have confined that number, in the first instance, to one chief protector, aided by four assistant protectors. I would propose that the chief protector should fix his principal station at Port Phillip, as the most convenient point from whence he could traverse the surrounding country, and be in personal communication with his assistants; two of whom should occupy the country to the northward and eastward, and the other two be stationed to the northward, and as far westward as the boundaries of the colony of South Australia. (The men to serve as protectors will be Mr. Dredge, Mr. Parker, Mr. Thomas, and Mr. Sievwright.)

It remains for me to explain my general view of the duties which will devolve on the protectors, and to refer to the points which will form the ground of instructions which you will issue to them.

1. Each protector should attach himself as closely and constantly as possible to the aboriginal tribes who may be found in the district for which he may be appointed; attending them, if practicable in their movements from one place to another, until they can be induced to assume more settled habits of life, and endeavour to conciliate their respect and confidence, and to make them feel that he is their friend.

2. He must watch over the rights and interests of the natives, protect them, as far as he can by his personal exertions and influence, from any encroachments on their property, and from acts of cruelty, oppression, or injustice, and faithfully represent the wants, wishes, or grievances, if such representations be found necessary, through the chief protector, to the government of the colony. For this purpose it will be desirable to invest each protector with a commission as magistrate.

3. If the natives can be induced in any considerable numbers to locate themselves in a particular place, it will be the object of the protector to teach and encourage them to engage in the cultivation of their grounds, in building suitable habitations for themselves, and in whatever else may conduce to their civilization and social improvement.

4. The education and instruction of the children, as early and as extensively as it may be practicable, is to be regarded as a matter of primary importance.

5. In connexion with the engagements, and as affording the most efficient means for the ultimate accomplishment of them, the assistant protector should promote, to the utmost extent of his ability and opportunities, the moral and religious improvement of the natives, by instructing them in the elements of the Christian religion, and preparing them for the reception of teachers, whose peculiar province it would be to promote the knowledge and practice of Christianity among them.

6. In reference to every object contemplated by the proposed appointment, it is exceedingly desirable that the protector should, as soon as possible, learn the language of the natives, so as to be able freely and familiarly to converse with them.

7. He must take charge of, and be accountable for, any provisions or clothing which may be placed under his care for distribution to the natives.

8. He will obtain as accurate information as may be practicable of the number of the natives within his district, and of all important particulars in regard to them.

These appear to me the principal points which demand attention in reference to this subject.

But it is of course not my intention to restrict you, in the instructions which you will have to issue to the protectors, within the topics on which I have touched, as your local knowledge and experience will doubtless enable you to supply omissions in the outline which I have given.

I have, &c.

(signed)     *Glenelg.*

## 4.2   8 June 1838. The Memorial.

*(Ibid.,* Vol. 34, 1839, Enclosure 1 in No. 6, p. 29.)

*A copy of a Memorial addressed to His Excellency Sir George Gipps, Knight, Governor-in-chief, and the Honourable and Executive Council of New South Wales.*

The Memorial of the undersigned Colonists, Landholders and Proprietors of Stock,

Respectfully showeth,

That your memorialists having a deep interest in the welfare and prosperity of the new settlement at Port Phillip, and in the peace and good government of this colony generally, conceive it incumbent on them to bring under the notice of your Excellency and Honourable Council the state of that part of the country, arising from the hostility of the aborigines.

That your memorialists have learnt with feelings of regret and alarm, that certain tribes on the road to and in the neighbourhood of Port Phillip have lately assumed a hostile attitude towards the settlers, and have committed many murders and other outrages upon them; that they are assembled in large numbers armed, and attacking such persons as are most unprotected and within their reach, so that many have been obliged to abandon their stations, leaving, in some cases, their flocks and herds at the mercy of the hostile tribes; and that the intercourse by land between this part of the territory and Port Phillip, if it has not already ceased, has become one of imminent danger to life and property.

That your memorialists are not aware of any aggression on the part of Her Majesty's white subjects which could have excited the blacks to commit the excesses and barbarities, of fresh instances of which almost every post brings the account, but believe that the natives, unrestrained by moral principles, and placing little or no value on human life, have been stimulated by their natural cupidity and ferocity in perpetrating the outrages of which they have lately been guilty.

That your memorialists feel, however, that an inquiry into the cause of these attacks on the lives and property of their fellow-subjects, peacefully pursuing an avocation sanctioned by the laws of their country, is not the question at the present time, but rather (their existence being ascertained beyond doubt) how most speedily and effectually a period may be put to these outrages.

That your memorialists are of opinion that these untutored savages, not comprehending or appreciating the motives which actuate us, attribute forbearance on our part solely to impotence or fear, and are thus rendered only more bold and sanguinary. This opinion, founded on past experience, will receive ample confirmation on reference to the history of this colony and the acts of its former governments. It is undeniable, that no district of the colony has been settled without, in the first instance, suffering from the outrages of the natives, and that these outrages continued until put an end to by coercive measures. Conciliation was generally used in the first instance, but invariably failed in producing any good effect, and coercion was ultimately found unavoidably necessary, which, if earlier adopted, would have saved much bloodshed on both sides. It is only when they have become experimentally acquainted with our power and determination to punish their aggressions that they have become orderly, peaceable, and been brought within the reach of civilization.

That your memorialists fear, that if adequate protection be not afforded by the Government, the settlers will undoubtedly take measures to protect themselves, as it is not to be supposed they will remain quietly looking on whilst their property is being destroyed, and their servants murdered; and your memorialists need hardly observe, that such a mode of proceeding would inevitably be attended with consequences of the most painful nature.

That your memorialists, in conclusion, respectfully entreat your Excellency and Honourable Council to take such energetic and effectual steps as will for the present repress, and for the future prevent, the aggressions of these hostile tribes, and protect the lives and properties of Her Majesty's subjects who are engaged in the laudable and enterprising pursuit of a pastoral life in the interior, and the pioneers of civilization, your memorialists being convinced that such a course will eventually prove to be the most humane and merciful.

Sydney, 8 June 1838.     And your memorialists will ever pray, &c.

(82 Signatures.)

### 4.3    23 June 1838. Sir George Gipps's reply to the Memorialists.

(*Ibid.*, Vol. 34, Enclosure 2 in No. 6, pp. 29-30.)

Colonial Secretary's Office, Sydney,
23 June 1838.

Sir,

I HAVE the honour, by command of the Governor, to acknowledge the receipt of a memorial, dated 8th June, addressed to his Excellency and the Executive Council, and signed by yourself and other gentlemen interested in the settlement at Port Phillip.

In reply, I am directed by his Excellency to inform you, that no person can have felt more concern or regret than he has at the accounts recently received from the southern parts of this territory. That in order to afford to the settlers in those districts all the protection in his Excellency's power, he despatched a party, consisting of an officer and 12 men of the mounted police, to the River Ovens, as soon as he heard of the late massacre of Mr. Faithfull's men, and that this party has since been increased to 21; so that with the seven that were originally at Melbourne, there will be a party of one officer and 28 mounted policemen, independently of the military force, which by a recent addition of 12, now amounts to 44; and that a discretionary power has been given to the police magistrate at Melbourne to cause parties of infantry to advance, if necessary, into the interior.

I am also instructed to inform you, that it is the Governor's further intention to establish posts at convenient distances along the road, from Yass to Port Phillip, in order to keep open the communication, and that a permanent addition will be made to the mounted police for this purpose.

Having thus explained the measures which have been adopted, and which his Excellency has reason to hope will be sufficient, Sir George Gipps desires it to be intimated to the gentlemen who have signed the memorial, that as he has the most positive directions from Her Majesty's Government to treat the aboriginal natives as subjects of Her Majesty, it is entirely out of his power to authorize the levying of war against them, or to give sanction to any measures of indiscriminate retaliation; and in order that no misapprehension may exist on this subject, he feels bound to declare, that nothing which has been done in this colony in former times, or in any other colony or place whatsoever, would, in his opinion, be a justification for departing from the strict obedience which is due to the orders of Her Majesty's Government.

It is doubtless only of late years that the British public has been awakened to a knowledge of what is owing to these ignorant barbarians on the part of their more civilized neighbours; but a deep feeling of their duties does now exist on the part both of the Government and the public, as may be proved by reference to the many inquiries which have been lately instituted on the subject, aud particularly by the unanimous address of the House of Commons to his late Majesty, adopted in July 1834, and by a Report of a Committee of the same House, made in the very last sitting of Parliament, both of which documents are of easy access to the public.

I am, however, directed to acquaint you, that there is nothing in the Governor's instructions to prevent his protecting to the utmost of his power the lives and property of settlers in every part of this territory, and that this his Excellency is determined to do. Sir George Gipps, moreover, readily allows, that after having taken entire possession of the country, without any reference to the rights of the aborigines, it is now too late for the Government to refuse protection to persons, who have come hither, and brought with them their flocks and herds on its own invitation, though at the same time, it must be evident that every wanderer in search of pasturage cannot be attended by a military force.

In conclusion, I am instructed to notify to you, that although the memorial to which this letter refers is addressed to the Governor and Executive Council, his Excellency has not deemed it necessary to take the advice of that body on it, as the line of his own duty is so clearly defined, that he feels neither doubt nor difficulty as to the course which he ought to pursue.

| | |
|---|---|
| Philip G. King, Esq. | |
| The Gentleman first signing the | I have, &c. |
| Memorial referred to. | (signed)   *E. Deas Thomson.* |

## 4.4   25 April 1838—21 July 1838. Sir George Gipps's reply to Lord Glenelg.

(*Ibid.*, Vol. 34, 1839, Enclosure 3 in No. 6, pp. 30-31.)

*"A statement of the principle outrages committed by or on the Aborigines . . . of which reports have been received since April 25th last."*

Your Lordship will observe that a great proportion of these acts of violence have occurred in the neighbourhood of Port Phillip, or on the road between the settled parts of this colony and that place, the reason of which is, that large herds of cattle and flocks of sheep have been recently driven through these extensive tracts of country, with a very insufficient number of people to guard them, often not more than in the proportion of one man to several hundred sheep. That under these circumstances predatory attacks should have been made on them by the natives, does not, I must say, appear to me in the least degree to be wondered at.

Your Lordship must be aware that it is quite out of the power of this Government to give to the proprietors or their flocks the protection they desire; even if we were restrained by no sense of humanity towards the blacks, the resources of the Government would be quite insufficient to keep military parties always in advance of persons who are migrating in search of pasturage, advancing often 50 miles in a single season, and, in the case of Port Phillip, having stretched to a distance beyond our former limits of between 300 and 400 miles in the last three years.

If proprietors, for the sake of obtaining better pasturage for their increasing flocks, will venture with them to such a distance from protection, they must be considered to run the same risk as men would do who were to drive their sheep into a country infested with wolves; with this difference, however, that if they were really wolves, the Government would encourage the shepherds to combine and destroy them, whilst all we can now do is, to raise, in the name of justice and humanity, a voice in favour of our poor savage fellow-creatures, too feeble to be heard at such a distance.

Your Lordship will not fail to observe, that of the outrages enumerated in the accompanying list, some took place 200 or 300 miles to the north of Sydney, others at more than 500 miles to the south, and some (at Geelong, the western limit of Port Phillip) at a still greater distance.

In order to keep open the communication between Sydney and Port Phillip, it is my intention, with the concurrence of the officer in command of Her Majesty's troops, to establish military posts on the road; and I forward a sketch, on which the places of these proposed posts are marked, they being, as your Lordship will perceive, the places where the road crosses the following streams on the way, viz. the Murray, the Ovens, the Violet Creek, and the Goulburn.

*To the North of Sydney*
*1.* ON the 2d May a report was received from Lieutenant Cobhan of the mounted police, stating that he had discovered the dead bodies of two men, named Gorman and Gale, who had belonged to a surveying party under Mr. Finch; and that he had captured a party of blacks, who were concerned in the murder of them. Two blacks were reported to have been killed in the affray.

*2.* On the 2d June a report was received from the Rev. Mr. Threlkeld, engaged on a mission at Lake Macquarie, stating that three aboriginal women had been murdered, by persons who were supposed to be in the employment of the Australian Agricultural Company.

*3.* A report was received on the 6th July from Mr. Foot, that in consequence of a horse having been speared at Mr. H. Dangar's station, a party of white men had assembled for the purpose of attacking the blacks; that they had taken 22 of them, including many women and children, and put them all to death. No official account has as yet been received of this atrocious deed, but a magistrate with a party of mounted police has been despatched in pursuit of the perpetrators of it. The scene of the atrocity is supposed to be not less than 200 miles to the north of Sydney.

*On the Port Phillip, or Southern Side of the Colony.*
*1.* Between the rivers Ovens and Goulburn, a large convoy of sheep and cattle, belonging to Mr. W. Pitt Faithfull, and under the charge of 15 white men, was attacked by a party of blacks, said to have been 300

strong. Seven of the white men were killed, and the rest, as well as the whole of the cattle, dispersed in all directions. This occurrence took place about 400 miles from Sydney, and 150 from Port Phillip.

2. On the 15th April the cattle station of Mr. Samuel Jackson, near Port Phillip, was attacked by about 50 blacks, some of whom had fire-arms; about 50 sheep were carried away, though some of them were afterwards recovered.

3. On the 22d April the station of Mr. John Gardiner, near Port Phillip, was attacked by a party of blacks, some of whom had fire-arms; they were, however, repulsed, and two of them who were subsequently taken were recognised as having been under the instruction of Mr. Langhorne, the missionary at Port Phillip. No lives were lost, though shots were fired on both sides.

4. On or about the same day a flock of 520 sheep, belonging to Mr. Kenneth Clark, was driven away from his station to a distance of seven or eight miles by the blacks. All were, however, recovered, with the exception of 43.

5. On the 6th May the flocks of Dr. Jonathan Clark were attacked by a party of blacks, who had dogs with them, and 20 sheep were carried off.

6. On the 19th May Thomas Jones, a servant in the employ of Mr. Bowman, was murdered by the blacks, about 60 miles from Port Phillip. On the preceding day a flock of sheep had been driven away from Mr. Bowman's station, though all were afterwards recovered, with the exception of four.

7. On or about the 22d May all the stations on the Burwan creeks, extending to a distance of more than 30 miles from Geelong, (on the western side of Port Phillip,) were attacked, for the second time, by a party of about 60 blacks. Several huts were plundered; one flock of sheep was driven to a distance of seven or eight miles, three were killed and 25 wounded. From another station 16 lambs were carried off, and from a third, six sheep and six lambs; and other mischief is reported to have been done to a considerable extent.

June 1. A black man, supposed to have been engaged in a murder committed some months ago, near Geelong, was drowned in an attempt to escape from the persons who were in pursuit of him.

June 9. Seven or eight blacks killed in defending a flock of sheep which they had carried away from the station of Mr. Yaldwyn, about 80 miles from Port Phillip. On this occasion the blacks are said to have defended themselves with great bravery.

N.B. A great number of less important outrages have come indirectly to the knowledge of the Government, or been reported in the newspapers. And it is said that a white woman, the wife of a soldier, has been murdered between Melbourne and Geelong, though no official account has been received of it.

## 4.5  November 1838. The Myall Creek Massacre.

(*Ibid.*, Vol. 34, 1839, Enclosure 1 in No. 8, pp. 40-41.)

*George Anderson's eye-witness account of the events before the Myall Creek Massacre, presented to the jury in Sydney.*

*George Anderson,* Examined.

I am assigned servant to Mr. Dangar; I was at his station at Myall Creek. as hut-keeper, for five months, in June. Mr Hobbs lives there as superintendent; he left home, to go to the Big River, in the beginning of June; when he left, there were some native blacks there; I have said there were 20, but I am sure there were that number, and upwards; I would not swear there were not 40. While master was away, some men came on a Saturday, about 10; I cannot say how many days after master left; they came on horseback, armed with muskets and swords and pistols; all were armed; I was at home when they came, and the stock-keeper; I was sitting with Kilmeister, the stock-keeper, in the hut; I saw them coming up; they came up galloping, with guns and pistols pointing towards the hut; I did not attend to what they said; they were talking to Kilmeister outside . . . the blacks were all encamped ready for the night; they were not more than two yards from the hut; this was about an hour and a half before sundown; there were plenty of women and children amongst them. The blacks, when they saw the men coming, ran into our hut, and the men then, all of them, got off their horses; . . . I asked what they were going to do with the blacks, and Russel said, "We are going to take them over the back of the range, to frighten them." Russel and some one or two went in; . . . I remained outside; one of them remained in; I heard the crying of the blacks for relief or assistance to me and Kilmeister; they were moaning the same as a mother and children would cry; there were small things that could not walk; there were a good many small boys and girls. After they were tied, I saw Russel bring the end of the rope out they were tied with, and gave it one of the men on one of the horses, I cannot say which. The party then went away with the blacks; . . . they were all fastened with one rope; it was a tether rope for horses in a field; it is a very long rope; they brought out the whole except two, that made their escape as the men were coming up; they were two little boys, and they jumped into the creek close to the hut; there was no water in it; they escaped at a dry part; one black gin they left with me in the hut; they left her because she was good-looking; they said so; I forget which; another black gin they left that was with Davy, . . . there was a little child at the back of the hut when they were tying this party, and when the blacks and party were going away, this little child, as I thought, was going to follow the party with its mother, but I took hold of it and put it into the hut, and stopt it from going. I had two little boys, the small child, two gins, and Davy and Billy; they all went away except these; the child was going after its mother. There was an old man, named Daddy, the oldest of the lot; he was called Old Daddy; he was an old, big, tall man; this Daddy and another man, named Joey, they never tied along with the rest; they were crying, and did not want to go; they made no resistance. Some of the children were not tied, others were; they followed the rest that were tied; the small ones, two or three, were not able to walk; the women carried them on their backs in opposum skins; . . . they were crying, in and out of the hut, till they got out of my hearing. They went up towards the west from the hut, the road way; Kilmeister got his horse ready, after he had done talking to them, and just before they were going to start; he went with them on horseback, and took the pistol with him; he was talking to them five or ten minutes; I did not take notice of what he said; I was frightened; . . .

Kilmeister went with them when they started; they were not in sight above a minute or so after they went away; about a quarter of an hour, or 20 minutes at the outside, I heard the report of two pieces, one after the other; the reports came from the same direction they went; the second was quite plain for any one to hear; . . . It was just before sundown, next night after, the same men came back to the hut where they took the blacks from; they were altogether of a lump, except Kilmeister, who was left behind; one of the party gave Kilmeister's saddle off his horse, and I asked him where Kilmeister was; he came in about 20 minutes after;

they stopt all night. I and Kilmeister slept together in one berth; the rest all slept in the hut; they were talking; I cannot recollect what they said. Next morning, three of them, after they had breakfast, took firesticks out of the hut, Russel, Fleming another, and Kilmeister another; and before they took the firesticks, Fleming told Kilmeister to bring the leg-rope with him that ropes the cows; . . . and they went in the same direction as they took the blacks and that I heard the two pieces. One of the men was left behind, and all the rest went with those who had the firesticks; one was left with me as guard, named Foley. While they were away, Foley and I were in the hut together, and the rest away; during the time they were away, I asked Foley if any of the blacks had made their escape; he said none, that he saw; he said all were killed except one black gin. Before the party came back, Foley drew one of the swords out of the case, and showed it to me; it was all over blood. During that time Davy and Billy came to the hut; in about an hour the other men came back to the hut; I saw smoke in the same direction they went; this was soon after they went with the firesticks; . . . they got upon their horses, and Fleming told Kilmeister to go up by-and-by and put the logs of wood together, and be sure that all was consumed; . . . They brought back no black gin they saved; the gins they left, and the two boys, and the child I sent away with 10 black fellows that went away in the morning. . . . I did not like to keep them, as the men might come back and kill them.

. . . I did not ask to have that gin left behind; . . . it was when they were going away when they undid one gin for me. They left Davy; he had been there a good while; he was more naturalized than the others; the others were as quiet as he; I did not dream they would take Davy. . . . I did not ask for the gin they left; I asked for one I had had before; she was a black fellow's gin. . . .

I had two examinations, as I wanted to speak the whole of the truth; I recollected more than I stated at the first examination. I have been here five years and better; I came for life. I never said this would get me my liberty; I neither expect nor hope for my liberty; I do not ask for anything, only for protection.

### 4.6   19 December 1838. Sir George Gipps's report on murder trials.

(*Ibid.*, Vol. 34, 1839, No. 8, Dispatch No. 200, pp. 34-35.)

*Governor Sir George Gipps reports on the trials that preceded the execution of seven men found guilty of murdering Aborigines without provocation.*

On the banks of the Big River there are several cattle stations besides that of Mr. Dangar, and it appeared on the trial, that for some weeks previous to the 10th June, not less than 50 blacks, of all ages and sexes, had been living at these different stations, (but mostly at Mr. Dangar's) in perfect tranquillity, neither molesting the whites, nor being themselves molested by them. In consequence of some old quarrels, however, or possibly from accounts having reached the place of occurrences in other quarters, a determination seems to have been formed by the white men to put the whole of the blacks to death. On the afternoon of Sunday the 10th June, a number of them suddenly surrounded the place, where more than 30 of the blacks were assembled; they tied them all to a rope, in the way that convicts are sometimes tied, in order to be taken from place to place in the colony; marched them to a convenient spot, about a quarter of a mile off, and put them all, with the exception of one woman and four or five children, deliberately to death. The following day, Monday, the 11th June, the same white men scoured the country on horseback, endeavouring to find 10 or 12 of the blacks, who having left Dangar's station on the morning of the 10th, had escaped the massacre. These 10 or 12 persons have never been seen or heard of since, and it is doubtful to this day whether they were not overtaken and murdered also.

The first accounts of these deeds of blood reached Sydney about the end of the month of June. I despatched, with as little delay as possible, a stipendiary magistrate (Mr. Day), on whose activity and discretion I could rely, and a party of mounted police, in search of the murderers; and Mr. Day, after an absence of 53 days, reported to me in person, that having come unexpectedly to the cattle station of Mr. Dangar, he had succeeded in capturing no less than 11 out of the 12 persons who were known to have taken part in the massacre. When Mr. Day arrived at the spot, some few scattered human bones only were visible, great pains having been taken to destroy the whole remains of the slaughtered blacks by fire; but undeniable evidence was procured of more than 20 human heads having been counted on the spot, within a few days after the day of the massacre; and the best accounts lead me to suppose that the number of persons murdered, of all ages and both sexes, was not less than 28. The 11 persons apprehended by Mr. Day all arrived in this country as convicts, though of some of them the sentences have expired. The twelfth man, or the one who has escaped, is a free man, a native of the colony, named John Fleming.

The 11 men were all brought to trial on the 15th of November, on an information lodged against them by the Attorney-general, containing nine counts. The first four counts charged them in various ways with the murder of an aboriginal black, named Daddy, the only adult male who could be identified as one of the murdered party; the five other counts charged them (also in various ways) with the murder of an aboriginal male black, name unknown. The jury on this occasion acquitted the whole of the prisoners. . . .

The Attorney-general immediately applied to have them detained on the further charge of murdering the women and children, none of whom had been comprehended in the first indictment; and this being done, seven of these men, on the 27th of the same month (November), were again brought before the Supreme Court, on the charge of murdering a child. On this occasion, the first five counts charged them simply with the murder of an aboriginal black child; other counts described the aboriginal child by the name of Charley. . . .

The seven men were consequently two days afterwards, on the 29th November, put on their trial for the murder of the child, and found guilty on the first five counts, which described the child merely as a black aboriginal, but were acquitted upon the counts which charged them with the murder of a child named Charley, sufficient proof of the name of the child not being adduced. . . .

The report of the judge (Mr. Justice Burton) who presided at the trial was received by myself and the Executive Council on Friday the 7th instant, when no mitigating circumstances appearing in favour of any of them, and nothing to show that any one of them was less guilty than the rest, the Council unanimously advised that the sentence of the law should take effect on them; they were accordingly ordered by me for execution, and suffered yesterday morning at nine o'clock.

## 4.7 21 December 1838. The Principal Gaoler's letter.

(*Ibid.*, Vol. 34, 1839, Enclosure in No. 10, p. 56.)

*Letter sent by the chief gaoler responsible for the execution of the convicted murderers of the Myall Creek Aborigines, to the High Sheriff of Sydney.*

Her Majesty's Gaol, Sydney,
21 December 1838.

Sir,

IN compliance with your suggestion to me yesterday, respecting the seven men executed on Tuesday morning, I have the honour to inform you, that frequently, during their confinement here, they each and all, at different times, acknowledged to me their guilt; but implied, that as it was done solely in defence of their masters' property, that they were not aware that in destroying the aboriginals they were violating the law, or that it could take cognizance of their having done so, as it had (according to their belief) been so frequently done in the colony before.

|  |  |  |
|---|---|---|
|  |  | I have, &c. |
| The High Sheriff, | (signed) | *Henry Keck,* |
| &c. &c. &c. |  | Principal Gaoler. |


## 4.8 1838. Captain Maconochie's observations.

(Captain K. H. Maconochie, R. N., *Thoughts on Convict Management and Other Subjects Connected with the Australian Penal Colonies,* A Lecture, Hobart Town, 1838, pp. 186-195.)

*This is a chapter from a lecture written by the influential traveller, Captain K. H. Maconochie, R. N., about the treatment of the Aborigines.*

It is difficult to consider the new Colonies now in the act of being established along the coasts of Australia, without feeling a deep interest in the native tribes about to be brought in contact with them. In every previous instance of such contact these tribes have been deeply injured; to such an extent, indeed, that it has been seriously and in truth, rationally and justly represented to a Committee of the House of Commons, enquiring into the subject, that even the Slave trade, with all its horrors has not been such a scourge to humanity as the English Colonizing system. Must these things then be here again acted? Because we want their territory, of which, it is true, they make but a very limited use, and which in their hands can never acquire its full value—must these other Black families be exterminated like their predecessors in similar circumstances? Or may not some scheme be devised, founded on the peculiarity of their condition and circumstances, calculated to preserve and improve them, while we also benefit ourselves? And may not some general principles be deduced from this scheme, and others similar, and be employed for trying even themselves—on which Native tribes may be managed generally, with advantage to themselves, and benefit to the European communities settling among them? To these two last questions I beg to offer some replies.

I.—It appears to me that were the natives in the neighbourhood of our Australian Colonies liberally enlisted in our public service, and regimented (like the Sepoys in India, the Black Troops in Western Africa, and the Hottentots on the Caffre Frontier), and thus formed into an active field police, we should be enabled by this hold on them both to preserve and improve them, and benefit ourselves essentially. They would require to be officered with white serjeants and corporals, who should be as much as possible interested in the successful management of their charge;—a light, convenient, and somewhat ornamental dress should be also given them;—and breaking them into small parties, they should be kept much in the field and on the move—at first hunting, with their other duty, but gradually acquiring more and more precise notions of military duty as their education proceeded. Their families, meanwhile, should be encouraged to settle in native villages under our protection;— their general habits should be there studiously improved;—their children should be educated;—and their fathers and husbands, who should be frequently allowed to visit them, and who would be receiving their own education at the same time in the field, would insensibly assist in this work. Perhaps one or two mounted commissioned officers should be added to the whole, who, attended by one or other of the little *pelotons* in turn, should ride about to inspect, encourage, train, and keep them in order. And the sum of benefit that might thus be derived, might, I think, be analized as follows.

*1.* A much more numerous, effective, and yet economical field police, could be thus maintained than by any other means. It would also be more steadily well-behaved than a prisoner police, otherwise so common in the Australian Colonies. Both natives and stock-keepers would be effectually restrained by it—for from the number and activity of its parties it would be almost ubiquitous. Occasions of irregularity and dissention would be thus kept down, and runaway convicts would be certainly arrested by it.

*2.* The relative *status* of the black population would be thus raised in the estimation of the community; and a more universally civil and conciliatory demeanor would consequently be maintained towards them. This is of great importance;—human nature is raised by courtesy and respect, and is certainly depressed and demoralized by contempt.

*3.* The affections of natives thus treated would soon be warmly engaged, to the whites generally, but especially to the Government so employing and advancing them; and between themselves and their immediate officers there would soon be the strongest ties. Their hearts would be proportionally light, and their improvement more rapid. They would be drawn upward both by feeling and ambition. Stupidity, obstinacy, or misconduct, would be crimes, not as regarded themselves only, but as they displeased such good masters; and the silken cord would, *as in every other case*, be more effectual than the iron fetter.

*4.* Their erratic habits, (the great stumbling block usually in the way of civilizing savage tribes) being on this system gratified, they would in other respects probably be thus much more teachable and scrupulously obedient than they are commonly found;—and habits of deference to command and direction, not requiring much sacrifice at first, would be confirmed by time, and might then be otherwise, and more highly directed.

*5.* A knowledge of, and taste for, European manners and civilization, would be thus extensively, yet silently implanted; and the habits of order, concert, and decorum learnt and practised in the field, would probably sooner pervade their huts, and family stations, than is now thought possible. It is thus that sailors and soldiers almost invariably make good settlers; and the liberated Hottentots settled at Kat-river astonished even the most sanguine by their steadiness and industry.

*6.* The observance of the forms of our religious worship, and gradually a perception of its truths, might thus also be early and extensively diffused. There is no strong counteracting superstition among the native Australians as in Africa and India.

*7.* Habits of neatness, decency, and cleanliness, usually repugnant to savages, yet without which it may be confidently said that no great moral improvement can be effected in them, would be more easily and early acquiesced in when imposed as points of military discipline, otherwise agreeable, than when differently suggested;—and spirituous liquors, and other improper indulgencies, could be thus more easily kept away.

8. The more distant native tribes, and even the members of the same communities not thus engaged, would be conciliated by seeing and hearing of this considerate, and as they would deem it, honourable treatment of their companions and equals. They would endeavour also not essentially to be left behind them. They would thus copy, as far as they could, their newly acquired habits, manners, and dress. They would try to get enlisted into their number; and for this purpose would recommend themselves to their common masters by activity, honesty, intelligence, fidelity, and such other virtues as were within their sphere. The whole imitative faculties of the race would be thus devoted to good, instead of, as now too often happens, to vice or folly; and the benevolent purpose for which a wise Providence has given to all savages a large endowment of these, viz.—to assist in drawing them up the first steps of improvement, before their reason can be interested in the task, would then be served by them.

9. The security which the organization of such a force would bestow on the infant communities setting an example of it, need not be insisted on. Surprise and insurrection would be almost impossible with a stirring, active, attached, native guard. . . .

II.—The next question, however, regards the general principles on which this, or any similar scheme, however modified by peculiar circumstances, should in the main be founded, so as to meet either the justice, or expediency of any case; and of these I think the following, not excluding others, are nearly incontestible.

1. When a new territory is occupied, and the original rights of the natives ranging over it are consequently infringed, the *first* claim to a share of its increased value is surely *theirs?* I do not mean that the proceeds of this should be gratuitously lavished on them (for that would be to injure, not to serve them); but they should be considered as having an admitted right to have such portion freely expended on them, as can really be shewn to be calculated to do them good. Even when this is deducted there will always be found in judicious colonization a large balance for ourselves; and besides that what will actually benefit the natives will benefit us also, this will give us a *right*, which, without it, it would be difficult to prove that we possess, to appropriate either the land, or the remainder.

2. The use to which we put the native portion should be of a nature to raise their relative *status* with regard to us, and not merely protect them in their inferiority. The first will make men of them, the second merely contemplates keeping them out of harm's way as children; and I do not think it possible to attach too much importance to the distinction.

3. Speaking generally, they should be encouraged to *intermingle* with the white population, and be employed *with* them, rather than have separate stations assigned them. It may no doubt be necessary occasionally, where enmity, jealousy, and their dividing and demoralizing fruits have long prevailed, for a time to qualify this position (as for example at present on the Caffre frontier); but as a principle it is not less certain than the others. Intermingling gives the attitude of confidence, separation that of distrust; and the feelings will follow their respective indications of whatsoever kind.

4. The employments selected for natives under this system, should, as much as possible, in the beginning be analogous to their original habits; yet they should not be allowed even from the first to act in them capriciously. The lighter the early tie the better; but there will be no real advantage gained till it become sufficiently heavy to be distinctly recognized. The first of manly virtues, and the foundation for all others, is the *self*

*command* implied by the voluntary performance of what is yet felt to be a task.

5. Much of the benefit to be derived from intermingling them with whites is founded, indeed, on this principle. They will imitate them in every thing, even in early submission to restraint; and the chief care will be that these whites shall give them as few worse, and as many other good, lessons as possible.

6. In dealing with human beings of all classes and states of society, much more virtue than is often admitted will be found to exist in a distinguishing dress. It operates both as an incentive and preservative; and habits of order, method, decorum, concert, union, are all reinforced by it. Among savages it cultivates also *amour propre*, (self-respect), a useful, sometimes irritable, but otherwise seldom steady principle among them. They are themselves, indeed, so sensible of the direct effect of a dress that many have a particular one for different occasions.

7. When some little authority can be blended with usefulness in employment, I am persuaded that there will always be found an advantage. Hence, though I would by no means insist on all savages, however different in circumstances, being treated precisely as I recommended the Australians to be, I yet think that the police will be found, generally, a good employment. (It has been found to answer extremely well on a small scale among the Van Diemen's Land Aborigines in Flinders' Island; and although less successful in New South Wales, that arises chiefly from the peculiarly imperfect manner in which it has been there tried). It should be a *preventive* rather than a *remedial* police, however; and I am certain that this distinction will be found an important one.

8. Wherever savages are employed, as much attention as possible should be paid to their own distinctions of rank. (Castes, on the contrary, I should be rather disposed to intermingle). Their chiefs should thus be made officers, or otherwise superior to, or equal with, some whites; and equality and amalgamation should in this way be studied as much as possible, without any factitious distinctions or difference even in the mode of protection. I most cordially agree with Captain Stockenstrom's opinion, that Protectorships are bad things, as implying inferiority; and that the forms of justice and protection should be the same to all.

9. A sincere, and not merely assumed, interest, should be taken in natives thus sought to be brought in. They cannot long be imposed on in this respect; and giving their own hearts, as they will all do, freely, their disappointment and resentment, when indifference is shewn to their *real* grievances, will always be proportionate. Their diseases therefore should be energetically attended to, their marriage ties and domestic usages should be respected, their children should be noticed as well as educated, their sports, and even in moderation their jokes, should be smiled at, their superstitions, if they have any, should be discouraged, and not rudely trampled on. Some tact, some firmness, some intelligence and discrimination will no doubt be necessary to draw a precise line between these attentions and an undignified compliance with pure caprices, which will impair respect, and do harm rather than good. . . .

11. I am also of opinion that in attempts to civilize and convert native tribes, systematic efforts should be always made to teach them English; and that translations, even of the Bible, into their own language are of very doubtful utility. The Creator himself seems to indicate this course, by the facility in acquiring languages which he has uniformly bestowed on savage man; and which is in truth but a branch of that great power of imitation with which he is universally endowed, the object of which has already been adverted to, and cannot be mistaken. But other strong arguments can also be advanced in favour of this course. The object is to raise

the native, not to descend to his level, or apparently even below it, by imperfect, and therefore necessarily in many cases ludicrous, efforts to use his jargon. In learning English, also, many ideas, abstract and others, will be acquired insensibly, the opportunity for conveying which is lost by communicating through the medium of native tongues. A habitual, yet gradual, and as is proved by the success of Classical education among ourselves, a beneficial exercise of the young native mind will be thus afforded, maturing its reason. The intellectual field into which it will thus be introduced will be more extensive than any labor of translation can afford. It is more calculated to excite imagination, to stimulate ambition, and to wean from barbarous associations. It would be easy, but seems unnecessary, to pursue the argument farther.

In conclusion—the great principles of native treatment are thus—their *elevation in the social scale, inter-mixture with ourselves, beneficial employment, religious conversion, instruction in our language,* and thereby progressive *development of their mind and understanding*; nor, I am persuaded, will any benevolent and *hopeful* spirit fail with them if it keep these ends in view. In considering the subject, however, the importance of *hopefulness* in dealing with them is well worthy of this separate notice. In the beginning it will be necessary in many cases even to "hope against hope;" for in this, as in so many other fields of moral labor, the first steps are the really difficult ones, being often long without their reward. Yet if persevered in they are sure of ultimate success. We see in children, up to a certain point, the same vacillation, unsteadiness, perverseness, inaccessibility to intellectual impression, and dislike to the effort of learning, with which savages are habitually reproached; and we may be assured that the same patient, persevering, parental, and *inventive* zeal which overcomes these qualities in the one, will not fail eventually to overcome them in the other also.

### 4.9   1838 and 1845. Sir Thomas Mitchell's observations.

(Major Thomas L. Mitchell, *Three Expeditions into the Interior of Eastern Australia; with Descriptions of the Recently Explored Region of Australia Felix and the Present Colony of New South Wales*, first edition, London, 1838, pp. 350-352, Vol. 2.

*Sir Thomas L. Mitchell, one of Australia's greatest explorers, believed in the intelligence and strength of character of the Aborigines he encountered.*

My experience enables me to speak in the most favourable terms of the Aborigines, whose degraded condition in the white population affords no just criterion of their merits. The quickness of apprehension of those in the interior is extraordinary, for nothing in all the complicated adaptions we carried with us either surprised or puzzled them. They were never awkward; on the contrary, in manners and general intelligence they appear superior to any class of white rustics that I have ever seen. Their powers of mimicry seem extraordinary, and their shrewdness shines even through the medium of imperfect language, and renders them, in general, very agreeable companions. . . . The bad example of the class of persons sent to Australia should be counteracted by some serious efforts to civilise and instruct these aboriginal inhabitants.

Lt. Col. Sir T. L. Mitchell, *Journal of an Expedition into the Interior of Tropical Australia in Search of a Route from Sydney to the Gulf of Carpentaria*, Longman, Brown, Green, and Longmans, London, 1848, pp. 412, 414.)

They have been described as the lowest in the scale of humanity, yet I found those who accompanied me superior in penetration and judgement to the white men composing my party. . . . It would ill become me to disparage the character of the aborigines, for one of that unfortunate race has been my "guide", "companion, councillor and friend", on the most eventful occasions during my last journey of discovery.

**4.10 21 May 1839. Sir George Gipps's notice to the commissioners.**

(*House of Commons Parliamentary Papers*, Vol. 34, 1844. "Copies of Extracts from Despatches of the Governors of the Australian Colonies with the Reports of the Protectors of Aborigines, etc., etc., New South Wales." Enclosure 2 in No. 3, pp. 20-21.)

*A notice published first on 18 September 1837, and again on 21 May, 1839, authorized by the then Governor of New South Wales, Sir George Gipps.*

"Colonial Secretary's Office, Sydney
18 Sept., 1837.

"The Governor having been informed by the reports of certain of the commissioners of Crown lands, that, at the stations beyond the limits of location, overseers and other persons in charge of cattle and sheep in those remote districts, are not unfrequently guilty of detaining by force, in their huts, and as their companions abroad, black women of the native tribes resorting to their neighbourhood, an offence, not only in itself of a most heinous and revolting character, but, in its consequences, leading to bloodshed and murder; His Excellency has been pleased to direct the commissioners to report the names of all persons whom they shall find in any way concerned in so abominable and unchristian a proceeding, in order that their licences may be immediately cancelled, and that they may be prosecuted under the Act, as illegal occupiers of Crown lands, or otherwise, as the law directs.

"By His Excellency's command,
"E. DEAS THOMSON."

**4.11 1 September 1839—29 February 1840. Assistant Protector Edward Stone Parker's first report.**

(Edward Stone Parker, "First Periodical Report from the Loddon District", in Edgar Morrison, *Early Days of the Loddon Valley*, Daylesford, 1966, pp. 13, 14, 15, 16.)

*Extract from the first Periodical Report from Assistant Protector Edward Stone Parker, from the headquarters at Mount Franklin, to Chief Protector Robinson.*

Several important facts materially affecting the condition and prospects of the aboriginal population, as well as the security of persons and property of the colonists have been forcibly brought under my notice. I beg most respectively to submit them to the consideration of Her Majesty's Colonial Government.

*1.* The first is the rapid occupation of the entire country by settlers, and the consequent attempts made to deprive the aborigines of the natural products of the country and even to exclude them from their native soil. The entire country of the Waverong and Witourong tribes with scarcely any exception, is now sold or occupied by squatters.

A considerable portion of the country ranged by the Jajowrong and Taoungurong tribes is also taken up by sheep and cattle runs.

All the available portions of the tracts that remain will speedily be absorbed in like manner by stock. The very spots most valuable to the aborigines for their productiveness—the creeks, watercourses and rivers—are the first to be occupied.

It is a common opinion among the settlers that the possession of a squatting licence entitles them to the exclusion of the aborigines from their runs.

Lately, Mr Munro, having pushed his stations on both sides of the "Coláband" and up the tributary creeks to Mount Alexander (Leanga nook) complained in a public journal that "the blacks are still lurking about the creeks—that they seemed determined to act as lords of the soil" etc., etc.

The plain fact is that this is their ordinary place of resort, as furnishing them with the most abundant supplies of food.

Precisely similar is the relative situation of the native and colonial population in other parts of the district—both parties mutually regarding each other as intruders. Are the territorial rights of the aborigines to be set aside by violence? Appointed as I have been by Her Majesty's Government specially to watch over the rights and interests of the natives, and to protect them from any encroachments on their property and from acts of cruelty, oppression and injustice, I feel it my duty respectfully but firmly to assert the right of the aborigines to the soil and its indigenous productions, unless suitable compensation be made for its occupation, by reserving and cultivating a sufficient portion for their maintenance.

*2.* Another fact consequent upon the foregoing is the diminution of the natural food of the aborigines.

Having in a former communication adverted to this, I need only now state that the facts then asserted have been fully corroborated by subsequent observation and enquiry and that I am prepared with ample evidence to substantiate those assertions.

The common result of this is that the natives resort to the outstations to procure bread, and, too frequently, under the excitement of hunger or cupidity, to take by force what is denied to their importunity.

They have acquired universally a taste for the white man's food—they tell me invariably they prefer it to their own wild productions.

This acquired taste might, and ought to be employed as a secondary means of their civilisation.

*3.* I have seen in my recent intercourse with the aborigines, considerable numbers of children, and I invariably find among them great quickness of apprehension and evident aptitude for instruction. It is my duty therefore to respectfully urge the necessity and importance of having these children, as much as possible, concentrated and at once brought under Christian instruction. Every moment lost in this manner is a postponement of the hope of their ultimate civilisation.

The old may be restrained but the young will certainly be reclaimed, if suitable means be at once employed.

*4.* It is my duty also to advert to the fact that I find it impossible to attach myself to entire tribes from the circumstance that the tribes are most usually broken up into small parties often ranging widely from each other in search of food. The only occasions when they assemble in any considerable numbers are when they resort to particular spots where some kinds of food may be abundant for a season, as to places abounding in fish or other articles of diet, and when different tribes meet to settle disputes by conflict or otherwise.

As these occasions are not of frequent recurrence it is becoming daily more necessary that the Protector should possess some point of concentration—some fixed station to which he may invite and bring aborigines.

5. Although indolence and dislike for constrained labor, are, in common with all savages, characteristic vices of the aborigines I am connected with, I am happy to state that many instances have come to my knowledge, where they have employed themselves to the satisfaction of the settlers and their own advantage.

I have found a man and boy, natives of an adjoining district, employed by Mr Piper as shepherds: they are both described as faithful and efficient servants. Several others have been named to me as occasionally employed in shepherding, washing sheep, packing wool, etc. I have not found among these who have visited my station any insurmountable repugnance of work, when properly encouraged and rewarded, and not barely commanded; but having no permanent station, no means of cultivation, and indeed up to the present time, no direct authority to issue provisions as a reward for labor. I am not in a situation to employ this method of promoting their civilisation.

In conclusion I beg respectfully to express my solemn and deliberate conviction that the present relative position of the aboriginal and colonial population must undergo a decided and speedy change to prevent the increase of predatory attacks on colonial property on the one hand and the continuance of a system of illegal punishment and indiscriminate slaughter on the other.

While I find it next to impossible from the desultory nature of my present official duties to employ the only efficient means of permanent civilisation, i.e. Christian instruction, I am painfully conscious that the wandering aborigines are sinking to a lower degree of moral degradation by the pernicious intercourse which they have with the vitiated portion of the lower classes in the colony.

I cannot draw the men away from the stations while they by pandering to the lusts of those employed on the stations can obtain more liberal supplies than I can furnish. The results of this vicious intercourse—disease, jealousy, brutal quarrels both with white and blacks, are rendering the condition of the aborigines more deplorable, and the property of the colonists more insecure.

Unless prompt and efficient measures are taken to concentrate and provide for the natives, I look forward with apprehension to the approaching winter as a period of aggravated outrage on both sides.

It is universally acknowledged to be a time of privation to the natives—that privation must increase with every successive season.

Concentrated, and their wants provided for, they might soon be brought under such restraints as would guard them against injury, and secure the property of the colonists from depredation. But left in their present state, to be beaten back "by the white man's foot"—to be excluded, perforce, from lands which many unquestionably regard as their own property, and from scenes as dear to them as our own native homes to us—despoiled, denied the right of humanity—classed with and treated as wild dogs—I can entertain no other expectation but that they will be driven to more frequent depredations, and exposed to more rapid and certain destruction.

I have the honor to be, Sir, Your most obedient servant,

Edward S. Parker,
Assistant Protector,

## 4.12 1840. Edward John Eyre's observations.

(Edward John Eyre, *Journals of Expeditions into Central Australia,* London, 1840, Vol. 2, pp. 153, 156, 158.)

*An extract from the journals of explorer Edward John Eyre, written as he crossed the interior of Australia.*

The character of the Australian native has been so constantly misrepresented and traduced, that by the world at large he is looked upon as the lowest and most degraded of the human species, and generally considered as ranking but little above the members of the brute creation. It is said, indeed, that the Australian is an irreclaimable, unteachable being; that he is cruel, bloodthirsty, revengeful and treacherous; and in support of such assertions, references are made to the total failure of all missionary and scholastic efforts hitherto made on his behalf, and to the many deeds of violence or aggression committed by him upon the settler . . .

I believe were Europeans placed under the same circumstances, equally wronged, and equally shut off from redress, they would not exhibit half the moderation or forbearance that these poor untutored children of impulse have invariably shown. . . .

Without laying claim to this country by right of conquest, without pleading even the mockery of cession, or the cheatery of sale, we have unhesitatingly entered upon, occupied, and disposed of its lands, spreading forth a new population over its surface, and driving before us the original inhabitants.

It is often argued, that we merely have taken what the natives did not require, or were making no use of; that we have no wish to interfere with them if they do not interfere with us, but rather that we are disposed to treat them with kindness and conciliation, if they are willing to be friends with us. What, however, are the actual facts of the case; and what is the position of a tribe of natives, when the country is first taken possession of by Europeans.

It is true that they do not cultivate the ground; but have they, therefore no interest in its productions? Does it not supply grass for the sustenance of the wild animals upon which in a great measure they are dependent for their subsistence?—does it not afford roots and vegetables to appease their hunger, water to satisfy their thirst, and wood to make their fire?—or are these necessaries left to them by the white man who comes to take possession of their soil? Alas, it is not so! all are in turn taken away from the original possessors. The game of the wilds that the European does not destroy for his amusement are driven away by his flocks and herds. The waters are occupied and enclosed, and access to them is frequently forbidden. The fields are fenced in, and the natives no longer at liberty to dig up roots—the white man claims the timber, and the very firewood itself is occasionally denied them. Do they pass by the habitation of the intruder, they are probably chased away or bitten by his dogs, and for this they can get no redress. Have they dogs of their own, they are unhestitatingly shot or worried because they are an annoyance to the domestic animals of the Europeans. Daily and hourly do their wrongs multiply upon them. The more numerous the white population becomes, and the more advanced the stage of civilisation to which the settlement progresses, the greater are the hardships that fall to their lot and the more completely are they cut off from the privileges of their birthright. All that they have is in succession taken away from them—their amusements, their enjoyments, their possessions, their freedom—and all that they receive in return is obloquy and contempt, and degradation and oppression.

**4.13 December 1842. A Missionary speaks of tribal warfare.**

(*House of Commons Parliamentary Papers*, London, Vol 34, 1844. Op cit., Enclosure No. 12. pp. 256-257.)

*Report of the Wesleyan Missionary, Mr. Francis Tuckfield, from the Sub-district of Geelong, Port Phillip, for the year ending December 1842.*

IN reviewing the society's operations among the aborigines of the district of Geelong, for the past year, it is painful to remark that the mission, for a considerable portion of the time, presented a rather gloomy and discouraging aspect.

The natives, in the exercise of their own barbarous customs, especially in their wars and revengeful and clandestine aggressions on each other, have been in a constant state of excitement and agitation. The mission establishment is known to be a kind of rendezvous for the surrounding tribes, whose forces have been weakened through European intercourse and it is an established law among the natives of the great Australian continent to revenge the death of their friends, by killing some one of another tribe; and it is a well known fact, that they always revenge where they are least likely to meet with resistance. The consequence has been, that the injured tribes around us have not ventured to come to the mission establishment but seldom, and when they have been there, they could not be prevailed upon to remain but a very short period at a time, fearing lest the more distant tribes should come upon them in their unprotected state. . . . On this very interesting occasion, the natives particularly complained of the want of protection, intimating, that as the white men had killed some of their fighting men, the great governor ought to send them the police to protect them from the violent and revengeful attacks of those tribes whose forces have not been so much weakened through the same cause; but as the natives are not amenable to British laws, and as no law has been framed to meet the exigence of their case, and especially as they have been allowed to butcher each other, and that in the presence of Europeans, with impunity, no promise of protection, such as they required, could be made to them. They however engaged, that if the present mission be continued, they would not leave it as they had been accustomed to do. Fresh arrangements were again made for the instruction of the young; six boys and four young men began to learn, in good earnest, the English language, the women attended to their needlework and other domestic arrangements, some of the men made themselves useful in grinding wheat at the mill, cutting and drawing of wood, &c., while others of them spent a portion of their time in hunting and fishing on the back ground. The whole were fed twice a day, and attended prayers every morning at seven o'clock. Thus they continued in peace and harmony (the average daily attendance on the station being 95) from November 28th, 1842, to January 4th, 1843, when a young man, by the name of "Derepderepbarn," from the Tollerbollock tribe, came in the evening of that day, about nine o'clock, to a breakwind, where there was a woman of the Dantgurt tribe sitting by her fire, and drove a large spear through her body, and immediately left the station. The poor unfortunate young woman groaned in an agony for a few hours, and then expired. A part of the Tollerbollock tribe were on the station at that time, but they declared they knew nothing of the felonious intentions of this young man, but they supposed it to be in revenge for a relative of his, who was murdered about fifteen months since. The following day (according to their custom of leaving the place at which a person is killed) they all left the station, deeply mourning over this most affecting circumstance, which had caused them to separate. Some of the young men, with one of the chiefs, came to the missionary, and promised to return in four weeks, lamenting at the same time over the absence of a law that would supersede their own barbarous customs, or a force adequate to keep the tribes in check, that they might live peacefully together.

It is an appalling fact, that all the murders which have been perpetrated on the Wesleyan establishment since its commencement have been on the Dantgurt tribe; a tribe which has suffered more through European inter-course than any other tribe with which the missionary is acquainted. Natives have been known to travel 120 miles for the purpose of revenging the death of some of their own friends, by taking the life of a Dantgurt native, solely because, through the paucity of their numbers, they were afraid to offer any resistance.

The Kolifon tribe, who are only about thirty in number, including men, women and children, would have been frequently in the same dilemma, if it were not for some humane settlers in the vicinity of the Lakes to have thrown around them the shield of protection. Some of the natives, therefore, in the settled districts are languishing and expiring under their own customs, which are rendered tenfold more aggravating and oppressive, through their intercourse with the white population, and under this yoke they groan, without any power of appeal.

It has been remarked, that we have no right to interfere with the natives so long as they exercise their own customs upon themselves; but we are not to suppose, that if we protect the natives from the violence of their fellows, that they will consider it an infringement on their rights; for this is what they want, and it is what they ask for; and some of them talk as if they believe it to be what they ought to have; and it is the opinion of the writer, that we are (to say the least of it) laid under a moral obligation to help the weak, as they cannot help themselves, and especially so, as we are the cause of their imbecility. It might be said, that upwards of 12,000 $l.$ are annually expended already, within the districts of Port Phillip, in support of a system of protection for the aborigines; but this system is to protect the natives from the aggressions of the whites, and not from the violence of hostile tribes. It is of the latter evil the natives in the settled districts most commonly complain; and complain they may; for the protectors have no power or authority to interfere. The natives on the outskirts of the territory suffer most from the whites; for in extending themselves they come in contact with fresh tribes; and in the absence of proper persons to effect a reconciliation, they are obliged to have recourse to arms for the protection of their wealth, which, in many instances, have proved to be sources of retaliation and bloodshed. . . .

### 4.14   14 August 1846. "The Blacks."

(*The Argus*, Melbourne, 18 August 1846, p. 2.)

*An article that appeared in the* Portland Gazette *and was reprinted in* The Melbourne Argus *soon after.*

"The Blacks."
These gentry are murdering each other in the most approved style towards the mouth of the Glenelg. They have got a quantity of fire-arms amongst them and appear very expert in their use.

**4.15 22 January 1852. The education of Aborigines.**

(*Queensland Parliamentary Votes and Proceedings*, Vol. 1, 1861, "Report from the Select Committee on the Native Police Force and the Condition of the Aborigines Generally". Appendix A, p. 565.)

*A letter sent to the Secretary of the Board of National Education, Sydney, by W. A. Duncan, Brisbane, concerning the education of Aborigines.*

*1.* If the subject of Education generally is surrounded by acknowledged difficulties, that of the Aboriginal youth of this Colony appears to baffle all human efforts, and it is with great diffidence that I offer the result of my reflections on this branch of the subject. Such as it is, however, I lose no time in laying it before the Board. It has at least the merit of having been arrived at after a careful study of the aboriginal character during several years. . . .

*3.* The next point to be considered is the availableness of the proposed school for the children of the aborignes—of their capacity for instruction there is no doubt whatever in my mind—in this respect I believe that they are quite equal to the white children; opinions quite at variance with this have, I know, been put forth, but they may generally be traced to persons who have occasionally suffered by the occasional depredations committed by the Native Tribes, and who, as some excuse for their illegal retaliation, seek to reduce their enemy to the level of the brutes. I have no such injuries to resent, and no affection to bias me on the other side, except that arising from regret at seeing a race of intelligent beings gradually swept from the earth by disease and violence, whilst all counter efforts to ameliorate their condition have proved abortive. With this well considered opinion of their natural capacity for education, I feel equally certain that by no human possibility can they ever be educated, unless their education be made compulsory. With the children themselves there would be little difficulty, but so absolute is the control of the parents, and older relatives of the children, over all their acts, and so numerous are their ceremonies, sports, and exercises, from which they dare not absent themselves, that unless the connection between the old and young is completely severed—an act repugnant at first view to all our special and political notions,—there is, I am convinced, no human power of civilizing or even of perpetuating the race, who, while they are rapidly disappearing by disease and other causes, receive but little increase in the natural way, in consequence of the promiscuous intercourse of their women with the white men.

*4.* If government should think proper to adopt this absolutely necessary step, and there is a precedent for compulsory education in Prussia, and other civilized states. I think all the other difficulties would vanish before ordinary perseverance. It would only be necessary to keep them at school until they were thoroughly grounded in the usual branches of elementary education, and well instructed in some branch of agricultural industry (say, for example, cotton growing for the boys, and cotton picking for the girls). By the time this were effected they would be at the age of puberty (which with them is early), they should then be regularly married from school, and some assistance should be rendered them to commence cultivating the soil on their own account. Magistrates and persons in the service of the Government should be specially instructed to protect them, until they became numerous and independent enough to protect themselves. With these and a few other precautions which would suggest themselves in the working of the system, I still think the Australian race might be preserved from the destruction to which it is now hastening apace, and to which preservation I repeat, the breaking up of the tribe habits, superstition, and influence, by the withdrawal of the young of both sexes, seems to me the first and necessary step. The mixture of the children of both sexes in the same school, would I think present no difficulty, but would, on the contrary, be greatly desirable.

5. The Native Police is an excellent institution, and I think it might be much improved, by having a school at each Police Station where they might be taught to read and write. That so much could be done with them as with the children, it would not be reasonable to expect, but something at least could be effected in the way I have mentioned.

Such are the suggestions which occur to me on the deeply interesting subject on which the Board have done me the honor to consult me; to which I can only add, that if I can be of any assistance to the Board, in carrying out their object, nothing will afford me greater satisfaction.

(Signed)

The SECRETARY
Board of National Education,
Sydney.

I have the honor,
&c., &c., &c.,
W. A. DUNCAN.

## 4.16 10 May 1854. Edward Stone Parker's lecture.

(Edward Stone Parker, *The Aborigines of Australia*, Melbourne, 1854. A Lecture delivered in the Mechanics Hall, Melbourne, 10 May 1854.)

*Part of a lecture delivered in Melbourne by Edward Stone Parker to a young Christian men's organization. Mr. Parker was a member of the Legislative Council of Victoria, and formerly assistant protector of Aborigines.*

. . . You have listened to the tale of the missionary or the traveller, as they told of far distant lands, where men grovelled in destitute barbarism, or in a semi-civilised heathenism, not less dark and deadly in its aspects, and your hearts have burned within you with pity for the suffering humanity, and desire to aid in its elevation. Your sympathies cannot be less deep . . . when the object of your pity is your "neighbour", and stands in full in your view, in all the abjectness of his social and moral condition. In the land in which we live is the highest civilization and almost the lowest barbarism dwelling in juxta-position. . . .

I think it must be deemed a subject of reproach, that though the aboriginal inhabitants of this land have been so long and so closely under our observation, there is so great an amount of ignorance as to their real character and habits, and capabilities for moral and intellectual improvement. . . .

The Physical Characteristics.

It is an opinion generally entertained that the native youth attain the attributes of puberty at a much earlier period than Europeans. I demur to that opinion. I have marked the development of children, whose birth I have recorded, and at twelve or thirteen years of age there were no greater implications of physical or mental progress than in their white brethren. . . . In fact, as the native-born youth of European derivation indicate a more rapid development than in the colder clime of our father land, I do not think that any real difference exists.

I am not an implicit believer in all the dogmas of the phrenologist. I think the science is, as yet, but imperfectly known. . . . but I can readily admit that a variation in mental development may become the occasion of a corresponding variation in the conformation of the head. . . . It is . . . interesting to observe the facial angle in the Australian aborigine approaches the Caucasian type, if indeed, it be not in some instances identical with it. The forehead is, however, generally narrow, and this narrowness is often characteristic of the whole head, indicating, according to the phrenologists, among other deficiencies, the absence of the quality called conscientiousness. So far as I have been able to investigate the subject, the greatest deficiencies in the development of the aboriginal cranium are in those organs which are regarded as indicative of moral qualities.

Geographical and Statistical Information.

. . . It is a great mistake to suppose that these different people take a wide range in their wanderings. . . . Sir Thomas Mitchell fell strangely into this error, when he supposed that his Sydney native, travelling with him to the previously unknown regions of Australia Felix, was able to communicate with all the different tribes he encountered even to the far Glenelg. . . . he either misunderstood his own supposed interpreter, or was grossly deceived by him, in fact scarcely one of his native names of localities in this colony have been verified. My own observations among these people, during a period of fourteen years, convinces me that the range of their migrations is ordinarily very limited. Very few of the natives of the Upper Loddon—the Jajowurrong—have seen the Murray; and only three or four natives of the Murray could ever be induced to visit the Loddon Aboriginal Establishment. In 1843, the Bolokepar, or Lake Boloke tribe, visited that establishment. But though the lake is not a hundred miles from the Loddon, the tribes had never previously met. One of the most intelligent of the Worngarragerra, (whose country by the way was even nearer to them than the Loddon,) said to me indignantly when remonstrated with for his unfriendliness, "Mainmait talle mainmait mirri-par-gar, mainmait malderrun; yurrong," that is "they are foreign in speech, they are foreign in countenance, they are foreign altogether—they are no good!" On that occasion I witnessed an interesting trait of native manners. The tribes were formally introduced and ceremoniously to each other by an old man of an intermediate tribe, naming each individual in succession, waving his hand towards him and at the same time giving his parentage, and sometimes a particular incident in the history of his family. Along the main river lines the communications may be more extended; but I am convinced that, ordinarily a native has been fearful of travelling far from his own district, except under the protection of the white man.

The fact that I have just adverted to is of some importance as showing the hopelessness of expecting a solitary missionary or two, or a single educational establishment, should exercise any beneficial influence on tribes remote from their own particular locality.

. . . In the year 1843 I endeavoured to take a nominal census of the aboriginal population extending from the Goulburn on the East to the upper Wimmera on the West, and from the great dividing range between the coast rivers and the interior waters on the South, and to the Mallee country on the North. I found then, and registered by name, in their respective families and tribes, about 1,100 individuals. . . . Taking the whole range of the colony of Victoria, I think 7,500 would be a close approximation to the number of the aboriginal population at the foundation of the colony. I doubt whether more than one third of this number exist now. . . . For several years past collisions between the races have been virtually unknown, with the exception of the Murray country where unhappily several murders of white men are believed to have taken place recently, chiefly of solitary travellers, some of whom are known to have been wandering about in a state of almost perpetual intoxication.

Among the causes that have been referred to as tending to the rapid decrease of the aboriginal population is one which I must notice as delicately as I can, because it ought to be and shall be refuted. It has the authority of a distinguished name, and has been frequently adverted to by various writers on the aborigines, as a statement implicitly credited, and by some writers on the varieties of the human race as an important and illustrative philosophical fact. Count Strzelecki asserts, that he has ascertained . . . that the aboriginal female, after cohabiting with Europeans, loses the power of bearing children to the men of her own race, . . . I give to that statement an unqualified and indignant denial. . . . Upon facts which have come to my own personal observations, not isolated, but of frequent occurrence, I base my denial.

And there is one dire evil doing its work of death among them as among those who call themselves a superior race; — . . . It is the deadly spirit bottle! If the vast mass of human life which has been sacrificed in this colony to this Apollyon of humanity, since the commencement of the gold discoveries, could be collected together, there would be found the bodies of the unfortunate aborigines among them, who once shrunk from the agent of evil as poisonous and destructive.

In the latter end of the year 1840 . . . several natives informed me confidentially that destruction was coming upon the white population . . . It was known that they were practising secret incantations with this object. The effects were described, graphically enough as producing dreadful sores, dysentery, blindness, and death. The "Mindi" was to come. . . . I was able to identify the threatened agent of destruction as the small pox . . . It is believed to be in the power of the large serpent "Mindi", the supposed incarnation of the destroying spirit, to send this plague forth in answer to the appeals and incantations of those who seek the destruction of their foes.

Language.
I have found the language to be copious in the terms expressive of physical objects and their attributes, but miserably deficient in psychological or metaphysical designations. . . . if you seek terms expressive of mental exercises or attitudes you are immediately at fault. For the sake of example, I have never been able to discover a term expressive of gratitude, and the natives say none exists. And so other terms expressive of virtuous emotions. They are unknown. This has been the greatest obstacle to the conveyance of religious truth to the aboriginal mind.

On this account I have long inclined that it is far more desirable to induce the natives to acquire English, than to depend upon aboriginal languages for conveying truth.

On the Subject of Government and Social Condition.
. . . I have already defined a tribe as a collection of families, nearly or remotely related to each other, and recognizing a common head or chief. The power of the chief, who is termed "Marmar", father, "Wooringarpil", leader or commander, "Kneyern Kneyerneet" or chief speaker, is very limited, unless the individual possesses intelligence and exhibits much prowess. His influence then becomes more extensive, and his authority respected. The association of the natives with the colonial population has had the effect of breaking up these relations to a considerable extent; and the rank of chieftain would soon be utterly lost, were it not for the egregious folly and heartless mockery practised by some old colonists, by inflating the savage pride of these individuals with the title of "king", and giving them as a badge of their ideal dignity, an engraved brass plate, and thus rendering them pitiable caricatures of human pride.

The tribes and nations maintain friendly relations with each other, by frequent meetings, at appointed times and places. Feasts are sometimes prepared, but the main business of the meeting is the yepene or corrobory, the native dance, which has been so often described.

To maintain communications with each other, the natives have appointed messengers, whose persons were held sacred, even when they went among their enemies. I have watched formerly with much anxiety, the return of these messengers from their embassy. If the result were peace they carried boughs, if war, their faces were painted as if going into battle. When individuals of other tribes thus arranged a visit, the etiquette if I may so term it, was remarkable. He scarcely looked, indeed, at the parties he came to see. Presently one of the elders would come up to him, bearing a kindled fire stick. He sits down before the visitor, and after some hesitation, begins to speak; but it is not till some minutes elapse that they get into cordial conversation. If the parties are very friendly a singular mark of respect is shown. They interchange languages if their speech differ; the visitor using the tongue spoken by his hosts, the host using that of the guest.

Individual and Family Life.

One of the darkest features in the aboriginal character is its gross sensuality. It is in my view the greatest obstacle to their improvement. I cannot portray, in an assembly like this, all the appalling details of the dark picture. Suffice it to say, that St. Paul's description of the vices of the ancient heathens, in the first chapter of the Epistle to the Romans, was but too forcibly applicable to the moral state of the aborigines, when I first went among them; and still I fear receives frequent and painful illustration. Polygamy was and is in existence among them. The females were betrothed or promised at an early age; and one great point of ambition for the Australian native was to get a number of wives. I have known as many as six appropriated to one man. . . . the strongest mark of friendship that could be displayed by one man to another, was to present him with one of his superfluous wives. . . .

The natives are generally much attached to their children, and their loss is to their mothers a time of fearful distress and excitement. It has been the custom here as in other parts of Australia for the mother to carry about for weeks the body of her lost one. And yet there is no doubt that infanticide prevailed to a fearful extent. Any deformed child was immediately destroyed. Among some tribes half-caste children were sacrificed. . . .

Religious Opinions and Superstitions.

. . . I am satisfied, from the minute enquiries I have made, from the aborigines that their religious notions were very few and very crude. . . . Amydeet (Jajowrong), amerjig (Witowurrong), are specimens of the designation applied to the white race. The same terms designate the separate state of the spirit when the body is dead. Hence the opinion, long prevalent, and fostered by the early settlers, but now I hope utterly exploded that when they die they would go to Van Diemen's Land, and "jump up white fellow." . . . It is well known that, on the first appearance of the colonists, the opinion was taken up, and long maintained among them, that they were their deceased progenitors returning to their former haunts. . . .

The natives in my earlier experience among them, never hesitated to avow their ignorance of religious matters. It was evidently a subject seldom in their thoughts. And I think it may be a hopeful circumstance, that, in seeking to impart religious knowledge to them, you have not to contend with minds much pre-occupied with strong prejudices and deeply rooted opinions. . . .

Let it not for one moment be supposed that there are any intellectual obstacles to the Christianization and civilization of these people. I have always maintained—and I still maintain—the obstacles are purely moral. It is their utter sensuality of their habits and dispositions that is the main hindrance to be overcome. . . . There are now a number of children and young people at the Loddon Institution, some of whom have been there for a considerable time, and their progress is very satisfactory. . . .

(Much stress has been laid on the apparently inveterate propensity of the aborigines to unsettled and wandering habits, as an insuperable obstacle to any efforts for their improvement. . . . But the causes of these wandering habits I have never seen adverted to. In the first place, the native has been accustomed to seek supplies of food in different localities, according to the season of the year, and the source of the aliment. . . . But the principle exciting cause of their constant wanderings may be found in the alarms and fears occasioned by their superstitions. Believing that his enemies could bring sickness and death upon him through the ground, he was always anxious to be continually shifting his locality, under the idea of escaping this evil influence. Hence the slightest appearance of sickness led to a fear that the ground was haunted and, if a death occurred, every dwelling place was directly changed. . . .)*

I now come to the FUTURE PROSPECTS of these unfortunate people, and what ought to be done for their welfare. Are they to be hopelessly abandoned, and not one effort made to promote their religious and social improvement? The reply of some will be, every effort has hitherto failed, and it is useless to make any further attempt to raise them from their voluntary degradation. I demur to this statement while I have before me families and individuals permanently civilized, actively industrious, and anxious to raise themselves in their social condition. The instances may be rare I grant, but they suffice to show that the work is not hopeless. It is too commonly the case to expect too much from the native. You expect that he will at your bidding give up all his preconceived notions, and at once fall into your way of thinking and your mode of life. He will never do this till he has an adequate motive, till he feels the force of some inducement strong enough to change the whole current of his thoughts and feelings. Religion alone can supply that motive—a conviction of its truth, an adoption of its principles, will at once place the foot of the aborigine on a higher step in the social scale, and it will require no constraint or persuasion to induce him to become settled and steady, and self-supporting. . . .

One other opinion as to the destiny of these despised people I must remark upon before I close. It is a common opinion, expressed too, in quarters often whence better notions might be expected, that they are a doomed race—that they must pass away. Nay, the opinion assumes a more daring form in the assertion that it is an appointment—the inscrutable decree—of Divine Providence that uncivilized races should perish before the march of civilization. I may admit to the probability of the event as to the Australian aborigines, but I deny its inevitable necessity. I want to know where the decree is written. . . . Do you not see that if the argument be worth anything that, if followed out to its ultimate consequences, it can be made to justify every outrage, and to palliate every crime?—God has suffered it, and therefore he wills it!

. . . Let men of the world say, if they will, "Let the people alone:"—"Let them die, as die they must," and as has been actually said to me,—"The sooner they perish the better." But let every Christian young man rise, and say with one voice, to the government, the legislature, and the

* The paragraph enclosed in brackets was omitted in the lecture delivered, through want of time.

nation;—occupy the land,—till its broad wastes;—extract its riches,—develop its resources,—if you will;—but, in the name of God and humanity, SAVE THE PEOPLE.

### 4.17 1860. The Lord Bishop of Adelaide examined.

(*South Australian Parliamentary Papers*, Adelaide, 1860, "Select Committee on Aborigines", p. 7.)

*The Lord Bishop of Adelaide firmly believed in his duty to civilize and Christianize the Aborigines, whatever the consequences.*

Question 97. Do you think it necessary for the saving of souls of blacks, that they should be Christianized, or do you suppose that the Almighty, in His General Providence, may not condemn those who are without the pale of the law, if, according to their own customs and belief they lead what is in their opinion a good life?
Answer: No. I do not think that a good life in their opinion is sufficient. It is necessary for their salvation to Christianize them if we can. We, if we have the opportunity to Christianize them, should do so. We should teach the heathen; and I think I should peril my own salvation if I do not try to teach them. What God will do, I do not know. I hope for the best, as He has given His Son to die for the sins of the world.
Question 98. Supposing that in endeavouring to Christianize them, you are in reality assisting to destroy them, do you not think that it would be inadvisable to injure their bodily health?
Answer: In the first place, I do not think that it does injure their bodily health, more than allowing them to live in their wild state; and secondly, I do not think it inadvisable to Christianize them; for I would rather they died as Christians than drag out a miserable existence as heathens. I believe that the race will disappear either way. . . .

### 4.18 9 May 1861. Royal Commission into the Native Police Force.

(*1*): *Lieutenant Wheeler's evidence.*

(*Queensland Parliamentary Votes and Proceedings, op. cit.*, Vol. 1, 1861. "Report from the Select Committee on the Native Police Force and the Condition of the Aborigines Generally", pp. 423-424.)

LIEUTENANT FREDERICK WHEELER called in and examined:—

*1.* By the CHAIRMAN: You are an officer in the Native Police Force? Yes.
*2.* How long have you been in the Force? Four years.
*3.* Where have you been stationed during that period? At Rockhampton, at Port Curtis, and down here.
*4.* How long have you been down here? Two years,—at Sandgate.
*5.* How many men are there in your detachment? Eight.
*6.* Are they the same men you had at first? No, the ten men I had at first bolted; that was at Rockhampton.
*7.* I refer to your present detachment? Yes, they are the same men.
*8.* Do you remember the affair at Coochin in December last? Nothing took place at Coochin; it was near Dugandan.
*9.* Were you sent for upon that occasion? Yes, I received four or·five

letters from settlers—Mr. Henderson, Mr. Compigné, Mr. Hardie, and others—telling me that the blacks had been robbing the huts, stealing the sheep, and threatening the shepherds. Mr. Compigné had left part of his run on that account, and brought the sheep to the head station.

*10.* Did you go up there with your detachment? I went up directly I received the letters to Mr. Compigné's station on the Logan.

*11.* Where is Dugandan? On the Teviot Brook.

*12.* What did you do when you came from Mr. Compigné's station? I went first to Mr. Compigné's, and from that to where the Albert runs into the Logan, but I did not find any blacks there. I then went over to the sea-coast, and followed it down to Point Danger. Finding no tracks there, I went over the mountains back again to Compigné's, and thence to Telemon; followed up Christmas Creek till I came underneath McPherson's Range and Mount Lindsay. I found the tracks underneath the ranges there, heading towards the large Dugandan scrub, between the Ten-mile and Fifteen-mile stations. I found the blacks in the large Dugandan scrub.

*13.* What did you do then? I dispersed them.

*14.* How did you know they were the blacks who commited the outrages? I followed their tracks for a fortnight.

*15.* Had you any other evidence—were any of them recognized by wearing clothes or blankets? They were all naked.

*16.* How many of them were there? The camps extended for about three miles; there were several different tribes; they had been congregating there for some time. They usually come down there before Christmas time; it is on the high road to Ipswich, between that and the salt water.

*17.* Had you any direct evidence to shew that they were the blacks who had committed the outrages complained of? The shepherds at Mr. Compigné's told me that the blacks had come down from the Telemon side of the range.

*18.* Had they been by the Bunya scrub? No.

*19.* Did they make any resistance? I only dispersed the Telemon mob.

*20.* Not the whole of them? No, none of the others.

*21.* What led you to disperse the Telemon blacks? They always do the mischief; the same mob had been robbing Mr. Collins's station at Telemon.

*22.* Were there any warrants out against those blacks? No. Warrants are never given out against the blacks for cattle-stealing, which is done by the whole tribe.

*23.* Did you recognize any of them? It was getting dark, but I recognized two or three of them.

*24.* Had you any information to prove that they were the same blacks who robbed Mr. Collins's station? No, I only know from what the shepherds told me, that a certain tribe of blacks committed the depredations, and that they had headed towards the sea-coast.

*25.* When you come into contact with the blacks in that way, have you a proper control over your troopers? Oh, yes.

*26.* Do they ever get out of your sight? Yes, when they go into the scrub; they then dismount and take off their trousers.

*27.* Did you go into the scrub on this occasion? No, I went round the scrub to get the Dugandan blacks away, so that they might not get shot.

*28.* How were you enabled to discern one portion of the blacks from the other? They form separate camps. Every squatter will tell you that the Telemon blacks are the blacks who do all the mischief.

*29.* I wish to know upon what evidence or appearance you acted in separating the blacks, dispersing one portion of them, and leaving the others? The Dugandan blacks never go over to Compigné's; it is always the Telemon blacks; they come from Captain Collins's station. It was just sundown at the time, and I got a boy (Jemmy Murphy) to shew me the different camps.

*30.* You say that you have proper control over your troopers—are they generally under the proper control of their officers? I cannot say; I have never been out with other officers.

*31.* At the time of this affray the troopers were out of your sight? Yes, they were out of my sight for about half-an-hour.

*32.* Do those troopers understand English sufficiently to comprehend your orders? Oh, yes.

*33.* Did you give them orders to go into the scrub? Yes.

*34.* What was the nature of those orders? I told them to surround that camp of Telemon blacks, and to disperse them.

*35.* What do you mean by dispersing? Firing at them. I gave strict orders not to shoot any gins. It is only sometimes, when it is dark, that a gin is mistaken for a blackfellow, or might be wounded inadvertently.

*36.* Do you think it is a proper thing to fire upon the blacks in that way? If they are the right mob, of which I had every certainty.

*37.* If I understand you aright, your instructions were to surround the camp, and fire upon it, and that the troopers were allowed to go out of your sight. Now, you must be aware if they received these orders, and were not under your immediate control, that there was considerable risk of loss of life, particularly of gins. Was there any necessity for such an indiscriminate slaughter upon that occasion? I don't think there was any indiscriminate slaughter: there were only two blacks shot.

*38.* But you did not see it? I was in the scrub, but I was away for about half-an-hour in another direction, to get the Dugandan blacks round me, to prevent their being shot.

*39.* I can understand this—if there are warrants out against certain men, and they take to the scrub, that your troopers are ordered to follow them, and, if they do not stop when called upon in the Queen's name, to fire upon them; but in this case there were no warrants out. I wish to know what induced you to give those orders? The letters I had received from several squatters, complaining that the blacks were robbing their huts, threatening their lives, and spearing their cattle and sheep.

*40.* What are the general orders of your Commandant? It is a general order that, whenever there are large assemblages of blacks, it is the duty of an officer to disperse them. There are no general orders for these cases; officers must take care that proper discretion is exercised.

*41.* Did you see any of the property taken from the shepherds? No, it was Mr. Compigné.

*42.* Was he with you on this occasion? No, I never take any white people with me.

*43.* Then it was on the evidence of Mr. Compigné that you surrounded the scrub and fired on the blacks? On that of Mr. Compigné, the Messrs. Collins of Telemon, Mr. Henderson of Tabragalba, Mr. Hardie, and other squatters.

*44.* How many dead bodies were there? I saw two.

*45.* Was not there a gin shot? Yes.

*46.* Don't you consider this is a very loose way of proceeding—surrounding blacks' camps, and shooting innocent gins? There is no other way.

*47.* When the blacks were called upon to disperse, did they offer any resistance? Yes, they threw everything they had at the Native Police.

*48.* But you were not present? I was with them when the gin was shot; I thought it was a blackfellow. I could not follow them at the time, and it is no use calling after them in the scrub.

*49.* Then it is clear they were not under your control when the gin was shot? That was a mistake; it was getting dark.

*50.* After this affair at Dugandan where did you go to? I went to Fassifern, following up the same track.

*51.* What occurred there? I came upon the tracks there; I think it was in the middle of the following day or the next. I found a small camp of blacks, and dispersed them.

52. What number of blacks were killed on that occasion? Two.
53. Did you see the dead bodies? Yes.
54. Was not one of them an old man? A middle-aged man.
55. Had he grey hair? Not particularly so.
56. Were you with the Police then? Yes.
57. With your troopers? Yes. I dispersed that mob on account of having received a letter from Mr. Hardie, stating that a mob of blacks had been threatening him, and that he could not get rid of them.
58. Had they been spearing Mr. Hardie's cattle? He said they had been spearing the cattle at Moograh, and threatening the lives of the men.
59. In fact, you saw nothing yourself? No. I could not waste time to see whether a cow or a bullock had been speared.

.     .     .

73. Are you often out on patrol? Almost always. I am now going to Durandur; the blacks are coming down for their blankets.
74. Are the accounts of the blacks in your district generally pretty good? Yes.
75. Have you generally found them troublesome? In some places.
76. Have they been quieter and better behaved during the last few years. Yes, considerably so.
77. Everywhere? Yes, we have driven them almost entirely away from the Logan. They generally go to the islands in the Bay, over the Dividing Range, to the boiling-down establishment, and to the townships.


**4.19  14 May 1861. Royal Commission into the Native Police Force.**

(2): *Captain John Coley's evidence.*

(*Ibid.*, pp. 424-427.)

CAPTAIN JOHN COLEY called in and examined:—

1. By the CHAIRMAN: You have been a resident in Brisbane a number of years? Nearly nineteen years.
2. Since the first occupation of the country? Since the latter end of 1842.
3. How long had the district been opened for settlement? About twelve months.
4. When you arrived? When I arrived.
5. You have seen a good deal of the Aborigines since your arrival? Yes.
6. What state were they in at the time of your arrival? The Brisbane tribe at that time numbered about two hundred and fifty; that was about the number, at that time, of the tribe.
7. Have they diminished since then? They are all gone since then—they are all extinct. The present blacks are the offspring of the Ningey Ningey and Bribie Island tribes.
8. Bribie Island? Yes.
9. You tell the Committee of your own knowledge of what the number of the tribe was on your arrival, that they have diminished since the settlement of the district? Quite so. They are all gone, altogether extinct.
10. To what do you attribute that? Well, it may be accounted for in many ways. Disease has carried off many of them; and I have known one black to have three wives in the course of eight or nine years, who were eventually all killed by his own hand, or the hand of some of his tribe.

*11.* Do you not think it is owing to the facility they have had for procuring liquor? That has much accelerated it. I have known others that have had two wives that shared the same fate in the course of six or eight years. I saw a great deal of the blacks when I first came up here. I built the first private residence in Brisbane, and they used to congregate about it, and I have seen sixty or eighty about the house at one time. Women were not then admitted into the settlement. They were kept out of Brisbane when it was a penal settlement.

.    .    .

*13.* You have said that the Brisbane tribe disappeared altogether. What, do you think, was the usage they met with during that time from the inhabitants of Brisbane? They were most kindly used.

*14.* You are aware that, during that period, several outrages in the neighbourhood of Brisbane, such as assaults, took place by the blacks? Yes, that is what they were generally fond of doing—assaulting women on the road some distance from Brisbane.

*15.* They were in the habit of doing so? Yes.

*16.* From your knowledge of the blacks, would you say that they have been ill-treated by the whites? To my knowledge, I am not aware of any attempt at Brisbane or Ipswich of that sort.

*17.* Have not white men been murdered by the blacks at Brisbane? Yes, in some numbers.

*18.* Have you any notion of the number that have been murdered by the Brisbane tribes, in the neighbourhood of Brisbane? I know that several were killed between here and Durandur, on the north road. The depredations were mostly committed on the drays, which were out two months or six weeks on a stretch. This I can tell, but the whole of the outrages can be traced in the Police Report which was forwarded to Sydney eight or nine years ago by Captain Wickham. It showed that up to that time one hundred and seventy-four white men had been killed by the blacks.

*19.* That is all over the District of Morton Bay? Yes.

*20.* Does it comprehend the Darling Downs? Yes. I believe that up to this time there have been two hundred and fifty killed—going over a space of nineteen years—in the Northern District. The blacks were severely chastised on account of these murders. That I know for a certain fact.

*21.* In what way have they been severely chastised? For want of police protection, the settlers had to protect themselves, and their retaliation was very severe.

*22.* By Mr. BLAKENEY: Did they retaliate by shooting? Yes, by shooting.

*23.* By the CHAIRMAN: Do you think that the establishment of the Native Police is an improvement on the old system of leaving settlers to protect themselves? I believe it has been. On the Kilcoy Station, owned by Mr. Evan Mackenzie, there were two white men killed, and an imported bull; and their retaliation was very severe on the blacks—they destroyed hundreds of them.

*24.* In what way? By shooting and poisoning them.

*25.* What with? With strychnine and arsenic, in flour.

*26.* Are you aware that strychnine goes by the name of Mackenzie among the blacks? I have heard so.*

*27.* The Mackenzie alluded to is not the Chairman of this Committee, but Mr. Evan Mackenzie? Yes.

* Mr. Mackenzie received a note from Mr. Plunkett, the Attorney-General of New South Wales, stating that he had received accounts of his having destroyed the blacks, and cautioning him, and informing him at the same time that if the complaint were brought before him officially he would have to take notice of it.

*28.* In your experience of the different murders of whites by the blacks, and of blacks by the whites, on which occurrence has the greatest stress been usually laid by the public and the press? Those that have received the greatest amount of notice have been the murders of the whites by the blacks—for instance, such murders as those of Mr. Gregor and Mrs. Shannon.

*29.* Do you remember that when some white men were murdered by blacks in the Bay, only the other day—a boat's crew of whites went with some blacks, and they were murdered, about eighteen months ago—has much notice been taken by the Government or the public press of this murder? Some by the press; little, or none, by the Government.

## 4.20 22 May 1861. Royal Commission into the Native Police Force.

*(3)*: *A. C. Gregory's evidence. Western Australian Education.*

*(Ibid.,* p. 447.)

*42.* Have not some attempts been made in Western Australia to improve the condition of the aborigines? Several attempts have been made; in fact, one constant and continuous effort has been made almost since the foundation of the Colony, in 1829.

*43.* Have those attempts been successful or not? I am afraid they can scarcely be said to have been successful; the success was only partial.

*44.* Will you explain to the Committee what has been done? In the first place, an attempt was made to collect the elderly natives together, and to teach them in schools, which was found to be altogether impracticable. Following upon this, an experiment was made to obtain and educate a number of young children; very young children were obtained; some of them were orphans, others were purchased from their parents; as many as possible were collected and brought in, funds for the purpose being supplied partly by the Government and partly by private enterprise. The school was conducted by the Wesleyan minister. But it was found that, when the children reached the age of thirteen or fourteen years, they began to die off, and at least fifty or sixty per cent. were lost in this way, until it became apparent that the system could not be carried on any longer. After careful enquiry, the Colonial Surgeon gave his opinion that the case was hopeless, and that the only way was to form a farm in the country, and give the children at least two or three days' schooling, and the rest of the week hard labour; and also to give them some coarser kind of food.

*45.* Was it the confinement or the large supply of food that affected them? The confinement was injurious, and the food they had been getting was, in fact, too good for them. On the farm, the system of teaching the children had to be almost entirely dropped, but, as far as it went, it was tolerably successful. When they arrived at a marriagable age, they were coupled off.

*46.* You are speaking of a kind of industrial school? Yes. It was necessary to send the police continually after the children, as they were always running away, and the windows of the school-house had to be barred. When they were caught they were flogged, to teach them not to run away any more, and shut up again. In fact, had it not been for a good purpose, the system which was adopted was one which might be said to have belonged to the barbarous ages.

*47.* Are those schools still in existence? Yes. Another school was afterwards formed, in which the system adopted was perhaps a better one. At King George's Sound, which is also in Western Australia, but in quite a different part of the colony, a school of very young children has been established by the Resident Magistrate and his wife, who are both very enthusiastic in the cause. None of the children are above twelve or thirteen years of age, and so far this school has been more successful than the other, and the health of the children much better; they have been allowed more open-air exercise, and have been more carefully attended to, and perhaps with a better knowledge of the peculiar character of their constitutions. I believe also in that district the habits of the aborigines are more nearly allied to those of the white population, and, consequently, they are more amenable to civilization.

## 4.21 27 June 1861. Royal Commission into the Native Police Force.

(4): *Lieutenant Carr's evidence.*

(*Ibid.*, p. 535.)

*83.* Have you had any instance brought under your notice of the rations of the black troopers being consumed, and of their subsisting without them? Yes, they are very frequently out of rations, when on duty.
*84.* For how long? I can remember their being without rations for as many as nine days, on one occasion.
*85.* How do you subsist generally? By the troopers providing me with food.
*86.* You and your men fare alike? Yes, on those occasions we live on roots, and a few odd opposums. On one occasion we were very badly off, when after blacks who had committed a very serious outrage; we could not act, as on other occasions, and shoot game.
*87.* You do not think white troopers would be able to do that? No, indeed, I do not. Another serious objection to having black trackers with a body of white men in the bush is, that there might be a row, which you might not hear of at the moment, and there would be nothing to prevent these trackers—who, of course, would be obliged to do all the duty of tracking, and to go out to find horses—if they took it into their heads, from walking off, and leaving me and my white men in the bush. That might take place in a strange country, and it might take us weeks to get back—if, in fact, we got back at all.
*88.* How is the service now supplied with regard to clothing? At present our supplies are not regular.
*89.* I believe January is the usual time for issuing blankets and clothing to the troopers? It has not been the usual time since I have been in the Force, but I presume it ought to be.
*90.* Have you up to this period received any blankets or clothing this present year? No.
*91.* Have the troopers suffered much in consequence? Of course, they have suffered from cold.
*92.* In what state is the saddlery supplied? The saddlery we have had to work with since I have been in the Native Police Force, seems to have been made for the purpose of cutting the horses' backs.
*93.* Is it very bad? Very bad. I saw the new saddlery for the Burdekin Police, of which I approved. I think it is a wondrous improvement upon the present saddlery.
*94.* In what state are the arms? Very miserable, indeed—very old, and half useless, almost.
*95.* Are you supplied pretty regularly with ammunition? We are out at present; in my division there is no ammunition, but I understand from the Secretary, that he has just made up some to send us.

96. Have you been obliged to make it, of late? Yes; it has been made at the Police Camp for the last three months.

.    .    .

153. You say a great many desertions have occurred in the Police Force? I have known of a great many.
154. Can you give the Committee some idea of what is the cause of this desertion? Many desert from disliking their officers.
155. On account of inefficiency on the part of the officers? I would not say inefficiency. I have known several desert from being rather severely treated.
156. What do you mean by severely treated—flogged? Yes, I think that desertions have taken place on various occasions on account of men being flogged.
157. There is no rule laid down as to your general guidance in reference to the punishment of troopers, by the Commandant? No, not expressly.

## 4.22 8 July 1861. Royal Commission into the Native Police Force.

(5): *Evidence of the Commandant of the Native Police, Mr. J. O'Connell Bligh.*

(*Ibid.*, p. 562.)

43. To your knowledge are the settlers, generally speaking, kind to the natives or otherwise? Generally speaking, kind—as far as I know.
44. Are any of the outrages committed by the blacks caused by injuries done them by the white people? I think so; perhaps not so much for what is usually termed bad treatment, as the violation of promises made to them by the whites of payment for work done by them. They take a great deal of offence at that; I think they feel it more sensitively than anything else.
45. Do you think it is the duty of the Government to give blankets and clothing to the blacks? I think it is a very good thing to give them blankets.
46. Can you suggest any better mode of distributing them? No, I think the present mode is a very good one; the blankets are distributed at the Police Station, or sent to the different squatters who apply for them.
47. Do you think that is a proper course? I think it is a very good plan, because the knowledge which the blacks possess that they will get blankets at the station tends to promote a friendly feeling towards the settlers.
48. Do you not think it would be better to entrust the blankets to the officers of the Native Police Force? I do not think so.
49. What is your reason for thinking so? Well, I never allow the blacks near my camp, and I rather think that would tend to bring them about. With regard to clothing, I think the blacks are far better without it—they only sell their clothes for grog.

52. Do you think any other force would be as efficient as the Native Police Force? Not after blacks, decidedly.
53. Do you think a mixed force composed of white men with black trackers would be as efficient? I am quite sure it would not.
54. Will you give the Committee your reasons? I am sure white police would not stand the same hardships as the black troopers do; they would not go on short rations, and if they were successful in finding the blacks in or near the scrub, I am quite sure they would see nothing of them

afterwards. I judge from my own experience; I can never keep up with the blacks, and it is very hard work for the native troopers. I generally keep one of my men with me in the scrub.

55. Do you think any means could be adopted to apprehend these depredators and bring them to justice? No; I never could apprehend them, except in open country, or at a station—never in scrub. I consider it impossible.

56. Will you state to the Committee the reason you cannot apprehend them in scrub? Because they move so fast that it is very difficult to see them. I don't think it would be possible to apprehend them in scrub. They go through it quite as fast as the native troopers; indeed they go faster, for the trooper is encumbered with his arms, and, although he only carries his carbine and pouch, it makes a difference.

57. Do you ever allow your troopers to fire upon the blacks except the blacks first attack them? No.

58. Do I understand you to say that they never fire on the blacks, except in cases where they have warrants out, and where there is no other means of apprehending them? Yes.

82. What are your usual means of supporting discipline in your force, supposing for instance that one of your men got drunk? I make the troopers fall in for punishment, and then punish the man myself.

83. With a riding-whip? Yes.

84. And you are quite sure the men would not stand being punished by the other troopers? Yes, when I first went out I used to make the other troopers inflict the punishment, but I found it would not do, they did not give half punishment enough.

85. What is the feeling among the troopers with regard to punishment? I think they know very well that they deserve it, and they take it as a merited punishment.

86. I suppose it is much the same feeling which schoolboys entertain? Yes.

87. Do you flog them on the back? Yes.

88. You take their shirts off? Yes.

89. I suppose the punishment is not really severe? Oh no, not very.

90. In what light do the wild blacks regard the Force—as butchers, or as fair enemies? I think as officers of justice, to punish them when they deserve it.

91. And are they not perfectly aware that by their depredations they incur some punishment? Yes, I am quite sure they are.

92. And they look upon us much in the same light as the New Zealanders do, and make war upon us in the same way? I think they do, and nothing but fear prevents them from carrying on a regular system of warfare.

93. And if we did not repel force by force they would drive us out of the country? Yes, I think it is the most merciful way of dealing with them.

94. Then, on the occasion of an attack by the blacks, the Force is necessary as much for the assertion of our superiority, as for the purpose of punishing them for their depredations? Yes.

95. And if we did not punish the blacks they would look upon it as a confession of weakness? Yes, that is exactly my opinion.

96. It is a question as to which is the strongest race—if we submit to them they would despise us for it? Yes. . . .

105. Who was this Mr. Bell? A squatter at Port Curtis.

106. Have you any idea of the meaning of his proceedings on the occasion you have referred to? Not the slightest; I was not flogging the man, as has been stated, in front of his house, but behind a woolshed at some distance from the house.

*107.* What was the offence for which you were punishing the trooper? His offence was this—I had told him to go after the horses, and I found him between the blankets. When I spoke to him he answered me rather sharply, and I struck him. Then we closed and had a little bit of a scuffle, in which he got considerably the worse of it, and I put the handcuffs on him, and was going to flog him when Mr. Bell interfered.

*108.* Had Mr. Bell signalized himself in any way as an opponent to the Force? No. and I was very much surprised at his interference.

*109.* I suppose if you were to overlook such an offence you would lose your influence with your men? Yes, I could not think of such a thing.

*110.* Is such insubordination frequent? No, it very seldom occurs.

*111.* On what terms do you generally live with your troopers? On very friendly terms, I am on much more familiar terms with them than I could be with white men.

*112.* Do they submit willingly to the restrictions imposed upon them? Yes very willingly, under proper management.

*113.* Do they keep their accoutrements clean? Yes.

*114.* And do they take great care of their firearms? Yes, most of them, some of them are rather stupid.

*115.* Do they understand the mechanism of their instruments? Oh yes, they have single-barrelled carbines, which are of very simple construction. The serjeant always takes them to pieces when the locks require to be oiled or looked into.

### 4.23  20 August 1864. "The Distribution of Blankets to the Australian Natives."

(*The Illustrated Melbourne Post*, Melbourne, 20 August 1864, p. 9.)

The annual distribution of blankets to the Aborigines generally takes place about the date of the anniversary of the Queen's birthday, so that our sable brethren have very excellent reasons for remembering the natal day of Her Most Gracious Majesty with feelings of the liveliest pleasure. Poor Fellows! It is but a sorry return for the millions of acres of fertile land of which we have deprived them. But they are grateful for small things and the scanty supply of food and raiment doled out to this miserable remnant of a once numerous people, is received by them with the most lively gratitude.

### 4.24  12 July 1865. Gideon Lang's lecture.

*Extracts from a lecture delivered by Mr. G. Lang, criticising the whites' treatment of the Aborigines.*

(Gideon Lang, *The Aborigines of Australia in their Original Condition, and their Relations with the White Man*, Melbourne, 1865, pp. 3-5, 37-41.)

*Punishment of the Whites.*—The Curator will seldom be able, for want of evidence, as the law at present stands in Queensland and New South Wales, to take any steps against the whites, and collisions will certainly occur until fear of punishment is brought to bear on the brutal cowards who now shoot the blacks because they are too much cowed to resist, and the law in no way can or will punish them. The only remedy is to adopt the law of Victoria—admit the evidence of the blacks. They are liars, no doubt, and have no idea of truth for truth's sake; but their evidence can be taken as it is here for what it is worth, like that of thieves and informers. When the blacks understood that the whites were liable to be punished, communication would instantly be made to the Curator; he would then examine the bodies; find if the bullets corresponded with those of the accused whites; trace the horses of the party to their place of residence or halt; examine their horses' tracts at the place of murder, and compare it with the horses' feet. He could thus get quite sufficient evidence in most cases to commit them, and, supported by the evidence of the blacks, enough to get them penal servitude, if not the gallows, which many of them have well earned.

Large bodies of blacks are now collected near Rockhampton, and, feeling their strength, will never settle on any country quietly until they are fought and beaten; but when that is done, it is sincerely to be hoped that some arrangement may be made for their having country assigned to them where they can live in safety. Dangerous as they now are, I can name gentlemen who are ready to accompany Mr. Morrill as a guard while he explains the terms on which they will be allowed to settle down at peace, which they will most thankfully accept. I persuaded a squatter in 1850 to have a conference, when he and I met some of the wild blacks in an open forest, each laying down our arms at a short distance. When they saw that I wished to make peace, it was painful to see their eagerness to be allowed to "come in" before the arrival of the black police, then expected. The squatter refused till he had shot a fine young fellow then present. I offered to take him as my guide, but nothing would move him, and they were left to the black police. After being hunted as they have been, they will submit to any arrangement that will secure them safety and a bare subsistence.

To conclude, the blacks have a tangible tribal government amongst themselves, and are sufficiently intelligent not only to make, but to enforce on the individual members of the tribe, any reasonable arrangement that may be proposed by the whites for the joint occupation of the country for pasture and hunting; and it is the duty of the Queensland Government to introduce and enforce some system that will at least give the blacks a chance of escaping summary extermination. In the country now under the jurisdiction of the Queensland Government, with its immense extent of hills, rivers, and coast, in a climate most suitable for the blacks, there are (judging from the large numbers—600 or 700—that collect occasionally in the settled parts) probably 30,000 or 40,000 aborigines, and it is awful to think that these are to be left, as at present, without law or supervision, to the haphazard mercy and management of every squatter who has capital or credit to take up country, and of every young scamp who may get appointed an officer of the Native Police.

WHAT IS THE ORIGIN OF FRONTIER WARS?

That question I shall endeavour to answer.

As nearly two-thirds of the Australian continent is still to be occupied, and that I believe the most numerously peopled by the blacks, it is a matter of grave importance, and a solemn duty for both the Government and the frontier squatters to adopt some system calculated to diminish, if not altogether prevent, those fearful petty wars, resulting in such destruction of property and life.

The causes are threefold:

*First.* That no Colonial Government has ever recognized any policy, authority, or property, tribal or personal, among the aborigines.

*Second.* They have been deprived of their hunting grounds without any provision being made for them, the country having been occupied by the white settlers with as utter a disregard of their interests, rights, and even subsistence, as if they had been wild dogs or kangaroos.

*Third.* From difficulties arising between the blacks and the pioneer squatters and their men.

The squatters and the blacks have been left to settle matters between themselves, and to "shake down" into peaceful joint occupation without any regulation or much interference on the part of the Government; and that very rough process and its results I shall now describe, previous to suggesting a remedy. Let me premise, however, by clearing away some popular errors.

In the first place, the idea is very generally entertained that, when the whites take up new country among the blacks, the squatters, as a body, commence the destruction of the natives as a matter of course, and without hesitation. Nothing could be more erroneous. It is of the most vital consequence to the pioneer squatter to keep on good terms with the blacks. He thereby secures all the bark required for his first rough huts and woolshed, besides valuable assistance for lambing and shearing. On the other hand, should he excite their enmity, he not only forfeits these advantages, but incurs such a heavy expenditure as would and has ruined many. He must then have two shepherds for each flock, and two hut keepers for each hut, all at exorbitant wages; and as the danger is an excuse for keeping close to the hut, the sheep are starved, and consequently there is a miserable lambing, and a very poor clip.

In the second place, it is not the interference of the white men with their women; they don't value their women enough for that. . . .

In the third place, more particularly in the case of sheep stations, the blacks are generally the aggressors, as to them such a mass of food as a flock of sheep, to be had without danger is irresistible, and a man's life is nothing. They kill the shepherd and steal the sheep, are followed and killed, and so a blood-feud is established.

The grand foundation of all the evil is the absence of any systematic provision, on the part of the Government, for the location of the blacks, when their country is occupied by the whites. Even when individual squatters have management enough to keep the blacks quiet, this renders a border war almost inevitable. Every year the white men advance, and occupy new country, often the entire area at once; and every squatter, on his own run, follows his independent plan of dealing with the blacks. Some allow them to remain quietly and come to the home station, which, with proper precautions, I believe the best system; and on cattle stations break the cattle into the blacks when breaking them into the run, which is very easily done. Others will at once drive them even from sheep runs, and shoot them down without further offence, wherever they are seen; but this is very rare, for the squatters as a body are most kind to the blacks, until war actually begins, and many of them even then.

If only sheep stations were in question the matter might more easily be managed, but the chief difficulty is with cattle, which are very often first put upon new country. The business of the white man is to get his cattle to settle on the station—always a tedious, difficult operation. They are at first yarded and tailed like a flock of sheep, and then allowed to take up their habitat on the different portions of the run, when they divide themselves into mobs, form their camps, and frequent particular water-holes. But all this preliminary work is liable to be undone, should any natives come upon the run, as the cattle detest the smell of them, and make off; and after being speared, they scatter in all directions, take to the scrubs, and become almost valueless. The usual practice is, to prevent the blacks from coming on the run at all, so that they are not only cut off from their own water-holes, but when the country is watered by one river or creek distant from any other, they are deprived of water altogether for more than half the year; every drink is at the risk of their lives, until they are driven, as they were on the Castlereagh, to perfect desperation.

As a large extent of country is taken up at one time, and this is done simultaneously on every station, they must go somewhere, a collision takes place, and the war begins. The blacks, thus driven to sheer desperation, then kill far more white men than is generally imagined. I have known thirty-two killed, in one small district, in about two years, and little known beyond it. The blacks are mercilessly shot down in turn, often without regard to age or sex, 156 blacks having been killed in the same district in the same time; and the blacks take revenge upon all, murdering even those who are kindest to them, until the cruelties practised on both sides are so atrocious as to be almost incredible.

The squatters most anxious to befriend the blacks are then placed in a very difficult position. When white men are murdered, it is indispensable to punish the murderer; but still the ordinary law is powerless, as the blacks never leave any survivor who might give legal evidence. The frontier settlers, however, can always obtain conclusive evidence from the natives themselves, and upon such testimony they are often obliged to act. The usual course is then for a party of whites, guided by blacks usually of another tribe, to start during the night, creep up close to the enemy's camp, wait till daybreak, and then commence the onslaught, in which, even when the greatest possible care is taken to avoid it, the women and children are sometimes shot. Everything in the camp is then destroyed, the blacks are scattered, destitute of the means of existence, and, of course, perfectly desperate. I must say this for the whites, however, that (although I have known brutal exceptions) whenever they can bring the blacks to a fair fight they do fight them fairly, and not unfrequently have been beaten, for the chances of such a contest are not so unequally divided as may be supposed. A blackfellow, with some eight or ten spears in his hand and some paddy-melon sticks, will throw them all while a white man is reloading after firing two shots; and I have known one man to be pierced in the thigh by two spears successively, thrown at seventy yards off. The attacks of the natives on the other hand are always sudden, and so carefully arranged, that when a white man is attacked his escape is almost hopeless, while his murderers are equally certain of escaping with impunity, and the whites become so furious that they often come in time to follow the treacherous tactics of the blacks with even greater cruelty than themselves.

## 4.25 July 1865. A challenge to Mr. Lang's statements.

(*Ibid.*, Appendix, pp. 74-75.)

*A letter challenging statements made by Mr. G. Lang when he condemned the behaviour of white settlers.*

. . . That collisions between the Native Police and the wild blacks will occasionally take place is inevitable, but that they occur so continually as Mr. Lang would appear to imply, is utterly untrue. Indeed, of late, the aggregate depredations committed by the blacks, and the consequent collision with them has been comparatively small. Mr. Lang would apparently wish it to be inferred that, in collisions with the blacks, the whites are always the aggressors, and that a desire exists, that they (the blacks) should be indiscriminately massacred and totally exterminated. I cannot believe that a man of Mr. Lang's 'colonial experience' can seriously maintain such a charge; it would be too foul a slander for any one in his position to utter. Mr. Lang, during his long career in Australia, cannot assert that he has ever known 'squatters,' in the true sense of this conventional term, as a body, guilty of cruelty to the blacks in any of the older colonies, and he cannot urge that the squatters of Queensland are of an inferior order, as regards education and character, to those of the southern colonies; and I would put it to his sense of propriety, whether men in any degree above the grade of the aboriginal himself, much more a class, the majority of whom are gentlemen in character, could be guilty of tacitly permitting the wholesale system of exterminating his charges would imply? I affirm, without fear of contradiction by those who are really practically conversant with the character of the blacks, that, as regards the question of aggression and extermination, the converse of the charge implied by Mr. Lang would be more nearly the truth amongst the savage tribes. Can Mr. Lang be ignorant of the Wills' massacre, under circumstances of atrocity certainly never exceeded in the history of any savages, and perpetrated upon a party who, one and all, from Mr. Wills, senior, downwards, had treated the blacks with the most marked kindness? Or does Mr. Lang forget the equally inhuman massacre of the whole of the defenceless Frazer family—mother and children, and household, some ten in number, on the Upper Dawson, which occurred some years previously? And how was it that these brutal murders took place? Simply from the absence of the police, who were even then not in sufficient numbers to act as the Native Police were originally intended, as a protective force. And in such cases of barbarous atrocity, is to be wondered at that retributive justice should be executed upon the murderers, whom it may not always be possible to identify individually, but for those diabolical acts the tribe to whom they belong, according to the laws of the savages, is well-known to be responsible? I deplore, as much as Mr. Lang, or the most enthusiastic Exeter Hall philanthropist, the necessity for bloodshed at all in our intercourse with the blacks; but I repeat, I utterly deny that in nine cases out of ten the whites are the original aggressors; and I anxiously look forward to the result which the Government are desirous of carrying out—that is, by the augmentation of the force, to render it sufficiently numerous to be employed as a continually patrolling force for the frontier districts, where by their presence, moving about from place to place, and on the principle that 'prevention is better than cure,' the causes of collision would in a great measure be controlled. . . .

### 4.26 5 August 1865. Mr. Cobham's amendment.

(*The Bulletin*, Rockhampton, Queensland, 5 August 1865, p. 85, in G. Lang, *op. cit.*)

*Report of the proceedings of a public meeting held in Rockhampton with His Worship the Mayor presiding.*

Mr. Cobham moved the following amendment to the motion:—
   "That in the opinion of this meeting it should be made legal for any proprietor or *manager* of a station, with the concurrence of *one* magistrate, to organize a force on any station *threatened* by aboriginals, or on which any outrage has been committed by them, to organize such force as may be necessary to disperse said blacks at once, and that no one engaged in such dispersion shall be liable to any legal penalty."

### 4.27 15 August 1865. An article condemning the treatment of Queensland Aborigines.

(*The Maryborough Chronicle*, Maryborough, Queensland, 5 August 1865, p. 84, in G. Lang, *op. cit.*)

Are the blacks to be dealt with as human beings, ignorant, brutal, and degraded, but human still? or are they to be treated as wild beasts.

Suppose the latter—an awkward supposition though, but necessary form what we read and hear sometimes of the doings, amongst the aborigines, of some of Her Majesty's subjects and servants.

The law, as it at present stands, deals with them as co-equal in all their rights and attributes, with a few trifling exceptions in colonial enactments, with the civilized race.

The Government do not deal with them after this law, so says the Chief Justice of Queensland. They have organized an illegal, but when properly officered, a very useful force. All depends upon the temperament and disposition of the officer. If he is a merciful man, and a man of intelligence and courage, he deals fairly but mercifully with them; if of a meaner nature, he indiscriminately slaughters them. It is an easier service, and he achieves the proud position of being considered a determined and active officer. Life and death, with no responsibility to human tribunal, is in his hands, without appeal, except to God. We cannot quarrel with this arrangement, because we cannot suggest a better.

## 4.28  1 November 1876. "A Skirmish near Creen Creek, Queensland."

(*The Illustrated Australian News*, Melbourne, 1 November, 1876.)

We have been favoured by a gentleman (who was travelling in the vicinity) with the drawings for our engraving of a skirmish between the Aborigines and Native Police of QLD on the Normantown Road, at Creen's Creek, about 150 miles from Georgetown. It appears that several hundred blacks had been holding a place called Bora, near Creen Creek and had attacked the telegraph station there. Two detachments of the QLD Native Police went to the rescue, under the command of Inspectors Armit and Poingdestre, they attacked the blacks, who resisted. The fight lasted a considerable time, but the blacks eventually were dispersed . . . The police officers say they have never met such a determined resistance from the blacks and that the Normantown road is a very dangerous one for travelling, as the Aborigines are numerous and vindictive.

## 4.29  24 March 1877. The objections of "A Mistake Creek Man".

("Letters to the Editor", *The Queenslander*, Brisbane, 24 March 1877, p. 18.)

SIR,—I observed in a recent issue of your paper a letter on the subject of aboriginals, signed "A Mackenzie Man". I cannot agree with him that the police should give orders to all blacks about Mistake Creek and Belyando to hold a corrobboree at the Mackenzie. They would certainly destroy game; but they would also kill other things; such as sheep, cattle, stick-up travellers, and perhaps commit murder, when they would have to be punished, and the parties that encouraged them there would be to blame. It is well known by all that have any knowledge of blacks that at all corroborees the mischief is planned. "Mackenzie Man" must also know this. Let "Mackenzie Man" try the blacks that inhabit the district he is in to kill the game, and watch the result. Before long they will tire, and recollect they are on their native ground. Strangers tire sooner; the blacks where "Mackenzie Man" resides will try to persuade him to get the other blacks to come to a corroboree, till they can steal gins, and then any mischief done they blame the strange blacks for, to get them shot, so that they will not be able to hunt them at a future time for taking their wives. I agree with "Mackenzie Man" that destroying kangaroo and wallaby is about the most useful object for them to be employed at; but let them come of their own free will, not to be ordered by anyone. It is well known by all blacks from Charters Towers to the Mackenzie what the squatters are giving the blacks already employed for killing wallaby; and if they do not come of their own accord, it would not be fair to make them. It is not fear of police stops them. If I am not mistaken in a previous communication "Mackenzie Man" said "Keep blacks away from towns and railway camps." In this I perfectly agree with him, as it is there they learn the value of money, which causes robbery and murder; and they also learn cunning to conduct their designs properly. As a proof, look at the Port Mackay blacks, and the murders they commit about once every two years. For the list of crimes committed by them lately read The Clermont Central Free Press, January 7, 1877; the narrative concludes thus:—"For the last two or three years the blacks have kept remarkably quiet in the central districts, and the troopers have been grumbling about having nothing to do. We fancy if the above report prove correct, there will be a little dispersing business to be carried out shortly. There can be no doubt that many an unfortunate traveller meets his end at the hands of our poor brethren, on the lonely bush roads, away out in the Never-Never country; and as this scrub has been the scene of so many outrages, we hope the authorities will not fail to give it a good scouring."

Long before any police can arrive there, the guilty blacks are most likely back at Port Mackay and in employment; so if any do get punished they are the ones that are not guilty of any misdemeanor; when they in revenge will kill somebody else, maybe a hundred miles from their own country, and months afterwards.

Such is all that can be achieved by letting blacks into towns to try and improve them. My idea is, keep them from all towns; punish them with great severity for anything they do wrong; punish any person ill-treating a black without cause severely; make any that comes into your employ ask when they want to leave, and when they do let them go at once; if they bolt punish them well whenever caught; and any person keeping a boy against his will to be punished. Let a black escape punishment when he ought to have got it, and watch the result. In less than a year he will be a thorough scoundrel, if not a murderer. Treat as I have stated, and mark the difference in twelve months.

A MISTAKE CREEK MAN.


### 4.30  24 March 1877. A letter from "Outsider".

("Letters to the Editor", *The Queenslander, op. cit.*, 24 March 1877, p. 18.)

Our Aborigines

SIR,—Will you permit me to draw the attention of your readers to some of the weak points in "An Old Queenslander's" article on the amelioration of our aborigines. Having twelve years' experience of the Queensland aboriginal in the different stages in which he exists at the present time, I think I can speak with a little weight in matters which concern their well-being. Like most writers on this question, "Old Queenslander" has greatly overestimated the psychological powers of this race. The mere fact of a few individuals having been successfully educated does not by any means authorise the inference that the whole race can in a like manner be raised to an intellectual level with the white man. "Old Queenslander" errs in one great particular: he believes that by kindness the blacks can be raised from their state of squalor and moral degradation. Now, Sir, anyone who has lived near the Australian savage is perfectly well aware that he believes kindness from a white man emanates from fear, and becomes more exactive in proportion to the amount of food lavished on him. "Old Queenslander" points triumphantly to the fact that the Victorian Government have, by the yearly expenditure of £8,000, succeeded in maintaining 577 aboriginals on their mission stations, and have *actually* sent a few of this number to take part in the cricket matches in the metropolis. Verily a great result obtained at such a price; and "Old Queenslander" would no doubt be proud to see the experiment repeated in Queensland. He is of opinion that by a course of good living and labor, with as much bodily freedom as may be compatible with the attainment of the second item, the Queensland blackfellow will eventually be raised from his present degradation and placed in a higher intellectual sphere, which will then enable us to teach, and him to grasp, the tenets of our religious faith. I have only to point at the aboriginal population of New South Wales, which "Old Queenslander" quotes as an example of the softening influences of intercourse between the races, as a contradiction to this assertion. The New South Wales black is a better man than the Queensland native, but simply because a century has elapsed since the white man put his mark upon him. Three generations have almost passed since then and it is not very strange that such a lapse of time should have done a little towards ameliorating a savage race. But there is another element at work, and one which "Old Queenslander" has entirely overlooked. The cases of South Australia, Victoria, and New South Wales, are in no way analogous to ours. In each of those colonies there are immense agricultural centres, which are covered with a population far exceeding any found on an equal area in Queensland, and it is to this fact, and to this alone, that the success of missionary stations in those colonies has been due. The blacks readily found employment among the farmers, and eventually would contentedly resign their roving life for the comforts offered to them in exchange for their services. And the exchange would be made all the easier as their country was in the hands of the whites, and every inch of it under cultivation. And this, Sir, is what I maintain has been one of the greatest obstacles we have had, and still have to contend with, in ameliorating the condition of our blacks. For what was done voluntarily, and at little cost, by the farmers of New South Wales and Victoria, will have to be borne by the, comparatively speaking, scattered population of this colony, and the burden is one which it would be impossible and impolitic to impose on a young colony like ours. Allowing that the blacks of the sister colonies are reduced to a mere remnant of once powerful tribes, it does not follow as a matter of duty that we should be forced to *entirely* maintain the thousands of aborigines in Queensland; and even if the colony did undertake the task, everyone who understands anything about the blacks knows that this course would only hasten their exit from off the face of the earth. Once impose restrictions on them, and they must succumb, for it would be quite as feasible to make a white man live after the fashion of blacks, in fact easier, from the superior adaptability of the latter to modified conditions of life, as to try and civilise an aboriginal, and make him a useful member of society. The great mistake which we make is the constant endeavour to make the duty go hand in hand with the cost, and get sufficient capital out of our creditors to pay our debt to them. I still uphold my plan, which you were good enough to publish in your issue of October 28, and which is being carried out in South Australia as well as here in Queensland, though it requires extending to become really useful in this colony—viz., the formation of depots in suitable localities, avoiding towns as much as possible, at which blankets, tomahawks, and clothing could be obtained by blacks, and in bad seasons rations as well. Have every article issued branded with the Government broad arrow and Q.G., and pass an Act making it felony to deprive blacks of any articles thus branded, by barter or theft. Increase the penalty for supplying grog to a black, and keep them out of all townships, where they are only taught every species of roguery by their more civilised countrymen and by the whites. Encourage the employment of aboriginal labor by respectable persons (there is little danger of such labor ever clashing with the white hands employed on holdings), and make it incumbent on all employers to have an agreement, such never extending over a longer period than, say, six months.

I think you will agree with me in believing that the blacks will derive more benefit in this manner than by shutting them in on runs or reserves, which, by the way, I defy "Old Queenslander," or anybody else, to successfully accomplish without having recourse to coercion. But I do not agree with him that because a portion of the aboriginal races may be brought together on a station, and induced to live there, we should acquire a little more right towards coercing the remaining portion than we now have. I fully concur with him in his belief that much good may be wrought upon the young of this and the next generation; but the adults of both sexes at present in existence must pass away ere the experiment can be successfully tried. I am of opinion that as we have acquired possession of their country we should do all we can to assist them, and think that the imposition of an "Aboriginal Tax" should be commenced at once, the funds thus raised to be used as Parliament may direct in ameliorating their condition. Nor do I think that the gentleman who would step forward and propose such a law would meet with any very serious resistance from the country. That such a step is becoming every day more imperative no one can deny; for the remaining portions of the colony which are still termed "Never-Never" country, will in the course of a few years have been wholly absorbed by the giant strides of our settlement; and when that time arrives, and the whole of the black race are, so to speak, in our palm, we would have a goodly sum which could be spent in such a way as to confer a lasting boon to these unfortunates. This would be a far easier method than the appropriation of an occasional small sum for aboriginal purposes, and I trust the day is not far distant when it may be realised.

I cannot close this letter without noticing an "Old Queenslander's" tirade against the native police. Are a whole body of gentlemen, holding appointments under Government, to be constantly attacked and villified by residents in large towns simply because they do their duty? Or is it fair to condemn all because two have disgraced themselves and their cloth by the commital of crimes at which everyone revolts? I, for one, cannot see in what manner these men have deserved the odium which is being constantly piled on their heads. Writers would show a great deal more good sense were they to strike at the fountain head, and force it to alter the system and remove the *mistery* in which the working of the native police has always been shrouded. They are supplied with arms and ammunition, and are drilled as an irregular cavalry corps, and yet when called upon to do their duty, they have to turn out and go to work like highwaymen. Why is this? Blacks are not such despicable opponents as you are led to believe, and can generally hold their own against the police. They will run if they get a chance, but can and do fight bravely if checked. We who live in the outside districts cannot see why the townspeople, who are maintained in a great measure by our exertions (for if there were no out settlements where would be the commerce?) should so perseveringly raise an outcry against the very men on whom we have to depend for the safety of our lives and property.

Trusting you will be able soon to report the commencement of a series of experiments for the amelioration of "King Billy,"—I remain, yours, &c.,

OUTSIDER.

## 4.31  1 May 1880. "The Way We Civilise."

*(The Queenslander, op. cit., 1 May 1880, p. 560.)*

*An incensed Queenslander writes a letter calling for some action to halt the extermination of Aborigines.*

The Way we Civilise.

WE republish in another column a letter originally printed in the *Cooktown Courier*. The writer lays bare a painful sore in our system of colonisation of which few of us are not conscious, but which we are apt in sheer disgust to ignore altogether. He uses strong language, but not stronger than that which is forced from every man who retains the ordinary feelings of humanity when brought in contact with the sickening and brutal war of races that is carried on in our outside settlements, especially those in the North. And there are special reasons why this subject should be again brought under public notice, so that we may at last adopt a line of conduct in dealing with the wretched aborigines of the colony which may reflect less disgrace on the community, and be more successful in saving our outside settlers from molestation.

It is necessary, in order to make the majority of the community understand the urgent necessity for reform, to dispense with apologetic paraphrases. This, in plain language, is how we deal with the aborigines: On occupying new territory the aboriginal inhabitants are treated exactly in the same way as the wild beasts or birds the settlers may find there. Their lives and their property, the nets, canoes, and weapons which represent as much labor to them as the stock and buildings of the white settler, are held by the Europeans as being at their absolute disposal. Their goods are taken, their children forcibly stolen, their women carried away, entirely at the caprice of the white men. The least show of resistance is answered by a rifle bullet; in fact, the first introduction between blacks and whites is often marked by the unprovoked murder of some of the former—in order to make a commencement of the work of "civilising" them. Little difference is made between the treatment of blacks at first disposed to be friendly and those who from the very outset assume a hostile attitude. As a rule the blacks have been friendly at first, and the longer they have endured provocation without retaliating the worse they have fared, for the more ferocious savages have inspired some fear, and have therefore been comparatively unmolested. In regard to these cowardly outrages, the majority of settlers have been apparently influenced by the same sort of feeling as that which guides men in their treatment of the brute creation. Many, perhaps the majority, have stood aside in silent disgust whilst these things were being done, actuated by the same motives that keep humane men from shooting or molesting animals which neither annoy nor are of service to them; and a few have always protested in the name of humanity against such treatment of human beings, however degraded. But the protests of the minority have been disregarded by the people of the settled districts; the majority of outsiders who take no part in the outrages have been either apathetic or inclined to shield their companions, and the white brutes who fancied the amusement have murdered, ravished, and robbed the blacks without let or hindrance. Not only have they been unchecked, but the Government of the colony has been always at hand to save them from the consequences of their crime. When the blacks, stung to retaliation by outrages committed on their tribe, or hearing the fate of their neighbors, have taken the initiative and shed white blood, or speared white men's stock, the native police have been sent to "disperse" them. What disperse means is well enough known. The word has been adopted into bush slang as a convenient euphuism for wholesale massacre. Of this force we have already said that it is impossible to write about it with patience. It is enough to say of it that this body, organised and paid by us, is sent to do work which its officers are forbidden to report in detail, and that a true record of its proceedings would shame us before our fellow-countrymen in every part of the British Empire. When the police have entered on the scene, the race conflict goes on apace. It is a fitful war of extermination waged upon the blacks, something after the fashion in which other settlers wage war upon noxious wild beasts. . . .

In the Cape York Peninsula the race conflict has hardly diminished in intensity since the whites began it by robbing and shooting the blacks on the occasion of the first rush to the Palmer. The struggle has been obstinate and fierce, and although an unusually large and costly body of police has been for years engaged in exterminating the aborigines, and few whites miss a chance of shooting any they may encounter, the strength of the tribes has not been broken. No doubt their numbers have been greatly thinned, but they have not been cowed. Consequently there is no part of Queensland in which more European lives have been lost, or where the bush is so thoroughly unsafe for the single traveller. It is difficult to estimate the extent of the loss that has been directly incurred, and still more difficult to calculate the indirect injury suffered by the district. Prospecting for minerals could only be carried on by well armed and equipped parties—and this in itself has been a serious drawback to the European miners. But the heaviest loss is being experienced now that the mining excitement has subsided. For, as the writer in the Cooktown paper says, there is plenty of good soil inviting settlement; but how many men dare fix their home in the bush when they know that neither their property nor their lives will be safe from the attacks of desperate savages, whose natural cunning has been intensified by their long struggle for life with the whites. Evidently settlement must be delayed until the work of extermination is complete—a consummation of which there is no present prospect—or until some more rational and humane method of dealing with the blacks is adopted. It is surely advisable, even at this the eleventh hour, to try the more creditable alternative, and to see whether we cannot efface some portion at least of the stain which attaches to us.

### 4.32  15 May 1880. "Sydney Aborigines, Past and Present."

(*The Illustrated Sydney News and New South Wales Agriculturist and Grazier,* Sydney, 15 May 1880, p. 23.)

The Aborigines of Australia are a doomed race. Found occupying one of the lowest stages of savage life when the shores of NSW became familiar with a presence of white men, their contact with the influences of civilization appears to have destroyed every possibility of their acquiring habits of self-reliance, or of preserving them from the debasing follies and vices which have effected such disastrous results among the "children of the wild" in other countries.

In a recent lecture on "The Aborigines of NSW," The Rev. J. B. Gribble, of Warangesda Mission, Murrumbidgee River contrasted the present condition of the blacks, after many years of intercourse with white settlers calling themselves Christians, with what it was in their primitive state. Then they were a free race with ample tribal territory, over which they could wander undisturbed. Their hunter craft and knowledge of the habits and resorts of game enabled them to obtain each day sufficient for the days needs. Indeed they lived in plenty. Their tribal customs and laws bound all members of the tribe together in friendship and they possessed a spirit of mutual assistance. The feeling of clanship was strong. The divisions of the tribe amounted almost to caste distinctions and the rules relating to courtship and marriage prevented intermarriage of those of near degrees of consanguinity and morality were well maintained.

But now their camps were scenes of abject misery. The settlers guns and the settlers dogs had harassed and destroyed their game, and semi-starvation was their lot. The poison of the grog shop had destroyed their natural acuteness, and the most horrible and loathesome diseases had spread from the vicious habits of the whites. The children in the camps were seldom black, but half-caste, sometimes almost pure white. The black and half-caste girls, ruined by the white man and caste adrift, were forsaken by the black men—their natural protectors—who went off by themselves or sought work among the stations, leaving the poor women a prey to the lawless waifs and strays of our civilization. The lecturer drew a thrilling picture of one camp recently visited by him, in which were eleven women and girls thus abandoned, with scarcely a rag to cover them, and not a morsel of food in their possession, their only hope of a supply being that two young lads had gone out to try and knock down a stray bird or two. Reference was made to the neglect of the blacks by the churches and government and instances were given of manifest cruelty and injustice by those in authority, the apathy of the police in the matter of supplying intoxicants, against which there were special legislation; the delay often occurring in the distribution of the one blanket — our only return for all we have taken from them — rendering the small boon almost nugratory. Our artist has illustrated the contrast between the Aborigines who formerly resided on the shores of Port Jackson and their representatives at the present time. In the country the difference between the old and the new order of things is not less strongly perceptible.


## 4.33  4 September 1880. "Black Vs. White."

(William Armit, "Black Vs .White", *The Queenslander, op. cit.,*
4 September 1880, p. 306.)

*Mr. William Armit discusses the cost of ameliorating the Queensland Aborigine.*

. . . Who that has seen the squalid wretches about towns will say they are as well off as when they lived in their savage state, or that their condition has been bettered by ever so little? We have a reserve at Mackay, and Mr. Bridgeman gives us an occasional report of its glorious success. But we also know that these same blacks have repeatedly made raids on the neighboring stations, fleeing back to the reserve to escape the well-merited punishment which would otherwise have been inflicted by the police at Nebo. The question of amelioration, after all, lies in a nutshell. It resolves itself in £ s. d. Now, is the Government prepared to place £100,000 on the Estimates for this purpose? I think not. And yet without an outlay far exceeding this sum we cannot hope to improve their position; and even then results can only be of the most transient nature. The Victorian Government placed their aborigines under the protection of guardians from July 1, 1851, to June 18, 1860, the aggregate sum expended under that system being £14,181. The results obtained were, however, very unsatisfactory. On the 18th June, 1860, a Board was appointed for the Protection of the Aborigines, and a sum exceeding £100,000 had already been expended on them in 1878. Taking the mean of a whole number of estimates we find that when the whites first settled in Victoria there were about 4,500 natives. Mr. Brough Smyth, from whose fine work I cull these facts, draws attention to the fact that, prior to the advent of the first settlers, a small-pox epidemic had greatly reduced their numbers. The total number of natives under the Board in 1876—that is, thirty-eight years after settlement—was 500. Thus we arrive at very startling facts. If the natives of a fine colony can by the sheer moral power of civilization brought to bear upon them as an ameliorating agent be reduced in thirty-eight years by 4000, at an expenditure of £114,500, what can we expect to effect in a like period with a native population of fully 20,000, one-half of which may be said to have hardly come into actual contact with our different systems? What, let me ask, would the advocates of amelioration give these savages in return for their dearly-loved freedom? Where and what are the sweets that they intend should replace their inborn love of the chase? How do they propose to overcome their nomadic instincts, to which may be traced their very presence on this continent? Imagine even a small tribe of blacks forced to live for a short period on one spot! Would not a fearful epidemic be the result? But no; a few enthusiastic humanitarians, philanthropists, call them what you will, actually desire to alter every condition under which these savages have for ages existed, and to change their very instincts by the mere force of a master will, as typified in the white man, expecting in their shortsightedness to transform what always has been the lowest grade of humanity into a useful and creditable element in the commonwealth. Could any scheme be more Quixotic! We find by actual tabulated facts that the closer we bring the opposing races together the faster the blacks die out; that the white man's kindness—mistaken kindness —is far more fatal to our blacks than his rifle; that the aborigines are utterly unsuited for protracted labor, and that they pine and die under confinement within defined limits. And still we wish to force all these fatal observances upon them under the so-called guise of humanity! Nothing that we can do will alter the inscrutable and withal immutable laws which direct our progress on this globe. By these laws the native races of Australia were doomed on the advent of the white man, and the only thing left for us to do is to assist in carrying them out with as little cruelty as possible, and to endeavour to extend the period of their action over as great a span of time as we possibly can. But any attempt on our part at coercive amelioration can only tend to expedite the final result, instead of lengthening their days in the land. It is not at all improbable that a mixed race would spring into existence could we conquer the tendency to infanticide which obtains in the tribes. As a rule half-bloods have a finer physique than the mother race, but four-fifths of these children are put to death and generally eaten. Were it possible to improve our blacks by the establishment of reserves—and an experiment might be tried at some suitable spot on our coast, where a dugong fishery or two would offer them employment, assimilating in some degree with their natural instincts —it would be our bounden duty to supply money and material for such establishments; but it becomes imperative to discover, first, whether such reserves will be of any use, and, secondly, whether the rate of mortality increases or diminishes under such a system. . . .

We must rule the blacks by fear, teaching them the uselessness of waging war on the settlers, and to do this the native troopers are far superior to white men, as they will follow and secure malefactors where a white man could not possibly penetrate. . . .

No white man should be permitted to cohabit with a gin, as is at present the case, unless he marries her. It is an everyday occurrence in the North to meet travellers and teams accompanied by a gin; even these men, in most cases, endeavoring to hide their degradation by dressing their sable Hebes in men's clothes and *passing them off as boys*. Such men have done more to foster the enmity between the races than any amount of patrolling. I have sketched here what I consider would be an improvement on the present system, being far cheaper than the substitution of white men; but one item should not be omitted in any scheme which may be eventually adopted: The force must be separated from the ordinary police, with which it has nothing in common. . . .

I would also encourage every attempt to collect information and materials from which a standard work of reference could be compiled. We know very little about the blacks, and that little is exceedingly fragmentary and based mostly on carelessly collected facts. The blacks will have disappeared from this continent before another century has come and gone. Their habits and customs are constantly changing or falling into disuse, since they came into contact with the whites; it therefore behoves us to obtain properly authenticated facts relating to everything connected with their past history. No one can be more fortunately situated for such work than Native Police officers, and the Queensland Government would confer lasting boon on the present and future generations of this country if they would sanction and foster any research tending to the fulfilment of so valuable an object. Our national Museum would soon be enriched by a vast and valuable collection, as varied as unique, illustrating the successive stages through which the aborigines have passed since our advent, enabling the student to arrive at definite conclusions, by comparison and classification. I have for eight years devoted all my spare time to such subjects, but was *forbidden to publish any information* which could give the public even the slightest glimpse into the doings of the Native Police. Why such a course should be adopted is inexplicable, and certainly does not reflect credit on those who were its initiators. I may refer your readers, *en passant*, to a graphically described patrol which appears in Mr. Brough Smyth's work on the aborigines of Victoria, vol. ii., pp. 336-339. Here we find that as far back as 1844-45 the blacks in the Port Macquarie district had to be terrorised into submission by a free use of the musket, the officer commanding, Mr. D—, chief constable, actually cutting off the tips of the ears as trophies, and bringing them in stowed carefully in his waistcoat pockets! . . .

Mr. Kennedy,* like Mr. Jack, fell a victim to his own misplaced leniency. When in cases like the above, the blacks become aggressive, gentlemen entrusted with Government expeditions have no right to hesitate in meting out such punishment as will most effectually deter such bloodthirsty savages from repeating their aggressions. The lives of such men, and of the party under their control, are of more value to the nation than those of a hundred blacks. Any leader failing to secure immunity from danger to his men is simply unfit for his post. As it turned out, we owe to a native who accompanied the hapless Kennedy the rescue of his expeditionary papers, when by the well-timed use of their rifles both he and his boy might have been saved, in spite of fever.

I will forward you a list of murders committed in this district by blacks, as a contra account to your column of "How we Civilise." I trust that you will succeed in bringing about the much-to-be-desired reform you advocate, and ameliorate both white and black, the former into unquestioned possession of the vast area of the colony, the latter off the face of the earth which they do not even serve to ornament. Having done this you will be in a position to exclaim with Hugh Miller:—"Thus the experience of more than a hundred years demonstrates that when a tribe of men falls beneath a certain level its destiny is extinction, not restoration."

WILLIAM E. ARMIT.
Normanton, July 26.

* an explorer

**4.34  15 July 1882. "Deputation of Blackfellows at Parliament House."**

(*The Leader*, Melbourne, Supplement, 15 July 1882, p. 5.)

Can these be blackfellows?—there must surely be a mistake. Where are the dirty opossum rugs, the waddies and the spears? Where is the restless, furtive, hunted look about the eyes, which we have been wont to regard as one of the most characteristic of aboriginal features, and as a sure index of the aboriginal nature? Neither in facial expression nor in outward garb is there aught here to indicate the presence of the blackfellow as we have hitherto known him. From each face there comes a calm, steadfast, civilised look; each of these manly figures is costumed in civilised and decent fashion; the attitude of each individual is not slouching but erect, as that of a self respecting man, conscious of his manhood. And how is it that these blackfellows (for we must call them such notwithstanding their civilised appearance) are represented here in the act of interviewing a Minister of the Crown, within the precincts of Parliament, and as presenting to the Minister a memorial? Strange to say too, the memorial has been actually concocted amongst themselves, has been actually written by one of their number, and is actually signed by every adult male of the community, whose sentiments are embodied in the document. Another strange thing is that when these blackfellows open their mouths it is not to give utterance to the yabber yabber which we associate with the blackfellows' tongue, but to express themselves intelligibly in decent English speech. They are able to make us understand that they feel deeply the injustice with which they have been treated for many years by the board which has professedly been appointed for their protection, but which, instead of protecting them, has threatened to deprive them of the land specially reserved for their occupation; and which has, apparently out of sheer spite, deprived them of the only manager they could trust and respect. All this is very remarkable, and our sole object in depicting it is to impress upon the minds of our readers how very remarkable it is. For who could have anticipated that these blackfellows, whom we have rated so low in the scale of humanity as to think them hardly worthy to be called men, would some day show themselves possessed of so much intelligence, and so much capacity for being trained and educated in our civilised habits of thought and methods of government, as to resolve of their own accord upon organising a deputation for the purpose of securing redress of their grievances? The interview took place in the great hall of Parliament House, on 5th July, while the Assembly was sitting. Mr. Deakin, member for West Bourke, introduced them to the Chief Secretary, explaining that the agitation which had been excited at Coranderrk by Mr. Green's removal from the management, about ten years ago, had caused the present deputation to come down to Melbourne, as it had led to similar deputations before, and that their object was to repeat the demands which they have been obliged to make on previous occasions. These demands were that the Central Board may be abolished and brought under the Chief Secretary's department, and that they may have Mr. Green re-appointed as manager. Mr. Deakin pointed out that the Central Board was still adhering to its often avowed intention of getting them removed from Coranderrk, and was also still persisting in its policy of antagonism to Mr. Green; and that consequently the disorganisation and distress prevailing at the station were bound to continue until the board's policy was reversed, and the rights of the blacks were respected and their wishes reasonably considered. Mr. Grant replied that he could not give any promise whatever, but would consult the Cabinet. He would not interfere, he said, with the board on any account, and they must go back and make the best of it; and he concluded by asserting that the agitation was all brought about by outside influence. This the blacks emphatically denied; asserting they had come unprompted by any one; in drawing up their memorial they had been unaided by any one; it was altogether their own idea; and they could only keep on coming down till they got what they wanted. Mr. Deakin reminded Mr. Grant of the repeated efforts of the blacks showing their earnestness in this matter that; Mr. Berry when in office had been favorable to granting their request, and that Mr. Grant himself has specifically promised to carry out Mr. Berry's intentions. Mr. Grant merely repeated that he must uphold the board, and that the blacks must obey. All the blacks said, in reply, was to deny once more the imputation that they were put up to it. Their last words, as Mr. Grant turned away, were:—"We suppose we must wait till there is another Ministry," Such is the case of the poor blackfellows of Coranderrk; and we may state our conviction that did the public but thoroughly understand it, they would sympathise with them in seeking redress, and determine forthwith that they should not have much longer to wait before getting it. The public, we believe, would recognise the great principle involved, that the blacks have rights which we are bound to respect, and that to allow them to be deprived of their rights would be a lasting stain upon the whole community.

### 4.35 26 December 1884. "Ration Day."

(*The Illustrated Australian News, op. cit.*, 26 December 1884, p. 210.)

Since the establishment of mission stations nearly the whole of the surviving aboriginal inhabitants have gone under their control, the blacks preferring to have a comfortable home and a regular supply of food to the hand to mouth existence of former days. But there are some members of the tribes who cannot shake off their nomadic habits and exchange their un-trammelled freedom for the white man's house but prefer the mia-mia and kangaroo and possum to the comforts of civilization. To them however the government allows certain privileges such as a supply of tea, flour, beef and blankets etc. which they obtain by applying for at stated intervals at the various mission stations. Our illustration gives a typical sketch of a party of black fellows who have come in for their rations. An old gin assisted by one of the other men is engaged in making the customary damper, while two others are occupied, one sampling a tin of jam (the present probably to the tribe from the missionary's wife) and the other in trying a piece of what appears to be unbaked damper. The old gin by the mia-mia is smoking a pipe in evidently blissful anticipation of what is to come, apparently entirely oblivious to the antics the picaninny is playing with its father, or of the evident gusto her left hand neighbour is disposing of the quart pot. As soon as rations are done, the blacks will probably disappear again into the bush, and return again at the next distribution of provisions.

### 4.36 1888. Alexander Sutherland's justification for killing Victorian Aborigines.

(Alexander Sutherland, M. A., *Victoria and its Metropolis, Past and Present*, McCarron, Bird and Co., Collins Street West, 1888, Vol. 1, pp. 28-29.)

Such a race, with such customs, could never have been numerous, and in spite of a kindly feeling to them for their good-humoured ways, we can scarcely regret that scenes of lust and bloodshed and cannibalism have come to an end, and that where these hours of midnight diablerie once filled the air with lamentations, there is now the decent little church, or the neat state-school, with human beings that have some ideal to live for, and some justification to plead for their existence. . . .

As to the ethics of the question, there can be drawn no final conclusion. Whether the European has a right to dispossess these immemorial occupants of the soil, or whether it is wicked that he should use his superior might in furthering his own interests at the expense of others, is a problem incapable of absolute determination. It is a question of temperament; to the sentimental it is undoubtedly an iniquity; to the practical it represents a distinct step in human progress, involving the sacrifice of a few thousands of an inferior race; he subtracts that as a small drawback to a vast good, and finds the balance enormously on the side of the good. But the fact is that mankind, as a race, cannot choose to act solely as moral beings. They are governed by animal laws which urge them blindly forward upon tracks they scarce can choose for themselves. If it is a divine law that the Anglo-Saxon people must double themselves every half-century, it must be a divine law that they are to emigrate and form for themselves new homes in waste lands. But every spot suitable for man's sustenance is held by some sort of human occupant; and, therefore, the Anglo-Saxon cannot choose but intrude upon the haunts of other races. When Victoria first felt the tide of immigration, England was peopled far beyond the then existing means of sustenance. Though trades extended and arts improved so as to yield employment for more and more, yet were there two hundred thousand human beings added to her population every year more than she could find food for. Had these stayed at home in deference to the claims which wandering savages might be supposed to have to forests that they merely hunted in, then for every savage so preserved, ten thousand human beings would have had to die by lingering deaths, the proximate causes many, but the ultimate cause the same distress from over-population; and the gloomy prospects that clouded the horizon in 1830 might have been a catastrophe of desperation in 1850. No Reform Bill could have prevented it.

In obedience to natural laws over which they had no control, seeing that they would not and could not brain their infants as the Australians did, the Anglo-Saxons sought these lands, and settled side by side with the natives. Their full justification lies in the fact that they recognized the claims of their sable brethren to subsistence from the soil, and though ruffianly individuals too often sullied the fame of their race by acts of cruelty, yet the wish of the whites as a community always was to secure, or, if necessary, to provide the means of subsistence to the aboriginals. Hence, as our future story will show, the appointment of protectors to guard the persons and rights of the native tribes; hence the formation of stations wherein the state supports and cares for them. But the altered conditions, which the white man's presence brought, have proved destructive to these poorly recuperative tribes. The vices which purge the civilized community of its inferior organizations, seized like a plague on the natives, and carried them off, as the small-pox did in the earliest years of settlement. Yet the actual hardship inflicted was not great. It was less a case of dying off than of failing to be born. The black man, indeed, paid the ordinary penalty we must all submit to; if he sadly regretted that he left none to inherit his blood we pity him, but our thoughts travel to the much harder scenes that would have been in city slums of the old world, and we are content with the balance.

Yet will there ever cling a pathos round the story of a vanishing race; and when we think of the agile forms that once held dominion over these widely forested lands; when we see them vanishing with terrible speed to be but a memory of the past, the contrast affects our feelings, even though our intellects refuse to be moved, recognizing the working of a law above that which man makes for himself.

## 4.37 13 December 1889. A. W. Howitt, on the Aboriginal tribe.

(A. W. Howitt, *On the Organisation of the Australian Tribes. An Anthropological Investigation*, in *Transactions of the Royal Society of Victoria*, Melbourne, 1889, Article iv, p. 136.)

*A. W. Howitt, an early anthropologist, describes the social organization of the Aboriginal tribe, showing a strong orientation towards the new theories of biological and social evolution.*

The principal points which thus stand out as prominent landmarks in this field of investigation are as follows:—

*1.* The group is the sole unit. The individual is subordinate in the more primitive form of society, but becomes more and more predominant in the advancing social stages. Thus group marriage becomes at length completely subordinate to individual marriage, or even practically extinct and forgotten where descent has been changed from the female to the male line.

*2.* An Australian tribe is not a number of individuals associated together by reason of relationship and propinquity merely. It is an organised society governed by strict customary laws, which are administered by the elder men, who in very many, if not all tribes exercise their inherited authority after secret consultation.

*3.* There are probably in all tribes men who are recognised as the Headmen of class divisions, totems, or of local divisions, and to whom more or less of obedience is freely given. There are more than traces of the inheritance by sons (own or tribal) of the authority of these Headmen, and there is thus more than a mere foreshadowing of a chieftainship of the tribe in an hereditary form.

*4.* Relationship is of group to group, and the individual takes the relationship of his group, and shares with it the collective and individual rights and liabilities.

The general result arrived at will be that the Australian savages have a social organisation which has been developed from a state when two groups of people were living together with almost all things in common, and when within the group there was a regulated sexual promiscuity.

The existence of the two exogamous inter-marrying groups seems to me to almost require the previous existence of an undivided commune, from the segmentation of which they arose. The evidence which I have collected, and which I have elsewhere noted as to the occasional recurrence of license, even in the class divisions themselves, is most important as indicating a reversion to ancient practice. The aborigines themselves recognise the former existence of the undivided commune in their legends, but I do not rely upon this as having the force of evidence.*

It seems to me that the once existence of such an undivided commune may well be provisionally accepted as being in the highest degree probable. The evolutionist is led to its contemplation logically. The special creationist may accept it as showing, if it pleases him to place the matter in that light, to what a pitch of moral degradation man had fallen from his once high estate.

* The Dieri and the Woeworung both say that their divisions were formed in consequence of a command conveyed from their great Supreme Being.

# 5

# The Aborigines in the Work Force

On all of the States' frontiers the lives of wealthy and poor were spartan and precarious. With labour difficult to employ and retain, especially after convict transportation ceased and the gold rushes began, and military or police protection often many hundreds of miles away, there were enormous advantages in quickly reducing the local tribes to a semi-starved and dependent position. Some could then be induced to work for a minimal amount of the poorest food (5.1-5.3). Sexual partners became available, and sheep and cattle killing could be controlled. Nomadic hunters very quickly succumbed to a changed way of life if access to water holes was blocked, game killed or reduced, and food-producing plants destroyed. In many instances the white man's distribution of food was simply exchanged for the more arduous methods of days of hunting in harsh and unyielding bush. Some white men chose to rid their runs of all Aborigines as quickly as possible, and the killing of blacks and some whites continued until the 1930s (6.5).

In 1892 the Western Australian Parliament considered that the frontier situation was serious enough to require the introduction of a Bill giving more protection to the State's Northern settlers (5.1). These men were losing sheep and cattle, but ironically, at the same time many were relying on the local tribes as unpaid stockmen and station workers.

In 1898 and 1899 two members of the South Australian Police Force officially complained of the situation where Aborigines were forced to labour for no pay, and a minimum of food and clothing, for any white man able to capture them, or offering liquor or opium (5.2, 5.3 and 5.5). Some saw the isolation of Aborigines on inviolable reserves as the final answer (5.4).

Towards the end of the nineteenth century it was becoming increasingly obvious that while the "full-blooded" Aborigine was "dying out", the "half-caste" community was increasing at a rapid rate. This question of the amelioration of the part-Aborigine became the most discussed aspect of the native problem, with "experts" agreeing that they should be rescued from their black mothers and trained as domestics and unskilled or semi-skilled workers (5.5). The exploitation of all Aborigine workers was being drawn to the attention of the public in Royal Commission inquiries (5.6) and public discussions.

Townsmen railed against pastoralists, and whites against Asiatics (5.5).

The Aborigine as a British subject equal before the law was a forgotten concept. In Western Australia, where many of the native populations lived, the law was used most effectively to exploit the Aboriginal worker. Never having benefited from the use of free convict labour to build public facilities, the Government was compensated by working the large and frequently falsely convicted Aboriginal prison population (5.6).

The same Royal Commission, commenting on this activity, also outlined the system whereby children and adults could be "bonded" all their working lives, without any guarantee of payment, training, or fair treatment.

The Last of the Tribe.—King Brown and Queen—Tewantin.
*Latrobe Collection.*

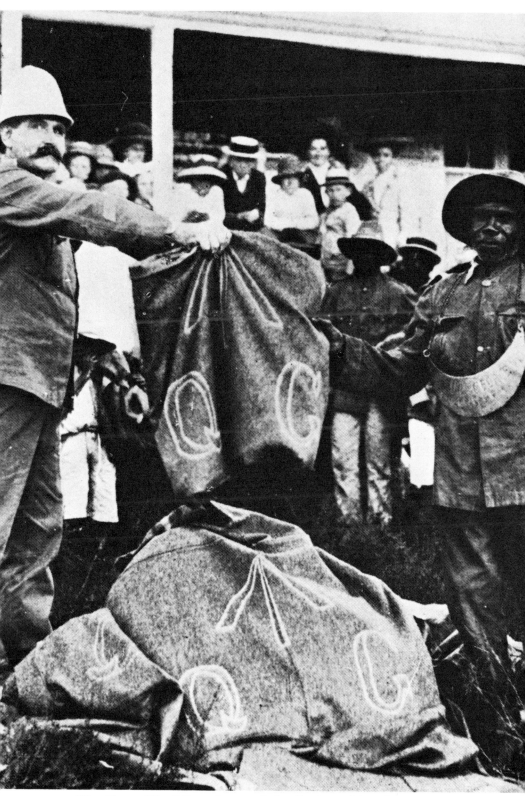

King George VI, of Ravensbourne, Cedar Creek, receiving blanket from Protector at Herberton.
*Latrobe Collection.*

1950's. An Aboriginal stockman from the Northern Territory.
*The Age.*

**5.1  14 January 1892.  Western Australian debate on settlers' protection.**

(*West Australian Parliamentary Debates*, Perth, Vol. 2, 1892, pp. 252-256.)
*The debate of a Bill to provide more protection for northern settlers in*

*Western Australia.*

Mr. Piesse: While admitting that the worthy settlers at the North deserve every protection—and I am sure the facts stated will receive the attention of the Government—it appears to me that the whole question is a very difficult one to deal with. As to providing extra police protection, I suppose that can easily be done, if the funds are provided; but the expense entailed must be very considerable. I think it is very necessary that the police sent up there should be well-chosen men, and West Australians, rather than new chums, unacquainted with the bush, or with the natives or their habits. If these men were supplied with sufficient horse-flesh, they ought to be able to do a great deal to help us out of the difficulties complained of. There is one other matter I should like to refer to, and that is with regard to hanging these unfortunate blacks. The hon. member for the Murchison said he would like to see them taken back to the place where a murder was committed, and there hanged in the presence of the other natives. No doubt that would have a good effect, but I do not think it would be a humane act to leave the bodies to hang there, unburied. It might deter others from committing depredations in that locality, but I think it would be a very inhumane act, and one unworthy of those who call themselves Christians. I have no great belief, myself, in what are called "Exeter Hall" principles, but we are dealing with the original owners of the soil on which we are now living, and no doubt we should show some justice towards them, and treat them in a fair manner. There is not the slightest doubt that much of the trouble now brought upon us was caused by the early settlers of the colony.

Mr. R. F. Sholl: No.

Mr. Piesse: In a great measure we are suffering now from some of the things that took place years ago.

Mr. R. F. Sholl: No. It is an unjustifiable assertion.

Mr. Richardson: Excess of humanity.

Mr. Piesse: As to the natives sentenced by the hon. member for the Murchison, and who, he says, were in an emaciated condition when he sent them to Rottnest, but when he saw them after coming out were fat and sleek, that does not seem to say much for the Murchison, for these natives must have been short of food when they were brought up for trial. They must have been robbed of their natural food, or they would not have been in the emaciated condition they were in, and perhaps this may help to explain their depredations. If these natives cannot find their natural means of sustenance, they must have recourse to the flocks of the settlers or starve. I do not blame the the settlers for crying out: I know they must have a great deal to put up with, and a great many losses, and I sympathise with them very much in their diffi-culties. At the same time I should like to see some humanity shown towards the natives. As to Rottnest, I cannot see how the Government are going to imprison natives in any other place except that island prison. You cannot keep them on the mainland without incurring great expense or working them in chains. They have been worked in chains on the mainland, and what was the result? The public cried out against the method of punishment, and it was done away with. Rottnest Island has been found to be the only suitable place for imprisoning them. These natives, when sent there, naturally gain flesh under the treatment they receive there, with regular food; and we must feed them. We cannot starve them. We must treat them as human beings, although we imprison them. Some re-marks were made by the hon. member for Newcastle in regard to the blankets supplied to the natives. The hon. member said that a native shepherd of his obtained six of these blankets, surreptitiously or by false pretences. I do not wonder at his wanting six blankets, if they were all of the same quality as I saw distributed in the Williams district. Six of them would only make one ordinary blanket. I had the curiosity the other day to weigh one of these blankets, and it only weighed 13 oz. How could you expect a blanket like that to keep an unfortunate native warm? We are well protected from the cold ourselves, and a 13-oz. blanket will not keep a native warm in winter. Whoever had the ordering of those blankets should have seen that they were such as would answer the purpose of keeping out the cold. These natives ought to be provided with proper covering. The least we can do is that. There is a large amount set apart for them every year, and it would be interesting to know how the money is spent. Perhaps the proper course would be to bring the matter under the notice of the Government, and possibly that may be done this session. The blankets now supplied are altogether unfit for the purpose for which they are wanted. I may perhaps have spoken a little heatedly on this subject of the treatment of the natives, but as a West Australian, and a West Australian of the second generation, I have some feeling towards these aboriginal natives of the soil, and I should like to see them treated properly.

Mr. Richardson: I do not think that many words are necessary to support this resolution. I think it commends itself to the House, and I do not suppose there will be much opposition to it. But I think the few remarks that have just fallen from the hon. member for the Williams (Mr. Piesse) are, without any intention on his part, calculated to mislead, and rather become a red herring across the trail. We are at present engaged in discussing a resolution for the protection of the settlers; the hon. member's remarks dealt with the protection of the natives. He pleaded for a certain amount of humanity to be shown towards the natives. I think the whole pith, the *crux* of this native question, and the whole of the difficulties surrounding it, may be traced, not to any lack of humanity, but to ultra-humanity. I think that what the settlers are suffering from is the result of an excess of humanity,—well meant, I believe, and honestly meant, but very much misguided, and no doubt the result of great ignorance of the whole question. I know from my own experience that few can compare with these settlers themselves in the humanity, sensible humanity, they have shown towards the natives,—not that stupid, maudlin humanity that would keep them idle and lazy, like the specimens we see parading the streets of Perth, who take good care they will never do a day's work so long as they can beg sixpences, which they spend at the first public-house they come to. That is what we are suffering from, an excess of this stupid kind of humanity. I know from my own experience that the difficulties which these Northern settlers are suffering from are quite unintelligible to residents in the town, or even in country districts where the natives are more or less civilised. I really do think these settlers themselves now deserve some little sympathy at our hands. For the last ten years the natives have had all the sympathy and all the protection, and I think it is about time we turned round and extended a little of that sympathy and that protection to the settlers themselves. I believe the whole difficulty has arisen from nothing else than some very misguided directions that were given to the police, and which made the police feel it almost their duty to coach these natives up as to what they should do, and what the settlers should do for them. Probably the natives, not understanding what was meant, looked upon the police as specially appointed by the Government to protect them in their roguery and in their depredations against the settlers. I do not say for a moment that that was the intention, but that has been the practical effect of this way of teaching the natives, and of our ultra-humane policy. I think it is about time we woke up to some common sense on this question, for there has been the reverse of common sense shown in the past, even by otherwise sensible men, on this subject.

Mr. Simpson: I have very much pleasure in rising to support the resolution submitted to the House by the hon. member for the Gascoyne, as the facts and the details he has given us are, I believe, unimpeachable. To my mind this question is beginning to assume rather ugly proportions. If we take the history of the colony for the last six months, it seems to me we have a stream of blood gurgling away from Kimberley to the Irwin—the blood of settlers "done to death" by natives. First of all there was poor Miller done to death at Kimberley. Within the last few days another death has been recorded, which I am sure has enlisted the sympathies of the members of this House, on the Ashburton. Then we have young Waldeck, on the Irwin, also done to death by natives. I think the best way to proceed in this matter is to start on the basis of teaching these natives the sacredness of human life. I do not address myself so particularly to the property aspect of the case, but human life must be held sacred at any price. We must bear in mind that the development of our colony depends largely on pioneering. Men go out, not in armed bands, or protected by the police, but with their lives in their hands, to discover and develop the pastoral, the agricultural, and the mineral resources of the colony; and the least we can do is to extend them some protection. We must bear in mind the proportions which this native difficulty is assuming. It seems to me to suggest that these pioneer settlers may be done to death at any minute by an absolutely useless nigger. The whole thing seems to me to resolve itself into what was once said by a distinguished Australian statesman, Sir Samuel Griffith; we must look the matter in the face, and decide whether the country where these native depredations are committed is to be a white or a black man's country. Men who reside there, and whose word is their bond, tell me they have known niggers spearing their cattle simply for the fun of the thing. Not because they were driven to it by drought or by hunger, but simply for fun. Rather ugly fun for the squatter, the man who has surrendered all the comforts of civilised life and faced the dangers and drawbacks of this almost torrid country. When these depredations are committed, these natives simply laugh at you. They know they are masters of the situation. There is, of course, the possibility of their being captured, but one must have a very large imagination to realise that possibility. But, if they are captured, what is the prospect opened out to them? A temporary but pleasant seaside sojourn at Rottnest. I think that Rottnest establishment is about the most grandmotherly thing, and the most silly thing, this colony can show, with its sleek and well-fed niggers. The hon. member for the Murchison has told us of what came under his own observation, when he came across a party of discharged natives from that charming nigger retreat. I may say that the last time I was out in the Never-Never country I saw a native prisoner who had started out with better clothes on than myself, but either the cut of them was not to his tastes, or perhaps they were a little too warm, and he first pitched away his coat, and later on his trousers. He had the decency to retain an undergarment which a paternal Government or the Aborigines Protection Board had supplied him with. He had some flour, also presented to him by the State, and that nigger, after capturing a few lizards, sat down to enjoy his repast, absolutely king, and supremely indifferent to our laws. He naturally felt the utmost contempt for the rights of property or the sacredness of human life, so far as the white man was concerned, and looked forward with positive gusto to the prospects of another sojourn in that agreeable retreat at Rottnest. I do not wish to use any bloodthirsty arguments about natives. I have seen good natives and bad natives, and I have a strong opinion about them. I think it will be a happy day for Western Australia, and for Australia at large when the natives and the kangaroo disappear. So far as their service on stations is concerned, although I know they are employed by some very level-headed men engaged in pastoral pursuits, still I think when those men come to make up their ledgers and reckon the cost of this kind of labor, the difficulty of management so as to get any satisfactory results, and the methods of conciliation one has to use, it is a question whether those engaged in pastoral pursuits would not do better without this class of labor, and employ some other form of labor more useful. My own idea about this native difficulty—I throw it out with all due deference to more experienced heads than my own, and to the Ministry,—but my own idea is that in these sparsely settled, out of the way districts, the settlers should distinctly understand that when they go there they have to be their own police. I do not think this colony has revenue enough to establish an extensive system of police protection in these far-away districts. I think all of us know that in the settlers in that part of the country where these depredations are committed we have a good class of settlers—a high stamp of men. I say sitting here as the representative of a constituency largely connected with pastoral pursuits, I should be only too happy to put into the hands of a board, appointed by the Government power to administer justice to natives in that part of the colony, without bringing these natives all the way to Perth. Let this board be composed of men in whom the Government would have confidence. I would also protect the natives. I would ask the Government to appoint a Native Defender in these districts, whose duty it would be to protect the natives, to see that however emaciated or decrepit a native might be he should be properly protected and receive British justice. I think this would be an economical and a good way of dealing with these natives. There is another point in connection with this native question: I would suggest for the consideration of the Government that the time has come when these natives should be distinctly told that they are to remain on the reserves set apart for them, and that if they go outside those reserves they do so at the risk of suffering pains and penalties. I think that would infuse the native mind with respect for the white man. We are told that it is because of the drought—at least it has been so suggested—that these depredations are committed. I have known droughts, so far as food is concerned, in cities; I have known it in Melbourne and Sydney. But I have never heard it suggested that this scarcity of food warranted a white man to steal a leg of mutton out of a butcher's shop without being punished for it. If a bad or dry season is to establish the rule that a nigger may kill a sheep or a bullock with impunity, I do not know where we are going to draw the line. The killing of one sheep or of one bullock or of twenty or a hundred, is only a question of degree. I think that in dealing with this matter all maudlin sentiment should be abolished. The time has come for drastic, exact, and positive measures, administered not with a light hand. The Government of the colony should accept the position without flinching and see that justice is done with an iron hand; and let the natives realise that while we are ready to treat them kindly and well so long as they behave themselves, they must also be made to understand that they must show an absolute respect for human life and property.

### 5.2  5 March 1898. Mounted Constable Thorpe's report.

(*South Australian Parliamentary Proceedings, op. cit.*, Vol. 2, 1899, "Select Committee of the Legislative Council on the Aborigines Bill", Appendix pp. 113-114.)

*Mounted Constable Thorpe comments on the employment and general condition of the South Australian Aborigine.*

Sir—In reply to your memo. of January 27th, 1898, I have the honor to report, for the information of His Honor the Government Resident and the Protector of Aborigines, as to the condition of aborigines, &c., &c.

At the outset, sirs, I might state that the condition of the aborigines from a health point of view, also their relations with the Europeans, is a most demoralising and deplorable one. Venereal disease in all its stages and forms is manifest, and to keep this horrible disease in check amongst the European and Asiatic people, some restriction should be placed upon these people, such as a fine or imprisonment in the lockup, if found frequenting the blacks' camps.

I feel sure that if half the young lubras now being detained (I won't call it kept, for I know most of them would clear away if they could) were approached on the subject, they would say that they were run down by station blackguards on horseback, and taken to the stations for licentious purposes, and there kept more like slaves than anything else. I have heard it said that these same lubras have been locked up for weeks at a time—anyway whilst their heartless persecutors have been mustering cattle on their respective runs. Some, I have heard, take these lubras with them, but take the precaution to tie them up securely for the night to prevent them escaping. Of course, sirs, these allegations are, as you know, very difficult to prove against any individual persons, still I am positive these acts of cruelty are being performed, and I think still worse.

Therefore I would most respectfully suggest that temporary inspectors (that is, persons with some pretensions of humanity in them) be appointed, say in each police district, such protectors to have power to engage the aborigines to squatters and other respectable persons; the protector to use his own discretion as to whether such persons of his own knowledge are fit and proper people to so engage such aborigines. The so-called traveller, with four or five horses, styling himself a *bonâ fide* stockman, I would debar of being allowed to have a blackboy or gin at all, for these are the very worst individuals; they are invariably illiterate and cruel, and live under the impression that after the blackboy has walked miles for his horses the proper and orthodox thing then to do is to bring him down with a stirrup-iron, whether the poor boy deserves it or not. These men are generally good horsemen, and carry firearms; the boys and gins know this, and through fear are compelled to suffer this perpetual hell. The next thing we hear is that the boy has cruelly murdered his tormentor. The police are then called upon to do their duty and arrest this terrible desperado (?) at any cost. Mostly all police officers with any bush experience know perfectly well that the majority of these boys, when once they are driven to desperation and murder, they eventually turn out very desperate, and will fight to the last to avoid arrest, or, as he may think, to undergo a repetition of his recent tortures. Thus the police are called upon to secure this unfortunate boy, in the doing of which they may be reluctantly compelled to take this boy's life to save themselves from being either killed or disabled for life with a spear. The boy naturally will treat us all as enemies, and will do his utmost to kill. I know from past experience that this is a very very sad duty to have to perform; still, when duty is to be done, sentiment must go down, it cannot be always avoided.

Still these tyrants, who goad these ignorant blacks on to destruction, very often get away unscathed. Probably the boy attempted to murder them; the police have to do their duty all the same. Lives may be sacrificed, and these fellows sit down quietly and "watch the fun," as they term it. The constable deputed to arrest the offender may in all probability have to take the life of the black in self-defence. Then it is generally paraded about that the constable is no protector of blacks; but little do these people think that the unfortunate constable who had to perform so dreadful an act perhaps felt miserable and full of sympathy for the boy, and very likely thought his tyrant should have shared a similar fate.

I have often passed these so-called stockmen (they are pure bush larrikins, and are the flashiest of the flash), on a bitterly cold morning, travelling over the plains on a cold winters' morning. They themselves were comfortably clothed and muffled, whereas their blackboys were a mere bundle of dirty torn rags, a shivering pinched-up mortal in a black skin. "Why don't you clothe your boy?" I have often asked. "Oh, he's only a b— nigger," is the reply.

By appointing temporary protectors the aborigines themselves would soon begin to know whom to look to for protection, and to whom they could state their grievances. I would begin at the bottom first, and totally debar any protector from keeping a lubra about the premises unless he was a married man. My reasons are obvious in this respect. He could not conscientiously do his duty whilst he himself had one about his premises. On the other hand, if at any time he had occasion to bring some offender to task, he would only get this thrown in his face; in short, he could not be an example to others.

It is all nonsense for some people to say that a boy won't stop unless he has a gin. My experience is that I could not keep a boy who had one; besides, once they took to a gin they then became lazy and useless, and I cleared them out and got another.

Then, sirs, the distribution of blankets to blacks on Her Majesty the Queen's birthday. This, I believe, in many instances is abused. The squatters are the first to benefit by it. They, as a rule, get one each for their boys, and probably gins. I have actually seen these on some stockmen's beds.

Now to obviate this expenditure—for I presume the province has to bear the brunt of providing these blankets—I would respectfully suggest that when squatters and others engaged any aborigines they be compelled to sign an agreement before a protector promising to feed and clothe in a proper manner and allow them, say, 5s. or 10s. weekly, such wages not to be actually paid to the boy or gin who earned it (and I can vouch some of them do honestly earn it at times), but be placed in some reliable hands, who will purchase food, clothes, and blankets for the aged and infirm and sick aborigines. Believe me, sirs, this would go a long way to ameliorate the sufferings of the poor old creatures; besides it would tend to cheer and comfort their reclining days.

Few people are aware what a very small scope of country some tribes are compelled to confine themselves on which to hunt for their food. It is a case of the weakest going to the wall, as the hostile tribes, such as the Wagites and Wombias, are very large. The Waggite tribe are so large that they hunt from the Georgina River, on the Queensland border, right out to the overland telegraph line near Tennant's and Attack Creeks. They can with impunity encroach on any of the preserves of the other and weaker tribes, and they dare not say nay. And so it is all through. The smaller tribes must remain on their small area of country; consequently the older people are in a semi-starved state. There are many cases of poor, old, tottering wrecks of blacks—all deserving cases—who would indeed be comforted by knowing that they could get some food and clothing, the result of their sons' and daughters' earnings. It would tend to create a better feeling all round. Besides, why should these station owners—mostly all wealthy people living at their ease in Victoria, New South Wales, and Queensland—be allowed to work their stations principally by the aborigines? Certainly in most cases they are well fed, but poorly clothed. I certainly think they ought to be made to allow each boy and gin from 5s. to 10s.

per week, or so much per month, the same to go towards providing their poor old fathers and mothers and sick friends with some of the comforts of this life.

The very fact of these squatters taking these young boys and girls from the old people thus deprives them of their children's assistance in hunting for food over these endless plains, and I can assure you, sirs, that in droughty seasons, such as have just passed, these old people, when alone, have very many miles to traverse before finding anything. I have frequently met poor old gins sitting down under a currant bush, fairly knocked up. She has, of necessity, to carry a big coolamon of water all the time, and after walking very many miles may only succeed in finding a few small lizards and an iguana occasionally. . . .

I think, sirs, that you will see the utility of my suggestion. These poor old people, how happy would they be, in their own humble way, to be able to sit down quietly at some waterhole and know that they had not to wander about, often hopelessly, in search of food.

I would also suggest that in the event of the squatters being compelled to engage the boys' gins, that the protector make quarterly or half-yearly visits to the stations, and ask the aborigines personally if they are contented, or have any complaints to make.

The protector ought, first of all, dispel every atom of fear from the blacks' minds and make them perfectly satisfied that the protector is his friend, and to impress upon such native that he need not re-engage when his time expires unless he so chooses.

Another very important question is the half-caste. Every father of a half-caste should be compelled to register the birth of such half-caste, and contribute towards its support through the protector. Some mean fellows think it a very clever and manly thing to saddle a young lubra with a half-caste child, then leave her to battle as best she can for its keep. Very probably, before being burdened with this half-caste child, the gin was earning her own living; but the moment she had a child no one would be bothered with her; and she dare not go amongst most of the bush tribes, or they would kill both her and her half-caste child. What then is this poor gin to do but to sit about and become diseased. One time the gins used to kill these half-caste children, but they have learnt to fear the consequences of such unlawful acts.

Another brutal thing I would like to bring under your notice, sirs, and that is bushmen cohabiting with young gins and giving them a loathsome disease and well knowing it. A very silly yet general impression exists amongst some ignorant bushmen that when suffering from gonorrhaea all that they need do is to impart the disease to some female, then the severity of such disease upon themselves will be greatly modified, or perhaps totally cured. Can you imagine anything so heinous? A very severe punishment should be meted out to these scoundrels. It is a pity that the Contagious Diseases Act does not obtain here. I have seen poor young gins, mere children between 11 and 14 years of age, suffering from syphilis in all its stages. The old blacks assured me that white men had run them down and ruined them.

These unfeeling brutes, called men, think nothing of cohabiting with young gins, while they themselves were actually suffering from venereal, yea, and syphilis too, not caring how much they spread it amongst their fellow creatures. And so it is year in and year out.

I think, sirs, that this is where these poor ignorant creatures deserve, nay command, our sympathies and assistance. It is the one word *fear* all through. No matter what it is these poor creatures have to submit to it is simply through *fear*. Wipe that from their minds, and show them that they have some friends to protect them from all these horrible cruelties that are daily heaped upon them, and I am sure and hope that their lot will be happier.

I think I am safe in saying that if protectors are appointed their first duties would be to go round and ask all the gins and boys if they are staying on of their own free will, and I feel sure one-half of them would say "No," and would gladly like to get away from their bondage. Of course there are many humane men out here whom I think would gladly engage their boys and gins in a proper manner, and pay a small wage as suggested by me.

No doubt they would require some protection should the boys or gins turn out incorrigible. In that case the easiest way would be to clear them out and engage others. Some men I know personally are not fit to have either a boy or gin, and I shall welcome the day that some form of statute will teach them so.

I have, &c.,<br>R. C. THORPE, M.C. (2nd class).

To His Honor Mr. Justice Dashwood, Government Resident (through Mr. Inspector Foelsche, Palmerston).

### 5.3   1899. Mr. Paul Foelsche's report.

(*Ibid.*, pp. 112-113.)

*A report from Mr. Paul Foelsche, an Inspector of police in South Australia, referring to the period between 1882 and 1899.*

The establishing of the Jesuit mission at Rapid Creek some fifteen years ago, and its subsequent removal to the Daly River, has to all appearance not met with the success the cause deserves or people may expect; but perhaps the rev. fathers have to contend with difficulties with which the casual observer is not acquainted. One thing appears to my mind conclusive, *i.e.*, their influence upon the natives as far as their condition is concerned does not extend far beyond the immediate neighbourhood of the mission station.

Here I beg to draw attention to a report, dated August 15th, 1882, relative to the condition, &c., of the aborigines in the Northern Territory, which I prepared at the request of the then Hon. Minister of Education for the information of the Jesuit fathers prior to their leaving Adelaide for here, which report, I presume, is filed in the Hon. Minister's office; and although written more than fifteen years ago, since when the condition of natives in the settled districts has considerably altered, yet it contains a good deal of matter still applicable to their general condition, as a perusal of the report will show.

At the time of writing the said report native men and women in and about Palmerston were in a fair way of becoming good and useful workers; at present they are, with very few exceptions, quite the reverse, and ladies find it difficult to get lubras to assist in household work, as they did some years ago; and the men as a rule pass their time away in idleness, and very few will accept work when offered them. But this is not so much the case up country and on the goldfields, where both men and women to some extent work for their living, although there is no perceptible difference in their general condition.

The cause of the present more or less contaminated condition of those natives who have come in contact with European and other races are various; but the principal ones are, in my opinion, their acquired fondness and craving for intoxicating liquor and opium, and the women's encouraged inborn inclination to prostitution. All the women are addicted to this vice, and even some of the young girls not more than 10 or 11 years of age indulge in it.

The severe punishment provided by law, and inflicted on conviction for supplying aborigines with liquor and opium, has not the deterring effect one would think it would have. With respect to these offences, colored races are the chief transgressors; but I am sorry to say there are many Europeans who deem it no offence to give natives a glass of grog occasionally, and some, I have reason to believe, do so regularly, and it is only when the native gets drunk that it comes to the knowledge of the police, hence many such offenders escape punishment.

No doubt liquor and opium has aided prostitution to the extent it is carried on, which is greatly encouraged by the men allowing their lubras to cohabit with anyone who gives them flour, tobacco, and in many cases money, so that they can while away their time in idleness. Outside the boundaries of the more settled districts, *i.e.*, pastoral settlements, a different state of relation exists between the Europeans employed on the stations and the aborigines; in many instances boys who assist in station work were, and perhaps are still, obtained by what is termed "running them down," and forcibly taking them from tribes to stations some distance away from the tribe, and young girls were and, I believe, are still obtained in a similar manner. This practice, I believe, was introduced from Western Queensland. I remember some eighteen years ago a Queensland squatter arrived on our goldfields with a mob of fat cattle; his only assistants were three or four so called black boys, but were in reality, as the squatter himself informed me, young gins dressed in men's clothes and obtained in the way stated. There are some stations on which nearly each man employed has his lubra, mostly obtained in a similar way and against the will of her relatives; as a rule they accompany the men when out on the run.

In some instances lubras are also detained at stations without the consent of their husbands or relatives, which was the cause of the attempt to murder in Charlie's and Joe's case.

There is strong reason to believe that natives so obtained are in many instances subjected to brutal treatment at the hands of those who capture and detain them, which, no doubt, often leads to retaliation and ends in attacks on—sometimes—quite innocent persons, and not unfrequently ends in serious wounding or murder.

More than half of the offences of violence committed by natives are attributable to detaining gins forcibly or otherwise. This, of course, does not apply to all stations, as some owners and managers do not permit such state of affairs to exist.

The indiscriminate wont of prostitution is undoubtedly responsible for the spread of venereal disease among the natives through contact with outside civilisation. This, together with other acquired vices, is already beginning to tell on the tribes in the more settled districts, which show unmistakable signs of decreasing in number.

During the last decade half-caste children have been on the increase, attributable to the increased intercourse of native women with European and other races. Such, then, is the present unexaggerated conditions of the aborigines and the relation existing between them and European and other races. The question naturally arises, what remedy can be devised in order that a better state of affairs may obtain. This is a question on which there is sure to be a diversity of opinion, and is a most difficult subject to deal with, and one hardly knows what suggestions to make. In my opinion nothing but severe measures will effect a desired change in the present state of affairs; and must be dealt with in a different way from dealing with aborigines in the south. The whole circumstances are different. But it will be difficult to make people who have not resided here for any length of time and given this question careful consideration see this.

The ex-Government Resident, the Hon. J. L. Parsons, in his last annual report, dated February 3rd, 1890, spoke very strong and plain on this subject under the heading "the aborigines," and urged, as the first duty of the State, to declare reserves for the absolute right and control of the natives. At his request I made a few remarks on this paragraph, which were printed with his report; and as I have seen no reason since to alter my opinion of what I then wrote, those remarks may be taken as part of this report, as some information may be gleaned from them, especially with regard to placing the natives on reserves.

I believe some reserves were declared, but nothing further has been done in the matter, and the scheme, in my opinion, may be looked upon as impracticable; but I think the system providing for the old, decrepit, and sick natives in vogue in the southern part of the Territory, which seems to work well, may be with advantage adopted here, namely, to establish depôts in the different parts of the settled country, usually at police stations, where the officer in charge is responsible for the proper distribution of rations and other suitable articles to those natives only who are not able, through age or physical incapacity, to provide themselves with food, &c., necessary to their existence, and to render monthly returns of such distributions as is done south; but no supplies should be given to those able to work for their living or procure food for themselves. In the most part of the northern portion of the Territory, especially all round the coast and on the numerous rivers and lagoons, there is an abundance of fish and game of all descriptions, and to supply those able to secure it only encourages laziness.

Then the gathering of numerous tribes and remaining during the greater part of the year in the vicinity of townships, especially as is the case at Palmerston, should be discouraged. With only short intervals, a good many of the Alligators, Woolners, and Minaedge tribes stay here from one end of the year to the other, and live principally on the prostitution of their lubras. As there is plenty of food obtainable in their own tribal country all the year round, they should be compelled to camp there, of course permitting them to pay periodical short friendly visits to the Port Darwin or Larrakeyah tribes, as they use to do in former times, about once a year. This would greatly lessen prostitution, drinking, and opium smoking, and improve their health. This could be effected by giving the police authority to clear them out and keep them away. At the first go off this, no doubt, would involve some trouble to do, but if persisted in they would soon learn to understand that they are not wanted here and have to camp in their own country.

Then something may be done for the half-caste children by compelling mission stations that have concessions from the Government, under certain conditions, to take in such half-castes and civilise them. They would then, when grown up, make excellent servants, and thus be raised above the ordinary condition of an aboriginal. I do not think there would be much difficulty in getting mothers to give up their half-caste children, for I believe any of them may be had for a bag of flour. Up to within a few years very few half-castes lived beyond the age of 12 to 15 years, and when inquiring after the whereabouts, as I generally do when missing any, the answer is "He been die along a bush"; but my opinion is when they get to a certain age they are taken away by old members of the tribe and knocked on the head.

Then, to further alter the present state of affairs, special laws will have to be passed specially adapted to this part of the Territory, and I venture a few suggestions with regard thereto; but I feel sure many of our legislators will not be able to so shape their ideas on this subject as to meet its requirements. But my suggestions can do no harm. Desperate diseases require desperate remedies, and so does this subject.

If a Bill is brought in, among other matters, provisions should be made as follows:—

1st. Aborigines should not be allowed to camp within the boundaries of any town or township. Police to have power to remove them.

2nd. They should not be allowed to wander or loiter about towns between sunset and sunrise unless *bonâ fide* employed by residents, the onus of proof to rest upon the employer, to the satisfaction of a justice or justices.

3rd. Persons harboring aborigines during night time, except *bonâ fide* servants under proper agreement.

4th. Persons harboring or enticing any aboriginal woman or female child on board boats while in harbor, except wives and their children of natives employed on such a boat under proper agreement.

5th. Persons taking away in boats any aboriginal female child or woman unless accompanied by the husband, or father, or relative of such child under proper agreement with such person.

6th. Persons employing aborigines and taking them outside the jurisdiction of the province without proper agreement.

7th. Any man or men having travelling with them any aboriginal female, unless accompanied by such female's husband or relative.

8th. All agreements between employer and aborigines to be approved of by the protector of aborigines.

9th. Proper rules and regulations for the guidance of the protector should be provided for, and his powers and duties defined.

10th. Punishment for such offences, heavy penalty or imprisonment.

Provisions should also be made for keeping a record of births and deaths among the aborigines as far as practicable, especially the birth of half-castes. Such record may be very useful in proving the age of females, especially half-caste, who at a very early age are in more demand for the purposes of concubinage than their darker sisters, of which Forster's case is an example. Such records would also assist in ascertaining whether the aborigines are increasing or otherwise. Officers in charge of inland depôts could furnish such records to the protector.

As the punishment provided by the Opium Act for supplying the drug to aborigines seems to have no deterring effect (ten convictions having been obtained since July 1st last, and only colored races being the offenders), the Act may be amended and corporal punishment added in addition to imprisonment, at the option of the magistrates hearing the case; and all natives found in places where opium is supplied to any of them to be liable to imprisonment.

Much more may be written on this subject, but this will suffice to show that unless something is done soon in order to bring about a better state of affairs, matters are likely to get much worse.

His Honour Mr. Justice Dashwood,
Government Resident,                I have, &c.,
Palmerston.          PAUL FOELSCHE, Inspector of Police.


**5.4 21 September 1899. Select Committee inquiry: J. L. Parsons' evidence.**

(*Ibid.*, p. 84.)

*The examination of the Honourable J. L. Parsons, one-time Government Resident, before the Select Committee inquiry of South Australia, where the establishment of Aboriginal Reserves is discussed.*

1908. We have it in evidence that things were much worse at one time than they are at present. I mean to say that the blacks are better treated now than they were formerly?—I can only say during the time I was Government Resident of the Northern Territory that I did all that lay in my power to protect the aborigines from treatment of this sort. In every case of attempted outrage or molestation we put constables on the track and endeavored to bring the offenders to justice. That was the policy of Inspector Foelsche and myself. We frequently failed because we could not overtake the accused persons.

1909. . . . Will you allow me in justice to myself to quote from my last report as Government Resident, dated February 3rd, 1890? I said—"During the period I have been Government Resident I have pressed upon successive Governments the absolute duty of the State to consider the conditions and provide for the future protection of the wild tribes who are living on this coast. Up to date all my suggestions, which have been printed in the Government Resident's annual or bi-annual reports, have passed without much attention from either Parliament, press, or pulpit. This fact, however, remains; there are thousands of aborigines here, who from a physical point of observation are fitted for all the conditions of an active, useful life. What will the Government do with them? I state most confidently that the first duty of the State is to declare reserves, and within these reserves to give the native tribes absolute rights and sole control." The country belongs to these people, and they are entitled to have a fair portion of it.

1910. You said the other day the blacks could live there now, even if there were no whites near them?—Perfectly.

1911. It would not be a hardship on them if they were driven a little way back?—If they could only be induced to go upon, say, Bathurst Island, and form a commonwealth of their own, it would be a most delightful solution of the difficulty. In the United States there were Indian reservations set apart, and it is only a natural right and a just claim of the aborigines of this country to have some of the best land given to them for their own use. It would be a difficulty to induce them to stop in any one place, because they are such wanderers. At the same time, if we do our best and get them to understand that "This is your country; you can live there, and you are welcome to the yams, the kangaroos, and the fish that are there. No one will be allowed to go there." We will have done our duty then, and I think this is the ideal and the right thing to do.

1912. *By the Chairman*—But would that be possible?—The difficulty, of course, would be the splitting up of the people into so many tribes. If you cannot do your absolute best, you must do what you can.

1913. How would they behave if the different tribes were placed upon an island?—I think they would fight. This is a problem much more easy to state than to solve; still, something ought to be done.

1914. *By the Hon. W. Russell*—You do not think it would be a hardship if they were kept separate from the whites?—They will not leave their own tribal country. These places are associated with great ceremonies. The Alligator River blacks have their own country, and if you meet members of the tribe they will say to you, "This is our country; we sit down here."

1915. You admit at the same time that through their contact with the whites they have contracted bad diseases which are the causes of their gradual dying out?—The Larrakeeyah tribe was very numerous, but it is now comparatively small. The tribes on the Alligator river away down towards the Roper River are numerous and vigorous. They stick to their own country.

1916. *By the Hon. E. Ward*—I have seen on the Adelaide River as many as 100 blacks approaching 6ft. in height marching in their warpaint with small men carrying spears and the lubras walking behind. Can they muster as many now?—Not now. . . .

**5.5    4 October 1899. Select Committee inquiry: F. J. Gillen's evidence.**

(*Ibid.*, pp. 100-101.)

*The examination of Mr. F. J. Gillen, "an expert on Aborigines", during the Select Committee into the need for a South Australian Aborigines' Protection Bill.*

2214. From a humane point of view, what is your impression of the work of the mission?—From that point of view excellent. I greatly admire the missionaries.

2215. How many missionaries have they at Hermannsburg?—Two, and their wives and families.

2216. Have they any day schools?—Yes; and services are conducted every Sunday in the native language.

2217. You think they are not doing any good to the blacks?—I do not think they have succeeded in making Christians of any of the blacks, not even of those whom they have had under their care since they were little things. I do not think it is possible to make a Christian of a South Australian blackfellow.

2218. Do you think that the mission is an honest attempt in that direction?—I am sure it is; and I have the greatest admiration for the missionaries. They are doing good, although they are not making Christians of the blacks. The missionaries are making the natives' path of extinction easier, and every man in Australia who is doing that for the blackfellow helps him.

2222. We have it in evidence that the missions have spent thousands of pounds and have got no return?—In Central Australia they have spent a lot of money, but some of the stations are remunerative.

2223. We have it in evidence that the Jesuit fathers have done excellent work?—They have abandoned their mission in the Northern Territory in disgust. They recognise that it is impossible to make Christians of blacks in that country, and some of the fathers have gone back to Europe. They spent £50,000 in the Northern Territory mission.

2224. It has not been a paying game to them?—No.

2225. And that mission has not been run on commercial lines?—No.

2226. What is the cause of this failure? Is not human nature the same in black and white?—First of all, the Australian aborigines are the lowest in the scale of barbarian races, as well as the lowest in human intelligence. Beyond that I cannot account for it. If I could do anything to uplift the blacks no one in Australia would be more ready than I. I have lived amongst them for the best part of my life, and I like them. They always treated me well.

2231. You do not think the Gospel is potent enough in the case of the blacks?—No. I think the missionary, in trying to make Christians of the blacks, destroyed all that was good in their organisation, and gave them nothing in return.

2232. You have seen the fruits of Christian teaching amongst them?— I have tried to find them, but have been unable to do so. I have lately published a book on the aborigines, in conjunction with Professor Spencer, of Melbourne, and in that I would like to have been able to say that the missionaries had succeeded in making Christians of the blacks. I approve of the existence of mission stations, because any institution which helps the old, the infirm, and the sick does good, whether it preaches Christianity or not.

2233. *By the Chairman*—Helps them physically?—Yes.

2234. *By the Hon. W. Russell*—Where is the difference between a black and white when launched into this world? Neither is educated?—No; but remember that we come of a race which has had the benefit of 1,800 years of civilisation.

2235. If a black and a white infant were brought before us would they not be on an equality in the matter of intelligence?—Yes; at that period of life. If you take a black child from its mother's teat, sent to Europe and educated it—even were the black to be a graduate of a university—and he returned to his place of origin, he would revert to barbarism. I have seen an instance where a boy has been taken away from the interior and brought down here to civilisation for six or seven years. He was pampered, fed well, educated and was always dressed well. On his return to the interior what happens? Off goes the clothing, and when I saw him he was smothered in red ochre and grease.

2236. Then it is not possible for them to be regenerated?—It is a matter of impossibility. A boy was taken from the interior eight or ten years ago and brought down the country. I believe he was on Hon. Mr. Tennant's station, and was taken down by one of that gentleman's managers. He was away for ten or twelve years, and when he got back to Charlotte Waters again he had almost forgotten his own language, and he could speak perfect English. One day he came to me and said, "I think I will go and get cut"—that means the process of circumcision and sub-incision which the blacks undergo—and I said, "Look here, Jim, you are a fool to submit to that." He said in reply. "Well, I can't put up with the cheek of the women and children. They will not let me have a lubra, and the old men will not let me know anything about my countrymen." Here was a young blackfellow quite civilised and yet he voluntarily underwent this awful ordeal. It is hopeless to try and regenerate the blacks.

2241. *By the Hon. G. McGregor*—Could you suggest anything instead of clause 11, that would give the protector of aborigines power to punish those who give opium and liquor to the blacks?—Clause 10 reads:— "Every aboriginal or half-caste employed by any person under the provisions of this Act shall be under the supervision of a protector, or such other person as may be authorised in that behalf by the regulations; and every employer of such aboriginal or half-caste shall permit any protector, or such other person as aforesaid, to have access to such aboriginal or half-caste at all reasonable times, for the purpose of making such inspection and inquiries as he may deem necessary." I would extend that clause by giving the protector power to prosecute in any case where he finds an employer illtreating a native.

2242. I am speaking of the administration of opium?—The clause could be extended to embody that too.

2243. Leaving out the word "premises," if clause 11 were read in conjunction with clause 10 would it not be to the advantage of the protector to have such a provision?—That presupposes that the permit system is indispensible. I do not think you can retain one word of clause 11.

2244. If we adopt the licensing system instead of the agreement scheme, as provided in clause 9, the person obtaining a licence can keep the blacks about his place if he wishes?—I understand I have already told the Hon. Mr. Russell that I see no objection to the licensing system.

2245. Would you permit those who had not a licence to harbor the blacks in their houses, boats, or premises?—It would be a hardship on the blacks if any settler was obliged to send them away.

2246. Do you mean that the settlers are in the habit of taking the blacks into their houses?—By no means.

2247. In the Northern Territory, particularly in or about Port Darwin and Palmerston, the Chinese often take the blacks into their houses and give them opium, but unless the police have actual proof of administration of the drug the Chinese cannot be punished. Clause 11 would make it punishable for the Chinese to have the natives in their premises. You have already admitted that the settlers do not usually take them into their houses, boats, or premises?—The settlers often use the young female aborigines as servants in their houses.

2248. Clause 11 would assist the authorities in punishing those who supply the blacks with opium and drink. If they could not prove administration they could prove them to be on their premises, and that would be deemed to be harboring?—I understand.

2249. Looking at it in that light, do you see any objection to the clause? —I do not. I think it is a good thing.

2250. You say the settlers do not harbor them in their houses in the bush?—Yes.

2251. What hardship would it be to the black or settler if the clause were retained?—Clause 11 says—"Any person who employs an aboriginal or half-caste otherwise than pursuant to a permit granted in accordance with the provisions of this Act or the regulations, or suffers or permits an aboriginal or half-caste to be in or upon any house, boat, or premises in his occupation."

2252. I am referring more particularly to the harboring portion?—If I engaged a lubra to attend to the work of my house it would be deemed to be harboring, unless I had a special permit.

2253. If the licensing system is adopted instead of the permit idea, the person having a licence could take the blacks into his house. Do you see any objection to that?—I have no objection to that.

2254. *By the Chairman*—On behalf of the Committee I wish to express our thanks to you for your attendance and for the valuable evidence you have given. I am sure we look upon your evidence as amongst the most valuable we have on record so far?—There is one matter I would like to suggest to the Committee, if they will allow me. I would like a clause in the Bill to give blacks access to all waterholes, and I think it would be advisable to insert a clause in the lease giving the blacks access to any part of the run,.

2255. *By the Hon. A. Tennant*—That is already the case?—I was not aware of it. In some places the blacks are driven away.

The witness withdrew.


5.6   **29 December 1904. Commissioner W. E. Roth's findings.**

(*Western Australian Parliamentary Votes and Proceedings*, Vol. 1, 1905, "Royal Commission into the Conditions of the Natives," pp. 6-32.)

*W. E. Roth, heading the Royal Commission into the Condition of the Natives, reports his findings after lengthy investigations.*

(2.) The Employment of Aboriginal Natives under Contracts of Service and Indentures of Apprenticeship.

Aborigines are employed with or without contracts, and under indentures of apprenticeship.

A. *With Contracts* (50 Vic., No. 25). The interests of the native are certainly not protected against the fitness or unfitness of his or her future employer, there being nothing to prevent the greatest scoundrel unhung, European or Asiatic, putting under contract any blacks he pleases. It must be admitted that it is permissible for the Minister (61 Vic., No. 5, Sec. 11) to cancel, owing to the employer's unfitness, a contract when once made, but as at the same time there is nothing to prevent an employer working a native without contract, such a prohibition is valueless.

B. *Without contracts.*—No action can be taken against an employer for working without contract, the commonest form of service. The proportion of natives under contract (already stated to be 369) to natives actually employed is one in twelve, as compared with the census taken three years ago by the police. Amongst the employers of the 4,000 natives thus estimated in service, there are many to whom the police would be prepared to object, but at present they are powerless to act. According to the evidence brought before your Commissioner, none of these natives throughout the North-West receive wages. There is a sort of code of honour (*sic*) amongst the pastoralists to the effect that one station owner, etc., does not interfere with his neighbour's blacks, the outcome of which is apparently to prevent them absconding. Being anxious to learn, if possible, what action was actually taken in order to bring such runaways back, inquiry was made from a pastoralist who, while denying that he either flogged or whipped them, admitted that he used no force further than the command that he had over them as being their "master"; yet this same gentleman had only a minute before stated that his reason for not putting his blacks under contract was that if they would not work of their own free will he always considered they were not worth having. Even without contracts the blacks are not free to come and go as they please. The assistance of the police is also invoked to bring such runaways back, an official acquiescence which is of course quiet illegal: the native is practically forced to work for his so-called master. While under such circumstances the absence of a contract does not prevent the employer securing and enforcing the services of the aboriginal, it relieves him of all responsibilities in the way of rations, clothing, and maintenance during sickness.

C. *Indentures of Apprenticeship* (50 Vict., No. 25, Part IV)).—Acting under instructions from the Aborigines Department, a Resident Magistrate "may bind by indenture any half-caste or aboriginal child having attained a suitable age as an apprentice, until he shall attain the age of 21 years, to any master or mistress willing to receive such child in any suitable trade, business, or employment whatsoever."

With regard to the most suitable age at which a child can be indentured as laid down by law, the Chief Protector considers this to be about six years. It being only permissive for a justice or protector to visit apprenticed children, your Commissioner is not surprised to learn that, with one exception no one knows of its ever being done.

No education and no wages are stipulated for in the indenture. The very spirit and principles of the Pearl Shell Fishery Regulation Act of 1873, which absolutely forbids a term of aboriginal service on the boats longer than twelve months, have been stultified by recourse to the system of apprenticeship: at Broome quite one-half of the children, ranging from 10 years and upwards, are indentured to the pearling industry and taken out on to the boats. The Chief Protector draws special attention to the fact that he cannot prevent male children being employed on the boats. One witness approves of the indenture system if under proper supervision, but objects to the clause in the Act referring to the assignment of apprentices on the death of the master: another considers it fairly useful if under proper restrictions: several express the opinion that the term of service up to 21 years of age is too long, the limits of age suggested varying from 14 to 18. Others object to the system altogether. One Resident Magistrate very ably expresses the present state of affairs as follows:—The child is bound and can be reached by law and punished, but the person to whom the child is bound is apparently responsible to nobody. Even the Chief Protector is obliged to admit the injustice of a system where, taking a concrete case, a child of tender years may be indentured to a mistress as domestic up to 21 years of -age, and receives neither education nor payment in return for the services rendered.

Your Commissioner recommends the legislation covered by Sections 19 to 21, and Sections 24 to 31, in the proposed Aborigines Bill. The sooner the indentures of apprenticeship are cancelled the better. In order to prevent the present abuse of maintaining the native only during a few months at a time and then turning him adrift to shift for himself, when if under contract he is prevented working for anyone else, provision should be made in Section 31 that if his leave of absence is extended beyond the limits mentioned therein the contract will lapse. If children of school age are in employment, and a school is available, the employers should be compelled to fulfil their duties in this respect as the legal guardians under the Education Act. The police should be instructed not to lend any assistance whatever in the way of bringing back runaway natives, except of course when armed with proper warrants. With a view to recouping the Government for the expense not only of granting aboriginal indigent relief, but also of benefiting the natives generally and the half-caste waifs and strays in particular, your Commissioner further recommends a minimum wage of five shillings per month on land and ten shillings per month on boats (Q. 1902, No. 1, Sect. 12), exclusive of food, accommodation, and other necessaries; the period of leave of absence to be also paid for.

(3) Employment of Aboriginal Natives in the Pearl-shell Fishery and otherwise on Boats.

Along the whole coast-line extending from a few miles South of La Grange Bay to the Eastern shores of King Sound, drunkenness and prostitution, the former being the prelude to the latter, with consequent loathsome disease, is rife amongst the aborigines. This condition of affairs is mainly due to Asiatic aliens allowed into the State as pearling-boats' crews by special permission of the Commonwealth Minister for External Affairs and allowed to land from their boats under conditions expressed in I. Ed. VII., No. 17, Section 3, Subsection K. The boats call in at certain creeks, ostensibly for wood and water, and the natives flock to these creeks, the men being perfectly willing to barter their women for gin, tobacco, flour, or rice; the coloured crews to whom they are bartered are mostly Malays, Manillamen, and Japanese; they frequently take the women off to the luggers. Direct evidence of this state of affairs comes from La Grange Bay, from Beagle Bay, where your Commissioner saw native women at daybreak returning on shore from the boats with presents of rice, etc., and from Cygnet Bay, where the disgraceful state of affairs and effects of disease on the aboriginal population are more fully detailed. One magistrate considers that the whites are just as much to blame as the coloured crews for the prostitution going on where the boats land for getting wood and water. As the result of their intercourse with aboriginal women, the boats' crews suffer a good deal from venereal disease, and the loss of their labour is severely felt by the pearlers. During about three months in the year the fleets lay up at Cunningham Point, Cygnet Bay, Beagle Bay, and Broome, as well as at other places: except perhaps at Broome, this laying-up season is taken advantage of by the more unscrupulous of the pearlers to swell the profits of the slop-chest by getting rid of their supplies of opium and of liquor, no small portion of the latter ultimately finding its way to the natives as payment for prostitution. A still greater evil, and one which may have disastrous results in the future, is that both the Malays and the natives, with whom they are at present allowed to consort, possess in common a certain vice peculiar to the Mahometan. It is highly probable that this habit, practically unknown amongst the autochthonous population of other parts of Australia, has been introduced along this North-West coast-line by Malay visitors during past-generations; the fact remains that these aliens are being admitted into the Commonwealth. Further North, beyond King Sound, along isolated patches of the coast-line, pearling vessels certainly do land, and their crews bring fire-arms ashore. A witness states that Asiatic crews may camp on shore while the boats are being overhauled, and also during sickness; according to the form of surety now issued by the Sub-Collector of Customs, Form No. 15, they can be engaged in any duties ordinarily connected with the vessels.

(4) The Native Police System.

Strictly speaking, there are no native police, and but little system in the departmental supervision of the trackers. A few trackers have been handed over to the Commissioner of Police as prisoners, under 50 Vic., 25, Sec. 33, but he is not aware whether they are ever visited by justices as is provided for by Sec. 35 of the same Act. Otherwise they are got "the best way we can," generally from stations in the neighbourhood, and being engaged in their native country seldom leave it. Trackers can come and go as they please, and are permanently employed if they like to stay: when the police want one they pick out what they consider is a good boy and put him on the list, but there is no signing on. During the course of his inquiry in the Northern and North-Western districts your Commissioner has only heard of one case where a tracker has been placed under contract; this omission to enter into agreement is apparently unknown to the head of the Police Department. Trackers are paid nothing, though two shillings a day and in some cases three shillings are paid to the officer or constable in charge of the station who provides the necessaries of life: the balance, if any, is handed over to the native. So far, no evidence has been adduced to show that they ever do get any balance, while all the police witnesses examined on the matter have been found to be paid on the lower scale. Out of this, the officer in charge has to supply not only necessaries of life, but also clothes, and sometimes, where the "double-gee" plant flourishes, boots. There is no trackers' camp at the police stations, the tracker, if single, being supplied with accommodation in the stable or on the premises. In the absence of any contract or other authority of office it seems almost questionable whether the tracker ought to assist in arresting, or be left in charge of, black prisoners, even while others are being arrested. The very fact of leaving black prisoners in charge of trackers has on at least two occasions led to shooting, with fatal results: one of these was in connection with the murdered gin referred to by the Resident Magistrate, Derby; the other led to correspondence (re death of Jumbi Jumbi) between the same gentleman and the Commissioner of Police wherein the former (3rd August, 1904) considered it undesirable that trackers should be armed. In the North-West they are still armed with Winchester rifles. That they are presumably used to firearms in these districts is reasonably deduced from the admission made by one of the police witnesses, that if the tracker is given a shot-gun he can find his own food.

(5). The Treatment of Aboriginal Prisoners.

When starting out on such an expedition, the constable takes a variable amount of provisions, private and Government horses, and a certain number of chains. Both he and his black trackers, as many as five of them, are armed with Winchester rifles. A warrant is taken out in the first place if information is laid against certain aborigines, but when the police go out on patrol, and the offence is reported, the offenders are tracked and arrested without warrant. Very often there is no proper information laid, in that it is verbal: when already out on patrol, there may be no information at all. Blacks may be arrested without instructions, authority, or information received from the pastoralist whose cattle are alleged to have been killed; the pastoralist may even object to such measures having been taken. Not knowing beforehand how many blacks he is going to arrest, the policeman only takes chains sufficient for about 15 natives; if a large number are reported guilty, he will take chains to hold from about 25 to 30. Chains in the Northern, not in the Southern, portion of this State are fixed to the necks instead of to the wrists of native prisoners. Authority for this is to be found in No. 647 of the Police Regulations, which states that "the practice of chaining them by the neck must not be resorted to except in cases where the prisoners are of a desperate character, or have been arrested at a considerable distance in the bush; or when travelling by sea, they are near the land to which they belong and it is necessary to adopt special measures to secure them. Even then the practice must not be adopted if it can be avoided." Children of from 14 to 16 years of age are neck-chained. There are no regulations as to the size, weight, mode of attachment, or length of chain connecting the necks of any two prisoners. When the prisoner is alone, the chain is attached to his neck and hands, and wound round his body; the weight prevents him running away so easily. According to the evidence of the Commissioner of Police, when there is more than one aboriginal concerned, the attachment of the chain would be to the saddle of the mounted police officer, but only when absolutely necessary; such an accident as a native neck-chained to a bolting horse has not yet happened, to his knowledge. The mode of attachment of the chain round the neck is effected with hand-cuffs and split-links; the latter bought privately, i.e., at the expense of the arresting constable, from a firm in Perth, and undoubtedly with the knowledge of the Police Commissioner. The grave dangers attendant on the use of these iron split-links, and the difficulty of opening them in cases of urgency or accident, are pointed out. The fact of the connecting chain being too short is also dangerous, because if a prisoner fell he would be bound to drag down the prisoner on either side of him; yet the Wyndham gaoler has noticed the length of the chain joining two natives' necks to be twenty-four inches, the cruelty of which he remarked upon to the escorting police. As far as one witness can find out from police and natives, the chains are never taken off when crossing rivers and creeks. In addition to the neck-chains, the prisoner may be still further secured with cuffs on his wrists (as your Commissioner has seen in photographs of constables escorting the chain-gangs), or on his ankles. Apparently unknown to the Commissioner of Police, chains are used for female natives not only at night, but sometimes during the day; these women are the unwilling witnesses arrested illegally for the Crown. The actual arrest usually takes place at daylight in the morning when the camp is surrounded, and occasionally the (armed) tracker is sent in by himself first. Accompanying the police may be the manager, or stockmen, who have volunteered to come, but as the manager does not prosecute and the stockmen are not called as witnesses, this voluntary action on the part of the station-employees may admit of another construction. For instance, of the two constables examined, one takes no precautions at night to prevent the assisting stockmen and trackers having sexual connection with the chained-up female witnesses and yet supposes such intercourse to go on: the other never watches his trackers, who might carry on in this way, and never takes any notice of these things—it would have caused trouble if he did. It is noteworthy that these same two constables, together with two others, are charged by natives with intimacy with the women: the females brought in as witnesses are usually young ones. About six or seven is the largest number of guns in the arresting party, perhaps such a quantity is accounted for by remembering that as many as 33 prisoners have been secured on the one occasion.

The larger the number of prisoners and witnesses, the better, pecuniarily, for the police, who receive from one and sixpence halfpenny to two shillings and fivepence daily per head, or as it is called in the North-Western vernacular "per knob". This expenditure is spread over four departments as follows:—The Crown Law pays for the witnesses brought to and from the court, the goals for sentenced prisoners in the police lock-ups, the police for prisoners from the time they are arrested until such time as they are convicted, and the aborigines for prisoners returning to their own country on expiry of their sentence. One constable admits making a profit, a corporal considers that this allowance acts as a temptation to bring in a larger number of prisoners and witnesses than other-otherwise, a civilian does not think so many cases would be brought before the courts if these allowances were not sanctioned, a Resident Magistrate has always been struck with the idea that this was the reason for so many natives being brought in at a time, etc. Your Commissioner is satisfied that the amount of purchased food, given to natives while on the road in, usually constitutes but a fraction of the native food supplied, e.g., lizard, kangaroo: notwithstanding the challenged statement of the police meat is not usually sold but given to the police on these North-Western stations. The daily amounts allowed per head are charged for under the heading of Aboriginal Prisoners' Rations Account, and the Treasury Paymasters, etc., at Wyndham, Derby, and Hall's Creek have been called upon to supply items. In less than three years up to date the amount so expended in the North-West districts of the State, North of Broome alone, has been £3,529 16s. 2d., and even this is incomplete, your Commissioner having reason to believe that certain of the claims are paid into private banking accounts, and so need not appear on the local Paymaster's list. Examples of the total amounts which certain of these constables, etc., have individually received are as follows:—J. A. Caldow, £259 6s. 9d. since January, 1904; J. Wilson, £462 2s. 7d. between March, 1902, and October, 1903, and £192 14s 7d. since July, 1904, it not having transpired how much he received between October, 1903, and July, 1904; J. Inglis, £29 17s. 1d. in October, 1902, and £165 16s. between April, 1903, and May, 1904; F. W. Richardson, £121 7s. 8d. between October and December, 1903; J. C. Thomson, £300 19s. 1d. between March, 1901, and May, 1904, with £33 9s. 5d. since then; W. Goodridge, £138 10s 8d. since April, 1903; J. O'Brien, £138 5s. 9d. between November, 1901, and August, 1902; A. H. Buckland, £215 12s. 6d. since March, 1903; M. Mulkerin, £335 6s. since November, 1901; J. P. Sullivan, £230 11s. up to September, 1904. Qne of these recipients alleges that such moneys are paid into the mess fund at the station, so that the profits are indirectly shared by other police officers. The number of aborigines brought in being the great desideratum, each having a money value to the escorting officer, it is not surprising to find that little boys of immature age have been brought in to give evidence, that children varying in age between 10 and 16 are charged with killing cattle, that blacks do not realise what they are sentenced for, that an old and feeble native arrives at the end of his journey in a state of collapse and dies 18 days after admission into gaol. (It is only fair to state that with regard to the cattle-killing children just referred to, some of whom were found neck-chained in the Roebourne Gaol, that, as soon as the attention of the Executive was drawn to them by your Commissioner, they were released.) Besides being half-starved, blacks are "hammered" on the way down. Any detentions on the journey in with the prisoners, or out with the witnesses, are also encouraged by this system of capitation fees. The Resident Magistrate at Wyndham complains of the constable's delay in bringing down six alleged cattle-killers and the four witnesses; of the corporal and lock-up keeper detaining discharged prisoners, etc., unnecessarily. Because rations are charged for to take the witnesses home again, it does not follow that they are escorted back; in some cases they are certainly not; in others, they may hardly have time to get to their destination before they are "rushed in" again by the police with another mob. It is no secret that the police say, if the ration allowance was cut down or taken away they would not arrest so many natives. By their own assertions, every native caught means more money in their pocket; reliable witnesses have heard such assertions made. At present there is nothing to prevent the constable arresting as many blacks as he chooses, while there is no limit to the number of witnesses he is allowed to bring in with him. With a view to avowedly justifying their action in bringing these large batches of prisoners into court—as many as ten or fourteen at a time—the police necessarily take care to make absolutely sure of a conviction, and, unfortunately, the Criminal Code Amendment Act of 1902 is the means of putting a suitable weapon into their hands. By 2 Edw. VII., No. 29, Sec. 5, "If an aboriginal native charged before justices with any offence not punishable with death pleads guilty, the justices may deal with the charge summarily. But no sentence of imprisonment imposed on summary conviction shall exceed three years."

To secure a conviction the accused are accordingly made to plead guilty—at the muzzle of the rifle, if need be. At this your Commissioner is not at all surprised, considering his firm conviction in the truth of a statement made him by a native lately released from goal, where he had served a sentence for cattle-killing, to the effect that one of the batch of prisoners originally arrested with him was shot by the escorting constable in the forehead, the victim in question being very sick at the time. Owing to the informant's lack of proper pronunciation, your Commissioner unfortunately cannot absolutely identify the murderer's name, though he has reported the matter to the proper authorities. With regard to the young women witnesses, their prostitution by the escorting police, the trackers, and stockmen, etc., who have aided in hunting them down, has already been referred to; partly for this reason and partly to gain their acquiescence in the subsequent court proceedings, their treatment on the way down, as compared with the men, is tempered with perhaps a little more mercy in the way of food and comparative freedom. Though these women are allegedly as guilty as the men, one constable states that he is acting under instructions in not arresting them; on the other hand, they are chained or otherwise prevented getting away; they are practically asked to turn informers; they are never cautioned in the proper sense of the term when giving evidence against their husbands, and thus do not in the slightest degree realise the harm they may be doing. The excuse made for bringing in these women at all is that the constable can get no other native evidence, or that "the grown-up men are those that kill the bullock; there are no young boys in the tribes; the squatters have them all". The accused male prisoners still less understand their position. On their arrest, which may even be before any evidence detrimental to them had been received, they are asked (apparently without being cautioned) whether they have killed a beast, but not necessarily informed with what they are charged; they do not at the time thoroughly understand what the charge is, but might a few hours later, evidently after the gins' evidence had been suborned. The police tracker is the medium of communication, occasionally has to converse through a second interpreter, and camps with the prisoners and witnesses before the case is brought into court. No witnesses are ever brought in for the defence. Furthermore, the pastoralist or station manager does not prosecute: he is generally very busy; it is a matter of domestic economy, he would be only too pleased to prosecute if he could do so with a minimum of personal inconvenience. It is quite intelligible that such an individual's personal convenience should be thus respected; the liability of the accused to a sentence of three years' hard labour, possibly in neck-chains throughout the whole of that period, is hardly worth consideration it is only a "nigger." The Resident Magistrate, Wyndham, states, "I think, and have seen it, that a man will plead guilty now for killing a beast some time ago: the native cannot separate two charges on two beasts, and will still have the same offence in his mind: if he kills a bullock once he will plead guilty to every subsequent charge of killing a bullock, no matter how often he will be charged with it." Thus, all to the advantage of the prosecution, when once the native has been induced to plead guilty, there is no necessity under this Criminal Code Amendment Act of 1902 for any awkward questions being asked concerning proof of identity or ownership of the beast, the actual killing, eating, or alleged removal of the carcase. One witness who has brought about, or perhaps over, 100 natives into Court does not remember any who have been found "not guilty"; under the circumstances already detailed, this is not matter for surprise. In two cases drawn attention to before the Commission where the accused pleaded not guilty they were of course remanded to Quarter Sessions; the charges were thereupon withdrawn on the application of the corporal of police on account of the expense of maintaining the witnesses.

c. *In the Gaols.*—Your Commissioner visited the gaols at Carnarvon, Broome, Roebourne, and Wyndham, and is able to place on record his high appreciation of the humane supervision and considerate treatment exercised by the gaolers over their aboriginal prisoners. Approximately, there are about 300 native prisoners in the gaols throughout the State. Two very degrading and yet remedial features of the prison system are the neck-chains, and their continuous use—morning, noon, and night—usually throughout the entire period of sentence.

At Wyndham, when boys aged from 14 to 16 have been charged with cattle-killing, the Resident Magistrate has cautioned, convicted, and re-leased them without imprisonment: at Derby, when a young boy comes into court the Resident Magistrate prefers to give a small sentence and to find him an employer. At Hall's Creek the whole brutality of the present system is brought into prominence when the acting Resident Magistrate sentences a child of 10 years of age to six months' hard labour for "that he did, on or about 10th September, 1904, near Cartridge Springs, unlawfully kill and carry away one head of cattle, the property of S. Muggleton, contrary to statute then and there provided." The same magistrate has sen-tenced another infant of 15 to nine months for killing a goat, and at least eight other children, between 14 and 16 years of age, to two years' hard labour for alleged cattle-killing. As already mentioned, four of the latter met with by your Commissioner in the Roebourne gaol have since been released. . . .

By 50 Vic., No. 25, Section 33, the Governor in Council may place an aboriginal prisoner "under custody of any officer or servant of the Govern-ment," who is thus responsible, and the prisoner is deemed to be in legal custody, wherever he may be employed or detained. Though this has been done within the last twelve months the Comptroller General does not con-sider the system a good one. So far the rules and regulations provided for by the Act, for the employment and safe custody of such prisoners, are conspicuous by their absence. An aboriginal prisoner is being lent out to a Resident Magistrate on doubtful legal authority. Others, on the instructions of such an official, are labouring outside the prison walls on public and municipal works and for local roads boards. In return for the work done for the Carnarvon Municipal Council they get a little tobacco, which, it is believed, is paid for out of the Mayor's private pocket. Although they may be improving the value of local and municipal property, no payment is received by the Government towards reducing the expense of their keep, or return-home journey when liberated, or even of covering the cost of their clothes which, on expiry of their sentence, the Aborigines Department has to provide. Furthermore, the Gaols Department Regulations Nos. 264, 266 preclude any gratuity being given, on release, to an aboriginal—another colour distinction—although he may be as civilised and appreciate the value of money as well as his European fellow-captive.

With regard to long sentences passed upon native prisoners, they are not considered beneficial. The blacks are far better in their uncivilised than semi-civilised state, and are a great deal of trouble after they come out of gaol. It does not do them the least bit of good, and does not stop them from killing cattle, the same blacks being brought before the Court again and again. Your Commissioner has also been informed that, according to the prison dietary, their taste for beef is still further cultivated. When blacks have been away from their native homes so long, they seem forgotten when they return; their tribes will have very little to do with them, and they often commit further crimes because in the meantime their women have been taken. It is doubtful whether the aboriginal prisoner understands his position, or knows that he is committing an offence when he tries to break gaol. One gaoler is of opinion that amongst the twenty blacks in his charge sentenced for cattle-killing, not one really understands what he is there for. Another, with seventy-two prisoners, thinks that about one-third of them know. Another states that when he took charge a great number of the prisoners were "myalls," and their idea was that they were there for road-making, but that as they became educated and get to gaol so often they now realise that it is for cattle-killing.

In the Kimberley District due care does not seem to have been always taken as to the identity of prisoners when first brought to gaol. Carelessness almost amounting to criminality is responsible for longer sentences having been exchanged for shorter ones, and for one case where a prisoner having two native names has really received two sentences on the same charge, while a fellow prisoner's name was on no warrant at all. When once in gaol, however, due precautions are taken in the way of attaching numbered metal tags to the chains.

(7.) General Treatment of the Aboriginal and Half-caste Inhabitants of the State.

A. *Women and Children.*—The Chief Protector has no power to enforce the protection, care, safety, and education of unprotected aboriginal women and children, nor to send the latter to mission stations, orphanages, or reformatories. The registration of the births of either half-castes or full-bloods is a matter of difficulty even in the settled districts. Of the many hundred half-caste children—over 500 were enumerated in last year's census—if these are left to their own devices under the present state of the law, their future will be one of vagabondism and harlotry. In speaking of the numerous aboriginal and half-caste children around Carnarvon, the Resident Magistrate says they will spend most of their lives in gaol or as prostitutes if something is not done with them. He would suggest their being sent to some reformatory or mission whether their parents wish it or not; but at present he has no power to deal with such cases. With regard to the 25 or 30 half-caste children around Broome, the officer in charge of police considers they should be taken right away; as long as they are left in their own district it is impossible for anything to be done with them. At Roebourne the Sub-Inspector of Police is of opinion that such children should be removed from the blacks' camps altogether: a shame that they should be allowed to run wild. At Marble Bar the Resident Magistrate suggests that the same means should be adopted with native waifs and strays as with white children: if they are bright and intelligent they should be sent at a suitable age to reformatories or schools, and in other cases be apprenticed to suitable employers to learn—girls domestic duties, boys, in that part of the country, stockmen's work. At Derby, the Resident Magistrate considers these are the people that should be got at. There is a large number of absolutely worthless blacks and half-castes about who grow up to lives of prostitution and idleness; they are a perfect nuisance; if they were taken away young from their surroundings of temptation much good might be done with them. He approves of sending them to properly organised and properly supervised schools, etc. The evils antecedent to the presence of half-castes in the neighbourhood of townships, which can be more or less controlled by the police, are increased on the northern and north-western stations where the patrols are necessarily less frequent: one station in the Fitzroy River District is credited with from 12 to 15 half-castes, varying from infancy to 21 and 22 years of age. Only occasionally does one hear of a pastoralist providing education to these waifs and strays. Unfortunately it is not compulsory for the reputed father to support his half-caste children. In the North-Western Districts the pastoralists have taken most of the native boys from the tribes; the blacks come in from the bush and get tobacco and food from the boys working on the stations; this leads to a lot of immorality with the women. There is no power to stop squatters, drovers, and teamsters taking these women and boys away. Women are to be seen on the roads dressed up as men. . . .

c. *Reserves.*—A grave responsibility rests upon the Executive in pursuing a policy of allowing large areas of country to be taken up and occupied without the slightest provision being made for the natives, who are thus dispossessed of their hunting grounds. The pastoralist gets a grant of land to raise sheep and cattle, and accordingly the kangaroo, the native food of the aboriginal, has to be got rid of. When these animals get scarce the blacks must kill the cattle or sheep. Another witness states that the natural herbage is eaten by stock put on the country for pastoral purposes, and the game is not so plentiful; the kangaroo hunters also destroy the natives' principal food. In the Sturt's Creek district, where a large number of cattle appear to be annually speared, the blacks can only get water where the cattle are watered; once they are driven from these places, they have nothing to live on; they could get food if they were allowed to stop where the cattle are, blacks and cattle will not agree, and the blacks are driven away; they must, live somehow, so they spear cattle. In another case, the natives are not allowed about the central paddocks, and the very fact of the stock being depastured on all the watered portions of the runs, quite deprives them of the chance of finding any of their natural animal food. In the North, the stock is gradually obliterating the natural native game. Under these conditions, the right reserved to the aboriginal by the Government to hunt for native food over the land when taken up by Europeans is of practically little worth; it has already been pointed out (when dealing with the question of wages) what obstacles may be put in his way when attempting to exercise this right, although possibly no actively hostile action to his presence need necessarily be taken by the station owner. The climax of refined hardship and abuse has so far been reached in the recent Dog Act of 1904, Section 29, where the black is not allowed to have more than one male dog unregistered, the ultimate and ill-concealed effect of such legislation being to prevent aborigines using dogs for hunting purposes, and so limiting still further the supplies of native food otherwise available.

In the same way that reserves are required for the exclusive use of the natives, so are others, *e.g.*, township sites, required for the use of the Europeans; blacks should not be allowed to enter the latter except under lawful employment.

Your Commissioner recommends the legislation dealing with reserves as expressed in sections 13 to 18 of the proposed Bill, and the proclamation of various townships, etc., in which aborigines, except in lawful employment, are not allowed to remain, as provided for in section 41. In the far northern unsettled districts the whole question of reserves resolves itself into one of either sacrificing many human lives or losing a few pounds derived from rents. So long as the land can be taken up at a few shillings per thousand acres, and no provision made for the dependent blacks who can and are being hunted off it, there certainly will be trouble. The stockowner naturally does his best for his cattle—one cannot for a moment blame him—while the protector exerts his utmost on behalf of his aborigines. In your Commissioner's opinion large northern reserves for hunting purposes are imperative not only on humanitarian grounds, but also on grounds of practical policy. The policy is not new, but already adopted in Queensland, and for many years past, on a much larger scale, of course, in Canada, the United States, and elsewhere. If the natives continue to be dispossessed of the country upon which they are dependent for their food and water supplies, by their lands being rented for grazing rights at a nominal figure—lands from which the lessees naturally desire to drive them —bloodshed and retribution will be certain to ensue, and the Executive, in its efforts to restore law and order, and in the cost of rations to make up deficiencies in the natural food supplies, will be ultimately put to an expenditure considerably in excess of the total rents received. Carrying the present practice of Might against Right to a logical conclusion, it would simply mean that, were all the land in the northern areas of the State to be thus leased, all the blacks would be hunted into the sea. The poor wretches must be allowed the wherewithal to live—their main hunting grounds and water supplies. They dare not voluntarily migrate elsewhere, as such action, according to tribal law, would constitute a trespass, punishable by death. Your Commissioner pleads again that large areas be resumed in the northern unsettled districts for the sole benefit of the natives, the location and extent of such reserves being dependent on local conditions, i.e., islands, large promontories, mountain areas, districts where the marches of several tribes meet, etc.; indeed, where the natives already are. In the settled districts of the State, of course, much smaller areas of country would only be necessary, because here the reserves, instead of being utilised as hunting grounds, would constitute sanctuaries and asylums for the indigent, the infirm, the children, and others on whose behalf it behoves the State to make special provision. As already mentioned, one of the main objects of section 15 of the proposed Bill is to give the Minister power to remove an aboriginal whose presence it is undesirable to continue in one particular district on account of his incorrigibility or proneness to crime, the evidence of which would not be sufficient to secure conviction in the law courts. In cases of tribal murder and cattle-killing such a power would be both economic to the State and merciful to the individual or individuals concerned. . . .

G. *Deaths, Burials.*—It would not appear to be anyone's business to notify the death of an aboriginal, whether under contract or not. At Derby, the Resident Magistrate has given instructions that in the event of a native dying without medical attendance within the limits of the townsite, a magisterial inquiry or inquest is to be held. Matters will be rectified by section 33 of the proposed Bill, which makes it incumbent upon the employer to give the necessary notice. By 61 Vict., No. 3, section 6, bodies must be buried in a public cemetery where one has been proclaimed, it being unlawful for a burial to take place elsewhere within a radius of 10 miles. In certain districts this has resulted in the contractors insisting upon burying natives. As the charges for burial are in some cases as much as £9 this would seem a useless expenditure, all the more so when prayers are put in as part of the contract at an additional cost of 10 shillings. The aborigines would appear to be always prepared to bury their own dead, and as they do not as a general rule die from any specially infectious disease, there can be no strictly valid reason for interment in a cemetery. Your Commissioner recommends that the provisions of section 9 of the same Act be availed of, and permission obtained from the Governor in Council to bury blacks in a more economic manner.

H. *Conclusion.*—In the settled areas of those portions of the State along which his investigations have led him, your Commissioner is satisfied that the natives, generally speaking, are not subject to any actual physical cruelty. On the other hand, the wrongs and injustices taking place in these areas, and the cruelties and abuses met with in the unsettled districts cannot be longer hidden or tolerated. Fortunately they are of such a nature that they can be largely remedied by proper legislation, combined with firm departmental supervision. My earnest prayer, on the eve of my departure from Western Australia, is that the next Parliamentary Session will see that the proposed Aborigines Bill of 1904, as originally introduced, supplemented with the recommendations contained in this Report, will become the Aborigines Act of 1905.

Attached hereto are the minutes of evidence taken (Appendix C).

I have the honour to be,
Your Excellency's most obedient servant,
WALTER E. ROTH,
Commissioner.

# 6

# The Twentieth Century and a
# New Deal for Aborigines

By the beginning of the twentieth century the Aboriginal tribes had
disappeared over much of the continent of Australia. A census taken
in 1930 showed that there were some 61,000 full bloods and 18,000
part-aborigines left. Those remaining tribalised were largely in the
north and west and remote desert regions. While some lived on
government stations and missions, others received rations or a small
wage in return for work on cattle stations. Squalid shanty towns nestled
on the outskirts of some country towns. Altogether, more than
11,000 Aborigines were in regular employment, although examples
of black people taking a respected place in the white Australian
community were rare. Aborigines could no longer be ignored, but they
rarely entered into the thoughts of the average urban Australian.

For many years the dominant theme behind official policy had been
to protect all Aborigines in their declining years from the degrading
influence of white and Asiatic culture. Accordingly, inviolable
reserves had been created in the remote parts of the different states.
Comparatively little was known about the social organization of the
tribal nomads, although men like Sir Baldwin Spencer did not
recommend changes in Government policy without first conducting a
survey of aspects of Aboriginal life previously misunderstood (6.2).

With the numbers of part-Aboriginals increasing yearly,
administrators began to think less about the eventual disappearance
of the black race and more about the education and training of their
half-caste children.

In 1913 a South Australian Royal Commission concurred with
Sir Baldwin Spencer and proposed reforms that would train the
Aborigine "so that he (would) become a full and useful member of
the community" (6.4). In 1928 Queensland's Chief Protector
Bleakley emphasized the importance of educating part-Aborigines
and isolating them from their darker-skinned relatives (6.8).

An inquiry carried out in Western Australia in 1935 did not reveal
any marked measure of success however (6.9). Training equipment
on Government stations was totally inadequate.

In 1925 a Department of Anthropology was organised at Sydney
University. Interest in the Aboriginal tribal culture grew, and in
1937, Donald Thomson, an anthropologist, recommended that if
any aspects of it were to be preserved, inviolable reserves had to be

set up in Arnhem Land immediately (6.11).

In 1937 the Commonwealth Department for the Interior, and a Select Committee Inquiry in New South Wales declared that the aim of their future policies would be to assimilate Aborigines ultimately into white Australian society (6.15).

For most of the country's Aborigines, life had hardly altered. Their life expectancy was far shorter than that of white Australians, infant-mortality rates were higher, diet and health was inferior, and legal, social, and economic discrimination was practised at many levels.

1914. An elderly Aborigine outside his shelter at Lake Tyers Aboriginal Settlement, Victoria.
*Ministry of Aboriginal Affairs.*

1950's. Cooking in the kitchen of a house at Lake Tyers Aboriginal Settlement.
*Ministry of Aboriginal Affairs.*

(*Ibid.*, p. 18.)

*Mr. W. E. Dalton, accountant and honorary secretary of the Aborigines Friends' Association, comments on the mission stations and the working potential of the mixed-blood population.*

369. What have you to say to the opinion expressed by Mr. South that the Government should take over the control of the mission stations? The Government would manage the industrial work and also see that the natives were looked after spiritually and educationally?—I quite approve of the missionary and educational part, but I do not favour the idea of the mission stations being under the control of one man or one Government. I think they should be under the control of a board. That would be, in effect, governmental control; but it would not be control by a Government official. You require human sympathy in dealing with the work at the mission stations. You must consider both sides. You cannot work the mission side without some regard to the industrial and *vice versa*. You have to bear in mind that 60 years ago the natives were practically animals crawling about in the bush. The half-castes are their children and usually, also, the children of the most depraved class of white men. They have not the heredity that other races have, and you cannot expect them to work on purely industrial lines. If you are going to have a four hours working day I think that the native could work beside the white man. He could not keep working for eight hours.

370. In asking my question I had the rising generation of half-castes and quadroons in mind, rather than the old aboriginals. Do you not think that the members of that rising generation are different in character from their parents on the maternal side?—Yes; but those people are the children of natives who were more or less animals 60 years ago, and their fathers were possibly the lower class of whites. As a rule, it is a low class of white who cohabits with a native woman, and their children have not the stamina and the proper conception of right and wrong that other children have.

371. I gather from what you mentioned that you think it would be beneficial to the natives if the Government took over the control of the stations provided a board of management were appointed?—Yes.

372. And the educational and spiritual welfare of the natives should be attended to as well as the industrial work?—Yes.

373. When Point McLeay was established there were not many half-castes?—That is so.

374. And to-day two-thirds of the natives there are half-castes and quadroons?—Yes; quite that proportion. There are, I think, about 300 or 350 natives at the mission and in the neighbourhood of the mission, and of those I suppose there would be not more than 60 or 70 full-blooded aborigines.

375. Do you think that the quadroon should be a burden on the State at all? Do you think that he has any claim on the State?—I think that the quadroon requires a good deal more sympathy than the blackfellow from one point of view. The quadroon is a person with the color taint in him for all time. And so has the half-caste and the octoroon. You gentlemen look on the half-caste population of South Australia as of no use on the face of the earth. The half-caste himself does not want to be here. But he is the white man's child.

376. *By the Chairman*—We are here to inquire into the condition of the half-caste and we approach the matter with an open mind. I think you are quite wrong in saying that we look on the half-caste as something different from what he is?—I withdraw it. I am speaking generally. The

blackfellow does not care for the half-caste; nor does the white man. The half-caste goes out with the intention of working. At Point McLeay for about 10 years we had a boot factory. We used to make the boots for the station and do the repairs. It costs us from £100 to £120 a year to teach the natives bootmaking. Several of them went out to find employment. We got a few into Murray's and Will's factories. Of the eight or 10 who went out there is only one man who is making any honest effort to earn his own living. His name is Rankine. The State has helped him to a certain extent. He married a white girl and he has three or four children. He has made a fine effort to earn his own living and keep away from the mission. For 10 or 12 years he has had no help from the mission. All the others drifted back. When the native gets among white people he is isolated. They do not like him; they will have nothing to do with him; and he gets lonely.

## 6.2    20 May 1913. W. Baldwin Spencer's new policy.

(Professor W. Baldwin Spencer, M.A., C.M.G., *Preliminary Report on the Aboriginals of the Northern Territory*, Department of External Affairs, Melbourne, 1913, Bulletin No. 7.)

*After nearly twelve months spent in the Northern Territory studying the problems associated with the contact between Europeans, Asiatics, and Aborigines, W. Baldwin Spencer submitted a preliminary report to the Minister of External Affairs.*

Morality and General Character of the Aborigines.
It is not infrequently stated by the white settlers that the natives have no morality. This is, of course, entirely untrue — that is, of aboriginals in their normal state, before they have been degraded by contact with a civilization that they do not understand and from which they need protection.
    Their moral code is a very different one from ours and certainly permits of and sanctions, practices which, in some cases, are revolting to us, but there are others, such as their strict law in regard to what woman a particular man may or may not marry, and vice versa, which it is a serious mistake to interfere with until we can give them something better and something that they can understand. Of course in many cases where the tribes, as in the immediate neighbourhood of Darwin, are not only demoralised, but decimated, the old rules cannot be enforced; but, except in these cases, the natives should be encouraged to adhere to them.
    It may also be said that generally speaking, the uncivilized native is honest, with probability not more exceptions than amongst whites; but that the so-called civilized aboriginal who has given up his old habits and become often a mere loafer, in many cases is not. . . . A native left in charge of property of any kind may generally be relied upon to prevent others from interfering with it. . . .
    On some stations there is undoubtedly difficulty in regard to the aboriginals both harassing and killing cattle. . . . In many parts there is practically little trouble, and it is only right to say that the personality of the white man counts for a certain amount. . . .
    On the other hand while it is true that, in some parts the aboriginal gives trouble, it is equally true that at present day, practically all the cattle stations are dependent on their labour, and, in fact, could not get on without it, any more than the police constables could. They do work that it would be very difficult to get white men to do and do it not only cheer-

fully but for a remuneration that, in many cases, makes all the difference at the present time between working the station at a profit or loss. . . .

The aboriginal is indeed a very curious mixture; mentally, about the level of a child who has little control over his feelings and is liable to give way to violent fits of temper, during which he may very likely act with great cruelty. He has no sense of responsibility and, except in rare cases, no initiative. His memory in many cases is wonderful so far as subjects are concerned that affects his life and mode of conduct. When once he has seen any place, or any particular natural object, he knows it for all time. If once he has heard a corroboree he knows the words and music and his memory in respect to native traditions is marvellous. It must be understood, however, that in proportion to the narrow sphere of their actions, there is as great a mental difference amongst aboriginals as amongst whites in their wider sphere. This is well recognized amongst the natives themselves. . . . The possessor of any particular capacity does not, except in very rare cases, secure any very direct personal gain from its exercise beyond the fact that he has a reputation for ability. Everything is communistic and even if a man is provided with an extra supply of food, or in recent years, tobacco, in return for something he has made or done, it is usually not long before it is divided amongst his friends. There is an equal distribution of profits quite irrespective of deserts.

Present Condition and Treatment of the Aboriginals. Aboriginals Living in Townships, Etc.

These natives have long since become degenerate and have lost all their old customs and beliefs. Many of them are employed by white residents to whom they are useful and by whom they are well treated. Since the passing of the Aborigines Act 1910, no permits to employ them have been granted to Asiatics. . . .

The supplying of aboriginals with opium and spirits and a wholesale prostitution of native women are common and constant practices amongst the great body of Asiatics and form the most serious evil that the Department has to contend with in the settled and more especially the mining districts. . . .

The Chinese quarters in Darwin, Pine Creek and more important mining areas are now declared "prohibited areas" and this restriction must be extended so as to apply to all other Chinese mining fields and quarters. The natives have so far been for years allowed to do exactly what they liked in regard to frequenting all parts that, without a much larger staff, and consequently more efficient supervision, it is difficult to make sure that they do not frequent any prohibited area. The Chinese are also very astute, and while undoubtedly there are not many aboriginals who venture into China-town in Darwin, there are amongst the lower Chinese many who find means of supplying the aboriginals with opium out in the bush. When, however the compound at Darwin, with its native houses, which is now in the course of formation, is complete and under proper supervision, it will be more easy to deal with the aboriginals and to prevent the Asiatics from coming into contact with them under the cover of night.

In order to meet the cases of the few reputable white settlers who live in prohibited areas and to prevent hardship or inconvenience in business matters, the plan has been adopted of issuing special permits in the form of brass discs that are given to employers of natives and enable the latter to enter a prohibited area when sent on business by their employers, who are responsible for the proper use of the disc.

Aboriginals Living on Large Pastoral Areas.

. . . Though comparatively few natives are employed on any station—the numbers in constant employment varying two or three to thirty or forty—

yet there is always a native camp in the vicinity of every station, where there is a smaller or larger group gathered together, attracted by the chance of securing food from the station. It is a constant occurrence on practically all stations where cattle are killed to distribute the offal and bones, often with plenty of meat attached to them, amongst the natives, who gather round the killing yard like crows around a dying sheep. Everything is eaten and every bone pounded up to get at the marrow. In addition to this there are many odd scraps distributed and the few natives who are permanently employed, unless special precautions are taken, will share what they receive with the others.

It is the natives on some of these large pastoral areas who are troublesome in the way of cattle killing, and yet on the other hand it is not too much to say that, under present conditions, the majority of the stations are largely dependent on the work done by black "boys".

Aboriginals Living on Wild Unoccupied Land.
Of these practically nothing is known. At the present time they carefully avoid coming into contact with any white man traversing the country. . . .

The Treatment of Aboriginal Women.
. . . I have already referred to the question of the Asiatics and their widespread habit of prostituting the lubras. The aboriginal's code of morality is different from that of the white man and he sees no wrong in lending his lubra. . . . Nothing is more patent than the rapid degeneration of the native in contact with Chinese. The lubra ceases to bear children, abortion being undoubtedly practised in many cases, and becomes a physical wreck.

In regard to intercourse between the whites and aboriginals, there is no such physical degradation of the lubras. It must be said very frankly that the absence of any women other than aboriginals in outlying districts is the chief reason for so many complaints in regard to the prostitution of aboriginal women, and so long as the absence of white women is the feature of the Territory, so long will it be extremely difficult, if not impossible, to put an end to this serious evil.

*It is most important that all Protectors should be married men and emphatically no one except a married man should be a Superintendent of a reserve or native station or settlement.*

. . . The practice that now obtains only too often of a white man, such as a drover or teamster, travelling over the country in company with an aboriginal woman who may have come of her own free will, together with a "boy" who is, or is supposed to be, her husband, or whom he has perhaps taken out of a camp, must be stopped.

Medical Officers, Hospitals, Treatment, Etc.
There were originally two medical officers associated entirely with the Department. Experience soon showed that this was inadvisable. The life led by the aboriginals is such that it is useless to attempt to treat them except in the very simplest way in the bush; in fact, any layman with a very slight knowledge and a few simple drugs could do all that is possible to be done for them in their camps. Any serious work can only be carried on in a properly-equipped hospital, and in many cases a native could only be detained for treatment by main force. I therefore suggested that the two medical men should be attached to the general medical staff, which would enable their services to be utilized for the benefit of whites as well as aboriginals, but that it should be understood that the services of one of them were to be especially at the call of the Aboriginal Department. . . .

In each hospital there should be special provision made for treating aboriginals apart from white patients. The services of intelligent half-castes could probably be secured as attendants. This provision need only be on a very simple scale, the wards taking the form of tents or bush shelters. The conditions in fact approximating as nearly as possible to their own native camp and open air life only under hygienic conditions.

Provision for Treating Contagious Diseases.

The question of how best to cope with the existence of various forms of venereal disease is one that must be seriously faced from the point of view of the welfare of both the aboriginal and white population. The native morality is such that the disease, once contracted, is bound to be widely disseminated amongst both aboriginals and white men of low morality.

In the first place as complete an examination as possible must be carried out (this is now in course of progress in the mining districts). The matter is a serious one, involving much expense, and, owing to the nature of the natives, is surrounded with great difficulties, but when it becomes practicable and the country is opened up, there will be no other course open but to follow the example of Western Australia and establish lock-hospitals for men and women to which, if necessary, they can be forcibly removed and where they can be detained until cured. The only possible situation for such hospitals is on islands, and two suitable for the purpose, one for men and one for women, could be selected in such a position that they could be under the charge of one medical officer. Special provision must be made in the Act in order to provide for the examination and removal of aboriginals to lock-hospitals.

Trial of Aboriginals.

During the past year I have been present in court whilst natives have been tried for various offences and have been much impressed with the unfair position occupied by aboriginal prisoners as compared with white men.

A very serious difficulty arises in the case of Australian aboriginals which is not met with in dealing with other savages such as the Maories. All the latter have a language that varies but little, whereas in Australia it is extraordinary how many entirely different dialects are met with. Each tribe has a dialect of its own, with the result that no one can attempt to master them all. So far as the words are concerned there is just as much difference between those in the language of two tribes such as the Larakia at Darwin and the Worgait at Point Charles, only a few miles away across the harbor, as there is between those in the French and German languages. No ordinary person can attempt to learn more than one or two and therefore for the most part verbal communication must be carried on, and evidence in court given in a kind of pidgin English, which is not altogether satisfactory, more especially in the case of wild natives who are in the position of either prisoners or witnesses.

It not infrequently happens that aboriginals are convicted on their own admission which they make without in the least realizing that such an admission, which may or may not be the strict truth, will send them to gaol. It is also little short of ludicrous to go into court the day before a trial and see the farce being solemnly enacted of a barrister and constable putting a witness through his facings in the box preparatory to his appearing before the Judge next day. I am not in the least imputing any wrong motive to the constable or barrister, because I know them to be or to wish to be quite fair and I realize the difficulties of their position when they have to deal with untutored savages who must be "coached"; but there is, it must be confessed, an element of danger in such legal proceedings. It is also only right to say that in every case of an aboriginal that I have seen tried in Darwin, whether before a magistrate or a Judge and jury, justice was most decidedly tempered with mercy, but as a safeguard I would recommend that (1) no aboriginal be allowed to plead guilty except with the consent of an official protector, and (2) no native should be convicted on evidence other than such as would serve to convict a white man accused of the same offence.

Necessity of Establishing an Aboriginal Reformatory.

Within the bounds of civilizations there can, of course, be only one system of laws, but whilst this is so it is imperative that an important change should be made in regard to the manner of punishing natives.

The Aboriginals Act as it stands at present does not provide for any definite punishment for aboriginals other than sending them to gaol in common with other offenders. There is, fortunately, under the Aboriginals Ordinance power given to the Chief Protector to authorize a police officer to take into his custody any aboriginal or half-caste and to deal with him as he may direct. It is most advisable for the Chief Protector to have some such general power as this in order to deal with cases, for example, where a man unlawfully takes a boy or lubra away from camp. That boy or lubra can be taken charge of by the officer and restored to his camp. The power is also most useful, because it allows a native who is guilty of some offence to be held in restraint without being sent to gaol, to which, of course, he cannot be committed by the Protector but only on the order of a magistrate after trial in Court. There are many occasions on which it would be most inadvisable for a native to be committed to gaol; in fact, experience has shown that in the first place sending an aboriginal to gaol has no deterrent effect so far as crime is concerned; and, in the second, he comes out worse than he went in. The average aboriginal thinks it no degradation or hardship to go to "Fanny Bay," the local gaol; many of them indeed regard it rather as a mark of distinction than otherwise and are proud to have been there.

Then, again, there are certain natives who without doing anything that actually renders them liable to be brought before a Court of law behave in such a way as to interfere seriously with the work of the protectors. For example, within the past few months one particular lubra who has considerable influence has been the means of decoying some of the young girls from the Roper Mission Station. This is not an offence against the law, as she did not actually remove them from the station and no prosecution could lie against her in a Court, and yet the effect in the minds of the natives of such successful defying of the authorities is very detrimental to the influence of the latter and to the welfare of the young natives.

It is essential that there should be some special reformatory institution to which aboriginals convicted of crimes, except homicide, should be committed rather than to gaol. A reformatory of this kind must be on an island in order to prevent easy escape. Here the offenders could be detained, and during their detention they should be employed in useful and profitable labour.

In addition to aboriginals committed to the reformatory on the warrant of a magistrate, the Chief Protector on a report received from the superintendent of a reserve or station, or of a protector, should be able to commit an aboriginal guilty of serious misconduct, which does not actually constitute an offence against the Act, to such a reformatory. In this case the committal should receive the approval of the Administrator, which will be quite a sufficient safeguard against any miscarriage of justice. Some such power as this in the hands of the Chief Protector is absolutely essential. I would suggest that either Field Island off the mouth of the Alligator River, or Peron Island off the mouth of the Daly be used for this purpose.

## Half-Castes

The half-castes are in a most unfortunate position. There may possibly be 100-150 of them in the northern and, approximately, the same number in the southern part, where also there are quadroons who may be regarded as belonging to the white population.

I think it may be said that though the half-castes belong neither to the aboriginal nor to the whites, yet on the whole, they have more leaning towards the former; certainly this is the case in regard to the females. One thing is certain and that is that the white population as a whole will never mix with half-castes. . . .

It must be remembered that they are also a very mixed group. In practically all cases, the mother is a full-blooded aboriginal, the father may be a white man, a Chinese, a Japanese, a Malay or a Filippino. The mother is of very low intellectual grade, while the father most often belongs to the coarser and more unrefined members of higher races. The consequence of this is that the children of such parents are not likely to be, in most cases, of much greater intellectual calibre than the more intelligent natives, though, of course, there are exceptions to this.

No half-caste children should be allowed to remain in any native camp, but they should all be withdrawn and placed on stations. So far as practicable, this plan is now being adopted. In some cases, when the child is very young, it must of necessity be accompanied by its mother, but in other cases, even though it may seem cruel to separate the mother and child, it is better to do so, when the mother is living, as is usually the case, in a native camp.

In a few instances, the fathers honorably recognise their responsibility and make provision for their half-caste children. In rare cases, they are adopted and brought up by whites, but, especially so far as the girls are concerned, this experiment is fraught with danger, owing to the temperament of the half-caste and to the fact that no white men, if white women are available, will marry a half-caste aboriginal. . . .

I have, after consideration of all the facts, come to the conclusion that, except in individual and exceptional cases, the best and kindest thing is to place them on reserves along with the natives, train them in the same schools and encourage them to marry amongst themselves. Any special cases in which a half-caste—a boy especially—shows any marked ability, can be easily provided for and he can pass on from a native to an ordinary school or to some other institution.

On the reserves the services of the more intelligent half-castes may be utilized in supervising the work of the aboriginals.

Provision could be made whereby the Administrator on the recommendation of the Chief Protector might allot special areas not exceeding, say, 150 acres to any aboriginal or half-caste who had proved himself capable of working the land for the benefit of himself and his family.

## General Policy in Regard to Aboriginal Affairs.

The care of the aboriginals of the Northern Territory should be made a national responsibility and any scheme devised for the purpose of preserving and uplifting them should be under the control of the Commonwealth Government. Subsidiary efforts by various bodies will doubtless be of great assistance, but in order that the work shall be continuously and adequately carried on in all parts of the Territory, it is essential that it shall be national in character and under national control.

I have already referred to the fact that the natives so far as their present distribution is concerned, can be divided roughly into four groups. From the point of view of dealing with them, they may be divided into two main groups—(*a*) aboriginals living in and about townships, and employed in the latter; (*b*) those living more or less in their wild state, and leading a nomad existence.

(*a*) *Aboriginals Living in and about Townships.*
These are practically limited to those around Darwin and Pine Creek and form a very small part of the aboriginal population.

These natives have so completely lost all their old customs that there is no difficulty in gathering them together into a village or compound, as is now being done in Darwin, at a convenient distance from the town. Up to the beginning of last year there were two main native camps within the town limits of Darwin, one on the top of a cliff known as the King Camp and the other on the beach below known as the Lamaru Camp. This division of the Larakia tribe into two such groups is of very old standing and in the choice of a new site has been recognised. There are to be two encampments one on the shore and one on the cliff above. The old ramshackle, dirty huts that the aboriginals made out of the remnants of corrugated buildings that years ago were scattered all over the township by a great cyclone, are now replaced by neat huts with walls of stringybark and roofs of iron.

In the compound there will be a school-house with a house for a teacher and his wife. Each native family will have its own house and there will also be separate houses for unattached men, women and visitors. The teacher will act as Superintendent of the compound and his wife as Matron.

Associated with each compound, there should be as at Darwin a garden on which employment can be found for a certain number of natives in the growing of fruit and vegetables. The whole compound must be fenced in and no one save aboriginals and officials of the Department should have access to it, except by order. Rations will be distributed to old and indigent natives, but otherwise the inhabitants should be self-supporting, as they will all be employed either in the garden or in business places or private houses.

In regard to those in employment in the garden a definite wage will be paid and the same is true of those employed in business or private houses in Darwin or Pine Creek, as the case may be. It will be necessary to fix a minimum wage and at each compound a register of aboriginals will be kept by the Superintendent and all applications to employ aboriginal labour should be made to him, and to him also all complaints by employers against aboriginals should be made.

A certain amount of the wages paid should be withheld by the employer and paid at fixed times to the Superintendent, who will place such sums to the account of the individual aboriginals in the Savings Bank.

In regard to those employed in private service in Darwin or Pine Creek, they will either be housed on their employer's premises or resident in the compound. In the former case, the accommodation provided must be approved by the Superintendent.

All aboriginals and half-castes should be either in compound or in their employer's quarters after sunset. A regulation should be passed forbidding them, except by special permit, to camp or wander about within the prescribed limits of any township between the hours of sunset and sunrise. Any aboriginal or half-caste infringing this regulation should be liable to be locked up by a police officer.

Any one, including all Government officials, bringing aboriginals or half-castes, except prisoners, into Darwin or Pine Creek, should immediately on arrival, notify a Protector or the Superintendent and should satisfy the Protector or Superintendent, as the case may be, that the accommodation provided for them is satisfactory. If he deems it desirable, the Superintendent or Protector may order them to be housed in the compound.

No native should be allowed to leave Darwin without the consent of the Superintendent or a Protector.

There is no doubt but that some of the natives, none of whom have been under any restraint up till the beginning of last year will, at first, resent any discipline, but with firm treatment this difficulty will be overcome. Natives should not be encouraged to come from outside parts into those compounds, but in view of the scarcity of labour for domestic purposes, it is probable that the numbers will have to be replenished periodically.

In consequence of the fact that the extension of the railway line from Pine Creek to Katherine Creek will soon be taken in hand, there is no need to make provision for a compound and native school at the former, which will probably become, when the line goes beyond it, merely a wayside station. On the other hand, for some time during the progress of the work, a considerable number of men employed in building the line will be located there and the aboriginals who now frequent the town and mining districts surrounding it must, as far as possible, be withdrawn on to reserves.

(b) *Aboriginals Living More or Less in Their Wild State, and Leading a Nomad Existence.*

The real problem is concerned with these who form almost the whole aboriginal population of the Territory. A considerable number of them, how-ever, have been periodically in contact with settlements, or with isolated whites and some with Asiatics.

I have previously pointed out certain features in regard to the habits, customs and beliefs of the aboriginals that will render it a matter of some, in fact, at first, great difficulty to segregate them on reserves but **in view of the settlement of the country for which provision is now being made, there is no other practicable policy but that of the establishment of large reserves, if the aboriginals are to be preserved, and if any serious effort is to be made for their betterment.**

It will not, however, be either necessary or wise to attempt to force them at present on to reserves in those large areas occupied by pastoral runs; but there are a large number, such as those in the Daly River District, and all along the line of mining townships, for whom the need of an adequate reserve on to which to withdraw them is urgent. Other reserves can be established as the need for them arises, but it is important while yet there are large areas of unoccupied land to have the fact recognised that certain areas are to be allocated for the use of the natives.

There are three essential requirements in regard to these reserves, and unless all three are complied with, they will be of little service.

(1) They must be of large size, so that different parts, if necessary, can be occupied by the members of different tribes, or groups of tribes.

(2) They must be of such a nature as to provide sufficient water and abundant native food supplies and be suitable for agricultural or pastoral work.

(3) They must be so located as to deal with groups of tribes that are allied in their customs and are more or less friendly.

A number of small reserves were created in 1892, and as a precautionary measure were re-gazetted during the year 1912. They are as follows:—

Manassie Reserve, 366 miles; Woolner Reserve, 366 miles; Larakia Reserve, 20 miles; Wangites Reserve, 388 miles; Woolwonga Reserve, 160 miles; Mallae Reserve, 100 miles; Mudburra Reserve, 579 square miles, and Mission Permit No. 2, 100 miles; Bathurst Island, or Wongoak Reserve, 786 miles. In addition to these, there is the Her-mannsburg Reserve in the Macdonnell Ranges.

These reserves appear to have been selected in a somewhat haphazard manner and are neither, for the most part, suitable in position nor adequate in size.

I recommend that under section 13 of the Aboriginals Act they be abolished, except the Bathurst Island and Hermannsburg reserves, which are both admirable ones, and others substituted for them.

Control and Equipment of Reserves.
Each reserve must be under the control of a Superintendent; in every case it is absolutely essential that he be a married man, whose wife will act as Matron and take a general oversight over the aboriginal women and children.

The Superintendent will be in supreme charge of the whole station and have the general direction of the work carried out. Every officer will be under his control. He must be a man capable of taking a general supervision over industrial work of various kinds and should be himself either a competent agriculturist or pastoralist, accustomed to dealing with stock, as the case may be, or experienced in some branch of industry. Considerable experience of aboriginals, though not essential, is hightly desirable. On some stations, such as the Alligator, agricultural work and stock breeding will be combined; on others, such as the Daly, agricultural and industrial work will predominate; and on others, such as the Newcastle Waters, stock breeding will be the main work. Each station will have to be stocked and equipped specially, according to its needs. There must be at least two white men, accustomed to the class of work required, to assist the Superintendent, both in the actual work of the station and, as far as possible, in taking part in the industrial training of the natives, both adults and boys; and it is highly desirable that these should be married men.

An important part of the station will be the school. At first it is probable that one teacher, assisted by the matron, will suffice; but if the station be a success more will be required. It is possible that these may be recruited from amongst the more intelligent scholars—half-castes, for example. There will be two classes of scholars. First, a small number who are the children of what may be called the station natives—that is, those actually and more or less permanently, engaged on the station, living in their own houses; second, a larger number, the children of outside natives, living in camps on the reserve, but not employed at the central station. Housing provision will have to be made for these children and they will also have to be maintained and kept away from the camps as far as possible. When once the stations are in working order, the cost of maintenance should be small, except in one or two cases, such as the Lake Woods station, where it may be difficult to grow food supplies. Each station will have to be rationed with the primary essentials, such as tea, flour, tobacco, &c., and clothing for the natives, though the latter should be as simple as possible.

Training in the Schools and on the Stations.
The teaching in schools should be of very simple character; it should include reading, writing, the elements of arithmetic and singing. The latter can be made to be of peculiar educational value in the training of aboriginals, owing to their universal fondness for it. In course of time each station should possess its own band.

Moral training should be given in the school on the simplest and broadest lines possible. It is, I understand, the intention of the various churches to undertake work in connexion with the aboriginals, each church working in a certain part of the Territory. I would suggest that the efforts of the churches could be best expended and would yield most valuable results, if they were devoted to the special training and subsequent maintenance of teachers who, after passing through this training, undertook the teaching work in the schools on the stations associated with the reserves. The salary of these teachers should be the same in every school and they should undertake both the mental and the moral training of the aboriginals.

The primary object of all stations must be to train the natives in industrial habits. Until such time as they acquire these habits there is no chance whatever of raising them from their present condition.

Apart from the elementary teaching above referred to, the main training should be industrial, simple agricultural work, carpentry, &c., and work amongst stock for the boys, domestic work and gardening for the girls.

Apart from a small number of men and women who will be fairly constantly engaged on the station, a number of the older men and women will come into the stations and will be useful to a certain extent, in a spasmodic way; but to attempt to train them systematically, or to influence them seriously from a moral point of view, will be merely wasting time and energy that could with great advantage be bestowed upon younger people, especially the children.

The older natives must be kindly treated, rewarded for any work that they may do, and looked after in their old age; but it is absolutely essential that all efforts should be directed towards the training of the younger generation. The children must be withdrawn from the native camps at an early age. This will undoubtedly be a difficult matter to accomplish and will involve some amount of hardship, so far as the parents are concerned; but if once the children are allowed to reach a certain age and have become accustomed to camp life, with its degrading environment and endless roaming about in the bush, it is almost useless to try and reclaim them. On the other hand, if they are once brought at an early age into a station and become accustomed, as they soon do, to station life—provided this be made attractive—then they will gradually lose the longing for a normal nomad life and will, in fact, become incapable of securing their living in the bush.

The teaching and training of aboriginals requires special capacity. A desire to uplift and help them though requisite in the teacher, is not in itself sufficient qualification for the work. If the care of the aboriginals is made a national matter, the Government providing land, equipment and either means for carrying on the various stations or subsidizing any of the latter as it does at the present time, then it is important that no one in any capacity as teacher should be allowed to work upon the stations except with the approval of the Government. In practice I would recommend the appointment by the Government of a small committee, which must be satisfied as to the qualifications of the proposed teacher.

Reserves and the Lands Ordinance.

Under the *Aboriginals Act* 1910, section 13, the Governor may—
  (a) Declare any Crown lands to be a reserve for aboriginals;
  (b) Alter the boundaries of any reserve;
  (c) Abolish any reserve;
and may (section 49 (k) ) make regulations authorizing the entry upon such reserves by specified persons or classes of persons for specified objects.

These conditions are radically altered in the Lands Ordinance, No. 8, 1912 in which no reference is anywhere made to the aboriginals or their relationship to the land. Under this Ordinance (Part III., Division 5, Miscellaneous Leases, section 43) the Administrator may, subject to the Ordinance and the Regulations, grant to any person a lease of any portion of Crown Lands, or of any dedicated or reserved lands, for any prescribed purpose, or for any purpose approved by the Minister.

Such leases (section 44) may be granted for twenty-one years, and (section 47) may be offered for sale by public auction.

The Administrator may also (Part V., Licences, section 49) grant licences to persons to graze stock on any reserved or dedicated lands for such period not exceeding one year, as is prescribed and may (section 51) grant licences to go upon dedicated or reserved lands and take therefrom timber, &c.

From the point of view of the Aboriginal Department, it is of primary importance that the reserves should be retained for the use of the natives, with the idea of isolating them and preventing them from coming into contact with other people. In this respect it is significant to notice that amongst the first applications for land in the Northern Territory, after the publication of the Lands Ordinance No. 3, 1912, was one for a lease of part of the Woolner Aboriginal Reserve. This was not granted, and though it is, of course, probable that the Administrator for the time being would refuse most applications, still the fact that the Ordinance now in force practically invites such applications is a serious matter and will always, unless the aboriginal reserves are especially safeguarded, be a source of anxiety to those who are entrusted with the work of the Aboriginal Department.

Proposed Amendment of the Aboriginals Act 1910 and the Aboriginals Ordinance 1911.
The suggestions made above require considerable amendment of both the *Aboriginals Act* 1910 and the *Aboriginals Ordinance* 1911 and if they meet with the approval of the Government I recommend that a new Act be drafted and regulations drawn up which will supersede the present Act, Ordinance and Regulations.

W. BALDWIN SPENCER
Special Commissioner and Chief Protector of Aboriginals.
20th May, 1913.

## 6.3 23 July 1913. E. C. Stirling's comments.

(*South Australian Parliamentary Proceedings, op. cit.,* Vol. 2, Paper No. 26, 1913, "Progress Report of the Royal Commission on the Aborigines.", p. 125.)

*Mr. E. C. Stirling comments on the health of the full-blooded community and the plight of the half-caste population, especially those on Government stations in South Australia.*

2599. If we establish a lock hospital, would it be to the advantage of the race for those people to be taken to that hospital and treated?—Yes; it would be to the advantage of the race.
2600. Is there any serious difficulty in the way of getting those people to the hospital?—The difficulty is with the natives who are living in their own encampment. To get hold of those natives you would need a very drastic system of inspection and examination. If the State is prepared to undertake that you would get the natives all right.
2601. Do you not think that the district trooper would hear of cases of venereal diseases?—No doubt he would.
2602. Could not the Government secure his services in getting hold of venereal cases and having them sent to a hospital for treatment?—There is no doubt that that could be done.
2603. Is it worth attempting?—I hesitate to give a very definite answer to that.
2604. In regard to cases inside the more settled areas, would you recommend it?—I think in that case you might do it without much trouble.
2605. Is it desirable that we should do it?—Yes; I think it is.
2606. *By the Hon. J. Jelley*—At Point McLeay I noticed that the physical condition of the blacks who were living in wurlies was worse than that of the natives who were living in houses. How do you account for that?— In the first place you have to be sure that you are starting with the same

material; and it is possible to have in a wurlie the same bad conditions as in a house. If you can establish what you say as a general rule it would require looking into, but it does not tally with what I have seen in the interior. It is possible to make a wurlie as close and beastly as any unventilated room. I would want to see the wurlie before I criticised the thing, and I would also want to see the people. To my mind it is a generalisation on too insecure grounds.

2607. At Point Pierce, where all the natives have houses, their physical condition is better than that of the best natives at Point McLeay?—I have not seen the Point Pierce station. The houses there may be all you could desire. The danger that applies to white people living in badly-ventilated rooms applies with greater force in the case of the blacks. The blacks have come from a life in the open air into a life where the atmosphere is frequently vitiated, and those are the conditions in which they are liable to contract pulmonary complaints. In that respect the blacks do not differ from ourselves. When we have returned to living in a house after we have been out camping, the first thing we do is to get a cold. In regard to the blacks read "tuberculosis" for "cold," and that is the point. Our race has established a certain amount of immunity to tuberculosis. We have had it amongst us; we live in an atmosphere of germs. I think it is very likely that no tuberculosis existed among the blacks here before the white men came. I hope you will not think that I am advocating that there should be no sort of habitation for the natives. What I say is give them rooms constructed on different principles from the rooms they have now. I am not saying that it is better for the natives to go back to wurlies, which are so often made up of filth and abomination. Give the natives proper houses, and introduce cleanliness and decency and order, which are all to their good, and all of which are absent from the wurlies.

2608. *By the Hon. J. Jelley*—If the natives are given the conditions you speak of is there any likelihood of increasing in numbers, so as to become a very great burden on the State?—That is a legitimate inquiry; but I think that the experience all the world over is that the black races die out in the presence of the white races. I do not think that what you say is a serious contingency. I think that with all you can do you cannot keep them beyond a certain time.

2609. Your experience in the interior of Australia brought you into touch with the troopers in the back country. Do you think it would be a desirable thing for the troopers to act in co-operation with the Aborigines Department in regard to the natives in the interior?—My experience of the police out-back has been very favourable. The troopers I have met out there have been sensible and decent men. I believe that they are men whom you could trust to act as your agents. I was very much struck with the capacity of those men who are stationed at distant places. It seems that their responsibility has given them a standing and a capacity that are very creditable. I believe they are as good men as you could possibly have.

2610. *By the Chairman*—Is there anything else you would like to bring under our notice?—I would like to refer to the half-caste children. My opinion is that the more of those half-caste children you can get away from their parents and place under the care of the State the better. I think you should take them at an early age. Supposing they were taken charge of by the State Children's Department it would be easier to deal with them if they were taken when they have the attractiveness of infancy. There is always something attractive in the infants of all races, whatever be the color. You would get people to take those children young who might be disinclined to take them when they were older. I think that is the best way to save the half-caste children—take them away from their surroundings. When they are caught young they are far less inclined to revert to their old state. There is a strong tendency among the half-castes when they have grown up to go back to the ways of the natives. They are far less likely to do that after they have had a long contact with civilization.

2611. *By the Hon. J. Jelly*—What would be a suitable age to remove them?—I think when they are about 2 or 3 years of age.

2612. *By the Chairman*—You would not recommend that they be taken away when they are absolute infants?—No; because then you would have the burden of them that all children are at such a young age. When they are a couple of years of age they do not require so much attention and they are young enough to be attractive.

2613. Do you think that their experience of two years with the black mother would seriously interfere with them?—No. There would not be time for them to establish habits and customs. I am quite aware that you are depriving the mothers of their children, and the mothers are very fond of their children; but I think it must be the rising generation who have to be considered. They are people who are going to live on.

## 6.4 1913. South Australian Royal Commission on Aborigines: committee report.

(*Ibid.*, pp. v, vi, viii, ix, x.)

*At the conclusion of the South Australian Royal Commission on Aborigines, the committee reported their wish to change the previous policy of protection to one of integration into the larger Australian community.*

Proposed Reforms.

7. The problem of dealing with the aboriginal population is not the same problem that it was in the early history of the State. There is no doubt that in the early days, and for many years afterwards, it was necessary for the Government to protect the native inhabitants; but, with the gradual disappearance of the full-blood blacks, the mingling of the black and white races; and the great increase in the number of half-castes and quadroons, the problem is now one of assisting and training the native so that he may become a useful member of the community, dependent not upon charity but upon his own efforts. To achieve this object we believe it is necessary for more direct Government control, and we therefore propose that the care of the aborigines should be entrusted to a central board assisted by local committees at Point Pierce and Point McLeay. We have given full consideration to the question of whether the work can best be carried out by a Government department or by a board appointed by the Governor, and have investigated both these systems of management in the other States. We are of the opinion that the appointment of a board of disinterested and qualified gentlemen will be more likely to bring about beneficial results than could be secured by direct Government control. . . .

The principal duties of the board will be to see that all aboriginal and half-caste children are educated up to the primary standard; to provide means for their being trained after they leave school for their future occupations in life; to see that the aboriginal reserves or leases are fully developed with the assistance primarily of the natives living on them; to assist young men to find outside work; to train them in habits of thrift; and to settle the most deserving on land as provided for in the 1911 Act. The education of the younger children is now satisfactorily carried out at Point McLeay and Point Pierce, but boys and girls, from 13 to 18 years of age, are practically neglected, and are allowed to waste the most important years of their life, from an educational point of view, in idleness. In the training of these boys and girls for future occupations there is great scope for the board and the greatest hope for the aboriginal race. The boys might be taught carpentry, blacksmithing, building, plumbing, saddlery, dairying, and general farm work, and the time of the girls might be occupied in sewing, dressmaking, household duties and laundry work, with a view to fitting them for outside situations. According to the means which are provided this technical training should be made compulsory on all boys and girls who have left school. The evidence points to the fact that the aboriginal parents have a strong natural affection for their children, but in some cases the best interests of the children are sacrificed by the manner in which they are brought up. For this reason we think the board should have power to take control of such children, or other children—at the desire of the parents—at the age of 10 and place them where they deem best, giving the parents such access to them as may be thought desirable. In Queensland an excellent system of encouraging thrift among the natives has been adopted by the establishment of a savings bank, controlled by the department, in which the natives are encouraged and to some extent are compelled to place their savings. Persons desiring to employ natives are compelled to enter into an agreement under which a certain proportion of the wages is sent to the department. When a native is working he must contribute not less than 2s. a week to his banking account, and he can put in as much in addition as he likes. The natives have also to contribute to the support of the settlement which is a home for them when they are unemployed. For instance, if a native is earning 15s. a week 5s. a week is sent to the department, 3s. to go into the general settlement fund and 2s. to go into the native's banking account. This banking system has worked so satisfactorily in Queensland that we recommend its adoption in South Australia. The Commission have given serious attention to the best means of improving the Point McLeay settlement, and have come to the conclusion that there are at present too many natives at Point McLeay to be supported by the area of land that will be developed for some years to come. Partly for this reason and partly as a means of training the natives in agricultural work, we consider it would be advisable to form a sub-station of Point McLeay, preferably in new undeveloped country near the Murray. On this sub-station such natives as are suited to agricultural work, preferably half-castes, could be employed. The Point McLeay settlement would still be regarded as the home of the natives, and the two places could be worked in conjunction. The Commission are of the opinion that the work of the churches among the aborigines has had a most beneficial effect so far as the moral and spiritual welfare of the aborigines is concerned, and for this reason we consider that the Government should provide all necessary facilities and financial assistance for the various churches attending to the spiritual needs of the people at the Mission Stations. It is also desirable that the co-operation of the Police Department should be enlisted in aboriginal work.

## 6.5   6 August 1926. Reverend Gribble's report.

(*West Australian Proceedings of Parliament and Papers*, Perth, Vol. 1, 1928, "Royal Commission into the Killing and Burning of Bodies of Aborigines in East Kimberley, and into Police Methods when Effecting Arrest." p. 10.)

*Letter sent to the Archdeacon of Perth and the Chief Protector of Aborigines, from the Reverend Gribble, Protector, and head of the Forrest River Mission, reporting an alleged massacre of natives.*

Sir,—The following is an account of recent happenings upon this aboriginal reserve. On 27th May last news was brought me by bush natives that the police from Wyndham had raided a native camp near the Pentecost River, south of here about 50 miles, and that a native named Umbilijie had been brained by a police tracker and his body thrown into the water from where it had been taken and buried by two native women. This old man was blind and decrepit. His son is among our mission boys. On the 28th. further news came in that Hay had been speared by a native named Lumbia. . . . (Memo. —Sentences expunged by order of the Commissioner.) Hay attacked Lumbia with his stockwhip and knocked him down with a blow on the head with the butt of the whiphandle. He still carries the scar of that blow. Jumping up he ran for his spear for up to that time he was unarmed. Getting his spear he drove it into the white man, who fell from his horse. An armed expedition set out from Wyndham, two mounted constables and two special police sworn in for the occasion, Messrs. Jolly and O'Leary. Overheu, Hay's partner accompanied the party on his own authority, I understand. On the 21st June a section of the police arrived at the mission, that is 13 days after leaving Wyndham. They informed me in the presence of a member of my staff that they had seen no natives. On the 23rd the rest of the police party, with Overheu and two natives, turned up. In the meantime I had learned where the wanted man was and offered to send two mission boys to pilot them, and also, told them that the natives were anxious for the man to be taken as they did not feel safe. On the 24th the Government launch came out with Sergeant Buckland on board. He disbanded the special police, having received orders to that effect. On the 26th the police with their trackers and our two boys left and returned on the 4th July with a number of native prisoners on the chain, and several women and children. Previous to this, on 30th June, rumours came in that the police, prior to their coming to us, had shot a number of natives somewhere near the Ernest River, a day's ride to the west. The police with their prisoners camped near us and I went to them and told them that as a justice of the peace and protector I would not allow them to take any innocent natives off the reserve. I sent for Mrs. Noble to act as interpreter, as none of the natives spoke English. From the suspected native Lumbia, his wife and another woman was obtained the same story that I had already heard from the natives. Lumbia confessed his guilt as to spearing Hay and to being the only man in the affair. The other prisoners were then released, and I took the prisoner, witnesses, Constable Regan and two trackers to Wyndham. In due course the inquest upon Hay was held. Lumbia was present and gave evidence as to how it all happened. The two women also gave evidence. Strange to say, nothing of the (expunged) story came out. It seemed to me that efforts were made to make it a cattle-killing affair. The Inspector of Aborigines was present on behalf of Lumbia and even he seemed anxious to keep out anything unsavoury. Lumbia was committed for trial on a charge of wilful murder. As a matter of fact, it was simply a dispute between an armed white man and, at the outset, an unarmed savage, for he had left his spear some distance away when the white man rode up. The savage won. On 6th July a native came to the station and reported that a number of men and women had been shot and burnt near the Ernest River, giving their names. Whilst on my way to Wyndham with bullocks for the works natives came to me with the same report. On the 12th August I left the mission for the Ernest River accompanied by Mr. Mitchell and several natives to investigate the reports which had become so persistent. We found the camp where the police had evidently been for some time. In this camp were unmistakeable signs of the presence of native prisoners. We could find no trace of these natives leaving that camp. I was confident that there had been a tragedy, though Mitchell seemed to think otherwise. On our way back I noticed some tracks coming down the range of hills and wondered what they were. On the 18th I took Mitchell back to Wyndham and, as I was leaving the mission, I told the Rev. James Noble to take certain men and go back and follow up those tracks. He did so and returned the day after my return from Wyndham. He had found the spot where a number of native men had been killed and their bodies burnt. He also found tracks of three native women who had been chained to a tree a short distance from where the men had been murdered. Their tracks were also in evidence right up to the spot where the men had been butchered, accompanied by one individual. Their tracks then led up the river accompanied by three shod horses' tracks. Mr. Noble was unable to follow these tracks far owing to the growing darkness. He also saw the trail by which the party of prisoners had been brought down from the police camp. He brought back a parcel of charred bones. On the 22nd August I left for Wyndham, taking Noble with me. I handed the parcel of charred remains to the medical officer there and sent you a wire. I then went and told Mr. Mitchell. Later in the day I asked him to go back with me, which he did. We left the same day and reached the mission early next morning, and left for the Ernest at noon. We went straight to the spot, being guided by Noble. Where the men had been done to death was a small tree to which the prisoners had evidently been fastened. Round this tree was a ledge of rock about a foot high. Dark stains were still visible, though great efforts had been made to clean up the declivity. Stones had been removed and the edges of the rock had been chipped. About 40 feet away to the north-east from this spot in the midst of the rocky bed of the flood-waters of the Forrest River was a large hole where a large fire had been. The fire must have been very fierce and large flat stones had been used to keep in the heat. When Noble found the place it had been neatly covered up, and large flat stones and a log placed on top. In the ashes were found a quantity of fragments of charred bones and other matter. In a shallow pool about 20 or 30 feet to the north of where the fire had been were small heaps of charcoal and in these we found small portions of skull and other bones. We then followed the tracks of three native women and three shod horses. We followed them about six miles up the bed of the Forrest River. Both Noble and myself had come to the conclusion that these women had been liberated and I said, "Well, we will follow on to the top of the sandbank." We did so and, as we surmounted the bank, we all received a shock for there, facing us, were the remains of a large fire at the foot of a tree. Close by I noticed where horses had been tied for some time, as evidenced by the tracks and manure, and close by was the spot where a small fire had been lit to boil the billy. Searching among the ashes we found a quantity of teeth and fragments of charred bones. The tracks of the women led right up to the spot and, although we followed the tracks of three horses away from the spot to the north-west, we could find no traces of native women's tracks. We returned to the mission after visiting again the deserted police camp. On 26th August I took Mr. Mitchell back to Wyndham. Inspector Douglas arrived in Wyndham on the 28th, and on the 30th, in his company, I again left the mission for the Ernest River. We went over the same ground and, where the women were burnt, we found a large stone behind the tree near where the fire had been, and on this stone dark stains and a few human hairs, which the inspector kept. We also found the trail by which the prisoners had been marched to the place of execution. There are some thirty native men and women missing. Reports have come in of other shootings of natives. At the time of the visit of the police here our nurses were treating a native with a shot wound in the leg. Another turned up with the back of his thighs full of shot. A woman named Loorabane has been reported as having been shot through the thigh. A woman, sister to one of our mission men, is reported as having been shot near Nulla Nulla Station and her baby brained by a Wyndham police boy. The brother asked permission to go and get her remains. He returned next day with two leg bones. Inspector Douglas is now on his way overland to make a thorough investigation by following up the tracks of the police whilst they were away. It has been a terrible affair. It has happened on the aborigines reserve in their own territory and in the name of the law. I sincerely trust that this awful tragedy of innocent men and women done to death in cold blood will lead to steps being taken to render such things impossible in the future. One of the women was blind.

Ernest R. B. Gribble, Protector.

## 6.6   1927. Reverend Gribble's suggestions.

(*Ibid.*, pp. 169-170.)

*Suggestions made by Reverend Gribble, head of the Forrest River Mission, concerning the treatment of native police and relations between police and Aborigines.*

169. As a protector of aborigines and as the head of the mission have you any suggestions to make?—I present the following—
Reforms suggested by Rev. E. R. B. Gribble in reference to police methods.
1. All expeditions for the arrest of native criminals to be accompanied by a protector if possible and a responsible police officer.
2. If a native is wanted by the police from a reserve the police must work with the cooperation of the superintendent of the reserve.
3. That trackers be not allowed to carry firearms, but that the police protect their trackers who, after all, are merely servants of the police.
4. That the custom of sending trackers armed to effect the capture of natives be discontinued and that the police do their own work of arrest.
5. That trackers be engaged over a term of years and trained for their own particular work, and be taught not to shoot but to help in seeing justice done to their own people.
6. Trackers not to be employed by the police in their own districts.
7. Trackers must be married men as far as possible.
8. As things are at present no native tracker's evidence be taken against his own countrymen.
9. Native witnesses not to be incarcerated in the same cell and on the same chain as the prisoner in whose case they are witnesses.
10. Better treatment of native witnesses and prisoners.
11. A native witness's evidence in a court of law (there is an abundance of unreliable evidence from whites in every court of justice at the present time) to have the same weight as any other evidence.
12. Night raids on native encampments by police be prohibited as in these encampments are always many women, children and old and helpless folk.
13. The travelling of native prisoners and witnesses to be seen to and reforms made.
14. That the police be prohibited from disposing to their own profit of weapons and curios taken from the natives. Also that the police be prohibited from disposing, to their own profit, of the scalps of dogs shot at native camps.

170. Would those suggestions make for the better welfare of the natives? Yes, under present conditions, though a good many would fall to the ground in the event of a segregation being adopted.
   . . . I have travelled with native police patrols from the east coast of Queensland to the Gulf of Carpentaria. I have listened to the stories told me by police officers at that time. I have come to the conclusion that the black tracker has been taught to murder, not white people but his own

countrymen. He is given a gun and taught to obey his white officer. He has been taught to conceal the truth and tell lies. From an experience of over 30 years in North Australia in missionary work amongst the natives, I would rather deal with bush natives than with a native who has had any connection with the police as a tracker. I feel sure that this inquiry will cause Australia to realise that the welfare of the natives is of far more importance than some of us have hitherto realised. At present the native is not the asset of the State; he is rather the asset of the individual who, shall I say, possesses him. This situation is not conducive to the best interests of the native. I need only remind Your Worship that it costs only 5s. to obtain a permit to employ an aboriginal, which in the North carries no wages with it, while on the other hand, it costs 7s. 6d. to register a dog, and the Government pays for the scalp of a dead dog the same amount that is paid for a permit to employ a native—5s. Without doubt a large number of natives have met their deaths during the time that this police expedition was in the district. It is to be remembered that the police themselves have stated that it was impossible for any party to operate without their knowledge. If such a thing can occur when police, custodians of the law, go out to arrest natives, what can be expected of others? Moreover, these happenings took place on the native reserve, the natives' own sanctuary, on country granted them by the Government of the State for their own use. This affair shows that they are not safe even in their own territory. In the past 14 years we have heard rumours and reports of similar occurrences, but at long distances from us. This, however, happened, as it were, in our own home paddocks.

### 6.7 4 May 1927. "Aborigines. A Dying Race. Grave Charges Laid Against the Whites."

(*The Sydney Morning Herald*, Sydney, 4 May 1927, p. 10.)

*A newspaper article deploring the condition of Aborigines in the north west of Australia.*

It has been alleged by a deputation which waited upon the Minister of Home and Territories (Mr. Marr) yesterday that the conditions affecting the lives of aborigines of North-West Australia were a disgrace to the Commonwealth, that in Wyndham the feeling against the native ran as high as the anti-black feeling in any American State. It was reported in the search for an alleged murderer in the North-West the police got a number of innocent men and held them in chains. One speaker said that it was rumoured that in the region if a native was considered a nuisance cyanide was put into his meat or arsenic in his flour. . . .

The deputation was representative of Church Missionaries and scientific bodies interested in the aborigine, and the Minister was urged to appoint a Royal Commission to inquire into the present status of the aborigines whom they alleged were gradually dying out as a result of contact with white civilization. . . .

In the Northern Territory numerous natives employed as stockmen rendered valuable service, and were well treated. In spite of that there was a kind of futility in regard to the race. They had no aim in life, and did not seem able to fit into white civilization, and went to pieces when in contact with civilization, opium, and disease taking their toll. For the twelve months ending June the 30th, 1925, there was a decline of 3149 natives.

It was only to the West of the Northern Territory and in the North--West of Western Australia that the very flagrant acts of cruelty were said to be committed. He had been told that drastic measures were taken against natives who killed cattle. . . .

## 6.8   1928. J. W. Bleakley's conclusions.

(*Commonwealth Parliamentary Papers*, Vol. 2, part 2, 1929. Chief Protector Bleakley, "The Aborigines and Half Castes of Central Australia and North Australia," pp. 1159-1197.)

*J. W. Bleakley, Chief Protector of Aborigines in Queensland conducted a comprehensive inquiry into all aspects of the mixed and full-blooded communities of Aborigines in northern and central Australia.*

*Compound at Darwin.*—The Aboriginal Compound at Darwin, though usually confused with, is a quite distinct institution from, the Half-caste Home, but each has suffered public criticism, some of which has been justified, but a great deal has been unfair to the officers doing their best under great difficulties.

*Domestic Labour.*—The presence of the compound at Darwin has been made necessary by the fact that, owing to climatic and other conditions, life in Darwin for many of the white families would be almost impossible without some cheap domestic labour, and the aboriginal is the only suitable labour of the kind procurable. This fact is admitted by all shades of opinion. But for this demand, the last place to be selected for an aboriginal institution would be a town where the presence of a large number of aliens and, until recently, a big meatworks, employing hundreds of men, presented so many of the dangers from which it is desired to protect these simple people. As the introduction of aboriginals as domestic labour was unavoidable, it therefore became necessary to provide effective protection while so employed, and a home for them when idle. As many employers proved unable to control and protect them at night, the rule now is that these servants, male and female, must return to the compound before dark and stay there until morning. No native is allowed in the towns of Darwin and Parap between sunset and sunrise, without a permit, and, by regulation, is liable to arrest and punishment if disobeying this order. Though drastic, it is a wise practice in the interests of the welfare of the native, as also is a rule forbidding them admittance to moving picture shows except at such times as the Chief Protector may consider the films suitable for showing to natives and not likely to lower their respect for the whites. . . .

*Aboriginal Clinic.*—The chief cause of dissatisfaction amongst the white neighbours is the presence of the clinic in the compound. Some fear exists that there is danger of infection from the venereal and other diseases under treatment there, perhaps per the agency of the aboriginals going backwards and forwards to employment. Whether such danger is real or not, there would appear to be serious objections to the presence of the clinic in the compound under present conditions. The buildings are all of galvanized iron, the larger huts used as the wards having concrete floors, many of which are cracked and uneven in surface. Though these buildings are kept as clean as their condition makes possible, they are in the same block as, and quite close to, the huts of the working natives. The patients are locked in the wards at night, the verandahs being enclosed with "K" wire, but, as the Superintendent and the Matron do not sleep on the premises and there is no night patrol, there is nothing to prevent contact between the diseased and healthy ones. . . .

*Proposed New General Hospital, Darwin.*—An alternative suggestion is that a new and up-to-date General Hospital be built for Darwin and the present buildings, which are certainly not modern, be taken over for the aboriginals. As the in-patient roll at the native institution is more than double that for the whites, the buildings would not be any too large. Unfortunately for this proposal, large expenditure has been incurred recently in a new maternity ward.

*Re-organization of Compound.*—With the removal of the clinic, the way would be open for a re-organization of the compound on attractive village lines. At present the accommodation consists of a number of small galvanized iron huts with ground floor, the occupants sleeping on the ground on their blankets. There are no separate quarters for single females. As the girls live in the huts with their "sweethearts" it has not been deemed necessary to place them in separate quarters under control. Where they are genuinely the tribal wives of the men it is quite natural and right they should live together, but this should be carefully ascertained and any loose system of "pairing" discouraged. It may happen that the woman sent up for service for a spell has left a native husband behind.

*Supervision.*—Though confined to the compound between sunset and daylight, there is not continuous supervision. The Superintendent and the Matron, who act in those capacities also for the Half-caste Home, which at present is in a house about one hundred yards from the compound, live in quarters between the two places, so there is only the fear of arrest and punishment to prevent the natives from breaking bounds or to check immorality with the women. Statements were made that such immorality was common, but the Superintendent advised that, although at one time there had been considerable trouble in that way, he was satisfied it did not exist to any extent now.

As, however, nothing is done to relieve the monotony of the hours at night, it would not be surprising if the native, having once tasted the pleasures of the town, and unable, like his educated white brother, to occupy his leisure time with reading or music, did break bounds occasionally. The native corroboree, though indulged in nightly, would not be sufficient for all, as a recent tally showed thirteen different tribes to be represented amongst the inmates.

It seems only fair, if these people are to be confined to their compound, that life there should be made at least comfortable and attractive for them. Encouragement could be given to them to improve their little homes, better the living conditions in them, and cultivate habits of cleanliness and neatness. The women, having opportunity to observe the living conditions of their place of employment, will be keen enough to emulate them, if given the chance, and take a pride in doing so.

*Religion and Education.*—Some local religious body might be given the opportunity to interest itself in the social life of the people by arranging religious services and entertainments. Simple night school instruction might also be imparted, and many of the natives would eagerly avail themselves of it. Their absolute ignorance places them at great disadvantage in their simple trading transactions. . . .

*Treatment.*—No evidence of serious ill-treatment was seen. It had been alleged that the natives on stations were practically in a state of peonage, but employers all held that if a native does not want to work it is useless trying to coerce him into doing so. The only redress possible is to stop his rations. The fact, however, is apparent that, with the loss of their only other means of subsistence, the tribe may become too dependent upon the station to be able to do anything else but yield to circumstances.

One fact, however, is universally admitted, that the pastoral industry in the Territories is absolutely dependent upon the blacks for the labour, domestic and field, necessary to successfully carry on. If they were removed, most of the holdings, especially the smaller ones, would have to be abandoned. One opinion was expressed that the lubra is one of the greatest of the pioneers of the Territories, for without her it would have been impossible for the white man to have carried on, especially where conditions were practically impossible for a white woman, and even where, as in the towns or in places in touch with civilization, the white woman has braved the climate and other discomforts, the lubra has still been indispensable to make life possible for her.

It is remarkable that, although recognizing their absolute dependence upon the natives, there has been no attempt made by the people on these holdings to elevate or educate them, though this should enhance their value as machinery. It seems to be the conveniently accepted notion that they are beyond redemption, that education spoils them, so there is no encouragement for ambition and the blackfellow, naturally lacking initiative and given no opportunity, has a hopeless outlook. Is it any wonder that he sometimes has little heart in his work and is branded as lazy and unreliable? Though any suggestion of improving the living conditions and wages of the young working natives is met by the objection that the industry cannot stand any increase in the cost of production, it is noted that, while some stations pay only with food and clothes, and others pay permanent hands the regulation 5s. a week, several seen in Central Australia claim to be paying from 10s. to £1 a week with food only. While one fairly generous employer supplied all his workers and their families with food, clothes, tobacco, and reasonable extras, and also fed all the camp people, his neighbour, not so kindly disposed, fed and clothed the workers only and took the clothes away from them when leaving. Yet these places were similarly situated as regards industry conditions.

An instance also came under notice of a trepang fisher, employing a number of natives under a licence, who, for weeks, had stayed in the town while the natives at his camp faithfully worked on, though run out of "tucker," catching and curing the fish, and forwarding it to him at the port to sell. Cases were quoted also of sleeper cutters, whose aboriginal labourers did practically all the cutting, carting, and stacking of the sleepers without any supervision by the employer. And these are the people often counted as unreliable and useless. This will be sufficient to show that the system which leaves the matter of reward for the labour entirely in the hands of the employer is not an equitable one. . . .

HALF-CASTES.

Perhaps the most difficult problem of all to deal with is that of the half-castes—how to check the breeding of them and how best to deal with those now with us. The solution of the first of these questions is just as important, perhaps more so, than the latter. As long as conditions such as exist now in the Territory continue, so this problem will face us. In a country where climatic and other conditions discourage the presence of white women, the evils of miscegenation will be evident.

*Position re Half-castes.*—Of the estimated native population in Central and North Australia of 21,000, about 800 are half-castes, the Central Australia quota being 306. Of these, 206 are in institutions, a few are in employment in the towns, perhaps 400 are employed on stations; the remainder, of which probably half are children, being in the camps attached to the stations or in the bush. These children should be rescued as early as possible. A few of the half castes born on stations have been sent by their putative fathers to boarding school for education, and a percentage of these have proved successful, one winning to the position of an outstation manager. Another man, seen in Central Australia, worked his own run and was well respected. Probably not more than 5 per cent. of the half-castes, other than those in the institutions, have received any education or know any other association than that of the blacks' camp. The majority are not even acknowledged by their fathers. Even where this doubtful benefit is accorded them, it is often only because of their usefulness as labour. On one North Australian run, which boasts fifteen half-castes of ages from one year to 36 years, seven at least bear the name of the owner, who was quite emphatic that half-castes should not be taken from the stations on which they were born as they made good labour. A case also came under notice in Central Australia where a white stockowner lived openly for years with a half-caste woman, who had seven children to him. Some of the children he sent away and placed in employment. Recently, however, he turned the woman adrift with a sum of money and married a white woman.. This half-caste woman and two of the younger children are now in the Alice Springs bungalow.

*Need for White Women.*—Efforts to check the abuse of these defenceless aboriginals and the breeding of half-castes will have little likelihood of success until conditions can be developed that will encourage white women to brave the hardships of the outback. One good white woman in a district will have more restraining influence than all the Acts and Regulations.

*Evasion of Law.*—Though strict laws forbid the employment or harbouring of single females by unmarried men, they are evaded by employing a "boy" to pose as a dummy husband. One man boasted of having a fresh "lubra" every week.

*Married Men as Protectors.*—If the officers in these vast outback areas are to be able to properly perform their difficult task of protecting the natives, they must not be placed in a position which may leave them in danger of not being able to fearlessly enforce the laws. Facilities should be provided for all Government officers, stationed in the bush, to be married men and have their wives living with them. The woman's influence and help will greatly enhance the value of their work. The Government then could justly take the stand, so essential for successful aboriginal administration, that no officer having abused the trust reposed in him should be allowed to continue in a position of control over natives.

If, in conjunction with this, the stations would provide similar encouragement for their men to marry, a big stride would be made towards the suppression of the present abuses and the reduction of the half-caste element.

*Policy necessary.*—A definite policy, framed upon understanding of the peculiar position and characteristics of the half-castes, and aiming at what is likely to be best for their future happiness and usefulness, should be formulated. Rescued from the camps and given opportunity for education and vocational training, they can be made an asset to the Territory. Left in their present position, they are more likely to be a menace, and, with what is an even more deplorable result, the increase of the quadroon element. All half-castes of illegitimate birth, whether male or female, should be rescued from the camps, whether station or bush, and placed in institutions for care and training. Even where these children are acknowledged and being maintained by the putative fathers, their admission to an approved institution for education should be insisted upon. The education should be simple in nature, but aimed at making them intelligent workmen and fitting them to protect themselves in business dealings. The vocational training for the boys should be in the trades already mentioned, as necessary for skilled station work, and, for the girls, the domestic arts to make them not only good servants but capable housewives. On completion of their training, those recommended as suitable for outside employment should be transferred to the control of the Chief Protector, who would satisfactorily place them and exercise supervision as long as might be necessary.

*Departmental Control.*—The provision in the present ordinances for departmental control of all half-castes, and even quadroons, where necessary, is a wise one, for these people, especially when uneducated, are generally as much in need of protection as the full blood, in fact are frequently more exposed to temptation and abuse.

*Measures for the future of Half-castes.*—Opinions vary as to what measure should be adopted for the future of the half-caste, but most people fail to make any distinction between the different breeds. The half-caste with 50 per cent. or more aboriginal blood or of alien blood cannot be fairly classed with the quadroon or octoroon. The latter should be separately considered.

Two suggestions have been put forward, viz.:—

    (*a*) Complete separation of the half-caste from the aboriginals, with a view to their absorption by the white race;

    (*b*) Complete segregation from both black and whites in colonies of their own and to marry amongst themselves.

Past experience, however, has shown that the half-caste, with few exceptions, does not want to be separated from the blacks, in fact is happier amongst his mother's people. He is not wanted by the whites, nor does he want to be pushed into a society where is is always an outcast. He should certainly be rescued from the degradation of the camps and given the benefit of education and training, but will be happier if raised to this civilization in company with the young aboriginals of his own generation.

*Marriage of Half-castes and Full Bloods.*—Like every one else, the half-caste prefers to marry where fancy dictates, and where there is freedom of choice it is frequently made from amongst the full bloods. Provided the latter have been lifted to an equally civilized plane, these unions are for the benefit of both sides.

*Object of training.*—The object of the training of the young half-caste should be to fit him to fill a useful place in the development of the Territory, for the industries of the country can readily absorb all trained labour, either black or brown, As the latter's associates will always be his mother's race, there seems little sense in trying to create a gulf between them.

*Exemption of superior type.*—Half castes showing the desire and capacity for raising themselves can be treated as special cases and given an opportunity to do so. As the superior type would probably be less than 10 per cent, to legislate for the whole on that small minority would only be courting certain failure.

*Marriage of half-castes to Europeans.*—Some of the superior half-caste or quadroons may help to solve the sex question, by marrying men in the outback not able to get wives of their own colour. Though one such marriage of a girl from Groote Eylandt appears to have been successful, most of the few unions of this sort observed did not seem to be very happy ones. The best type of white man is not anxious to outcast himself in this way, preferring, if he must, to satisfy his lust with casual lubras until able to return to white society.

*Suitable missions for half castes.*—The two missions, Bathurst Island and Goulburn Island, could receive children from the western and northern areas of North Australia, Hermannsburg Mission those collected in Central Australia, and Groote Eylandt those from the Gulf side, the destination of the children, as rescued, being decided by the Administrator.

Half-caste Bungalow, Alice Springs.

After inspection of the above institution on 17th July, 1928, the following interim report was furnished from Alice Springs, by request, to the Secretary for Home and Territories:—

    "*Unsuitability of present buildings.*—I have the honour to report having inspected the 'Bungalow' Home for half-castes at Alice Springs and inquired into the proposal to erect another more suitable building for the inmates elsewhere. No comment by me is necessary as regards the present buildings, as I have already gathered that your Department is convinced—

(a) the buildings are unsuitable;
(b) the present site is also unsuitable;
(c) immediate removal is highly desirable.

*Proposed Half-caste Colony.*—The important question first to be considered is whether the establishment of an institution on the lines suggested, viz., a separate mission or colony for all crossbreeds of aboriginal blood, who are to be segregated from both whites and blacks, is a sound proposition. From my past experience of these people, I am of the opinion it is not. There is every probability that it will fail to achieve the object aimed at and, in any case, will create a second colour problem likely to prove troublesome in later years. Before giving the grounds for the above opinion, I would point out that the inmates of the present home are composed of four classes, viz.—

(a) three-quarter-caste aboriginals;
(b) half-caste aboriginals;
(c) quadroons;
(d) octoroons.

*Reasons against separate colony.*—Inquiries from all classes of persons with experience of dealing with aboriginal half-castes, such as station owners, missionaries, police, &c., only confirm my opinion that, without appreciable exception, the half-caste of 50 per cent. or more aboriginal blood, no matter how carefully brought up and educated, will drift back to the aboriginal, where naturally he finds the atmosphere most congenial to him. Educated aboriginals and half-castes, who have married back amongst the full-bloods on missions and settlements, when questioned, were emphatic in the opinion that these people were happier amongst their own race.

The above is sufficient at this stage to indicate my reasons for recommending that action be not taken to establish an expensive institution.

*Suggested Mission Home.*—The Hermannsburg Mission, within easy reach of this centre, is willing to receive all half-caste children of 50 per cent. or more aboriginal blood, provided a reasonable extra allowance is made for the expense of feeding, clothing, housing and educating them. I think an allowance of 3s. 6d. a week per head would be acceptable and reasonable.

*Quadroons and Octoroons.*—Quadroons and octoroons, under 10 or 12 years of age, should, where such can be done without inflicting cruelty on the half-caste mother, be placed in an European institution, where they can be given a reasonable chance of absorption into the white community to which they rightly belong. The earlier this is done the better for them, before they have been irretrievably leavened with the aboriginal influences, which would make themselves felt even in a segregated crossbreed establishment.

There will be sure to be some little difficulties of adjustment in connexion with the present inmates, but they can confidently be left to the discretion of the Administrator here, who possesses all the necessary qualities of sympathy and tact to deal with them.

The above suggestion will not immediately deal with all the 64 cases at present in the home, but about half can be so disposed of, and perhaps 12 or 14 more, if the mothers can be persuaded to agree to parting with their quadroon and octoroon infants. It was not deemed advisable at this stage to approach them on the matter.

With regard to such children, from a discussion of the matter with the Director of the Child Welfare Department in Adelaide, it was learnt that there would be no difficulty in arranging the admission of such children to suitable orphanages there, under the Salvation Army or some other religious body, at the expense of the Federal Government, and his department would be willing to assist with the necessary inspections of the children. Of the balance of the children in the home, suitable employment could, without difficulty, be found with carefully selected employers, in this Territory or in South Australia, for another 12 between the ages of 13 and 30.

*Reception Home suggested.*—For some time, and probably permanantly, a suitable home will be necessary for the section that cannot be happily provided for otherwise. Some such institution will be required to receive half-castes rescued from the bush and, by reports obtained, there is still a number to reckon with and, doubtless, always will be whilst present conditions exist in this territory, where the vast station areas make the employment of white married stockmen impossible.

The Home, as now proposed, would be in the nature of a Reception Home for half-castes until they can be suitably provided for.

The original building plan could be greatly modified and accommodation for 30 inmates should meet all needs. One good middle-aged married couple, able to manage the home with the aid of the adult half-caste women, and impart simple instruction in general, manual and domestic subjects to the inmates awaiting employment, should be ample. If a satisfactory water supply is obtained, the boys could be employed raising fruit and vegetables for home consumption and attending the necessary dairy stock for milk and butter needs. In a good season, stock fodder could perhaps be grown and conserved, but agriculture on any large scale would be hardly practicable, owing to the poor rainfall. The girls, if provided with sewing machines, could be profitably occupied in making garments for themselves and for issue to the indigent camp natives through the Protector's office.

It has since been recommended that this Home be placed under the management of a mission body, on condition that—

(a) Half-castes sent by the Government Resident for temporary shelter be received;

(b) The mission co-operate with the Government Resident as regards suitable employment for or marriage of the inmates as opportunity arises;

(c) Suitable education and domestic training be provided.

*"Removal of Present Bungalow.*—In the meantime action should be taken, without delay, to remove the inmates of the present home to a safer place. If water can be obtained at the site now suggested, about seven miles away, I would unhesitatingly recommend the immediate erection of temporary dwellings (which would afterwards serve as workshops, laundries, storesheds. &c.) and the transfer of the 'Bungalow' inmates as soon as these are ready. I understand that the Administrator estimates he has sufficient material for all the buildings required, temporary and permanent, including accommodation for the officer placed in charge, and the only important expense will be the cost of erection. Advice of the Works Department is being obtained by him as to the possibility of recovering and using some of the material now at Jay's Creek site.

*Aboriginal Camp, Alice Springs.*—Another matter, to a certain extent linked with the 'Bungalow' question, is the existence of a fairly large camp of aboriginals about half a mile from the town, where about 60 indigent natives are regularly supplied with relief. Although this camp is in a creditably clean and sanitary condition, it is obvious that its proximity to what, shortly, will be a fairly busy centre with the coming railway construction camps, makes it a certain source of trouble. As the inmates of this camp are all members of the same tribe as the natives on Hermannsburg Mission, it would be no hardship to them if all were removed to that institution to receive their relief with the other inmates.

The Missionaries are willing to receive them if allowed the necessary rations or equivalent value. They would be in much safer and healthier surroundings. Some of them also are parents of half-caste children in the Bungalow.

*Holiday Camp for Working Natives.*—As in the past, natives employed on outlying stations have used this camp, when in town on holiday or awaiting fresh employment (and incidentally helped the old indigents to eat their rations). Suitable provision could be made for them by utilizing some of the material of the present bungalow for the erection of a hut, with fireplace and sanitary convenience, where they could be ordered to camp and be out of the town, while near enough for police control.

The foregoing proposals have been considered in conference with, and with the assistance of, His Honour the Government Resident, and he authorizes me to say that they have his full concurrence.

*Suitability of Mission.*—Subsequent inquiries, of a similar nature, in regard to the sister institution in the north, have only confirmed the opinions expressed in the above. Hermannsburg Mission is favourably placed for giving these young half-castes the vocational training, especially the stock and bush work, to fit them for employment as skilled station hands in their own territory. Financial assistance, however, would be required to enable them to provide the additional accommodation, furniture for the children, and the plant to give the required manual and domestic training.

Recommendations.

It is therefore recommended that—

(1) The original proposal for a Half-caste Home at Jay's Creek or other site be not proceeded with;

(2) All the children in Alice Springs Bungalow of 50 per cent. or more aboriginal blood, or with a preponderance of other dark blood, be transferred to Hermannsburg Mission;

(3) Quadroons and octoroons, where such can be done without hardship to the mother, be placed in an European institution, such as the Salvation Army Homes in Adelaide, and arrangements be made with the Child Welfare Department there for inspection;

(4) As many as possible of those remaining be placed in suitable employment locally, under supervision of the Chief Protector;

(5) An industrial home, with provision for 30 inmates, be established at a site selected about 7 miles from Alice Springs, if water can be found there, for cases not eligible for (2), (3) and (4), and to receive half-castes rescued from the bush until they can be otherwise arranged for;

(6) Temporary buildings be erected at (5) to enable early removal of the bungalow children to be effected, owing to approaching Railway Construction Works;

(7) The whole of the aboriginal camp at Alice Springs be removed to Hermannsburg Mission;

(8) A special grant of £500 be made to Hermannsburg Mission, to provide the necessary additional accommodation, furniture and plant, for care and training of the half-caste children;

(9) The industrial school be supervised by the Administration, and likewise the eventual hiring of the trainees to employment.

*Leper Lazarette, Darwin.*—Much public criticism has been levelled at this institution which is situated about 2 miles from Darwin on the other side of the harbour. Though under the control of the Health Department, the inmates are practically all aboriginals and half-castes. There is no proper accommodation for these patients, who have erected rough bush huts for themselves. Neither is there any competent nursing supervision, an intelligent quadroon, himself a patient, gives what attention he can, under the direction of the Health Officer. The sexes are not divided, one young female patient "living" with the quadroon attendant.

Everything possible and reasonable is provided for the patients in the way of food, clothing and amusements.

The condition is very unsatisfactory, but apparently nothing can be done to improve matters until the proposal, submitted some time ago, that the old Quarantine Station be given for use as a Lazarette, is decided upon. This should be dealt with as early as possible.

Mission System.

These missions are all working on right lines; the officers making themselves conversant with the native language and customs and endeavouring, without unduly pressing the white man's civilization upon them, to induce them, by the education of the young, to see the advantages of the settled and industrious life.

Although the evangelization of the people is their basic object, its true relationship to and dependence upon, the social and industrial education of the race is wisely recognized. None but the old, the sick, and the young are fed without doing some productive work to earn it.

*Objections to Missions.*—Objections are frequently voiced against the establishment of mission stations as a measure for the protection of the primitive aboriginal. Anthropologists have expressed the view that such institutions, by encouraging them to leave their tribal grounds for the reserve, cause disintegration of their tribal life and eventual extinction. That, where men, even with practical ideas, but without the essential sympathetic understanding of natives, are placed in control, they do harm by allowing religious enthusiasm to over-ride the native culture. Another objection is that, in the eagerness for spiritual results, harm is done by gathering natives together for purely religious teaching and bringing them up as pensioners. Also that, unless such work is adequately supported, once commenced, an injustice can be done to the children by drawing them away from the bush life and its training in bush-craft and then, having to abandon the work, leaving them stranded. The contention of the objectors is that, beyond reserving for their use suitable and sufficient country and protecting them from outside interference, nothing should be done to interfere with their living their own life in their own way.

*Necessity for Institutions.*—These views, though born of sincere desire for the welfare of the natives and worthy of earnest consideration in any measures for the betterment of the race, apparently overlook certain important facts. The native, once having come into contact with the white man or alien and acquired a taste for his foods and luxuries, is not likely to longer remain a contented savage. There are few places now left of which it can be said that the natives are absolutely uncontaminated, and it is doubtful if any exist where they do not need protection from the unscrupulous, waiting to exploit their hunger for such luxuries. The disintegration of tribal life, already encompassed by the encroachment of the white man, has created the need for something more, in the way of protection and relief, than can be afforded by a Protector they seldom see and very often are afraid of. And this need can best be served by an institution, conducted by experienced men, with benevolent motives, who, while avoiding the dangers feared by the sceptics, can win the confidence and trust of the people, by ministering to them in sickness or distress and generally exercising a watchful eye on their welfare.

*Advantage of Mission System.*—In conditions such as exist in the Territories, this work, though recognized as the responsibility of the State, should as far as possible be placed in the hands of subsidized missionary organizations.

In the first place, the cost of management is less, and the missions can obtain the type of worker who undertakes the work from missionary, and not mercenary, motives and is likely to have more sympathy with the people.

The Government, with its tremendous task of developing the country, would be unwise to burden itself, and its already overtaxed machinery, with the worry of management of a number of charitable institutions. Far more effective work can be done by the Administration if it can confine itself to the direction of the work required.

The mission bodies now operating are keen to undertake such work and co-operate with the Government for the betterment of the people. . . .

*Quadroons and octoroons.*—As already indicated, the crossbreed with a preponderance of white blood should be considered separately. Their blood entitles them to be given a chance to take their place in the white community and on as favourable a footing as possible. That this may be successfully accomplished, the children should be removed from aboriginal associations at the earliest possible age and given all the advantages in education and vocational training possible to white State children, to minimize as far as possible the handicap of their colour and friendless circumstances.

To avoid the dangers of the blood call, employment should be found where they will not come into contact with aboriginals or aboriginal half-castes. In spite of such precautions, however, a few will doubtless drift back, and it may be found advisable to allow, even encourage, the marriage of such difficult cases with crossbreeds of darker strain.

Those quadroons and octoroons removed too late to receive the benefits of early separation and special training, but who have been placed in domestic service in towns beyond the State, should be given every possible opportunity to improve their condition, if possessing the character.

While official supervision and control is essential in their own interests, any appearance of branding with the aboriginal stamp should be avoided, so as not to hamper unduly their upward progress. For instance, a rigid application of the regulation rates of wages for aboriginals would be manifestly unfair, as, with equal opportunities for learning, many should prove as useful and valuable as the average European servant.

The evidence in one southern city, where a number of such crossbreeds have been placed in service, was that employers willingly paid direct, to good servants, the difference between the aboriginal regulation rate and the ruling wages for similar work to State children.

Where suitable official inspection of these is available, the fixing of rates of wages, supervision of the spending, portion to be banked &c., could be well arranged between the inspector and the employer.


Recommended Policy.

Summarized, the policy should be:—

(1) To check as far as possible the breeding of half-castes by:—
   (a) strict enforcement of laws for protection and control of female aboriginals;
   (b) encouraging immigration of white women into the Territories;
   (c) removal of obstacles to having married men in positions of control over, or on places employing, aboriginals.

(2) Collect all illegitimate half-castes, male and female, under sixteen years of age, not otherwise being satisfactorily educated, and place in Aboriginal Industrial Mission Homes for education and vocational training.

(3) Make education of all half-castes under sixteen years of age compulsory.

(4) Education to aim at making them intelligent and able to protect themselves in business dealing, and the vocational training to fit them to fill a useful place in the labour for development of the Territories.

(5) Transfer those with preponderance of white blood to European institutions at early age, for absorption into the white population after vocational training.

(6) Keep official control of all crossbreeds in employment, but avoid hampering social progress of those under (5) by too strict application of aboriginal regulations.

(7) Grant exemption, by certificate, to those who, after education, prove of superior character and capable of managing their own affairs.

Proposals put Forward for Future Administration.

Of the numerous suggestions made with a view to improvement in future administration the following might be separately surveyed:—

(1) Establishment of a native state with self-government;
(2) Complete segregation of all wandering natives;
(3) Establishment of cattle stations like Moola Bulla in Western Australia;
(4) Compulsory general education of aboriginal children;
(5) Education in citizenship;
(6) Formation of Aborigines Advisory Board;
(7) Employment of trained anthropologist for scientific study.

*Native State.*—The proposal for the formation of a self-governing Aboriginal State, though condemned by many as fantastic and impracticable, still has the virtue of having been born of a sincere and wide-spread desire for the upliftment of a downtrodden race.

In the form put forward, it is, in many directions, impracticable, and shows a lack of administrative experience of the characteristics and limitations of the natives, as it evidently, to quote one criticism, proposed to thrust upon them a social machine they cannot understand.

In presenting the scheme, it is claimed that the natives are becoming extinct, because:—

(a) the sources of native food supplies are being encroached upon;
(b) past methods of government have failed—demoralizing instead of uplifting the people;
(c) mission effort has not been adequately supported.

The proposal therefore is:—

(a) To reserve country where tribes are still intact.
(b) Include only tribes now occupying the territory to be reserved.
(c) No outside natives to be forcibly included.
(d) Members of State to have perfect freedom of movement.
(e) Government at first to be by native tribunal under benevolent white direction.
(f) White adviser, teachers, missionaries, and industrial instructors.
(g) Severe laws to safeguard against any contaminating outside interference.
(h) Native tribunal to be empowered to deal with contagious diseases.
(i) Ultimate entire self-government under Native Administrator.
(j) Representation in Parliament.

The above scheme evidently assumes that the natives have, or can be expected to develop, qualities that they have never so far displayed. They have no conception of democracy as understood by civilized nations. Their native laws and customs seem to utterly fail to conceive any idea of combination or federation of tribes for mutual government or protection. Each tribe is a separate and distinct group, with its own language, customs, and laws environing its peculiar totem, and has interest in nothing outside of those associations. Any interference with the government of the tribe by an elected tribunal, even if such body could be created, would be bitterly resented.

The educated full-blood native, David Unaipon, indicated by the petitioners as a likely leader in such a movement, was most decided, in discussion on the question, that his people would never voluntarily change their tribal customs and laws for any form of national government. To press such a system upon them would only result in chaos, for the different tribes would not agree.

The freedom of egress and ingress to be allowed would endanger the security of the State, by leaving them exposed to temptations or the introduction of diseases and vicious characters from outside.

Without those ideas of federated self-government, the proposal can, in the main, be melted into a comprehensive scheme for the greater protection and betterment of the primitive races, on lines more suited to their present circumstances, but possible of development, by gradual education, to partial if not whole self-dependence.

*Complete Segregation of all Wandering Natives.*—This suggestion, though excellent in theory, cannot be put into practice, except gradually, without committing the error it is desired to avoid—ruthless disintegration of the tribal life. The shielding of the race from the evils of contact with the civilized races is urgently necessary, but until, through the education of the growing generation, the tribes are induced to voluntarily seek the sanctuary of the benevolent institutions established for their care, it will be better to concentrate effort on the amelioration of the lot of those suffering from detribalization and the tightening up of the machinery for moral protection.

Any wholesale herding into reserves in strange country would be unwise.

*Establishment of Cattle Stations for Aboriginals.*—Although this proposal, if properly managed, is an excellent one from the point of view of revenue raising, it misses most of the essentials of institutions for the betterment of a primitive people. The raising of cattle only may provide the beef needs and the revenue for other expenditure, but food, though the most important item, is not the only essential consideration.

Twenty able-bodied men and half a dozen women would provide all the labour necessary to run the largest cattle station likely to be established, and, if that was to be the only industry developed, the remainder of the inmates would be just kept in idleness. Any system that pauperizes the native, or produces for him without effort on his own part, is not likely to succeed in uplifting him.

An institution, to be successful, must be able to find profitable occupation for all its able-bodied inmates in industries productive, as far as possible, of their own needs and that will also provide practical vocational training for the young; as for instance—

    (*a*) cattle breeding for beef, milk, butter, and animals for heavy haulage teams;

    (*b*) cultivation of fodder crops for dairy stock and working animals;

    (*c*) also of vegetables, fruit, poultry, eggs, &c., for food;

    (*d*) saw milling for material for improvement of living conditions;

also such useful trades as building, carpentry, blacksmithing, saddlery, plumbing, wheelwright work, butchering, and numerous others, all in daily need on a large self-contained institution, and skill in which enhances the value of the labour hired therefrom.

*Compulsory General Education of Aboriginal Children.*—This would only be practicable where it had been possible to gather them into institutions. As already explained, the instruction should only be of a simple nature, and aim chiefly at domestic and manual training. Until the Territory is further developed and facilities for the education of white children are provided, any attempt at compulsory education of even the children of station camps would be out of the question. The rescue of half-castes from the camps and education in institutions should be compulsory.

*Education in Citizenship.*—The aboriginal of the Territory, though quite equal physically and mentally to his cousins in the more advanced States, is still in a very primitive condition, and it would be useless attempting to educate the present generation in the duties and responsibilities of citizenship as practised by the white man's civilization. If, by benevolent dealing, their confidence can be won and the young people trained to appreciate the settled family life, develop the desire for self-dependence and pride in its part in the village betterment, learn something of the spirit of social service, that will be a great stride in citizenship for one generation. It is too soon yet too look forward to any higher development in self-government.

*Formation of Aborigines Advisory Board.*—This suggestion emanates from certain bodies in South Australia, interested in a similar board in that State, where the different philanthropic associations have taken an active interest in the aboriginal question. Unless such a board is composed of persons with expert scientific or administrative knowledge of aboriginal characteristics and conditions, it would be of little value and only calculated to hamper administration.

Such a board, to be effective, should contain a trained anthropologist, a medical expert in diseases peculiar to natives, and officers and missionaries experienced in aboriginal administration, who should all have first hand knowledge of Territory conditions. Their duties should be confined to advising on matters of policy.

*Employment of Trained Anthropologist for Scientific Study of Race.*— The Chair of Anthropology of the University of Sydney has undertaken some work in collection of anthropological data and has placed several of its students at places in North Australia and Queensland to study and record the culture of the most primitive tribes. It is certainly important, from a scientific point of view, that records of this fast dying race should be saved while the field for research still exists.

The knowledge obtained would be of important value also in future policy and administration.

## 6.9   24 January 1935. Commissioner H. D. Moseley's report.

(*West Australian Parliamentary Votes and Proceedings, op. cit.,* Vol. 1, 1935, "Royal Commission on Aborigines", pp. 4-13.)

*Following a Royal Commission, Commissioner H. D. Moseley reports the situation that he found among Aborigines, especially those engaged in the pastoral industry of Western Australia.*

The Social and Economic Conditions of Aborigines and Persons of Aboriginal Descent.

In the North (or Kimberley Division of the State) the natives, except where living in their natural state in the unsettled areas, are chiefly to be found either on pastoral leases or Government Stations, or at Missions. . . . In the case of natives on pastoral properties (cattle and sheep) they experience conditions which as nearly as possible, approach their natural life. They certainly have a place in the country to which they belong—an important consideration from the point of view of the native: their work takes an appropriate form—in the bush amongst stock. . . . In the main they want for nothing: they are well fed and clothed and the huts in which they live, made of bush material, bags or sometimes flattened petrol tins, are suitable to their needs; anything more would not be appreciated by them—indeed, they would not be used. . . . I have seen numbers of these station camps, and have seen no sign of unhappiness in the natives. During the day the men work on the run, the women—or some of them—are employed in or about the homestead. . . . Bearing in mind the number who do nothing, it is not a cheap form of labour, but it suits the pastoralist who by looking after the old people, keeps the young people on the property and has labour available when it is needed. It would be difficult if not impossible to obtain white labour when such labour is required only during a portion of the year. . . . In the Kimberleys the native is not paid and, bearing in mind the experience of one district of the North West it appears to be of no great disadvantage to the native; he has not acquired, and I doubt if (generally speaking) he ever will acquire, any real sense of property: he will give away anything he has and, as he has never had money, and would not recognise it if he saw it, he is not being deprived of anything. One could not, even with extreme imagination, visualise a native of the Kimberleys settled on his own property: of what other use would money be to him? He and his dependents are fed and clothed and cared for when sick— . . . and he wants for nothing. . . .

The number of blacks employed on stations in the Kimberleys cannot be far short of 2000. They are probably to be found on 70 or 80 pastoral stations. If their happiness is to continue, they must obviously be allowed to remain on those stations and any attempt to remove them for more thorough training would not only be cruel but producive to no good effect: it would be impossible to expect privately owned stations to be responsible for the necessary training and education of blacks. So, for the present, further endeavour to take these station blacks to a higher degree of living seems impracticable. . . .

I have already mentioned that in the North few half-castes are to be found on the stations. That is a gratifying fact but one difficult of explanation: for it is regrettable that my investigations have satisfied me that in certain parts of the North intercourse between the white man and the aboriginal woman exists to a degree which is as amazing as it is undesirable. This is a matter of some delicacy to discuss, but it is right that it should be discussed. I have been told by men long resident in the Kimberleys that it is unwise to be familiar with the natives, that the natives lose respect for the white man who fraternises with them: that principle—possibly a good one—is obviously disregarded when the desire for sexual intercourse is uppermost. . . . white people living in native countries in time lose any feeling of repulsion for colour. I do not know if that feeling of repulsion has ever existed in the State; it certainly does not amongst those who have lived among blacks and I hope it never will. On the other hand, if a feeling of repulsion against this practice of cohabiting with native women can properly be exhibited, then I think those who otherwise would have followed the lead may be deterred from contributing to the increase of half-castes.

Leaving the Kimberleys and turning now to the North-West, ordinary living conditions of the natives are similar to those of the Kimberleys, though in some cases rather more pretentious habitations are found. I have mentioned, however the fact that in the Kimberleys the native is not paid for his labour. That system in so far as pastoral work is concerned, obtains as far South as Wallal, on the Ninety-Mile Beach. South of that and generally throughout the Pilbara District, it is the usual practice to pay the natives employed on stations. The custom which has apparently been in force for about 20 years is universally condemned amongst the pastoralists, but all agree that it is now too late to alter the existing state of affairs. The objection to the payment is based on assertions made by the pastoralists that the native has no idea of the value of money, that he is an easy victim for unscrupulous itinerant hawkers and that it encourages him in his gambling desires, which are firmly fixed. He will of course, gamble without money: for a game of cards he will divest himself piece by piece of his clothing to enable him to continue the game; but, with money, his gambling instincts are aroused to the fullest extent. . . . The fact remains, . . . that as things are at present the money he earns is not the slightest use to him. He has developed a character which is, to my mind, entirely artificial. His holiday— . . . calls for greater preparation than the walk-about of the Northern native. Instead of discarding his clothes and starting out with his spears to hunt game, it is often found that this North-Western native packs his suit case and, having padlocked the front door of his hut, gets into this turnout (in a few cases even a motor car) and sets out on a holiday vastly different to that of his former days. It is I think without doubt merely an imitation of the white man. It cannot be regarded as an indication that he is really trying to improve his method of living. If it were so one would notice improvement in other and more appropriate directions. . . .

Those natives of the Murchison are of a different type; here closer settlement prevails and the natives are apparently more civilised. . . . In some cases they still live in camps—in others they have more elaborate accommodation near the homesteads. They are cleaner in appearance and better dressed; they speak English more correctly—pidgin English, fortunately is not so often heard. Almost without exception those employed on stations are . . . described as good station hands. But, of course they need close supervision. The women with equal supervision make competent domestic servants, and those on stations where the natives have died out or are few in number feel their absence. The men are all paid wages . . . and here . . . the system works well. With few exceptions however the natives do not save their money. They do not actually waste it, gambling is not noticeable to any extent; but they have an insatiable desire to spend their money. They buy dresses for their women and are attracted by the hawkers wares. . . . on many stations their buying is closely supervised.

Constitution of the Settlement. (At Moore River.)
The settlement comprises:—
1. A compound at which are located young people sent there for a variety of reasons, and people taken from their parents sent to the settlement for education and protection.
2. A camp for indigent natives and their families, situated some 300 yards from the compound.

The Compound.
*Accommodation.* The dormitories present from the outside a dilapidated appearance. Inside at present there appears to be adequate room, but remembering the numbers who at this time of the year sleep on the verandahs, I should say that, during the winter months, the rooms are far too crowded. . . .

The dormitories are vermin ridden to an extent which I suspect makes eradication impossible. . . .

There are no means of keeping the inmates in the dormitories at night. The doors are locked, but latticed walls are easily broken and many cases are on record of girls visiting the camp a few hundred yards from the compound after they have been placed in the dormitories for the night.

. . . While it remains part of the settlement, it should be made impossible for the inmates of the compound to have any communication with (the camp). At New Norcia Mission I noticed that all the openings to the dormitories were guarded by strong link mesh netting, I was told that this was effective, and a similar expedient for Moore River was suggested by the superintendent, Mr. Neal, in his evidence. It should in my opinion be attended to at once, and the compound should be patrolled at night by a responsible person, not a native policeman. . . .

There is no accommodation for the compound children during rainy days other than the dormitories. Those of school age cannot in wet weather use the bough shed which in summer is used as a classroom . . . the matter in my view requires urgent attention. . . .

The hospital is a substantial building, but two additional wards are necessary. The nursing sister declares that a labor ward is a necessity, and whatever name may be applied to it, it certainly seems to me necessary as one ward is common to men and women. There is no isolation ward, and the one bathroom is used as a surgery. The need of an isolation ward was made apparent by the presence of a child, suffering from syphilis, on the verandah and mixing with other children.

*Equipment.* With the exception of the work done in the sewing room, in which I am informed clothing is made for all indigent natives throughout the state, and a small amount of sand brick making, nothing is being done in the way of vocational training because no equipment is provided. . . .

The equipment in the dining room is deficient, and with few exceptions, the children had no implements of any kind to aid them in eating. Judging by their dexterity in the use of their fingers. I am afraid they have little knowledge of any other method, though I did an experiment with a child and one of the few spoons available. I am told that there had been a sudden disappearance of spoons, and that more had been ordered. I hope the children will not experience great difficulty in manipulating them.

*Food.* Here there is much room for improvement. Powdered milk for children is obviously useless . . . No vegetables are grown at the settlement, and a totally inadequate supply is imported.

There is an insufficiency of meat, and, if articles as fruit and eggs were occasionally supplied, fewer children would go to the hospital. This view is supported by the doctor and nursing sister.

Punishment of inmates: . . . I was shown a place of detention commonly called "the boob" and I disliked its appearance very much. A small detached "room" made of posts driven into the ground, floor of white sand, scarcely a gleam of light, and little ventilation, and I was told that inmates have been incarcerated in this place for as long as 14 days. It is barbarous treatment, and the place should be pulled down. If detention is necessary, . . . it should be carried out in a more suitable place and the maximum period of 14 days prescribed by regulations, considerably reduced. Records of such punishment should be sent to the Chief Protector.

The Camp

It seems obvious to me that it should be removed to some other site immediately. Nothing more detrimental to the work of the settlement can, in my view, be imagined. Many of the inmates are, in the Superintendent's opinion, useless, and they seem to be, with few exceptions of the poorest type. I was unable to obtain the numbers of inmates in the camp, but 102 full rations are issued daily, a child receiving half a ration.

The inmates of the compounds are admitted for protection and education, and I found them living within a few hundred yards of a collection of useless, loafing natives, content to do nothing and always ready to entice the compound girls to the camp. It would be better that the grown-up people should be sent away and the children taken from their parents and put in the compound. . . .

My report on the Moore River Settlement will have conveyed my opinion that the place is not suitable. It will be of no practical value unless means are found of employing the inmates fully. . . .

The other Government native stations, all of which are situated in the Kimberleys, are Moola Bulla and Violet Valley in the East Kimberleys, and Munja, which is at the head of Walcott Inlet. Permanently attached to these stations are approximately 400 natives.

Dealing with Moola Bulla, one of its objects, as I have already mentioned was to reduce the amount of cattle killing by natives. It can be assumed that it had no other purpose, which may be gathered from its present operations. . . . its chief object is to keep natives usefully occupied by helping to grow cattle and, incidentally sheep. . . . It is true that, unlike the private properties, Moola Bulla takes an interest in the elementary education of half-caste children. . . . but, if (it) is ever to assume the stature of a properly equipped Government Native Settlement, then I feel that far more should be done for the people in touch with the Station. I have pointed out earlier the difficulty in the way of having any form of organised training on private properties. The Aborigines Department should be, and no doubt is grateful in reflecting that part of its burden is being shouldered by these pastoralists in keeping so many natives usefully employed, and in caring for the old and infirm natives from whom they get no tangible return. But after inspecting three Government Stations in the Kimberleys, all established with the object of benefiting the blacks, I am left with the firm conviction that far more is needed. . . .

At Violet Valley, it may be said quite frankly that no work is done . . . but perhaps, there is little that can be done here, and its existence may be justified if, in fact, as I am led to believe, cattle killing by natives is less prevalent since its establishment. The number of natives in touch with this Station is small, probably no more than 40, and no half-caste child has been born on the station during the last eighteen years.

Munja Station offers scope for work of a different class from that of Moola Bulla. Here there are according to the Manager, hundreds of acres of good agricultural land in the vicinity of the homestead. Why is this not turned to good account? . . . There are 700 natives in touch with the station, 140 are permanently there and 60 are worked. The Station equipment for agriculture consists of a three-disc plough and a set of harrows. No Adviser in Tropical Agriculture has visited Munja in the eight years the present manager has been there. . . . It seems so obvious to me that at both Moola Bulla and Munja a great deal more should be done to train natives. The experiment may in some instances be a failure. On the other hand, I am confident that a great deal of success will be achieved. But in both these places whatever scheme for the advancement of the native is adopted, it must be thorough and complete. There must be no half measure; a half educated native presents greater difficulty than one with no education at all.

### 6.10  22 November 1937. R. R. Brain's report.

(*New South Wales Parliamentary Papers*, Vol. 7, 1938-40, Select Committee pp. 615-617, 623-625.)

*The examination of Mr. R. R. Brain, one-time superintendent of an Aboriginal Government Settlement in New South Wales. He tells of education and employment conditions, housing and health, and the Aboriginal psychology.*

233. How many inmates were there at the mission?—118, I think.

234. How many were full-blooded aboriginals?—The percentage was fairly high—between 20 and 30 per cent. I think the number connected with the station reached about thirty-eight full-bloods.

235. The remainder were half-castes?—Quarter-castes and eighth-castes. There were not so many actual half-castes.

236. Do you really understand the psychology of the native?—I believe so. I got on well with them.

237. How did you find the mission when you went there?—Generally speaking, the health of the people was fairly good.

238. There was no hospital there?—There was a hospital there at that time. There had been one for years, but it was closed down two or three months after I went there.

239. Why?—I believe through lack of funds. Moreover, the doctor would not stay there, and they could not get another medical officer. We took over on the 27th July, 1934. The hospital closed late in November or early in December.

240. What happened to the people who were ill?—We took them to Collarenebri.

241. There is no doctor there?—Yes, an excellent one. . . .

245. What was their principal complaint?—At Angledool it was eye trouble mostly. But there was evidence of malnutrition amongst some of the children. That was rectified. One man suffered from tuberculosis, and had been bedridden for nearly two years. He died, but the people there were generally healthy.

246. How was the malnutrition rectified?—By supplying extra foodstuffs and green vegetables.

247. Did you make a complaint to the Board?—No, not at that stage. We also had an outbreak of whooping-cough in December, which was mentioned this morning by Sister Pratt. The children were run down. I think there were ninety-four cases of whooping-cough, the eldest being a man of 35 or 40 years of age, and the youngest a child of 3 or 4 weeks' old. I wrote to Head Office and said that I had talked things over with Mrs. Brain, that the children were run down and were in need of extra food supplies. I submitted orders for such things as oatmeal, rolled oats, peas, beans, macaroni, sago, and so on, and I received approval, the goods arriving as soon as possible. Besides that a considerable quantity of cod liver oil and Parish's food was given the children, and their health definitely improved. About April or May, 1935, the Chief Inspector of Schools visited the station. He remained about an hour and a half, during which time he looked around the station and expressed the opinion that he had seen no children looking healthier at any aboriginal station he had visited. The photograph of tomatoes the Committee saw this morning was taken during the whooping-cough epidemic. . . .

249. Would you attribute the malnutrition to which you have referred to neglect?—No.

250. Then to what cause?—Possibly the need for certain things is not appreciated.

251. Does that mean neglect?—I would not say it was neglect.

252. *Mr. Horsington.*] It might have been due to ignorance?—Possibly. I do not think the manager at the time was capable of wilful or criminal neglect. He is not in the service now.

253. *Chairman.*] You said there was a good deal of eye trouble there. To what do you attribute the cause?—The doctors say it is definitely due to a germ. Trachoma is the name of it, but there are other troubles, too. Probably infection is spread by bush flies, and it can be carried in dust.

One child takes it to another. As Sister Pratt said, the heat and dust are tremendous contributory factors in its spread. . . .

254. Did you notice much syphilis there?—No. none that I could recognise.

255. When the hospital was closed, what happened?—Mrs. Brain was .the only nurse in the district, and she was called out even to attend serious cases amongst whites. There was a doctor at Goodooga, 32 miles away, but going there was unsatisfactory, and it was a bad road, impassable in wet weather. To Collarenebri the distance was 54 miles.

256. What was the condition regarding food allowance when you went to Angledool?—The normal ration was issued.

257. Do you consider it was adequate?—That is arguable. If people are able to augment their rations I think it was quite a fair ration. But I cannot say that I agree with it. It was a dry ration consisting of 8 lb. of flour, 2 lb. sugar, ¼ lb. baking powder, 2 lb. potatoes, 12 oz. onions, 12 oz. jam, and there was meat twice a week.

258. That is a week's ration for an individual?—Yes. A child would get half that amount. Twice a week there was 2 lb. of meat for an adult. Then there was the question whether elderly persons or children were in need of anything else, and literally there was no limit. At Angledool I ordered a good deal of cornflour, and the orders were always fairly large. There was always oatmeal and rolled oats. For a person in need I took it for granted that I was free to act, and they got cornflour or extra rice. A good deal of condensed milk was also used at Angledool. That was given to people in ill-health and to weaklings.

259. How did you get your medicines? Did you have authority to purchase them?—We ordered them by requisition through the Government Stores Department. The supply of Parish's food was never refused. Two things were expensive—codliver oil and olive oil—but they, too, were always supplied when necessary. On one occasion I was only able to obtain half quantities for a time because the stores were short of supplies.

260. Did you call for tenders for supplies?—At Angledool I did for certain things. Most of what was wanted I got on office orders from Sydney, including sugar, salt, and lime. At Angledool the tin huts were whitewashed inside with lime once a week. We called tenders for flour and for meat. At Angledool we killed the sheep ourselves. . . .

264. Were the aboriginals capable of properly cooking the food supplied to them?—Definitely they were not. While the children showed evidence of malnutrition Mrs. Brain cooked at least one full meal a day for every child on the station. She prepared eighty-seven meals a day for those children, apart from their rations.

265. A good hot meal with vegetables?—Yes.

266. Have you any suggestion to make to overcome that difficulty so that the aboriginals can benefit from the food given them?—I can make no suggestion off-hand. They like the inside of a sheep—the "moobil" or intestines—better than any other part. As the Committee probably know, tripe eaten by the white man has to be scrubbed and cleaned before it is considered edible. During the time Mrs. Brain was sick and away I visited a child who had been ill and asked her if she had had anything to eat. "Yes," she replied, "I have had quite a good tea. I have had 'moobil.' "

267. What were the housing conditions like at Angledool?—Very bad.

268. What were the huts like?—They had been condemned by the Board years before I went there, and the Board was preparing plans to improve the position. The huts contained two rooms, and were built of galvanised iron, with a fireplace, but they were not lined. It is extremely cold in the west during the winter, and, frankly, in summer they must have been like hell.

269. Did the aboriginals live in the huts or did they camp out?—They lived in them. In summer they would go down to the river.

270. Was there no lining in the huts?—No. I once put bagging in, but it was unhealthy.

271. Had they plenty of ventilation?—There were four windows and doors in each hut, but ventilation is something about which the aboriginal requires to be educated. In winter time they all get inside, and you will find them sound asleep and their heads covered by blankets while the doors and windows are closed. In some cases they put boughs about, and at Angledool some have grown creepers.

272. What educational facilities are there?—I was the teacher at Angledool, and we had a fine little school there. I think there were twenty-four or twenty-five children there when I took over, and the number was increased to thirty-nine. When the Chief Inspector visited the school in April or May, 1935, there were thirty-eight there. That is a matter I should like to discuss with the Committee later on. I was not trained as a school teacher, and I believe it is a job for the expert.

273. Were the aboriginals engaged by station owners through you?—Always, I think.

274. Were they indentured?—No, but we had apprenticeship for children between the ages of 14 and 18 years. I have a grouch in connection with the employment of aboriginals, but it does not affect the Board's administration. Outside employment is better than having the children doing nothing at the mission station. But the difficulty is when an employer wants a man for only two or three weeks. He would employ him on the basic wage, £2 2s. a week and his keep for two or three weeks, and then the man would return to the aboriginal station and have to wait perhaps two or three weeks longer before he got any more work. The employment was intermittent. An employer employing a white man could not do that.

275. When the aboriginal was engaged by the man on the land, was he paid full wages or was some of it put into a trust fund?—No, they were paid full wages.

276. About the female labour. Some of these girls are sent out to the station?—As apprentices.

277. What wages do they get?—I believe I had better leave that to the Secretary of the Aborigines Protection Board. They commence at 1s. 6d. a week pocket money.

278. I can answer that question. Part of it is paid as pocket money and the balance to the manager, and it is forwarded to the head office in Sydney quarterly, where it is banked in the name of the apprentice.

279. What is the balance? Is there a recognised standard?—Oh, yes. In arranging the placing of the boys and girls, I send a movement form to the head office and a contract form to the employer with the conditions set out and the money to be paid. The details are worked out by the head office.

280. You should surely know what they are to receive?—I believe they get 1s. 6d. pocket money, and the 2s. paid to the Board which is banked on their behalf, plus food, clothing and medical attention.

281. What is the clothing?—They have to go out fully equipped, and the clothing has to be kept up. The manager should, if possible, keep in touch with the apprentices from time to time. The police in the district visits the place where they are employed regularly.

282. Who is responsible for the clothing?—The employer.

283. The amount the child is entitled to is really 3s. 6d. a week, food and clothing?—For the first year.

284. How old would they be then?—14 years.

285. Medical attention is also the employer's responsibility.

286. Do they get it?—Generally speaking. They are supposed to get it.

287. A princely salary all right!—If they only get 6d. a week, the girls would be a great deal better off on the station than in any environment I have seen. It is a workable method, but it is not the best, and it would be a good thing to improve it.

288. You say they are fully equipped when they go to a station as apprentices?—Yes.

289. What is the equipment? What are they supplied with?—Roughly, two of everything.

290. There must be a uniform system of equipping them when you send them out to a station like that?—There should be a uniform system; but I am sure when it is adhered to it is actually laid down that each child gets issued four complete suits of clothing, two in winter and two in summer. At Angledool we get the material and have it made up. Mrs. Brain and a half-caste used to do it when I was there. The clothes were made in the clothing factory.

291. What is your experience with regard to this indentured labour of boys and girls? Have many of them returned to the mission before their time was up?—Yes.

296. In your opinion, is the apprenticing out of boys and girls a good method of dealing with them?—Yes; as things stand at present, with the stations' existing resources; because it is better by far than having them in the environment of the aboriginal station—an environment which I am prepared to tell the Committee is putrid. I worked in a shearing-shed as a young lad of 14 years, as a wool roller. Then I served during the war, but I have heard filthier filth from aborigine boys and girls of from 4 to 5 years of age than I ever heard in those places. . . .

298. On the whole, can you believe the aboriginals?—No. During my time I did everything that was humanly possible for the good of those people. I never had an apprentice run away but that I immediately went out to find where he was. On one occasion I took a girl to Brewarrina Police Station, where she made a statement that appeared to be absolutely water-tight. I subsequently showed it to Mr. Cookson, the Police Magistrate, who said, "It reads true." Yet that same girl said she told us a tale in order to get back to the mission station to play rounders.

299. Is that an exception or is that the rule among these people?—That case itself would be an exception; but as far as telling the truth is concerned, the aboriginal people are not truthful.

300. Taking them on the whole?—Taking them on the whole, if a lie will fit in they will not tell the truth.

301. If it so happens that the Committee eventually visits these stations, is it your opinion that if we come into contact with these people, and they are asked questions, it means we must weigh their answers and try to consider actually what the truth is, and not take their statements for granted?—Yes, I can quote concrete instances. On 11th August last year, two members of the Aborigines Protection Board, the deputy-chairman and another member visited my station. One woman told both of these men that I had not issued rations to her children. . . . and we found that the husband of the woman at that time had three weeks' rations at Angledool. He had been issued extra rations, apart from those issued to his family because he was going to Queensland for cattle. We called this woman in and asked her why she had not told the truth. She replied, "I do not know why I told them that—simply because there were no doors and no windows in my hut." I believe something of that was reported by these two gentlemen as against me.

302. *Chairman.*] There is also a possibility of other people not telling the truth?—That is so, but I take it that if these people have a complaint they are likely to express it obliquely.

**6.11 December 1937. Donald Thomson's recommendations.**

(*Commonwealth Parliamentary Papers, op. cit.*, Vol. 3, 1937, No. 56, p. 805.)

*An anthropologist, Donald Thomson, studied the Aboriginals problems and made the following recommendations to the Commonwealth Government.*

The object of my own recent undertaking in the field was to make a survey of the present position and to present a plain, unbiassed scientific statement of the facts. As an anthropologist, I may point out that the continuation of the present system will lead to such and such an end or that the result of such and such a policy will be so and so, but the decision and the ultimate responsibility for the action or the failure to act rests, of course, with the Government.

Although it is admitted that the problem of dealing with the aboriginals in the future is a complex and difficult one, I believe that the immediate problem that faces the Government, and the first moves, can be stated in simple terms. The real issue at the present time seems to be a decision as to whether the system in the past, of permitting the almost unregulated disorganisation and disintegration of native culture is to be permitted either in the same, or in some modified form, or whether the Government is prepared to face the alternative, which is a real attempt to save the remaining natives. This will admittedly require definite and even drastic measures.

It is not difficult to prove by a review of the facts that the end of the system of the past can only be decay and ultimate extinction. It is admitted that the second policy requires strong measures, and that neither this, nor any one policy will meet with universal approval. . . .

An unbiassed review of the history of white contact with, and influence upon, the aboriginals over the past 150 years leaves no room for doubt that it is unfavourable to the natives. The conclusion is inevitable that they have suffered everywhere at first disorganization of their social order, degradation and ultimate decay. Government institutions, missionary, educational and other endeavours to help and to uplift these people have not been able to arrest the decline. . . .

Unfortunately accurate figures are rarely forthcoming, but where they are obtainable they reveal a rate of decline that is even more appalling than is generally realized. I have quoted exact figures for a station in North Queensland which show that under favorable conditions, and under full protection of a sympathetic Presbyterian Mission at Mapoon, and of the Queensland Government, a community declined, in only 30 years, from more than 400 to less than twenty. A general review of the conditions all over Australia, and the comparative data available, show that the decline has almost everywhere proceeded at the same appalling rate. . . .

There is still another aspect of this problem. I do not think that even among those whose avowed policy is deliberately to stamp out the native culture—and I can cite examples of this policy which I have seen in operation—for example, in the "dormitory system" practised on certain mission stations—the effect is ever followed to its logical conclusion. I think that it should always be remembered that in making black white men of these people we do them the greatest of all wrongs, since with our rigid adherence to the "white Australia" policy, we are not prepared to admit them to real social equaliy, which would obviously be the only possible justification for such action, even if for biological and cultural reasons, it were workable.

Preliminary Recommendations.

I recommend therefore that the Commonwealth Government adopts as its initial policy the following essential measures, which can later be elaborated and extended.

(1) That the remnant of native tribes in Federal Territory not yet disorganized or detribalized by prolonged contact with alien culture be absolutely segregated, and that it be the policy of the Government to preserve intact their social organization, their social and political institutions, and their culture in its entirety.

(2) That the native reserve Arnhem Land be created an inviolable reserve for the native inhabitants, and that steps be taken at once to establish and maintain the absolute integrity of this reserve.

(3) That similar steps be taken to render inviolable any other reserves in which the native population remains undetribalized.

(4) That legislation, similar to that obtaining in the Mandated Territory of New Guinea for the protection of the native populations be imposed, and for the punishment of offenders against the established policy of the Government.

(5) That steps be taken to remove the anomaly by which watering depots have been established on the native reserve for the convenience of pearling vessels (known to be manned chiefly by aliens whose presence is inimical to the welfare of the native population), that this authority be rescinded and that these depots be abandoned.

## 6.12 1937. Ration allowances on Government settlements in New South Wales.

*(New South Wales Parliamentary Papers, Sydney, Vol. 7, 1938-39-40, "Select Committee on the Administration of the Aborigines' Protection Board", 1938, p. 736.)*

*Officers' Rations*

18. Rations according to the undermentioned scale will be issued to managers and other officers on the Board's stations, viz.:—

| | PER WEEK |
|---|---|
| Flour | 8 lb. |
| Tea | ¼ lb. |
| Sugar (white) | 2 lb. |
| Meat | 7 lb. |
| Potatoes | 7 lb. |
| Soap | 1 lb. |
| Butter or | 1 lb. |
| Jam | 2 lb. |

Where butter can be made or potatoes grown on the stations, they must be taken from the station supply.

*Free Issue of Rations.*

19. (a) Rations consisting of 8 lb. of flour, 2 lb. sugar, and ¼ lb. tea per week will be allowed to all aged, infirm, or sick Aborigines. Children attending school may, at the discretion of the local committee or guardian, be allowed half rations, and the issue of such rations will be withheld in any case where children do not attend regularly. On the Board's stations, and at reserves where specially authorised, meat up to 7 lb. per week, ⅛ lb. tobacco, and salt and soap are to be issued as required.

(b) Rations are not under any circumstances to be issued to the able-bodied without special reference to the Board. The men must go out and obtain employment, and be made to understand that they must support themselves and their families.

(c) In cases of special urgency, rations not exceeding a week's supply may be issued in cases not authorised, but the particulars must be at once reported to the Board.

(d) A quarterly return of all rations issued shall be furnished to the

Board, giving particulars of the names, ages, sex, and caste of the recipients, and the reason for the issue.

(*e*) A supply of medicines and such medical comforts as rice, sago, arrowroot, oatmeal, and maizena shall be kept in stock at the Board's stations, and issued to any Aborigines who may be sick or otherwise in need of the same, but the circumstances of such issue must appear on the quarterly returns of rations issued.

*Supply of Clothing*

20. The following clothing will be supplied annually to Aborigines throughout the State, in such cases as may be considered necessary, viz.:—
Men and Youths.—One coat, two pairs trousers, two Harvard and two flannel shirts—the coat and trousers to be of diagonal tweed.
Boys—Two knicker suits (serge), two Harvard, and one flannel shirt.
Women and Girls.—One winsey and two print dresses, one winsey and one flannel petticoat, two pairs calico drawers, and two calico chemises
Infants (boys to three and girls to four years).—Two diagonal tweed frocks, five petticoats with bodices, and two Harvard shirts.

*Requisitions for Supplies.*

21. All supplies must be obtained upon requisition under contracts taken by the Board, or the Stores Supply Department. The Regulations under the "Public Service Act, 1902," relating to the "Mode of obtaining Supplies, "Receipt, Custody, and Issue of Stores," etc. shall be strictly observed.

In all cases where articles are not obtainable under contract, local offers in writing should accompany requisitions.

On the first day of July of each year, managers of stations shall submit an estimate of the quantities of ration tea and soap required for a period of twelve months, showing the stock on hand at that date, and (in the case of soap) the quantity required for each quarterly delivery in the months of November, February, May and August respectively.

*Medical Attendance.*

22. Before issuing orders to Aborigines on the Government Medical Officer, the Board's managers and the Police shall satisfy themselves that the cases require the attendance of a doctor. Where necessary the patients are to be sent to hospitals subsidised by the Government.

## 6.13 1937. Powers and duties of the Aborigines' Protection Board of New South Wales.

(*Ibid.*, pp. 747-748.)

The Act provides that the Board shall, subject to the direction of the Minister, be the authority for the protection and care of aborigines under the Act, and shall exercise general supervision and care over all the aborigines, and over all matters affecting the interests and welfare of aborigines and protect them against injustice, imposition and fraud. Its principal powers and functions may be summarised as follows:—

(i) With the consent of the Minister, to apportion, distribute and apply as may seem fitting, any moneys voted by Parliament, and any other funds in its possession or control for the relief of aborigines.

(ii) To distribute blankets, clothing and relief to aborigines.

(iii) To provide for the custody, maintenance and education of the children of aborigines.

(iv) To manage and regulate the use of reserves set apart for the use of aborigines.

(v) It may appoint the managers of stations and such other officers as may be necessary.

(vi) It may appoint local committees consisting of not more than seven or less than three persons to act in conjunction with the Board and also officers to be called guardians of aborigines. It may also dispense with these persons and bodies.

(vii) It may remove from reserves any aborigine or other person guilty of misconduct, or who, in the opinion of the Board, should be earning a living away from the reserve.

(viii) It may apply to a Police or Stipendiary Magistrate for an order directing any aborigine who, in the opinion of the Board, is living in undesirable conditions, to remove to a reserve or place controlled by the Board, or if he is only temporarily resident in this State to return to the State from whence he came.

(ix) Only with its consent can an aborigine be removed or caused to be removed from New South Wales to any place outside the State. Before giving its consent the Board may require that a bond be entered into.

(x) It may fix such terms and conditions as it deems to be desirable for the employment of infant aborigines and may collect and institute proceedings for the recovery of any wages payable. In the event of a child so apprenticed refusing to go to the employment, the Board may remove him to some home or institution for the purpose of being trained. If of the opinion that the moral or physical well-being of the child is likely to be impaired by continuance of the apprenticeship, the Board may, after due inquiry, cancel the indentures. It may also lay a complaint if of the opinion that the employer is not complying with the conditions of the indenture, or is unfit to have further control of the apprentice.

(xi) It may assume full control and custody of the child of any aborigine if, after due inquiry, it is satisfied that such a course is in the interest of the moral or physical welfare of the child.

(xii) If of the opinion that any aborigine is not receiving fair and proper treatment; is not being paid a reasonable wage; or that his moral or physical well-being is likely to be impaired by the continuance of his employment, the Board may terminate same and remove the aborigine concerned to such reserve, home or other place as it may direct.

(xiii) It may require an employer to pay the wages of any aborigine to some officer on its behalf where it appears to the Board that such arrangement is in the best interests of the aborigine.

(xiv) It may institute all actions and other proceedings against any person for recovery of wages due to an aborigine.

(xv) It may cause any aborigines who are camped or are about to camp within or near any reserve, town or township to remove to such distance from the reserve, town or township as it may direct.

(xvi) It may authorise the medical examination of any aborigine and may have him removed to and kept in a public hospital or institution for appropriate treatment, or to undergo such treatment as and where provided.

(xvii) It may institute action to recover the cost of maintenance of an aboriginal child from its near relatives.

(xviii) It may inspect or authorise the inspection of any station or reserve on which aborigines are located, and any buildings, or any other matter or thing thereon.

(xix) It may institute proceedings for a penalty in respect of offences against the Act and the Regulations.

**6.14 1937. Public Service Board's General Policy recommendations.**

(*Ibid.*, p. 768.)

*A summary of the Public Service Board's views and recommendations following the Select Committee Inquiry in New South Wales.*

(a) The ultimate aim of the administration should be the gradual assimilation of aborigines into the economic and social life of the general community, and this can be brought about only by a vigorous policy which will ensure a close study of each individual and family with a view, as soon as they are fitted by education, training and personal qualities, to their being aided to establish themselves outside stations and reserves under the control of the Aborigines Protection Board.

To achieve this result, the present policy of aggregating aborigines on stations under the immediate control of qualified persons is the proper one, but the policy should be directed to ensuring that every available facility is fully utilised for their education and training. As the individuals become fitted to take their place in the general community, steps should be taken to remove them from the stations to desirable surroundings, their places on the stations being taken by those most advanced, and so on, until in course of time problem cases only are retained on the stations.

(b) To carry out this general policy, there should be on the Board persons qualified by training and experience to bring to bear on the problem all necessary knowledge. To this end there should be included in the Board membership representatives of the controlling Department (the Chief Secretary's), of the Departments of Public Instruction, Health and Police, an expert in agricultural development, a member who has specialised in social and anthropological work, and an executive member who will also be the principal officer of the Board's staff, devoting the whole of his time to the work of the Department. The title of this Board, it is considered, might well be altered from the present title to that, say, of Board for Native Affairs.

(c) Full use should be made of the specialised services available in other Departments to ensure that the best results are obtained in the use of the Board's property, not only from the point of view of increased production, but as a vital means of training aborigines in various types of work. For example, it is essential that the services of the experts of the Department of Agriculture be utilised to ensure the production of suitable crops, of milk, butter, etc., to augment the ration supply and so improve the general health of the aborigines, as well as to train them in rural pursuits; of the medical, nursing and inspectorial services of the Department of Public Health, and of local authorities as a means of surveying the whole problem from the point of view of health and living conditions; of the Forestry Commission's experts with a view to ensuring the proper conduct of the sawmilling operations and so obtain the maximum output and the best results in the training of aborigines in sawmill activities; of the officers of the Police Force in reporting upon individual cases, and acting as agents for the Board; of the Department of Public Works and its organisation in connection with the erection of buildings, pumping plants, and in general oversight of such operations, thus relieving the Board's inspector for the more legitimate inspectorial activities; of the trained inspectors of the Child Welfare Department in supervising apprentices and other non-adults.

(d) In order to overcome the antipathy of the general community to the aborigines, which represents one of the principal difficulties in dealing with the problem, use should be made of local committees of public spirited citizens for such purposes as employment, recreation and social work generally.

(e) No new stations should be established until a complete survey has been made of the existing stations, with a view to determining their suitability from the following points of view:—
  (i) Habits of the aborigines;
  (ii) Suitability of location, having regard to health, water supply, availability of employment off the station, availability of training facilities,
and a reasonable standard of comfort provided on existing stations.

(f) In connection with the education of the aborigine children the Education Department should permit (and encourage) their attendance at ordinary schools, and they should not be debarred from such attendance, except under very exceptional circumstances. This will assist in the ultimate solution of the problem and, provided the headmasters of schools with considerable numbers of aborigine children are carefully selected, should cause no difficulty in administration.

## 6.15  13 July 1938. Citizen rights of Aborigines.

(*Ibid.*, "Report and Recommendations of the Public Service Board of New South Wales", No. 13, p. 758.)

*A report by a select committee into the administration of the New South Wales Protection Board.*

It has been said from time to time that Aboriginals should be given full citizen rights. Briefly as far as can be seen at present, the majority of Aborigines, as defined by the Act,* have all citizen rights except the following:
  (a) They cannot exercise franchise at Federal elections.
  (b) They are prohibited from obtaining liquor.
  (c) If Aboriginal blood predominates they cannot receive maternity allowance or old-age or invalid pension from the Commonwealth Government. (Incidentally an Aboriginal, if resident on the stations, as already stated, is not eligible to receive the old-age or invalid pension.)
  (d) Residents on stations have been debarred from receiving relief work provided by the Government of this State.
  (e) Family endowments payments are in general, made to Aboriginals by means of orders for goods instead of in cash.
  (f) Certain restrictions may be imposed on Aboriginals in accordance with the provisions of the Act.
The Commonwealth Electoral Law is not a matter which can be dealt with by the State Government. The denial of old-age pensions, and invalid pensions and the maternity allowance under the Commonwealth Law to those in whom Aboriginal blood predominates together with the denial of old-age pensions to any Aboriginal resident on a station, . . . might well be taken up with the Commonwealth Government.

The last named provision, viz. the non-payment . . . of the old-age pension appears . . . to be a matter requiring urgent consideration. The effect, . . . has been to cause many aborigines living on a station under supervision, to live . . . under conditions that are not a credit to the community, and which are certainly not in the interests of the Aborigine.

Generally speaking the restrictions imposed by the present law of this

* The Act: Aborigines Protection Act, New South Wales 1909-1936.

State are in the interests of the Aborigines, and at the present time the Public Service Board's inquiries indicate that in general the opinion is that they should not be lifted, even though there are numerous Aborigines who might with justification be placed on an equal footing with the general community.

The general opinion of those most competent to speak appears to be however that their education has not yet reached the stage where the restrictions can be lifted as a general policy, without harmful effects on the majority.

**6.16 7 December 1939. Politicians discuss the Native Compound at Darwin.**

(House of Representatives, Commonwealth of Australia Parliamentary Debates. 1939-40. Revised Estimates, 7th December 1939. pp. 2364-2367.)

*The accommodation and health of the Aborigines is considered as well as their ability to contact white servicemen.*

Mr. McEwen.—

The aborigines and half-castes in the Northern Territory are the responsibility of the Commonwealth Government. When I visited Alice Springs about eighteen months ago I found there a half-caste institution situated a mile or two out of the town. It consisted of the old telegraph station which, judging by is appearance, was built long before I was born. That old building is the only shelter provided for the half-caste population at Alice Springs. There I saw a state of affairs which honorable members will find it difficult to believe—120 half-caste children, and 13 or 14 adult full-blooded and half-caste women, the parents of some of the young half-caste children, living in that most deplorable old building, which, when it rained heavily, took in the water almost as if there were no roof at all. The dormitories were a disgrace.

Mr. BARNARD.—Why did not the honorable member initiate reforms when he was Minister?

Mr. McEwen.—I did initiate reforms, and my complaint is that they were not carried out. As I have said, 120 children were being accommodated in two dormitories, where they slept on two sets of wire mattresses. The first set, which accommodated 36 children, stood 1ft. 9in. from the floor, and 2ft. 4in. above their heads as they lay was another set of mattresses accommodating another 36 children. The building was roofed with corrugated iron, and had a concrete floor, so that it must certainly have been too hot in summer and almost unbearably cold in winter. I know many stud stock breeders who would not dream of crowding their stock in the way that these half-caste children were huddled in this institution at Alice Springs. After I had inspected the place, I recommended to the Government that a new institution be built; that it should be removed from the present site, and taken out a few miles where facilities could be provided for the inmates to accustom themselves to some useful work on a cattle property so that they would be fitted to take jobs later on. I prepared tentative plans and estimates, and submitted them to the Government. To-day, I see that there is not one penny on the Estimates to correct the deplorable state of affairs that exists at Alice Springs. It is a shameful thing to allow it to continue. At Darwin, I found that about 50 half-caste girls, ranging from children three or four years old to young women, were accommodated in a small weatherboard cottage of not more than five or six rooms, the kind that normally would be regarded as suitable, perhaps, for a minor official, his wife and two children. Not only were these 50 girls living in this place, but the building also served them for a school. The dividing walls had been torn out, and stretchers were packed over the whole of the floor as closely as they could be put. For their schooling, the girls huddled on a narrow strip of verandah which was not accommodating beds, and there they were taught. I have since been informed that even that building has been taken over by the administration or the defence authorities, I do not know which, and the girls are being accommodated— under what conditions I do not know—in the compound for aborigines. That is the very opposite of what has been agreed upon as the proper care of half-caste people, the idea being to raise their status by keeping them away from the aborigines. I could not, without being unparliamentary. express the shame I feel that no money has been provided on the Estimates this year to correct that state of affairs. In the school at Alice Springs, 120 children, with their three teachers are accommodated in a building which consists of two rooms, each 30 feet square, and a verandah.

Mr. HOLLOWAY.—And 80 per cent. of them are suffering from sore eyes.

Mr. McEWEN.—That is probably correct. The verandah has a galvanized iron roof only 8 feet high and 30 to 40 children sit in class under this verandah in the intense heat of a Central Australian summer. It is not unknown for children to collapse while in class. I appreciate the financial difficulties of the Government during wartime, but there are some things which no financial stringency can excuse, and included among them are the things to which I have just drawn attention. . . .

Mr. FROST.—

The honorable member for Indi referred to the new compound at Darwin, at which half-castes and full-blooded aborigines were accommodated. The old compound is now being used for hospital purposes. The new compound should have been located miles away from where it is. It is too near the aerodrome, where 300 to 400 of our young men are to be trained for the Air Force. It is a disgrace to the Government that the compound should be located so close to the aerodrome. It is well known that many of the half-castes and aborigines in the compound suffer from venereal disease. Some of them are in a bad state. The only mark that distinguishes the diseased persons from others in the compound is the red trimmings on their clothes. It is a disgrace to the Government that the compound should be located as close to the aerodrome as it is, seeing that we are sending our boys there for Air Force training.

Mr. McEWEN.—The honorable member is making a grave reflection upon our young men.

Mr. FROST.—I am simply stating the facts. If the honorable member for Indi cares to close his eyes to the facts, I do not intend to do so. He was partly responsible, I suppose, for placing the compound where it is.

Mr. McEWEN.—The honorable gentleman is again wrong.

Mr. FROST.—If that is so, I withdraw the remark. I do not desire to do any honorable member an injustice. I reiterate, however, that we should not be sending our boys into a training camp so close to the filthy compound in which these natives and half-castes are living.

Mr. McEWEN.—The honorable member does not seem to have much confidence in our young men.

Mr. FROST.—I have reared a family, and I try to see things as they are. Everybody must realize that, as the compound is so close to the Air Force camp, our boys will be subjected to serious temptations with which they should not be confronted. A young and innocent boy may make a mistake and suffer for it all his life. He may even be ruined. The honorable member for Indi, while he was in office, should have taken steps to remove the compound from its present site. We should not set such a temptation in the way of our young men. Parents may have brought their boys up strictly only to find that, at a time when they are serving their country, they are led astray. The natives and half-castes should be accommodated many miles away from Darwin and not close to the centre of the town. . . .


## 6.17  30 June 1943.  Aboriginal Employment.

(*Annual Report on Aborigines and Rations,* issued during the year ended 30th June, 1943, for the North-Western Division, Police Station Oodnadatta, South Australia.)

*Extract from an annual report on Aborigines from the Oodnadatta Police Station, South Australia, explaining the employment situation for Aborigines.*

All aborigines desirous of employment in this district can be employed, mostly by pastoralists. During the past year there were not sufficient aborigines offering themselves to fill positions open to them. Conditions of employment offered by various owners and managers of pastoral properties are quite satisfactory. A number of men are in employment doing odd jobs in the town.

The number of male aborigines capable of doing stock work appears to have fallen off during the last few years. From enquiries made this would appear to be largely due to the fact that a Mission Station (i.e., Ernabella) is situated on the eastern boundary of the Aborigines' Reserve and natives will not leave that locality to obtain employment when they can obtain rations in exchange for dog scalps. From personal observation I find that the aborigines are not taught stock work at that Mission as is done by a Mission in the Northern Territory (i.e., at Hermannsburg). This is to be deplored at the present time owing to the shortage of white labour due to war-time conditions. In the course of patrols through the various stations I find that aborigines employed on those stations are treated with consideration and are allowed their periodical walkabouts.


## 6.18  December 1944.  Newsletter from the Ernabella Mission for Aborigines, South Australia.

(*Ernabella News Letter,* Ernabella, December 1944, pp. 1-3, 4.)

. . . We are feared that groups of the younger men were going East and forsaking their nomadic life, and perhaps were losing their skill in hunting and were in danger of becoming detribalised.

Mr. Love makes answer to our fears.*

"There is a tendency on the part of a large part of the native population to make their hunting journeys to the East. . . . They also do visit the cattle stations and some few of the people are employed casually on the stations. During these visits most of the people live on their hunting. . . .

They come back here with a great collection of old ragged clothes, presumably obtained from their compatriots who are employed and clothed on the stations. Here is one problem for us: we must make Ernabella more attractive than any other station. The attractions are mainly white man's clothing, and white man's food, the latter being a long way second.

Ernabella has to make it possible for the people to get clothes to buy for themselves if they wish. If not, they will get rags elsewhere.

* Mr. Love, Mission superintendent.

At present war-time restrictions make this difficult. Later they can buy from the proceeds of dingo scalps, or earn from labour given at Ernabella.

. . . We can, and intend to, keep the children unclothed; the young women will not go naked again, nor can we make them do so. The men are not so particular, but greatly like clothes.

All of the people at Ernabella are nomadic. None stay here for long at a time, let them continue to be nomadic.

Can a nomadic hunter be a Christian? I believe he can. Then what do we want to do for our people? Beware that, in our zeal to do much for them, we do not err in doing too much *to* them.

Ernabella will never be able to employ more than a comparatively small proportion of the people permanently. They do not want to be permanently employed. Let them go off into the bush again. . . .

. . . We have young men in all stages. They spend their years of adolescence under the charge of their tribal elders rather than of the missionaries. I think we must acquiesce for some years to come at least, and never seek to break the authority of the elders; but in due time to win the elders, too, to the way of Christ."

### 6.19 1944. A Certificate of Citizenship.

(*Statutes of Western Australia*, Perth, 1944, "Native (Citizen Rights) Act", 1944, No. 23, 8° and 9° Geo vi., pp. 88-91.)

*Western Australian legislation defining the terms on which a Certificate of Citizenship might be granted to an Aborigine.*

4. (1) Any adult person who is a native within the meaning of the Native Administration Act, 1905-1941, may make application for a Certificate of Citizenship to a resident or stipendiary magistrate or Government Resident in the magisterial district in which he resides.

(2) Such application shall be in the prescribed form supported by a statutory declaration signed by the applicant to the effect that he wishes to become a citizen of the State, that for the two years prior to the date of the application he has dissolved tribal and native association except with respect to lineal descendants or native relations of the first degree, and—

    (a) that he has served in the Naval, Military or Air Force of the Commonwealth and has received or is entitled to receive an honourable discharge; or

    (b) that he is otherwise a fit and proper person to obtain a certificate of Citizenship.

(3) Every application shall be accompanied by two recent written references from reputable citizens certifying as to the good character and industrious habits of the applicant.

5. (1) Before granting any application brought under the provisions of the preceding section, the magistrate shall be satisfied that—

    (a) for the two years immediately prior the applicant has adopted the manner and habits of civilised life;

    (b) the full rights of citizenship are desirable for and likely to be conducive to the welfare of the applicant;

    (c) the applicant is able to speak and understand the English language;

    (d) the applicant is not suffering from active leprosy, syphilis, granuloma or yaws;

    (e) the applicant is of industrious habits and is of good behaviour and reputation;

(3) At the hearing of the application, whether or not the Commissioner appears in support or opposition, the magistrate may direct the production of all relevant papers and other documentary evidence and may call for such reports and order the summoning of such witnesses as he may consider necessary.

If the Commissioner appears he may be granted an adjournment not exceeding two months within which to make all necessary enquiries.

(4) If a magistrate grants an application he shall thereupon issue under his hand a Certificate of Citizenship in the prescribed form. Such certificate shall have affixed thereto a photographic likeness of the applicant in the manner of a passport.

6. Notwithstanding the provisions of the Native Administration Act, 1905-1941, or any other Act the holder of a Certificate of Citizenship shall be deemed to be no longer a native or aborigine and shall have all the rights, privileges and immunities and shall be subject to the duties and liabilities of a natural born or naturalised subject of His Majesty.

Nothing herein contained shall deprive the holder of the right to property or benefit accrued prior to the granting of the application, or of any property which would accrue to or devolve on him if a Certificate of Citizenship had not been granted.

7. (1) Upon complaint of the Commissioner of Native Affairs or any other person, a magistrate may suspend or cancel a Certificate of Citizenship if he is satisfied that the holder—

(a) is not adopting the manner and habits of civilised life; or
(b) has been twice convicted of any offence under the Native Administration Act, 1905-1941, or of habitual drunkenness; or
(c) has contracted leprosy, syphilis, granuloma or yaws.

(2) Upon suspension or cancellation of a Certificate of Citizenship the person concerned shall lose the full rights of citizenship conferred by such Certificate and shall be deemed to be a native or aborigine for all the purposes of the Native Administration Act, 1905-1941, or any other Act.

(3) A Certificate of Citizenship may be suspended for a fixed term or for an indefinite period subject to the right of the native to prove to a magistrate that his conduct and character justify a renewal of the Certificate.

**1966. An Aboriginal child takes a bath. (7.9).**
*The Sun.*

**1967. Aboriginal Settlement at Dareton, New South Wales. (7.11).**
*The Sun.*

# 7

# Becoming an Australian Citizen

With the 1950s came increasing concern for Australia's image overseas as a protector of minority groups' rights. Men like Sir Paul Hasluck stated that any claims made by Australia as an interested nation "are mocked by the thousands of degraded and depressed people who crouch on rubbish heaps throughout the whole of this continent" (7.1). In 1951 a meeting of Commonwealth and State ministers agreed that the future policy should be to direct all Aborigines towards full citizenship. In 1961 the Commonwealth decided that all adult Aborigines should receive the right to vote if they so wished (7.3), and everywhere discussions were directed towards changing the black man into a working-class Australian as soon as possible. "Half-castes" became citizens automatically, and "full bloods" could apply for citizenship if they considered themselves able to manage their own affairs (6.19).

In the 1960s the way was being opened for Aborigines to achieve the Governments' stated goals, however increasing numbers of blacks and whites were questioning the validity of this objective. Sociological and demographic studies showed that in fact assimilation was proceeding only slowly. There was increasing evidence to show that some Aborigines wished for a separate community and identity of their own (7.15-7.16).

Aborigines were becoming more vocal. They supported their equal-pay claims, and in 1963 Yirrkala tribesmen protested about the resumption of reserve land without having been consulted (7.6). The question of land rights of indigenes had been debated for many years overseas, but finally it came to worry Australian politicians (7.7).

A referendum held in 1967 to give Federal Parliament the right to pass laws for the welfare of Aborigines was overwhelmingly supported by 5,700,000 Australians. It indicated the attitudes of the majority were in sympathy with the Aborigines, but the speed at which real measures were taken was criticized by the press and opposing politicians. Australian Aborigines still had one of the highest infant death rate in the world, general health was at an appallingly low level, and the lack of education and motivation

1965. King Brumby. (7.8).
*The Sun.*

1971. A woman at Yalata Aboriginal Reserve,
South Australia, eats kangaroo meat.
*Mrs. I. M. White.*

1971. A woman and children at Yalata Aboriginal Reserve, South Australia.
*Mrs. I. M. White.*

hampered the adult worker (7.19).

The Queensland Aborigines and Torres Strait Islanders' Affairs Act, remained one of the few documents still discriminating against the black people, although it met increasing opposition in 1970 (7.22). Judging public feeling correctly, Prime Minister Mr. Gorton announced that all discrimination against Aborigines would be eliminated in the lifetime of his Parliament (7.26).

This same year saw Aborigines writing and speaking on their own behalf, not as people cast in the mould of white, middle-class respectability, but as an aggressive, frustrated group trying to inform their fellows and the white Australian that Aboriginality was something to be proud of (7.15, 7.16, 7.18, 7.27).

1971. Pre-school-aged children receiving their daily ration of cereal, milk and vitamins. Yalata Aboriginal Reserve, South Australia.
*Mrs. I. M. White.*

1967. Demonstration supporting the Aborigines' Land Rights claim.
*The Age.*

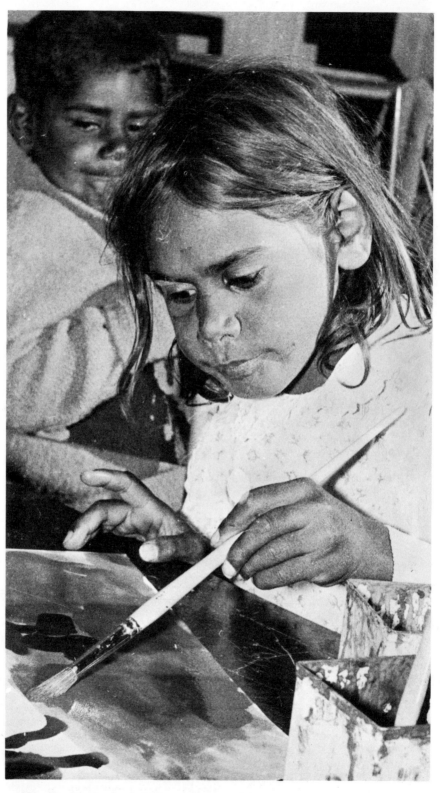

1972. Aboriginal school children enjoy an art lesson.
*Ministry of Aboriginal Affairs.*

(Paul Hasluck, "Speech from the House of Representatives", 8 June 1950, in *Native Welfare in Australia. Speeches and Addresses by the Hon. Paul Hasluck, M.P.*, Perth, 1953, pp. 5-12.)

*Extract from a speech delivered in the House of Representatives by the then Mr. P. Hasluck.*

According to the census that was taken in 1944, there were then in Australia 71,895 persons who were classified as aborigines. That total included 24,881 who were classified as half-castes. Approximately one-third were classified as nomadic and slightly less than one-third were classified as being in employment. Of the remainder, also approximately one-third, the majority were either in supervised camps or were looking after themselves in various stages of transition from bush life to the life of the white community.

. . . the problem today is not a problem of protection. In the old days when they were a primitive people living under primitive bush conditions, the problem chiefly was to set up a barrier between them and the invading white community. Those days have gone, and the nation must move to a new era in which the social advancement rather than the crude protection of the natives should be the objective of all that is done in this sphere. We must either work for the social advancement of the aborigines or be content to witness their continued social degradation. There is no possibility now of our being able to put at least two-thirds of the aborigines back into bush life. Their future lies in association with us, and they must either associate with us on standards that will give them full opportunity to live worthily and happily or be reduced to the social status of pariahs and outcasts living without a firm place in the community. In other words, we either permit this social evil to continue or we remedy it.

. . . a total of approximately 72,000 aborigines living in an expanding community of approximately 8,000,000 whites is so small that it is manageable. We have on our hands a serious but not a frightening problem. The total number of aborigines constitutes a social group within but not of the white community. Therefore, that group can, and must, be managed. Unless we tackle this problem now it will increase in seriousness. . . .

The fundamental point to be recognized is that in this matter we must deal with not one problem but several problems. I shall illustrate that point by referring to the conditions of those natives, approximately 20,000 who are classified as being in employment. That number can be sub-divided into six, or seven, classifications. First, there are those natives who live on cattle stations in the north under tribal conditions and whose subsistence with that of their families is provided by station owners. They live a bush life and during a large part of the year, when they are not needed for mustering, they go walk-about and resume their full tribal habits. In the north-west of Australia natives are employed mainly on sheep stations. Because of their tribal background many of them are attached by their own choice to particular stations. They receive wages and largely follow the habits of white workers, although their standards of living are certainly far below those of any white stockman or boundary rider. In the areas farther south the natives in the sheep country may be contrasted with those living in the agricultural areas under conditions roughly approximating those of the white workers, but enjoying a lower social standard, and suffering the disability of social outcasts. There are also natives who are under the protection of missions or government settlements. Then there are those who find regular employment, receive award rates of wages, and live in their own homes. Finally, there are natives who, perhaps, not being so steady in their habits, follow seasonal labour or take contract work, as the fancy moves them or as their need for some new commodity arises. These are only some instances that indicate the wide variation in the types of employment followed by natives classified as "employed" and the extent of this national problem. Any uniform plan to cover all natives in employment which disregarded these wide differences in the competence of various groups of aborigines, their conditions of work and their manner of life would be certain to cause conflict and confusion, and would give neither satisfaction to ourselves nor benefit to the aborigines. . . . I know that the Australian Constitution leaves responsibility for aborigines with the State governments, and that the direct legislative and administrative powers of the Commonwealth in respect of aborigines do not extend beyond Commonwealth territories. . . . I merely ask the Commonwealth Parliament as the supreme voice of the Australian nation, to ensure that, irrespective of where the constitutional powers lie, the practical task of the betterment of the conditions of the natives throughout the Commonwealth shall be undertaken. . . .

My plea for action by the Parliament is reinforced by a consideration of the attempts that have been made in the past to do precisely what I am now suggesting this Parliament should do. The subject of native affairs was raised at the Conference of Commonwealth and State Ministers in 1936, and in 1937 a conference of Commonwealth and State representatives in Canberra drew up a number of admirable principles and made some exceedingly sound recommendations. Any action that may have followed that conference was so slight as to bear little relation to its decisions. Again, following discussions that took place at a conference of Commonwealth and State Ministers in 1947, when this subject was raised by Mr. (later Sir Ross) McDonald, the Minister for Native Affairs in Western Australia, a conference of Federal and State officials was held at Canberra in 1948. That conference made recommendations that all members will agree were fundamentally sound and showed its recognition of the seriousness of this problem. Once again, the action that followed bore little relation to the extensiveness of the recommendations. With those past experiences in mind, I submit that, if we agree, as I hope honorable members do agree, that this Parliament should act in this matter, we should consider more than the simple passing of another resolution or the initiating of another conference. We should consider starting a new era in which direct, positive and effective action is likely to be taken. . . . it is necessary to make a reappraisal of the role of this Parliament in the problem of native welfare and to give a lead in the formulation of a joint national programme.

There also seem to me to be other arguments why the Australian Government should make its voice heard in this matter. The Commonwealth Parliament is the custodian of the national reputation in the world at large. Our record of native administration will not stand scrutiny at the standard of our own professions, publicly made in the forum of the world, of a high concern for human welfare. We should be condemned out of our own mouths if those professions were measured by the standard of native administration accepted in Australia today. When we enter into international discussions, and raise our voice, as we should raise it, in defence of human rights and the protection of human welfare, our very words are mocked by the thousands of degraded and depressed people who crouch on rubbish heaps throughout the whole of this continent. Let us cleanse this stain from our forehead or we shall run the risk that ill-intentioned people will point to it with scorn. When we have done that we shall be able to stand with greater pride and more confidence before the world as a self-respecting nation. . . .

Before concluding I wish to refer to the work of the Christian missions in Australia. The 50 government institutions care for 9,300 natives and 54 Christian missions care for approximately the same number of natives. Government institutional staffs total 283 and mission staffs total 219. It is plain, therefore, that if it were not for the Christian missions Australia would be doing only half as much in respect of the welfare of the aborigines as it is now doing. In addition such voluntary organizations as the Flying Doctor Service also extend their benefits to aborigines. I realise that there are good missions and some missions that may not act as wisely as they might, but generally speaking all missions bring into the field of native administration a body of devoted and zealous workers whose zeal and sense of vocation cannot be, and never will be, matched by the ordinary methods of Public Service recruitment. Any government should accept with gratitude the services of so dedicated a body of people. Furthermore, the Christian missions enlist behind their efforts the support, interest and sympathy of the whole community.

The motion before the House attempts to cover the grounds that I have rapidly sketched in brief outline. In the first place it is based on two propositions which are as follows:—(a), that the Australian Government exercises a national responsibility for the welfare of the whole Australian people and therefore should co-operate with State governments in promoting the welfare of aborigines; and (b), measures of native welfare should be directed towards the social advancement as well as the protection of aborigines. The motion then goes on to say that co-operation should include additional provision of finance. It then asks that in order that effective administrative action may follow, the Government should prepare definite proposals to place before the State Premiers and thus accept the role of co-ordinator and energizer in matters relating to native administration. Finally, the motion lays down the principle that due regard be paid to the following:—(a), State administration of native affairs; and (b), co-operation with the Christian missions. It does not attempt to prescribe the methods that the various administrations should adopt. Any one who has had first-hand knowledge of the native problem will agree that the present conditions of the aborigines are so diverse, and the possibilities for their advancement are so dimly seen that the programme can best be worked out in relation to the day-to-day tasks of routine administration. We cannot hope for a sudden transformation or to hit upon a single plan that will transform the position overnight or that will immediately reform this great social evil. We know that discouragement will be encountered and that the response to various demands will be different from what we may hope for, and that in such circumstances this programme for the benefit of the aborigines will have to be worked out bit by bit and day by day over the course of several generations.

## 7.2    18 October 1951. Mr. Hasluck's report on the Native Welfare Conference.

(*Ibid.*, "The Native Welfare Conference", 1951, pp. 13-19.)

*A report on the Native Welfare Conference held in Canberra in September 1951, in which the Minister for Territories, Mr. Hasluck, speaks of segregation and assimilation.*

Mr. Speaker—I wish to inform the House of the results of the Native Welfare Conference held at Canberra on September 3rd and 4th. The purpose of this conference, which took place at the invitation of the Commonwealth Government, was to allow an exchange of information and a pooling of experience between those who are actively engaged in native administration in Australia, and to seek agreement among them on the objectives of native policy and the methods by which those objectives may best be served. The Governments of New South Wales, Queensland, South Australia and Western Australia accepted the invitation to attend. . . .

Before reviewing the conclusions of the Conference, however, I would ask Members to look back over the past century and a half in order that the present conference may be seen in its place in Australian history. Broadly speaking, the history of native administration in Australia falls into three periods.

Initially, there was a brief period, at the time of first settlement in the various Colonies, when the aboriginal inhabitants of this continent were regarded as having equality before the law with other British subjects and when the missionary purpose of bringing to them both civilisation and Christianity was uppermost in men's minds.

Then, after the inevitable clashes which followed the extension of settlement into tribal lands and after the discouraging failure of early attempts to convert and instruct the savage, there came a longer period when the aboriginal was regarded as being in a special class by himself, neither amenable to the law nor in practice able to enjoy the equality which had been accorded to him in British theory and Christian faith. Administration during this period was based on the idea of protecting the aborigines from the harmful effects of white settlement, either by placing them apart in reservations or by making special laws and regulations to control the natives themselves and the actions of the white man towards them. During this period, the attitudes of white Australians were shaped chiefly by the fact that the primitive aboriginal and the detribalised aboriginal, who had learnt only a smattering of European ways, did not follow the same habits of life as the rest of the community, were not restrained by the same beliefs and customs as the white people but had beliefs and customs of their own, and could not look after themselves and earn their own living in the normal way. Therefore, the white people took measures to protect the native people from injury and to supply their wants but did both on a lower scale than would have been thought fitting for the rest of the community.

During this period, there was considerable neglect of the aboriginal, due largely to the acceptance of the idea that his inevitable end was to live a low and primitive life until his race died out, and that, by his very nature, his own needs and consequently his rights, were less than those of other people. Our actions during this period were redeemed by acts of kindness and compassion but not by any faith or hope, nor did they offer to the aboriginal of the future any place in life more attractive than that of being the dumb object of pity until he died.

During the past half-century, however, this second period has been giving place to a third period in which the idea of protection yields to the idea of the advancement of social welfare of the natives in order that they may live the best life of which they are capable and that they may eventually find a fitting place as members of the Australian community.

This change has been taking shape slowly for at least half a century, and the conference recently held in Canberra is the culmination of the activities of many Australians, both official and private, who have been working for many years to bring about a new understanding of this great Australian social problem, and a clearer recognition of the claims of the aboriginal as an individual.

The recent conference was, in a sense, the inheritor of a conference of officials which was held at Canberra in 1937, following discussion at a Premiers' Conference, and of a further conference of Federal and State officials held at Canberra in 1948 as a consequence of a move initiated at the Premiers' Conference in 1947 by the Minister for Native Affairs in Western Australia. The special significance of the recent meeting is to be found in the fact that it was a conference of Ministers and that the scope of its discussions and its conclusions were wider in range and more definite in purpose than at the earlier meetings.

Because there is a good deal of misrepresentation, both inside Australia and overseas, on the subject of Australian treatment of native peoples, I should like to remind Honourable Members that the genesis of this move for the advancement of native peoples and the foundations of our policy are distinctively Australian. The foundations of our policy are two principles which Honourable Members on both sides of the House will recognise as abiding and treasured principles of our Australian life. The first one is the principle of equality of opportunity. All of us in this Chamber know Australia as the "land of opportunity," and as the land of "the fair go," and, having ourselves benefited from the rule that a man should be able to live the most useful life for which his capacity fits him, we will also share in the idea that these phrases and these ideas should have a single meaning for all who dwell within our borders. The second great and abiding Australian principle which our grandfathers and fathers valued and handed on to us was that, in this country, there should be no division into classes but that men should stand on their own worth. That, too, is a principle which leads to the logical conclusion that the coloured people who live in Australia should not be regarded as a class but as part of the general community whenever and as soon as their advancement in civilisation permits them to take their place on satisfactory terms as members of that community.

These two characteristic principles of Australian democracy are the foundation of Australian native policy and the justification of that policy. . . .

It will be seen that the two principles to which I have briefly referred relate in part to the rights of the individual and in part to the general well-being of the community. On the one hand, we in Australia want to give the chance of a happy and a useful life to all our people; on the other hand, we want to build a society in which there shall be no minorities or special classes and in which the benefits yielded by society shall be accessible to all. Such an Australian society will not be completed until its advantages cover, too, our aboriginal people.

While we state that as the ideal, however, we have to recognise that many years of slow, patient endeavour will be needed before the ideal can be realised. By various causes, large numbers of these people are not, in fact, in a condition today to enter into the full advantages of life in an Australian community. At the time of the coming of the white man these isolated beings were a primitive people, a people still living at a level of material culture similar to that of the Stone Age in Europe, and we cannot expect them to leap in one generation across a great valley of technical change through which the rest of mankind struggled slowly for thousands of years. Too frequently sympathisers with the aborigines or advocates of their cause are ignorant of or put aside the stark fact that large numbers of them are not at this moment capable of entering the general community at an acceptable level or of maintaining themselves in it. There are many coloured persons who have already learnt from the white man how to live acceptably after the manner of other Australians and are in fact doing so, but there are many more who by reason of ignorance and primitive habit certainly could not do so.

One fact that is too often overlooked is the wide diversity in their condition. At one end of the scale is the primitive tribesman, a nomad who wanders naked in his tribal territory, hunting and gathering food, wholly bound by tribal custom and belief. Ascending the scale will be found people in all stages of contact with civilisation and of progress in education.

We can declare the same ideal for all of them but, if we are to be realistic, we will recognise that the rate of progress towards the attainment of that ideal will be very slow for many of them, that their immediate needs vary greatly according to their present condition and that the methods by which their interests will be best served must change from group to group and from period to period.

The recent Native Welfare Conference agreed that assimilation is the objective of native welfare measures. Assimilation means, in practical terms, that, in the course of time, it is expected that all persons of aboriginal blood or mixed blood in Australia will live like white Australians do. The acceptance of this policy governs all other aspects of native affairs administration.

Seeing that the policy of assimilation determines the shape of other administrative measures, it calls for close scrutiny. What are the other possible courses open to us? One alternative to a policy of assimilation is a policy of complete segregation of natives under conditions lower than those of the rest of the community. In examining this alternative, the first point to be recognised is that contact between the natives and the white people has now gone so far that in no part of this continent are we dealing with a virgin problem and more than two-thirds of the natives are either detribalised or well on the way to losing their tribal life. In spite of the creation of large aboriginal reserves for the primitive tribes in the North and Central Australia, contact with the remaining third is bound to increase at the volition of the natives as well as through the activities of the missionary, anthropologist and official. Even if we wished to place the remnant of tribal natives into some sort of anthropological zoo in the isolated corners of the continent, it is extremely doubtful whether we could arrest the curiosity that is daily extending their knowledge of white ways.

The second point—and I make this without apology either to the cynics or the scientists—is that the blessings of civilisation are worth having. For many years past, people have been rather nervous of using phrases about carrying the blessings of civilisation to the savage for fear that they might be accused of cant and humbug. The world today, however, is coming around again to the idea that inevitable change can be made a change for the better. We recognise now that the noble savage can benefit from measures taken to improve his health and his nutrition, to teach him better cultivation, and to lead him in civilised ways of life. We know that culture is not static but that it either changes or dies. We know that the idea of progress, once so easily derided, has the germ of truth in it. Assimilation does not mean the suppression of the aboriginal culture but rather that, for generation after generation, cultural adjustment will take place. The native people will grow into the society in which, by force of history they are bound to live.

The third point is that the large body of natives who are already losing grip on their tribal life or have lost it altogether will be left spiritually as well as materially dispossessed unless something satisfying is put in the place of their lost tribal custom.

Thus, segregation at a lower level of civilisation than the rest of the community is out of the question for two-thirds of the coloured people and would be of only negative value and possibly of temporary duration for the remainder of their race.

Another alternative is segregation on standards which, in the course of time, may improve to a stage similar to that of the rest of the community. Such segregation could take place in settlements and missions solely occupied by natives. The objection to this policy is that, if it succeeds, we will build up in Australia an ever-increasing body of people who belong to a separate caste, and who live in Australia but are not members of the Australian community. We will create a series of minority groups living in little bits of territory on their own. The more the method succeeds, the more awkward it will be, for it will result in the very situation in Australia which we have always sought to avoid, namely, the existence of a separate racial group living on its own. In pursuit of a policy of assimilation, the settlement and the mission station can be used for the advancement of the native peoples and as a refuge for those of them who need protection during a transitional period. Some of those who cannot complete the transition may live and die on settlements, but those who have the strength and capacity to develop their abilities more fully should have freedom to enter into a larger life in the general community.

This leads us to the major argument for a policy of assimilation. It is a policy of opportunity. It gives to the aboriginal and to the person of mixed blood a chance to shape his own life. If he succeeds, it places no limit on his success but opens the door fully. Segregation of any kind opens the door into a peculiar and separate world for coloured people only.

I propose to lay on the table a report of the proceedings of the Native Welfare Conference, so I will not recapitulate the various decisions here.

The final decision of the Conference was to create a Native Welfare Council composed of the Ministers in the Commonwealth and State Governments who are concerned with native welfare.

Out of the discussions of this Council, we hope to see emerge practical and effective proposals for nation-wide action. The executive responsibility in native affairs remains with each of the Governments in respect of its own territory. The Council represents a bid for a better native policy and a bid for closer Federal-State co-operation and mutual assistance to that end. . . . I feel that I can express to honourable members the common thought of those who took part in the discussions. We have set ourselves a humane task; we have founded our resolve on a faith in the capacity of human beings; we have shaped our plan on the best traditions of democratic life in Australia. We want all those who are trying to build a better Australia to join with us in this effort. We want to make sure that every one living in our country will be able to have a happy and a useful life— a life worthy of a human being.


## 7.3  1961. A Select Committee's recommended changes to the existing law regarding the voting rights of Aborigines.

(*Commonwealth Parliamentary Papers, op. cit.*, 1961, Vol. 2, "Report from the Select Committee on the Voting Rights of Aborigines", pp. 1-5.)

1. On the 18th April, 1961, upon the motion of Mr. Freeth (Minister for the Interior), the House of Representatives resolved—
That a Select Committee be appointed to inquire into and report on—
(*a*) whether the entitlement to enrolment and the right to vote presently conferred by the *Commonwealth Electoral Act* 1918-1953 on persons referred to in section 39 of that Act should be extended with or without qualifications, restrictions or conditions to—
(i) all aboriginal natives of Australia, or
(ii) aboriginal natives of Australia included in particular classes, and, if so, what classes;
and, if so,
(*b*) the modifications, if any, that should be made to the provisions of that Act relating to enrolment or voting to provide for enrolment and voting by aboriginal natives or any particular classes of aboriginal natives. . . .

4. The aboriginal people are increasing in numbers. Changes have occurred in the customs of the great majority which ensure, in the words of one of our witnesses, "that they will never tend to die out again". Their children are numerous and healthy right across the north of this continent. Education in hygiene is reducing the incidence of disease, and prolonging life, while the birthrate is rising and marriage is tending to be influenced by Christian concepts. Unlike traditional aboriginal marriage it is becoming in more and more cases a partnership between young people of no great disparity of age. The aboriginal people are a permanent part of the Australian community. This makes imperative the recognition of their proper status, and the planning of their integration into the Australian community. Your Committee, while limited by its terms of reference to the franchise, recognizes that the franchise alone is not enough. It hopes that the exercise of the franchise by aboriginal people will lead to policies which meet their needs.

5. Somewhat differently placed are the Torres Strait Islanders. They are a concentrated population. They are not nomadic. They have a high percentage of literacy. The increase in their numbers may give the islands a local problem of over-population. They do not at present possess the Commonwealth franchise, except for ex-members of the Torres Strait Islands Regiment, most of whom appeared to be unaware of their entitlement until your Committee's visit. They are not ethnically related to the Australian aboriginal people, nor is their language similar to that of any aboriginal tribe. They do not feel themselves to be part of any aboriginal community.

6. As well as persons who are fully of aboriginal descent or who are Torres Strait Islanders, there are people of mixed European and aboriginal descent not enfranchised. Many of these have been entitled to the Commonwealth franchise since a definition was set out in a memorandum of the Attorney-General's Department of 25th January, 1929. (*See* paragraph 33.)

7. The declared policy of the Commonwealth Government towards the aboriginal people is that they should be gradually integrated into the European community.

8. Over the past five years the majority of the remaining nomads have, of their own volition, come to the settlements and missions scattered throughout the Commonwealth and your Committee considers that there are now fewer than 2,000 aborigines living in their traditional tribal cultures, out of contact with European civilization.

9. As the nomadic aboriginal adults are moving to the settlements and missions, gradually renouncing their nomadic and semi-nomadic lives, their children attend school where their integration commences.

10. It was demonstrated to your Committee that any policy other than integration of the aboriginal people into one Australian society would be impracticable.

11. Your Committee believes that integration does not necessarily mean the loss of aboriginal tribal culture or a division in tribal relationships but, however desirable it may be in theory to endeavour to preserve the tribal form of society, it is abundantly clear to your Committee that the tribes themselves are making continuing voluntary contact with European civilization and that in the course of a few years, there will be no aborigines living in the completely tribal state.

12. As a situation of complete integration is inevitable, your Committee considers that the aim of the Commonwealth should be to assist integration to continue as smoothly and speedily as possible.

13. The aborigines need a considerable capital investment in education,

including technical and agricultural education, in industries, land tenure and housing.

14. Your Committee found that the period between the ages of 14 and 21 is a difficult one during which more needs to be done for the aboriginal youth and suggests that every effort should be made by the Commonwealth Government to ensure that free secondary and technical education is readily available to all aboriginal children in all States of the Commonwealth, and assistance towards social integration between schooling and employment, in order, amongst other things, to prepare them for the franchise.

15. In respect of housing, it appears to your Committee that it is beyond the resources of the States and the Northern Territory to house satisfactorily even a small percentage of their aboriginal populations and it is suggested that the Commonwealth Government give deep and sympathetic consideration to this major aspect of integration, for purposes of stability of domicile.

16. Your Committee received evidence which indicated that many people believed that the Commonwealth Government should assume full responsibility for the welfare of all people of the aboriginal race. Others considered that Commonwealth assistance to the States for aborigines should be more generous. Your Committee draws the attention of the Government to these matters for its earnest consideration. . . .

THE STATUS OF THE AUSTRALIAN ABORIGINAL PEOPLE

22. In the early history of European settlement in Australia there were sometimes conflicts between the Colonial Office and the local Colonial authorities and settlers concerning the status of aborigines as subjects of the Crown of the United Kingdom. These conflicts clarified the position of the aborigines as British subjects, although, because of their ignorance of the laws and customs of the settlers, they were never able to derive much protection from that status. At Federation there was no doubt of their status as subjects of the Queen and some were on the rolls of Victoria and South Australia.

23. The Constitution clearly envisages the people of the Commonwealth as being "Subjects of the Queen, resident in any State". The meaning of the expression "people of the Commonwealth" would doubtless be today "natural born or naturalized subjects of the Queen permanently residing within the limits of the Commonwealth of Australia". The franchise to elect members of the Senate and the House of Representatives in the Commonwealth of Australia is one expression of the rights of subjects of the Queen, permanently residing within the limits of the Commonwealth of Australia, in the case of the House of Representatives, and the right of "subjects of the Queen permanently residing in any State", in the case of the Senate.

24. The people of the Australian aboriginal race, notwithstanding the implications of the wording of a Statute of one State, are all, without question, natural born subjects of the Queen, permanently resident within the limits of the Commonwealth of Australia. . . .

THE LAW OF THE COMMONWEALTH OF AUSTRALIA.

32. The Commonwealth Electoral Act was amended subsequent to the appointment of your Committee and the relevant sub-section of Section 39 of the *Commonwealth Electoral Act* 1918-1961 relating to the Australian aboriginal people now reads as follows:—

"(6.) An aboriginal native of Australia is not entitled to enrolment under Part VII. unless he—
    (a) is entitled under the law of the State in which he resides to be enrolled as an elector of that State and, upon enrolment, to vote at elections for the more numerous House of the Parliament of that State, if there is only one House of the Parliament of that State, for that House; or
    (b) is or has been a member of the Defence Force.".

33. A definition of "aboriginal native", for Commonwealth electoral purposes (and in respect of Section 127 of the Constitution), was provided by the Attorney-General's Department to the Chief Electoral Officer by memorandum dated 25th January, 1929, and it is this definition which is still used by the Commonwealth Electoral Office. An "aboriginal native" is defined as a person in whom aboriginal descent preponderates and "that half-castes were not 'aboriginal natives' within the meaning of Section 127 of the Constitution".

34. Your Committee by applying this definition, has established the fact that thousands of such people in Queensland and Western Australia, who are already integrated into the community and are not living in the tribal state, have the right to be enrolled and to vote at Commonwealth elections but are unaware of the fact. . . .

## RECOMMENDATIONS.

41. Your Committee recommends in respect of the existing law of the Commonwealth—

(1) That, because the aboriginal people in New South Wales and Victoria have long been integrated into the Australian community, early administrative action be taken so that the compulsory provisions of the Commonwealth Electoral Act relating to enrolment and voting be applied to them.

(2) That wherever it is relevant for the Commonwealth Electoral Office to act upon the definition of an Australian aboriginal, that definition should be that which is the practice in the Northern Territory, namely, a person entirely of aboriginal descent.

(3) That early action be taken by the Commonwealth Electoral Office to inform aboriginal and Torres Strait Islander servicemen and ex-servicemen, and people entitled to the franchise under the terms of the Attorney-General's memorandum to the Commonwealth Electoral Officer of 25th January, 1929, of their entitlement to be enrolled and to vote.

## 7.4 1962-1967. South Australian legislation on Aboriginal reserves and institutions, treatment of diseases, and employment.

(*South Australian Statues*, Adelaide, 1962, No. 45 Elizabethae ii Reginae, "Aboriginal Affairs Act", pp. 134-146.)

## RESERVES AND INSTITUTIONS

18. The Governor may by proclamation-
   (a) declare any crown lands to be reserved for Aborigines;
   (b) alter the boundaries of any reserve;
   (c) with the consent of the owner declare any other lands to be a reserve for Aborigines. . . .

20. (1) In order to promote the welfare or facilitate the training of Aborigines, the Minister may refuse the entry of any Aboriginal or group of Aborigines into an institution.

(2) If any Aboriginal or person of Aboriginal blood agrees to enter or remain within an institution with the approval of the Minister for purposes of training, the Minister may declare a trainee.

(3) An Aboriginal who enters an institution after a refusal of entry by the Minister, and any trainee declared under subsection (2) of this section who refuses to remain within an institution until he completes his training to the satisfaction of the Minister, shall be guilty of an offence.

(4) No Aboriginal shall be kept within the boundaries of an Aboriginal institution or removed from any such institution without the consent of the governing body of the institution concerned. . . .

PROVISIONS FOR THE TREATMENT OF CONTAGIOUS OR INFECTIOUS DISEASES.
25. (1) The board may, by notice in writing, authorize any legally qualified medical practitioner therein named to medically examine any Aboriginal.

(2) Such notice shall be sufficient authority to the practitioner to enter any premises where such an Aboriginal is, or is suspected to be and to medically examine such Aboriginal in such manner as the practitioner deems necessary.

(3) If the practitioner on such an examination finds that the Aboriginal is suffering from a contagious disease he may order the Aboriginal to undergo such treatment in any hospital or otherwise as he may direct.

(4) Such order shall be sufficient authority for any officer of the department or any member or the police force to take such action as will enable a legally qualified medical practitioner to treat such Aboriginal until such practitioner shall discharge him.

(5) It shall be the duty of such practitioner, when in his opinion the Aboriginal is free from such contagious or infectious disease to report the fact to the board.

(6) Any Aboriginal who refuses to be examined or to be treated after order made as aforesaid, or who attempts to avoid treatment as aforesaid, shall be guilty of an offence against this Act.

EMPLOYMENT OF ABORIGINALS.
26. Every person shall allow any member of the board, officer of the department, or member of the police force to have access to any Aboriginal employed by such person, and to enter any house, vessel, boat or premises where such Aboriginal is or is employed, at all reasonable times, for the purposes of inspection and inquiry.

## 7.5    12 July 1963. The Policy of Assimilation.

(*Commonwealth Parliamentary Papers*, Vol. iii, 1962-1963, "Aboriginal Welfare, Conference of Commonwealth and State Ministers, Darwin, July 1963", p. 651.)

*The Statement of Policy issued by a conference of Commonwealth and State ministers about Aboriginal welfare, in which the ministers spell out "The Meaning of the Policy of Assimilation".*

Conference of Commonwealth and State Ministers held in Darwin, on 11th and 12th July, 1963, on Aboriginal Welfare.
STATEMENT OF POLICY
*The Meaning of the Policy of Assimilation.*
The policy of assimilation means that all Aborigines and part-Aborigines will attain the same manner of living as other Australians and live as members of a single Australian community enjoying the same rights and privileges, accepting the same responsibilities, observing the same customs and influenced by the same beliefs, hopes and loyalties as other Australians. Any special measures taken for Aborigines and part-Aborigines are regarded

as temporary measures, not based on race, but intended to meet their need for special care and assistance to protect them from any ill effects of sudden change and to assist them to make the transition from one stage to another in such a way as will be favourable to their social, economic and political advancement.

In making this statement attention should be drawn to the rather loose use of the term "citizenship" in reference to the status of Aborigines who are excluded from provisions of special State and Territory statutes and to their assimilation into the community.

Australian Aborigines are Australian citizens by virtue of the *Nationality and Citizenship Act* 1948-1960. In most States and Territories there is specific legislation designed to promote their welfare and afford them special assistance, but such statutes can in no sense derogate from their citizenship in the sense of their status as Australian citizens. The Commonwealth and State Governments are working actively for their social, economic and political advancement so that the need for special legislation will disappear.

*Methods of Advancing the Policy—*

(i) Extension, where applicable, of Government settlement work to encourage nomadic and semi-nomadic Aborigines to adopt a more settled way of life and to make health services, better standards of housing and nutrition, schooling, vocational training and occupation available to them and their children, to enable their progressive advancement.

(ii) Provision of health services including particularly child welfare services.

(iii) Provision of education at all levels, to the greatest extent possible, in the same educational institutions as are available to other Australians and, in addition where necessary, in special primary and pre-schools for Aboriginal and part-Aboriginal children.

(iv) Continual improvement in housing and hygiene standards on Government settlements, missions, rural properties, and in towns and assistance towards provision of and training in the use of improved housing facilities particularly in town areas.

(v) Vocational training (including apprenticeships) and employment, particularly in ways which will assist Aborigines and part-Aborigines to make a contribution to the advancement of their own people—teaching assistants, nursing and medical assistants, patrol officers, welfare officers, &c.

(vi) Encouragement of social and sporting activity both among Aborigines and part-Aborigines and participation by them in general community activity.

(vii) Extension of welfare work, particularly to assist those people living in or near towns to adjust themselves to the life of the community.

(viii) Welfare services provided for other members of the community to be available to Aborigines and part-Aborigines (child, family and social welfare services).

(ix) The further removal of restrictive or protective legislation.

(x) Positive steps to ensure awareness in the community that implementation of the policy of assimilation is possible only if Aborigines and part-Aborigines are accepted into the community and that the community plays its full part.

(xi) Further research into special problems associated with the Aboriginal welfare programme.

It is recognized that some of these methods may not be applicable in every State of the Commonwealth and that methods may vary from State to State.

## 7.6 1963. Petition of the Yirrkala people.

(*Commonwealth Parliamentary Papers, op cit.*, Vol. iv, 1962-1963, "Select Committee on the Grievances of Yirrkala Aborigines, Arnhem Land Reserve, p. 952.)

*Following the excision of some* 140 *square miles of their Reserve area, the Yirrkala people petitioned Federal parliamentarians.*

TO THE HONOURABLE THE SPEAKER AND MEMBERS OF THE HOUSE OF REPRESENTATIVES IN PARLIAMENT ASSEMBLED
*The Humble Petition of the Undersigned aboriginal people of Yirrkala, being members of the Balamumu, Narrkala, Gapiny and Miliwurrwurr people and Djapu, Mangalili, Madarrpa, Magarrwanalinirri, Gumaitj, Djambarrpuynu, Marrakula, Galpu, Dhaluayu, Wangurri, Warramirri, Maymil, Rirritjinu tribes, respectfully sheweth—*
1. That nearly 500 people of the tribes are residents of the land excised from the Aboriginal Reserve in Arnhem Land.
2. That the procedures of the excision of this land and the fate of the people on it were never explained to them beforehand, and were kept secret from them.
3. That when Welfare Officers and Government officials came to inform them of decisions taken without them and against them, they did not undertake to convey to the Government in Canberra the views and feelings of the Yirrkala aboriginal people.
4. That land in question has been hunting and food gathering land for the Yirrkala tribes from time immemorial; we were all born here.
5. That places sacred to the Yirrkala people, as well as vital to their livelihood are in the excised land, especially Melville Bay.
6. That the people of this area fear that their needs and interests will be completely ignored as they have been ignored in the past, and they fear that the fate which has overtaken the Larrakeah tribe will overtake them.
7. And they humbly pray that the Honourable the House of Representatives will appoint a Committee, accompanied by competent interpreters, to hear the views of the Yirrkala people before permitting the excision of this land.
8. They humbly pray that no arrangements be entered into with any company which will destroy the livelihood and independence of the Yirrkala people.
And your petitioners as in duty bound will ever pray God to help you and us.

(*English translation*)
Certified as a correct translation. Kim E. Beazley

## 7.7 1963. Commonwealth policy on Aboriginal reserves.

(*Ibid.*, p. 957.)

*The Commonwealth's policy concerning the utilization of proclaimed Aboriginal reserves, by those prospecting for minerals. Special reference is made to the Arnhem Land Reserve.*

RESUMPTION OF PORTIONS OF THE ARNHEM LAND RESERVE
25. During the 1920's and 1930's, the general public was becoming interested in aboriginal affairs, and many bodies pressed for the reservation

of large areas as sanctuaries for nomadic tribes, particularly in the south-west of the Northern Territory and in Arnhem Land.

26. Having proclaimed the Arnhem Land Reserve, the Government considered that the fact that the Aboriginals Ordinance (forerunner of the Welfare Ordinance) provided that persons should not enter reserves without permission, indicated that it was the intention of the Ordinance to ensure that reserves should be used solely by Aborigines.

27. It was not intended that the lands included in the reserve should be handed over absolutely to the Aborigines, and that, if a payable gold or mineral field were discovered in a reserve, such a field should be worked and the area withdrawn from the reserve. It was suggested that any valuable discovery of gold or other mineral substance made within the boundaries of an aboriginal reserve should carry an obligation to pay the Crown a specified amount by way of royalty or other charge and that any such moneys should be utilized for the benefit of Aborigines.

28. Nevertheless, reserves were proclaimed for the express purpose of providing the Aborigines with adequate land to meet their hunting and other requirements in order to preserve the aboriginal race. If the area of these reserves was to be reduced by allowing portions to be withdrawn from time to time for developmental purposes, the object of the reservation would be defeated.

29. It was considered that the large area left unreserved should have been ample to enable development to proceed, at any rate for a number of years to come, without encroaching on the small reserved area, and that therefore, before any encroachment was made upon the aboriginal reserves, the possibilities of developing the unreserved areas should be exhausted.

30. The fact that although permits had been granted on many occasions in the past for large prospecting parties to enter reserves, but that no important mining discovery had been made in the reserved area, was also taken into consideration.

31. In 1948 the Minister for the Interior approved the resumption of Truant Island, lying 30 miles south-east of Cumberland Strait in the Wessel Islands, for uses as a pearling base, in order that pearlers could make full use of the pearling season without the necessity for taking their luggers on the long trips back to Darwin to refuel and re-supply. Truant Island was chosen as the most suitable spot as it was not occupied by any Aborigines and its isolated position rendered visits by Aborigines from neighbouring islands or the mainland very difficult.

32. The present thinking in regard to aboriginal reserves is summed up in the statement made by the Minister for Territories (Mr. Hasluck) on the 6th August, 1952—

"A policy of assimilation and the measures taken for the education and care of natives means that less dependence is placed on reserves as an instrument of policy than was placed on them in the days when it was considered that the interests of the natives could only be served by keeping them away from white settlement."

33. That part of the Arnhem Land Reserve which had been revoked from the Coburg Peninsula Flora and Fauna Reserve and added to the Arnhem Land Reserve in 1940, was resumed in 1962. The balance of the Flora and Fauna Reserve was also resumed and a new Flora and Fauna Reserve, consisting of these two parts, was created.

34. On the 13th March, 1963, an area of 140 square miles was excised from the Arnhem Land Reserve on the Gove Peninsula. This area had been prospected for a number of years and it had been established that there were vast deposits of bauxite there. The Government's policy of assimilation assumed that the development of reserves should take place, provided that the Aborigines shared in the benefits of the development. Cabinet had decided in 1952 that prospective miners on reserves would have to

put up a very strong case, and also show that no injury would be suffered by the Aborigines, before they would be allowed to enter on the reserve.

35. Where the Administrator of the Northern Territory considers that parts of a reserve should be resumed for mining purposes, he must forward to the Governor-General, with his recommendation, a statement setting forth the effect of the resumption on the welfare of Aborgines in the reserve.

36. The statement in respect of the excision from the Gove Peninsula was as follows:—

"The object of revocation of the part of Arnhem Land Reserve recommended to His Excellency the Governor-General in Council is to permit large scale bauxite mining operations in the area.

The area to be revoked constitutes a small portion (140 square miles) of the total area of the Reserve which is over 35,000 square miles.

The revocation will not adversely affect aboriginal wards resident within the area and their rights and needs are adequately protected and catered for. Specific proposals have been made in this regard and they will be adopted as the development of mining activities shows the need for them.

The mining operations will offer training and employment opportunities for wards in the area, which would not otherwise be forthcoming and will contribute towards their assimilation in the Australian community."

## 7.8  8 April 1964. Mr. Beazley comments.

(*Commonwealth of Australia Parliamentary Debates*, House of Representatives, 25 February to 16 April, 1964, Vol. H. of R. 41, pp. 1-1226. "Questions, Aborigines", 8 April, 1964, pp. 821-822.)

*Mr. Beazley speaks of the new moves to grant Aborigines equal drinking and other privileges without immediate consideration of the inequality of wages.*

Mr. SPEAKER (Hon. Sir John McLeay).—I have received a letter from the honorable member for Fremantle (Mr. Beazley) proposing that a definite matter of public importance be submitted to the House for discussion, namely:—

The need for all Commonwealth instrumentalities including the armed services, to pay aborigines employed by them a wage at least equivalent to the award rate as fixed by the Arbitration Commission for a worker similarly employed who is covered by awards; the need for the extension of the protection of Arbitration Commission awards to aborigines employed privately in the Northern Territory; the need for unemployment, sickness and tuberculosis benefits to be paid to aborigines in the Northern Territory at the same rate as for other citizens and to be as readily available to them.

·        ·        ·

Mr. BEAZLEY (Fremantle).—Articles have appeared in the press on the proposals that were presented to the Legislative Council for the Northern Territory by the Director of Welfare, Mr. Giese. He introduced a battery of legislation, which was summed up by the Melbourne "Age" in these words—

'The sweeping legislation introduced in the Northern Territory Legislative Council by the Director of Welfare (Mr. Giese) on Wednesday abolishes the concept of protective wardship for the majority of the Territory's 18,000 full-blood aborigines and would end at a stroke social and legal restrictions which have been represented for years as valuable and necessary.'

When we have examined the proposals that have been put before the Legislative Council for the Northern Territory, we have been disturbed to see that the question of the wages paid to aborigines has been deferred to some undefined date in the future. We feel that on wages turns the question of eligibility for certain social services at European rates, such as the unemployment benefit and the tuberculosis allowance. The select committee on the grievances of Yirrkala aborigines found that no aboriginal in the Northern Territory receives the unemployment benefit and that tuberculosis allowance at the rate of £1 a week is paid to aborigines who, if they were Europeans, would receive the allowance at the rate of some £12 a week.

Adequate wages confer freedom of movement, as distinct from theoretical freedom of movement, and social freedoms which in practice do not exist without an adequate income. The Government, through its officers in the Legislative Council, is sweeping away what might be called paternalistic legislation, but the ability of aborigines to dispense with paternal protection depends on their ability to support themselves with adequate wages. The legislation does not yet touch wages. While aborigines receive inadequate wages the final impression given by the policy being pursued in the Northern Territory is that it ends up only with the prospects of ill-health, poverty and degradation. . . . Of something like 5,000 aborigines in the Northern Territory, only about 50 receive award rates of a European standard. The Commonwealth itself is employing aborigines in a civil capacity in the armed forces at much less than award rates. It is also employing aborigines on settlements at less than award rates. For instance, when I was at Maningrida a tractor driver, whom I admit receives his keep, was being paid £3 10s. a week for his services. No aboriginal in the Northern Territory receives unemployment benefit although many are palpably un-employed.

The changes being proposed in the Legislative Council are many. . . . The dramatic items that have been highlighted in the press are, first, that aborigines may drink alcohol and enter hotel bars; secondly, in native settlements drink will be made available under supervision; thirdly, aborigines may cohabit with Europeans without marrying them. The whole assumption underlying this in the speech of the Director of Welfare was, of course, that European men will have access to aboriginal women without marrying them, not vice versa. The fourth proposal is a touching little one which provides that aborigines may buy methylated spirits provided an unpalatable additive goes into the fluid. It was indicated that something would be done in future about wages but it seemed to relate only to wards' awards. . . .

Everyone may have an opinion about priority of need. I believe that these proposed priorities are wrong. Aborigines need access to the Arbitration Commission before they need access to the bar and the brothel. Those who have lost their tribal life clearly need a standard of living long before they need methylated spirits, the right of promiscuous intercourse, the freedom to be prostitutes for white men or the right to enter a bar. We are seeing in Western Australia, where legislation concerning wages is defective, how some of these things are working out. The press has been full of reports about aborigines being paid in cheap wine. On the streets in certain sections of Perth we see today aboriginal women, who obviously come from homes with no income, standing around waiting to be picked up by affluent white men in cars.

The assumption underlying these priorities that have have been sub-mitted to the Legislative Council of the Northern Territory is that aborigines want the dregs of our civilization before they want what belongs to their dignity. If this is, in fact, the priority of values which has been allowed to develop among them, then we will be disgraced before God and mankind. I do not know what thinking emanating from the Department of Territories devised these priorities but it seems to be a defective concept that liberty and depravity are synonymous. Vital aspects of real liberty are being ignored.

## 7.9  29 July 1965. "Aborigines on Stations."

(*The Sun*, Melbourne, 29 July 1965, p. 32.)

There are 50 Europeans on the property, 10 families and 159 working aboriginals.

The chief aboriginal is a tall, stately-looking man called King Brumby and he wears a plate about his neck.

King Brumby, though, has a rival—Jabiru.

Recently Jabiru went for citizenship papers and he received some how-to-vote papers.

Jabiru sensed that they were very important and asked Mr Millar to lock them in the safe.

Thereafter he answered not to Jabiru but to "Mr White."

King Brumby was furious. He called Jabiru "that civilised b——."

To restore King Brumby's loss of face Mr Millar had to do something fast.

He gave him a letter of introduction to his daughter in Melbourne, also to be locked in the safe.

That taught the "civilised b——" a thing or two.

## 7.10  29 September 1966. "Aboriginal Settlement at Lake Tyers."

(*Ibid.*, 28 September 1966, p. 1.)

Marion Carter, 3, seems to be enjoying her bath at Lake Tyers settlement. But the bath is a cut-down 44-gallon drum, and the family's clothes had been washed in it before Marion stepped in.

Professor Donald Thomson, Professor of Anthropology at Melbourne University, on Monday described conditions at Lake Tyers as "grim and heartbreaking."

## 7.11  20 June 1967. "Poverty among Aborigines of the Murray Valley."

(*The Sun, op. cit.,* 20 June 1967, p. 8.)

In the Murray Valley, a place of lush, rich orange groves and vineyards, there are two sets of values.

One is on the surface: The wealth of the area and its beauty—both obvious.

But there are also other values—not as obvious, but real just the same. And they deal with poverty.

Poverty, in a very real and tragic sense, stalks coldly through the whole of the Murray Valley.

You see it everywhere: from the pathetic little collection of huts across the river from Swan Hill to the aboriginal settlement of Manatunga, about half a mile out of Robinvale where the aboriginals walk aimlessly around because there is no work for them, and not the slightest prospect of work.

Everybody—from the Aborigines Welfare Board to the Aborigines Advancement League and local welfare workers—admits the Murray Valley is an economically depressed area for unskilled workers.

And the aboriginals, because of lack of education and perhaps bad treatment, are about the most unskilled of the lot.

The only work is seasonal, fruit-picking and grape-picking. And right now, when the leaves on the vines are golden and ready to drop, there is NO work available.

At least 200 aboriginals live around Robinvale—100 in the Rumbalara-style settlement, Manatunga, the rest in humpies.

One welfare worker told me the situation was "tinder dry" and likely to get worse if something couldn't be done to provide employment.

"They are crying out for houses and work," he said.

"One family living by the river in a humpy has been after a house for 16 years, but the board hasn't done anything."

But it is not until you drive the 14 miles into NSW from Mildura to Dareton that the real disgrace of the situation hits you.

Pastor Doug Nicholls told me he thought Dareton was "a national disgrace—something that should be on our conscience."

The settlement has been there for at least 35 years, and no improvements have been made in that time.

There is no water, there are no toilets, no houses—just tin and chicken-wire

For drinking water, the people walk more than a mile with buckets to the house of a local farmer who lets them use his rainwater tank.

The people who live there are friendly, kind and gentle (the local police, who have an excellent relationship with them, say the only trouble is the occasional drunk, who remains polite to the last), but they are beaten, depressed, apathetic.

But not the younger ones. They go to school in Dareton, see the houses in the cool tree-lined streets of the towns, and then go home to their rubbish tip, the dirt, flies and beds on the floor.

THEY are ashamed. And pretty soon, unless something is done, THEY will be beaten, depressed and apathetic—because at present they face the same circumstances that beat their parents. . . .

Janette —— 16, faces this daily contrast between her "home" and the town.

She lives with her parents and five brothers and sisters in a tin one-room humpy. She sleeps with her two sisters in the back of a rusty, abandoned car.

Janette works in Dareton at the Save the Children Fund's local headquarters, where she looks after other similar, but younger children.

Janette left school last year after finishing sixth grade. Her mother accepts the blame for her poor school record.

"She missed a lot of school," Mrs. —— said.

"When the irrigation channels are dry there's nowhere to wash the clothes . . ."

She added sadly: "It doesn't look good to send them to school looking dirty."

Janette also missed school because when the fruit season is over, her parents often move to Pooncarie, on the Darling River, trying to make money trapping rabbits.

And school doesn't really matter when you don't know where your next meal is coming from.

It was impossible to talk to Janette. She was embarrassed and ashamed, and talking only made it worse.

Although Dareton is in NSW it is largely Victorian in many ways—and the Victorian Aborigines Welfare Board seems to have shown more interest in it than its NSW counterpart.

The chairman of the board, Mr. J. H. Davey, went to Dareton five years ago at the invitation of a Save the Children Fund officer in Mildura.

What he saw revolted him.

"I wrote a stinking report to the NSW department," he said yesterday. "They didn't even have the courtesy to acknowledge it."

In Swan Hill, a hard-working committee is trying to make up for what its members say is the board's "neglect" of aboriginal problems in housing, education and employment.

### 7.12 30 April 1968. A Parliamentary question on "Black Power".

(*Commonwealth Parliamentary Debates, op. cit.*, Vol. H of R 58, pp. 1-1108, "Questions", 30 April 1968, p. 886.)

*Mr. Jarman addresses to Mr. Wentworth, the Minister for Social Services and Aboriginal Affairs, a question dealing with the likelihood of "Black Power" becoming established in Australia.*

Mr. JARMAN—I address my question to the Minister for Social Services and Minister in Charge of Aboriginal Affairs. Has the Minister seen the reported statement made at a memorial service to Dr. Martin Luther King in Sydney recently that 'black power' was a possibility in the future of Australia? How seriously does he view the possibility of future unrest of a potentially violent nature amongst the Aboriginal population? Is he aware of the existence of any organised attempt to create such unrest?

Mr. WENTWORTH—I have seen the statement to which he has referred. In my view there is no reasonable possibility of 'black power,' so to speak, arising in Australia. However, I am aware of the disruptive attempts of certain people to create differences of opinion and outlook between our Aboriginal people and the people of white descent. I deplore these efforts. I deplore entirely the efforts of certain people to create in Australia, as they have succeeded in creating in the United States, differences that could lead to violence. I do not believe that these efforts will succeed here. I assure the honourable member and the House that the Government will do everything in its power to provide for the advancement of our Aboriginal people, to ensure that they receive justice in every way and to prevent the emergence of conditions that could be used as an excuse for creating differences in the Australian community. The Government regards the Aboriginals as Australians in the same sense as all other Australian citizens.

### 7.13 9 August 1968. Mr. P. J. Nixon's statement.

(*Ibid.*, Vol. H of R 60, 1968, pp. 1-1907, 13 August to 10 October 1968, "Ministerial Statement, P. J. Nixon", 9 August, quoted 13 August 1968, p. 22.)

*Statement by the Minister for the Interior, Mr. P. J. Nixon, M.P., urging that the question of land rights be considered in a wider context than the emotional plane on which it is frequently presented.*

### NORTHERN TERRITORY—ABORIGINAL LAND RIGHTS
The Government is in favour of Aboriginals gaining title to land but believes that this should be under the land tenure system which applies to the rest

of the community and under conditions which will give them real prospects of improving their position in life.

The Government's aim is to ensure in the most effective way possible that all of the opportunities which the Australian community offers for a full and satisfying life are open to every Aboriginal and that all Aboriginals are equipped to take advanatge of those opportunities in the way which most appeals to them.

Singling out the issue of land rights and pressing for areas of land to be granted to groups of Aboriginals in remote places would not serve this purpose. On the contrary we could end up with a series of depressed Aboriginal communities tied to a form of sub-standard living with a barrier between them and the rest of the Australian community. Separatism and segregation of Aboriginals would create here problems now being faced in other countries.

The Aboriginals in the Northern Territory are not deprived of land rights. A substantial part of the Territory—nearly one-fifth—had been set aside by reservation for the use and enjoyment of Aboriginals. Government efforts are being concentrated on the best way of establishing Aborigines on the land in economic areas.

This is being done by an examination of resources of reserves to assess the opportunity for development and land settlement. Legislation to provide for titles of land on reserves to be granted to Aboriginals is at present before the Legislative Council for the Northern Territory. Funds will come from royalties for mining and forestry projects on reserves which are paid to a special trust fund to assist Aboriginals. Also the Prime Minister has announced that a special fund will be set up to provide capital assistance for Aboriginal enterprises. As further land is required Aboriginals will be given opportunity to obtain economic blocks. The Aboriginals' future in the Northern Territory is not a bleak prospect—it is a prospect of great promise.

Government policies are directed towards the objective of the assimilation of Aboriginal Australians as fully effective members of a single Australian society. The Government wishes to avoid measures which are likely to set Aboriginal citizens permanently apart from other Australians through having their development based on separate or different standards.

Demands for land grants built up from protests, with only vague generalisations about intended use, and with no thought about how the people could live at a reasonable standard and what opportunity there is for the children, will be detrimental to Aboriginals.

So far as the claim made on behalf of some of the Gurindji tribe in the Territory for rights to traditional land is concerned: it is by no means clear that the Aboriginals themselves had in mind an area of 500 square miles on which to run their own cattle station. They were asking for a residential area where they and their families could live with possibly the opportunity to run a contract droving and mustering business if any of them so wished. The Government has answered this proposal by agreeing to establish a residential area on Crown land at Wave Hill where facilities for education and medical care of Aboriginals in the area have been established for some years; and to provide land to run horses if any of the people set up as contract musterers and drovers. In time this residential area will be developed as a town to serve the needs of all the people in this part of the Territory.

Neither Wattie Creek nor the site for the township is known to contain sites which are of special sacred significance. As previously announced, arrangements are being made to ensure that Aboriginals who have been living at Wattie Creek will not be disturbed in their occupancy should they wish to remain there. The laws of the Northern Territory also protect the rights of Aboriginals who wish to camp, roam or hunt anywhere on the pastoral properties in the Northern Territory.

There are perhaps 130,000 people of Aboriginal descent in this country—there are about 20,000 full-blood Aboriginals in the Territory. A signficant proportion of people of Aboriginal descent are living and making their own way in the community without special assistance. The majority however need some form of assistance and guidance. They all have a legitimate claim to participate in this assistance—no one group has a greater right than the remainder. Whatever is done for one must be capable of application and be applied to all who might seek the same help.

Some Aboriginals will find their future as land-owners. Others will choose to follow a different vocation. The Government's approach is that those who want to take up land and work it in the same way as other Australians do should be assisted to secure land under normal titles. Those who want to find their future in other occupations should also be assisted where necessary.

Land rights should be regarded not as an end in themselves but a means to an end. The ultimate end the Government seeks is full participation by Aboriginals with other Australians in the life of a single Australian community.

## 7.14 13 August 1968. Mr. Whitlam's comments.

(*Ibid.*, Vol. H of R 60, 1968, E. G. Whitlam, Debate, 13 August, pp. 15, 16, 17.)

*In a Parliamentary discussion the Leader of the Opposition, Mr. E. G. Whitlam, comments on the Government's actions since the holding of the referendum the previous year.*

Mr. WHITLAM (Werriwa—Leader of the Opposition)—Fifteen months ago, on 27th May last year, the people of Australia, in the most massive expression of the general will ever known in this country, gave this Parliament the power to pass laws for the welfare of Aboriginals. The referendum was not designed merely to remove discrimination against Aboriginals; its purpose was to give the National Parliament and the National Government authority to grant especially favourable treatment to them to overcome the handicaps we have inflicted on them. Ninety-one per cent of the formal votes cast favoured the proposal. This was more than a mandate: It was a virtual command by 5,700,000 Australians that the National Government should take a lead to promote the health, training, employment opportunities and land rights of Aboriginals.

Four months elapsed before the Government appointed a Commonwealth Council for Aboriginal Affairs. The late Prime Minister set up an Office of Aboriginal Affairs in his Department. The present Prime Minister (Mr. Gorton) appointed the present Minister-in-Charge of Aboriginal Affairs (Mr. Wentworth) at the beginning of March. This gave rise to hopes that the new Government would indeed strike out on a new and national approach to Aboriginals. . . .

On 12th July the Prime Minister addressed in Melbourne a conference of Commonwealth and State Ministers responsible for Aboriginal affairs. . . . In his address the Prime Minister said:
"I believe that the Minister and the Council, in their relations with the States, should seek to discharge three main functions.
  1. To allocate funds from the Commonwealth to the State for Aboriginal advancement, using State machinery to use these funds for an agreed purpose to the greatest possible extent.

2. To gather information regarding Aboriginal matters (especially welfare) and to act as a clearing house for such information both as between the various States and as between States and Commonwealth.
3. Where appropriate to assist the States in the co-ordination of their policy and in setting the general direction of the Australian approach to Aboriginal advancement."

Not one of these three items required an amendment to the Constitution. All that has happened is that the States are to receive specific grants rather than general grants to pursue their present policies. It was always open to the Commonwealth under section 96 to make such specific grants. The change is a change of bookkeeping, not of policy. As far back as 1965 full blood Aboriginals were included for the first time with the rest of the population of the States in the population figures governing the calculation of Commonwealth grants to the States which we colloquially call income tax reimbursements. This change had particular advantages for Queensland and Western Australia, where most full blood Aboriginals reside. The Government has thus, through its leader, revealed to the world that the referendum was just a sop to the Australian conscience and international opinion. . . .

Nothing indicates better that there has been no real change, that there is no new policy, than the fate of the Minister-in-Charge of Aboriginal Affairs. In a spirit of optimism and goodwill, he went to Wave Hill in April. . . .

Later the Minister submitted to Cabinet a proposal to detach 8 square miles of Vestey's Wave Hill property consisting of 5,186 square miles—the biggest cattle station in the world—to enable the Gurindji people to run and break in brumbies. . . .

On 2nd July the Cabinet rejected the Minister's proposal. Clearly, the Country Party and the Minister for the Interior have determined the Government's policy on this matter. . . . The Minister for the Interior has subsequently made quite misleading statements about the nature of the original request from the Gurindji and the Government's response to it. He said in Darwin on 8th August:

They were asking for a residential area where they and their families could live with possibly the opportunity to run a contract droving and mustering business if any of them so wished.

This is a thoroughly false statement of the wishes of the Gurindji. The Minister-in-Charge of Aboriginal Affairs at least must know how false it is. The Minister for the Interior went on to imply that the Government had partially met the request. He said:

"The Government has answered this proposal by agreeing to establish a residential area on Crown land at Wave Hill where facilities for education and medical care of Aboriginals in the area have been established for some years and to provide land to run horses if any of the people set up as contract musterers and drovers."

This is a proposal altogether irrelevant to the original petition of the Gurindji and it does nothing to meet the wishes or needs of the people now congregated, not at Wave Hill but at Wattie Creek. All that the Commonwealth is doing is providing basic amenities that it would be morally and legally bound to provide in any case. It is cruel enough to raise false hopes and to dash them: It is more cruel to pretend that the Commonwealth has gone some way to meet these hopes.

The real intentions of the Minister for the Interior were shown later in his statement of 8th August. This is the real statement of the Government's policy on Aboriginal land rights as far as the Country Party is concerned. The Minister said:

"Some Aboriginals will find their future as land owners. Others will choose to follow a different vocation. The Government's approach is that those who want to take up land and work it in the same way as other Australians do should be assisted to secure land under normal titles. Those who want to find their future in other occupations should also be assisted where necessary."

This is a spurious and brutal statement. It is a statement that would have graced any Legislative Council in Australia in 1868. It disgraces this Parliament in 1968. It is the cry of the squatter through the ages: 'Keep off.' If this policy had prevailed there would have been no Australian Country Party today. For more than a century, almost all land settlement in Australia has been made possible only by special government assistance. We have assisted soldier settlers. Governments have provided opportunities for settlers in the brigalow lands in the last few years at a cost of $26m. We annually subsidise dairy farmers by $31m to enable them to stay on the land. We subsidise wheat farmers to enable them to trade with China. Since 1954 there has been a Northern Territory (Lessees Loans Guarantee) Act under which a man can obtain a guarantee of $60,000 to enable him to take up and work a lease. One man has obtained such a guarantee. Is he an Aboriginal? We subsidise overseas companies to enable them to take over vast areas of our oil and minerals. The entire history of land development in this country has been characterised by special government assistance. But, according to the Minister for the Interior, no special assistance can be given to Aboriginals to help them to recover 8 square miles of their own tribal lands and to apply on it the skills in which they specialise.

Nothing demonstrates the unreality of the present policies more than the constant use of the word 'choose' to describe what should happen to Aboriginals. The Minister for the Interior says: 'Others will choose to follow a different vocation.' The Prime Minister says:

"The policy of assimilation seeks that all persons of Aboriginal descent will choose to attain a similar manner and standard of living to that of other Australians and live as a member of a single Australian community."

How can there be a real choice unless special assistance, especially favourable treatment, is given? How can there be true choice until there are good health, proper education, decent housing, and adequate employment opportunities at award rates?

The health of Aboriginals is an indictment of this country. In 1963 a survey carried out under the auspices of the Australian National University and the Australian Institute of Aboriginal Studies showed that there was an infant death rate of 208 per 1,000 live births in central Australia. The report on the survey stated that this 'must be among the highest infant mortality rates in the world'. The Aboriginal infant mortality rate is about ten times greater than that among other Australian infants. The incidence of leprosy among Aboriginals in the Northern Territory is among the highest in the world. In 1960 members of an American-Australian scientific expedition said that in four places they had visited in the Northern Territory 'leprosy is considered endemic'.

Very few Aboriginals complete a secondary school education. It is estimated that in the Northern Territory, 5,400 Aboriginal children and 7,100 other children are of school age. There are, however, twice as many other children receiving primary education as there are Aboriginal children receiving it, and there are four times as many receiving secondary and post primary education. There is one Aboriginal child receiving assistance to study outside the Territory and there are nearly 200 other children receiving similar assistance. For years the Commonwealth pleaded that it did not have the constitutional power to adopt conventions of the International Labour Organisation and Unesco to legislate for Aboriginals in relation to the principal matters set out in the terms of this proposal for discussion.

The Commonwealth now has unquestioned power but has not applied the conventions. What is needed is a policy of equal rights and special privileges. If we cannot reverse history, we must redress it. The Commonwealth now has full power to do this but still fails to exercise this power.

## 7.15 11 January 1969. An Aborigine attacks white attitudes (1).

(*The Koorier*, Melbourne, Vol. 1, No. 4, 1969, p. 6.)

*An Aborigine attacks the attitudes of white Australians and calls for a recognition of the black race and a pride in Aboriginality.*

MODE OF MIRRIGAN
Had the opportunity of seeing what our average run of the mill gubbah knows of the injustices of the Koorie here in the free Australia.

It was during the afternoon tea break. I was chewing my bit of goanna fat when a few of the gubs started a conversation with me about the Koorie and his problem (not *theirs* please note).

Why can't he go to school like every other Australian?

Why can't he pick himself up from the gutter?

Why does he always go on walkabout?

Why is he lazy?

*All this from men.* Men who should be capable of understanding and knowing simply by reading the newspapers.

After letting their questions come fast, heavy and often and almost choking on the piece of meat, I finished my tea and then opened up on them.

First I thanked them for their support in the referendum. I thanked them for actually recognizing us as worthy of being in the homo sapien class. Thanks for nothing!

The gubs are the *only* race in the world who won't ratify the I.L.O. Convention 107 adopted at Geneva in 1957, a part of which reads:

". . . the right of ownership collective or individual of the members of the (indigenous) populations concerned over the lands which these populations traditionally occupy shall be recognized".

Koorie, black people all I say to you what have we to thank the gub for if he won't even abide by a policy of justice accepted by races of his own bleaching.

Australoid brothers and sisters raise your voices every where you go and tell every gub who will listen what terrible wrong he is doing to the downtrodden blackman or one day it might be too late.

Be proud of our race which has dignity. Remember black *is* beautiful.

## 7.16 27 January 1969. An Aborigine attacks white attitudes (2).

(*Ibid.*, Vol. 1, No. 5, 1969.)

*The same Aboriginal writer warns the white Australian of the Aborigines' intense feelings of hatred and repression, and at the same time calls fellow black men to take pride in the Aboriginal race.*

MODE OF MIRRIGAN
My point today is the purpose of my controversial (I hope) articles to date, and it is a three pronged attack.

Firstly I am hoping to create an awareness of the Koorie as a race. This seems to the average gub a silly point.

Why try and create tension and racial strife where there is none, in comparison to America and England?

To this I say there is much to be learnt for you, the white overlord. The tight spring-loaded tension is here among the Koories. The only thing that the gub can thank his lucky stars for, is that he managed, throughout his rule to suppress the Koorie to such a bitter extent, that he killed the blackman's individuality as a race, dignity, national pride and unity, but bear me out and recognize the fact, as has been proved throughout even the white man's history, that with the return of dignity and national pride comes the burning desire to be free and this spells *trouble*.

Secondly, I hope to shake up the "integrated" black-white man into making him feel his guilt in turning his back on his less fortunate brethren, who through their own uneducated resources are striving to hang onto what is theirs by birthright. I would trade one native for *six* "integrateds", who have smothered their ancestors with the white blanket. You know who I mean, so if the cap fits. . . .

The third point is simply this. For the gubs who feel antagonism towards me and hate me I say thank you, for at least in showing your hate towards me, you honour me by not hiding behind apathy.

## 7.17  4 March 1969. Mr. Wentworth's reply.

(*Commonwealth Parliamentary Debates, op. cit.*, Vol. H of R 65, pp. 923-2174, 9 September to 26 September 1969, "Ministerial Statement", 18 September, pp. 1561-1563.)

*Dr. Mackay addresses a question to the Minister in Charge of Aboriginal Affairs, Mr. Wentworth, referring to a press statement which inferred the desirability of sterilising Aboriginal males.*

Dr. MACKAY—My question is addressed to the Minister for Social Services. Has he seen reports that the honourable member for Capricornia proposes surgical procedures to limit the birth rate amongst certain Aboriginals and other under-privileged families? . . .

Mr. WENTWORTH (Minister in charge of Aboriginal Affairs)—My attention has been drawn to a letter on this subject which was written by the honourable member for Capricornia and which appeared in the Press. I think I can say in fairness to the honourable member that he did not, as far as I can understand, advocate compulsory sterilisation of Aboriginals. . . .

The honourable member did say in point of fact that he regarded Aboriginals as second-class citizens—as people, if I remember the phrase, whom the main stream of life had passed and who could not possibly catch up. He therefore thought that their birth rate should be reduced and in particular he advocated sterilisation for this purpose. He went so far as to suggest that the campaign for sterilisation should be backed by colour films and television campaigns so that there would be some measure, perhaps not of compulsion, but of moral compulsion put on Aboriginals to submit themselves to sterilisation. These are concepts which I think the Government would certainly reject and which I for one would consider to be rather in the totalitarian groove that the honourable member has mentioned.

## 7.18 April 1969. "What Does the Future Hold?"

(*The Koorier, op. cit.,* Vol. 1, No. 9, 1969, p. 6.)

*An article in an Aboriginal newspaper accuses the white Australian of his past and present treatment of the Aborigine.*

What is in store for him? What has he to look forward to? Like thousands of other Aboriginal children the future is about as bright as the past.

His parents, like many others try desperately to give their children something to look forward to. They work hard to live by the white man's standard, but they lack the spirit of competition, the required ruthlessness of the pale brothers. They refuse to rise on the social ladder at the expense of others.

These complacent, satisfied people, called the Australian Aborigines, had until the advent of whites, a social structure and way of living envied by a great many people. Yet these same people seek to destroy this because they are unable to attain this form of living themselves. We, the Aborigine, scream that we want to choose our own way of life, but still governments and white people generally resist us. You white people cried when Russia invaded Poland, you applauded when Israel reclaimed their land by force, you condemned the Reds when they overran Czechoslovakia. Yet when an Aborigine even so much as whispers Black Power, he is ridiculed and condemned. Yet weren't we also invaded? Weren't also our people slaughtered and enslaved? Aren't we still oppressed by white dominance?

Even to this day the whites are still maintaining the wholesale destruction of the Aborigine. Some facts to bear this out are: the high infant mortality rates—the figures are that one in every six Aborigines die in infancy; the enormous percentage of Aborigines in Australia suffering from leprosy; the absence of full-bloods in Victoria; and the last remnant of the Tasmanians, namely, Truganini.

Truganini's bones lie in a coffin-like box in the basement of the Hobart Museum. She was refused the right to a burial and even in death she suffers at the hands of the white man. Is the Tasmanian Government scared that their white society will show its true colours by doing again what their sadistic and scavenger ancestors had done to the body of Bill Lanney. I accuse the white man of murder, rape, invasion and sacrilege.

THE PROSECUTION RESTS

## 7.19 1969. Dr. H. C. Coombs' statement.

(Dr. H. C. Coombs, in *Ibid.,* Vol. 1, No. 11, 1969, p. 9.)

*Dr. H. C. Coombs, Chairman of the Commonwealth Office of Aboriginal Affairs, addresses the Australian College of Physicians on "Aboriginal Health".*

### ABORIGINAL HEALTH

I have tried to present the available data as objectively as I can, refraining from comment or attempts to lay blame. Perhaps one could summarise the picture somewhat along these lines: If an Aboriginal baby is born today—

1. It has a much better than average chance of being dead within two years.
2. If it does survive it has a much better than average chance of

suffering from sub-standard nutrition to a degree likely permanently to handicap it—
   (a) in its physical and mental potential;
   (b) in its resistance to disease.
3. It is likely in its childhood to suffer from a wide range of diseases but particularly E.N.T. and respiratory infections, from gastro-enteritis, from trachoma and other eye infections.
4. If it reaches the teen ages it is likely to be ignorant of and lacking in sound hygienic habits, without vocational training, unemployed, maladjusted, and hostile to society.
5. If it reaches adult ages it is likely to be lethargic, irresponsible and, above all, poverty-stricken—unable to break out of the iron cycle of poverty, ignorance, malnutrition, ill health, social isolation, and antagonism: if it lives in the North it has a good chance of being maimed by leprosy and wherever, its search for affection and companionship may well end only in the misery of V.D.
6. If it happens to be a girl it is likely to conceive a baby at an age when her white contemporary is screaming innocent adulation at some "pop" star and she will continue to bear babies every twelve or eighteen months until she reaches dougle figures or dies of exhaustion.
7. And so the wheel will turn.


## 7.20  18 September 1969. Mr. Wentworth's statement.

(*Commonwealth Parliamentary Debates, op. cit.*, Vol. H of R 62, pp. 1-1404, 25 February to 23 April 1969, Questions, 4 March, Dr. Mackay, p. 319.)

*Mr. Wentworth's ministerial statement regarding the growth of tourism in areas of significance to Aborigines.*

Mr. WENTWORTH (Minister for Social Services and Aboriginal Affairs): From the tourism point of view the Government recognises that the rich traditional culture of the Aboriginal people is of great interest to many visitors—both domestic and overseas. Many visitors wish to see something of the Aboriginal way of life. However, only a handful of the Aboriginal citizens of Australia today live for even part of the time in their traditional manner, and most of these people live in remote and inaccessible places.

I must make it clear that it is not the intention of the Government to permit or encourage the presentation of Aboriginal Australians as "tourist attractions", to be looked at and photographed as though they existed to satisfy the curiosity of other people. In all its consideration of the role of Aboriginals in the developing tourist industry the Government has considered the interests of the Aboriginal Australians first, and will respect their right to privacy ahead of the interests of the tourist industry or of tourists themselves. The Government recognises, however, that, particularly in outback areas of central Australia and to some extent in northern Australia, the tourist industry is, and will develop further as an important source of livelihood for the residents. In many places the permanent resident population is predominantly Aboriginal and there could be material advantage for Aboriginal residents as well as for the industry in their greater involvement in the industry, as owners and operators of services for tourists, as producers of goods for sale to tourists, and as employees in the industry.

In any development of the industry within the Aboriginal reserves and in developments involving Aboriginal residents outside reserves, the Government considers it essential that nothing should be done without full consultation with, and the agreement of, the Aboriginal residents. Within the reserves in the Northern Territory no development of the industry will be permitted unless it is planned in consultation with the residents, with their consent and for their material benefit. Subject to these limitations the Government seeks to involve the Aboriginal communities in the development of any services for tourists and other visitors in or near the areas of those communities. It is envisaged that the funds available for the establishment of Aboriginal business enterprises from the Commonwealth Capital Fund for Aboriginal Enterprises, the Northern Territory Aborigines Benefits Trust Fund, and other sources will make it possible for Aboriginal communities to benefit from the development of tourism when they wish to and in ways which they decide. . . .

One of the Government's major concerns in relation to sites where there are rock paintings or engravings, stone arrangements and the like is to ensure their preservation. Where there are living Aboriginal people with a continuing concern for such sites, their interests must remain paramount. Under legislation in the Northern Territory it is possible to declare sites to be prohibited or prescribed areas, and action has been taken to identify and protect a number of sites in particular areas where they may be exposed to the risk or damage or interference. Many such sites, especially within reserves, are presently protected by their remoteness and difficulty of access. The Government is alive to the need to protect and preserve such sites both inside and outside reserves and to consider the interests of the Aboriginal people in any planning for tourist development near such places.

I conclude by again stressing that the Government is concerned to protect Aboriginal antiquities from deliberate and accidental damage and to preserve the interests and respect the wishes of Aboriginal communities and individuals in the development of their participation in the tourist industry. It is concerned to ensure that Aboriginals should secure the maximum material benefit from their participation in the industry in ways which enhance their status as Australian citizens with uniquely interesting cultural traditions.

### 7.21  18 March 1970. Senator Keeffe's statement.

(*Ibid.*, Vol. S 43, Senate Debates, 26 November 1969 to 7 May 1970, Debate on Aborigines, 18 March, Senator Cant, p. 382.)

*During a Commonwealth Parliamentary debate, Senator Keeffe discusses the use of alcohol on Palm Island, an Aboriginal settlement.*

. . . A couple of young boys took a boat to the mainland. Supposedly they were on a fishing expedition but they did not go fishing; they went to the mainland and picked up a little bit of alcohol. I might say that alcohol is a pretty scarce commodity on Palm Island at present but in comparatively recent months you could buy a bottle of very cheap wine—what Australians commonly refer to as plonk—for $10. A bottle of methylated spirits was available to residents of the Island for $5 a bottle. You could not get beer for under $2 a bottle. Alcohol is not allowed on the Island except for white residents for medicinal purposes; I think that is how it is described. It is not allowed for anyone whose skin is not white. Significantly the rum running, if you like to call it that, was done by white people running boats to the Island and making an exhorbitant profit. Every so often a white man is caught and fined $50 or something like that, but that is his licence fee for the year.

In this case the boat was impounded for three months. My approaches to the Director were successful in getting two or three weeks taken off the three months, and I was requested by the Director to give the man concerned a lecture and to tell him that it was not to happen again. This state of affairs does not only apply to this settlement; it applies to other settlements. This same iron hand of discipline is exercised over the inhabitants in almost every government settlement in Queensland in the same way as you exercise discipline over a cow or on a poultry farm.

### 7.22 30 June 1970. The Queensland Director of Aborigine and Islander Affairs' Annual Report.

(*Ibid.*, pp. 2056-2057.)

*A portion of the Annual Report submitted by the Director of Aborigine and Islander Affairs, Queensland, complaining of the interference by interested outsiders.*

The year, however, has not been uneventful. It has been significant that an increase has occurred in the numbers who seek to attain notoriety by advocating an "Aboriginal cause".

These advocacies have been generally of a "pressure group" nature, some of their most vocal proponents being from other States, and without any real responsibility or indeed consideration for the persons affected by the doctrines espoused.

Those most vociferous have generally also been noticeable by a lack of any real personal contribution or involvement particularly in the welfare field.

While introduction of new ideas is both welcome and beneficial, it is considered that such ideas should be constructive; however, some performances experienced during the year can only be described as regrettable, unconcerned and mischievous.

People of Aboriginal ancestry, as a result of a lack of public interest in the past, have enough difficulties of their own and these, together with those arising out of an apparently remorseful public conscience, are more than sufficient. The introduction of radical and subversive activities do little other than add to this burden and can constitute a definite hindrance to the progress of Aboriginal Queenslanders.

It would seem also that the period has confirmed the emergence of an "elite" group who might be described as "professional" and/or "Pseudo" Aborigines, many of whom advocate particular doctrines but who have either become isolated from the main stream of Aboriginal people or have, in fact, never been in close contact or consultation with the wider segment of Aboriginal Queenslanders who consider themselves truly Aborigines.

### 7.23 4 November 1970. Abschol's summary of the Aborigines and Torres Strait Islanders' Affairs Act, 1965.

(Abschol, University of Queensland Group, St. Lucia, Queensland, in *Ibid.*, Vol. S 46, 13 October to 4 November 1970, pp. 1047-2122, Debate on State Grants (Aboriginal Advancement Bill), p. 2052.)

*A summary of the Aborigines and Torres Strait Islanders' Affairs Act,* 1965, *prepared by Abschol, a group working on behalf of Aborigines at the University of Queensland.*

## THE ABORIGINAL AND ISLAND AFFAIRS ACT OF 1965

The following summary does not cover all of this act. It is intended to deal only with those parts which are very important or particularly objectionable. Emphasis is given to those provisions which cause most complaints among Aborigines.

The basic philosophy of this act seems to be that the Aborigines it covers must be closely controlled by the Department of Aboriginal and Island Affairs (hereafter referred to as the department). No meaningful form of self-determination is permitted. Apparent attempts at this are aborted by the close departmental control exerted.

In reading the act, or this summary, it is important to bear in mind the people with whom it deals. Aborigines on reserves have grown up believing that they had no rights at all and that they must always obey the white staff on the reserve. Under the previous acts and other directors this belief was very close to being correct. Even if this is no longer so this upbringing ensures that the Aborigine is unlikely to argue with any decision of the manager and is very unlikely to go as far as to appeal against his decision. This becomes more apparent when we consider the possible penalties for any such opposition—removal from the reserve, transfer to the other end of Queensland, complete loss of income and thus food (other than what can be obtained from friends) or house arrest for an indeterminate period. The Aborigine knows these things can occur because he has seen them happen or knows of some-one to whom they have happened. Some of these do not occur often but the threat is always there.

It is also important to realise that the Aborigine on the reserve has very little formal education—perhaps 5 years of schooling would be the average for the adults. Thus even where the act does give him some rights, e.g., the right to appeal, he is unlikely to know this and is probably unable to use them. The difficulty of access to the reserves for outsiders ensures that he does not learn to exercise these rights. Thus while it may be true that the Queensland Full Court will take action against abuses of power by the administrators of the act it is highly unlikely that any Aborigine will bring before them a complaint.

30,000 Aborigines and Islanders are subject to this act.

In this summary "The Manager" refers to the official of the Department of Aboriginal and Island Affairs who is in charge of a reserve or settlement.

"The District Officer" refers to the official of the Department of Aboriginal and Island Affairs who is in charge of one of the districts of Queensland. This may or may not include one or more reserves.

"The Director" refers to the official in charge of the Department of Aboriginal and Island Affairs. He is subject only to the Minister of Aboriginal and Island Affairs, the political head.

Declaration under and exemption from the act.

The 1965 act differentiates between those Aborigines to be assisted and those not requiring aid. A period of twelve months was set aside during which the director could "declare any Aborigine, part-Aborigine or person having a strain of Aboriginal blood to be an assisted Aborigine" (Sect. 17). With this went the power to declare under the act any of the children of assisted Aborigines if they had "not attained or not apparently attained" 17 years of age (S.19).

After the transitory twelve months, admission to the act was, if voluntary, by an application to the Director (S.18). Also included in the act are provisions for compulsory entry under the act. Thus if the Director or any authorised officer finds a person "has a strain of Aboriginal blood" and "should in his best interest be declared" he may require him to appear in court and to answer the complaint and to be further dealt with according to law" (S.20). The court may declare the Aborigine as needing assistance and put him under the act. In addition when an Aborigine or part-Aborigine comes before a court the presiding officer may declare the Aborigine to need assistance and put him under the act "whether or not such person was convicted of the offence with which he was charged" (S.21).

Exemption from the act may be declared by the Director at his own discretion or upon receipt of an application for exemption. If such application is refused an appeal can be made to a magistrate's court as discussed later.

Two important points should be made to clarify the situation. Members of Parliament continuously receive requests for help to get out from under the act. It is also notable that Aborigines refer to the "unassisted" as "free men" and talk about getting their freedom when making application for exemptions. This shows the degree to which they feel oppressed by the act.

This is not to say that all assisted Aborigines want to be exempted from the act. As things stand exemption means that the Aborigine must leave the reserve. Many Aborigines have lived there all their lives and still want to. They don't like the restrictions under which they live but prefer them to being forced to leave their home. The restrictions, after all, are only what they are used to.

The reserves.

Within the preliminary to the 1965 act, Parliament specified that all existing reserves were to continue as such (S.4(11) ). It is important to examine the extent and generality of the powers assigned to the Manager and to the department.

The most general powers are contained in Regulations 10-13 and apply to "every resident on or visitor to" the reserve. Thus all must "conform to a reasonable standard of good conduct" (R.10), must "obey all lawful instructions of the Director, District Officer, Manager, Councillors or other officers of such Reserve" (R.11) and must not do "any act subversive of good order or discipline on a Reserve" (R.12). Even when a non-resident is authorised to be on the reserve, he may not "interfere with the normal duties or activities of any assisted person" (R.16). Naturally the Manager as the senior officer would be the one to decide, at least in the first instance, on what is a reasonable standard of conduct, what acts subvert good order and what interferes with normal duties.

The wide scope of these powers is easily susceptible to misuse and gives to the manager almost absolute power over the actions of all on the reserve. Colin Tatz, in his article "Queensland Aborigines, Natural Justice and the Rule of Law" (Australian Quarterly, Sept. 1963) quotes many documented cases of breaches of similar regulations in the act then in force. He shows how they were used to deal with such diverse topics as arson, assault, bribery, drunkenness, theft and trespass.

The regulations not only authorise the manager to eject anyone "who enters or remains on a Reserve without the Manager's authority (R.13) but also make it an offence for anyone to bring onto a reserve "anything which in the opinion of the Manager" is likely "to disturb the peace, harmony, order or discipline of such reserve" (R.17).

Section 34 gives the Director power to forcibly move an assisted Aborigine not living on a reserve onto any reserve in Queensland. The Director may remove an assisted Aborigine from the reserve by cancelling his certificate of entitlement (R.24) or may, on the recommendation of an Aboriginal Court, transfer him from one reserve to another (S.34). The wishes of the assisted Aborigine need not be considered. Appeals against each of these decisions may be made as discussed below. No non-resident of a reserve can enter it without permission of the manager (R.13). This means that a non-resident Aborigine, born on a reserve with perhaps parents still living there, cannot enter without permission. Nor can the parents leave the reserve to visit the son without permission (R.70). These two provisions cause more complaints than any other in the act.

Detention in a dormitory can be enforced by the Manager, Aboriginal Court or Visiting Justice (R.70). Acts which are punishable by detention include attempts to escape or illegally leave the Reserve; "failure to carry out instruction in hygiene, sanitation or infant welfare", being guilty of immoral conduct or committing an offence against discipline. The basic philosophy of the act, that of control of the people it covers, is shown by the definition offered as an offence against discipline (R.70). Breaches are seen as failing to obey "lawful instructions", behaviour which is offensive, threatening, insolent, insulting, disorderly, obscene or indecent", wilful damage, being either idle, careless or negligent at work or "IN ANY OTHER WAY OFFENDS AGAINST DISCIPLINE OR GOOD ORDER OF THE RESERVE OR COMMUNITY".

The maximum term of detention before review is six months. Further detention requires a report to the Director. If the Director and Manager so wish there is no limit to the period of detention. The Manager has the power to release the detained person at any time (R.70).

Aboriginal Councils.

The Aboriginal Councils seem a liberal attempt to develop self-management on the Reserves. R.21 defines their role as that of "local government of the Reserve" and, as such they are responsible for the "good rule and government" of the Reserve or Community. The most pleasing aspect is the acknowledgement of cultural influences—such government is to be "in accordance with Aboriginal customs and practices". Furthermore, the Council is given the power and authority to make By-laws, such as "regulating and controlling peace (R.22), including setting maximum penalties which can be used in the Aboriginal Court (maximum of $40 and/or 14 days imprisonment).

Other powers include passing By-laws to determine "the direction, administration and control of the working and business of the local government of the Reserve". R.22 (See also R.23), it can also pass resolutions (R.20) and levy fees, rents and dues (R.25). Despite the apparently wide powers assigned to it, the Council is continually subject to the Director. No By-Law can have effect until approved by the Director (R.28), and each order or resolution is subject to the will of the Manager, who may suspend it, "either for an indefinite period or for such a period as he may specify". R.31(1). The normal appeal mechanism applies.

All communal income (rents, fines, dues) is paid into a Community Fund (R.45) and "A disbursement shall not be made from a Community Fund unless the manager approves" (R.46). Thus the manager controls all the council's finance and has another effective method of blocking any of its actions that he wishes to. No appeal mechanism exists.

The council consists of 4 assisted Aborigines only 2 of whom are elected. The other 2 are appointed by the Director.

Any assisted Aborigine who has been convicted of an offence against the Act, Regulations or By-Laws in the previous two years is not eligible to stand for election (R.33). The scope of the powers allotted to the manager give him a considerable degree of control over such convictions and thus over who is eligible to stand for election.

The Director may remove any of the members of an Aboriginal Council (R.19).

Aboriginal Courts.

The courts are to consist of at least two Aboriginal Justices of the Peace (if the community does not have 2 J.P.'s then at least three members of the Aboriginal Council will then form the Court). (R.48). Its power is defined as (a) hearing and determining complaints for offences against any By-Law or regulation and imposing penalties and (b) hearing and determining any action set out in "The Magistrates Court Act of 1921" in which the amount involved does not exceed two hunderd dollars. The Court can only act in relation to assisted Aborigines and only within the reserve in which it is constituted.

The members of the court receive no training in their duties. Usually they do not fully comprehend the proceedings and are easily influenced by anyone who does. This, plus their natural desire not to get into the bad books of the Manager, gives to him considerable control over their activities.

Aboriginal Police.

Regulations 67-69 allow for the establishment of such a force. Their role is seen as that of assisting "the maintenance of good order and discipline on and supervision of a Reserve or community". The Manager not only may make the rules regarding the Police Force but can also "promote, disrate, suspend or dismiss any policeman" (R.69).

The power of the police is to "arrest and bring before an Aboriginal Court" any assisted Aborigine who breaches the act or the regulations, or a "lawful command" of the Manager. The police also have the power to arrest any assisted person who is to be removed (S.34) by the order of the Director. No effective training is given to the Aboriginal Police.

Appeals.

Appeals to a magistrates court are available for more decisions which the act allows the department to make on behalf of the assisted Aborigine. This appeal must be made in writing. Considering the high rate of illiteracy of Aboriginal adults (average education is about 5 years at school) this implies the heavy dependence they must place on white employees of the department for assistance in their appeal against decisions of the department.

Perhaps the most telling argument against the effectiveness of the appeal mechanism against administration decisions is that it is very rarely used. This is despite continued complaints about these decisions. It may be that the basic reason for this is that since the Manager controls every aspect of the reserve and the life of its residents, accepting his decisions is a small price to pay to avoid antagonising him.

Appeals are also available against decisions of the Aboriginal Court. The procedure is similar except that the first court of appeal is the District Officer, and the second, the Visiting Justice.

Funds.

The sense of control over nearly every aspect of the assisted Aborigines life is further extended in the financial sector with the provision of a series of Funds.

In addition to the Community fund already mentioned, the Aboriginal Welfare Fund is set up, which is to be "maintained for the general benefit of persons having a strain of Aboriginal blood" (R.4). The money is derived from the proceeds of any transactions by the reserve e.g. produce such as cattle. At no stage is there any indication as to what form "general benefit" might take.

The department can take complete control of the financial affairs of an assisted Aborigine, exercising all powers which he himself would otherwise have (S.38). All his income is then paid into a trust fund account which is operated on by the Director or his delegate who allocates to the Aborigine such funds as he (the Director) decides "are required by the said assisted person or are necessary for payment of his just debts".

Appendix A.

It has been claimed by some that the discretion allowed to the director or manager of a reserve are not unusual and that various officials have similar discretion over white citizens. Thus the governor can dismiss a white council just as the director can dismiss Aboriginal councillors. The difference is that the governor has no direct connection with, say, the town council of Toowoomba and will act only if something very unusual occurs while the manager is the administrator of the reserve and may act to prevent opposition to his policies.

The list below gives powers the department can exercise over the assisted Aborigine that no official has over the white community without court intervention.

Transfer from one part of Queensland to another.

Full control over the income of the person.

House arrest for an indeterminate period without trial.

Wages set by government regulations rather than by the industrial courts or by agreement.

The Department can force a man to leave his job.

Appendix B.

Form No. 15—Queensland.

"The Aborigines' and Torres Strait Islanders' Affairs Acts, 1965 to 1967" Regulation 74.

### Wage Rates

The minimum rate of wages payable to assisted persons employed under "The Aborigines' and Torres Strait Islanders' Regulations 1966" in addition to food and accommodation shall be as follows:

(a) General station hands—
Drover in charge, head stockman or stockman in charge of out-stations, general station hands, drovers, musterers and stockmen—
In accordance with the Station Hands' Award.

(b) Youths under the age of 21 years—
Experience—In accordance with the Station Hands' Award.
Inexperienced Trainees—
During first year of employment—$13 per week.
During second year of employment—$15.00 per week.
During third year of employment—$17.00 per week.

(c) Employees other than General Station Hands, but including house-boys, yardmen, employed at or about a dwelling-house—
Adults—$23.00 per week.
Under 21 years—$19 per week.
Under 20 years—$17.00 per week.
Under 19 years—$15 per week.
Under 18 years—$13.00 per week.

(d) Male employees not specifically herein mentioned—The same rates as prescribed in the preceding item (c).

Abuses of this power are common. The following Memorandum was written by the District Officer in Chillagoe to the District Officers in Cairns and Mareeba, and was dated 16th April, 1969.

Dear Sirs.

D . . . . D . . . . of Chillagoe is travelling to both Cairns and Mareeba and is expected back in Chillagoe in approximately 6 weeks time.

D . . . . is a waster and it would be appreciated if only small amounts were given for pocket money.

A/c. as at 31/2/69—$1,981.72.

Yours faithfully, . . . . District Officer, Chillagoe.

It is frequently not possible for an assisted Aborigine to obtain record of his bank account. Requests for such a record are simply not answered or are answered with incomplete information.

The power to take control of the finances of an assisted Aborigine can be a powerful method of punishment. Thus in Normanton as a result of a brawl in a hotel, the two combatants had their allowance withheld for a month. As this was their only source of cash income for the families, the persons concerned were left to fend as best they were able, off the charity of the rest of the community.

Employment.

Any assisted Aborigine working outside a reserve can be withdrawn from this work by the Director (R.72).

The District Officer or Manager can demand that the employer of an assisted Aborigine pay the wages, in full or in part, directly to said District Officer or Manager (R.73).

The wages rations and accommodations paid to the assisted Aborigine other than those cases covered by an award are laid down by the Department of Aboriginal and Island Affairs and are set out in schedule 15 (R.75) Appendix B.

Examples of the wages paid on reserves are the following figures for Yarrabah in 1969.

Yarrabah was then on a cash economy so everything must be provided from the wages—

Weekly Wage

Truck Driver—$18.00
Tractor Driver—$10.00-$16.00
Labourer—$8.00-$16.00.
Mechanic—$22.00
Painter—$14.00
Ganger—$18.00-$23.00
Carpenter—$18.00 (probably trained on Reserve)
Police Constable—$10.00-$16.00.

It is difficult to see how a man can keep his wife and, perhaps six children on $10.00 a week. That malnutrition is so widespread on Queensland reserves (e.g. see Dr. Stewart, Department of Childrens Health) is hardly surprising. It is also difficult to understand why a labourer on a reserve is only worth one-third as much as a labourer elsewhere.

(e) Cooks and Domestic Servants—

Cooks—Male (cooking for 13 persons or more)—In accordance with Station Hands' Award.

Cooks—Male (having less than three years' experience)—$24.00 per week.

Cooks—Female (cooking for 10 persons or more)—In accordance with Station Hands' Award.

Cooks—Female (having less than three years' experience) (cooking for 10 persons or more)—$18.00 per week.

(f) Domestic Servants—Female—

Having three years' experience (over 18)—$15.00 per week.

Not having three years' experience (over 18)—$11.00 per week.

15 to 18 years—$10.00 per week.

(g) Slow, aged, infirm or retarded workers—General station hands and

(g) Slow, aged, infirm or retarded workers—

General station hands and stockmen—$28.00 per week.

Youths under 21—$14.00 per week.

Or such rate as shall be determined by the District Officer in writing with the approval in writing of the Director of Aboriginal and Island Affairs first obtained.

(h) Married Couples—
   Husbands in accordance with regulation scale of wages for particular occupation in which engaged. Wife at regulation rates.
(i) Horse and Saddle Allowance—In accordance with Station Hands' Award.
(j) Employees engaged by the hour shall be paid one-fortieth of the appropriate weekly rate, plus 15 per cent. There shall be a minimum of three hours' pay and one meal shall be provided.
(k) The value of keep for all purposes, including the computing of payment to employees working overtime or on annual leave shall be deemed to be $2.50 per week.
(l) Food and accommodation shall be supplied to every employee in accordance with clause 75 of "The Aborigines' and Torres Strait Islanders' Regulations of 1966". Provided that where it is not possible for the employer to provide food and accommodation as aforesaid the employer shall pay the employee an extra allowance of not less than $2.50 per week.

General.

Notwithstanding anything herein contained, a District Officer shall claim higher rates than the rates hereby prescribed when he is satisfied that the ability of the assisted person warrants such higher payment.

## 7.24  4 November 1970. Senator Keeffe's complaint.

(*Ibid.*, p. 2059.)

*Senator Keeffe complains during a Senate debate that Aboriginal children suffer poor health and subsequently are disadvantaged at school.*

In the so-called settlement areas that are allocated to Aboriginals outside most Queensland country towns, particularly in the western areas, we find fairly large numbers of children. For instance, the Cunnamulla reserve has a population of 300 or 400 people. I notice that somebody has been there recently and has said that the Government is doing all it can. I was there a few weeks ago, and what I saw is a disgrace to the Australian community. It is a disgrace to the Queensland Government and the Commonwealth Government, because the people are expected to live in shanties without proper facilities to carry out ordinary personal hygiene. A percentage of the children, probably as high as 60 per cent, show signs of either malnutrition or all the other kiddies' disease that catch up with youngsters who are forced to live in ill-ventilated homes. This is an area where there is a tremendous amount of cold weather and hot, dry summers. Flies and all the diseases they bring are rampant. We need 30 houses in that area alone to overcome the housing shortage. We can multiply this number of houses by virtually every western and northern town in Queensland, and if one made a survey of the Northern Territory one would find that the need is even greater. . . .

First of all, we could improve the health of Aboriginal children. An Aboriginal youngster who suffers from a lack of food or a lack of proper food obviously has a handicap at school. That has been proved, and I do not propose to go through all the documents relating to it today. There will be other opportunities in this Senate when I will be able to do so. Obviously, this is one of the big problems. Aboriginal children just cannot keep up with white children in the school or with other Aboriginal children who are receiving a better diet. This is where the first problem starts.

Secondly, having provided Aboriginal children with some sort of an education, the next big problem is to provide job opportunities for them, because they are not being provided. The number of Aboriginal youngsters undergoing secondary education represents a very tiny fraction of the total number of Aboriginal children who ought to be receiving it. I think that throughout Australia, only 5 or 6 Aboriginal children are undergoing university education, and this is a disgrace to this country and to the Government.

## 7.25  4 November 1970. Senator Gair's comments.

(*Ibid.*, p. 2063.)

*Senator Gair comments on the education of Aborigines, their employment, land rights, and protective/restrictive legislation.*

The availability of education facilities is vital because until we get the Aboriginal children and train and educate them they will continue to behave as they have done in the past. My wife and I have taken them into our home and protected them. My wife particularly has taken a great interest in young women who have been in our service. She has always emphasised how important it was for them to be among the best of their people and not to associate with the cheap class hanging around the Adelaide Hotel, South Brisbane in great numbers misconducting themselves in public view.

They have a responsibility to themselves. These people, particularly in their teenage years, need some guidelines and protection from the evils of the world today because they are regarded as easy prey by a lot of unscrupulous people. I have seen them come to Brisbane from Cherbourg into the service of various people, and unless those girls are given some maternal protection and advice and not allowed to roam the streets until all hours at night it is not long before the majority of them return to Cherbourg in a pregnant condition. There they have their babies who again become a responsibility on the State and on the Commonwealth. Education is vital if we are to train these people to a state of responsibility that will enable them to take their place in any phase of our community life. Much has been written and said about making land available to them—giving them grazing properties to conduct. Some Aboriginals are quite bright. Most of them may be reasonably good stockmen but I question whether they have the business acumen to manage a cattle station or a sheep property.

Senator Keeffe—Is that not our fault?

Senator GAIR—I agree. Education is the important thing. It may be found necessary for many years that they have to operate such properties with the guidance and direction of persons qualified to conduct the business side of such undertakings. If young men, particularly those who have applied themselves in school and who show promise, are taken in hand by the authorities and trained in the management of a station or any other business for which Aboriginals are naturally fitted and which will enable them to live in the country, something could be done. However they must be young enough to be trained. I feel that all governments have failed to a great measure because of their inclination to adopt a paternal attitude to these people, as instanced on settlements where they are given foodstuffs sufficient to enable the maintenance of a family without requiring them to accept any responsibility. Few have been asked to take on a responsible job. I exclude those who have joined the police force at Cherbourg or other settlements.

The Government endeavours to create social functions for the Aboriginals who have their own public halls, radios and television sets. They have school balls, adult balls and debutante balls. I remember an occasion when a little girl who worked for us was decked out by Mrs. Gair and sent to a debutante ball where she was received by Mr. W. M. Moore who was then Minister for Health and Home Affairs. The people at Cherbourg live happily and I sometimes wonder whether we have not been too paternal and too protective. It may have been better had some of these people been discharged from the settlement and left to work out their own destiny. If we have erred at all it is only because of our solicitude for these people. No government wants to regiment them but to protect them.

If finance is to be made available let us hope that it will be expended judiciously and in the interests of these people. I support that part of the amendment, which refers to the abolition of all discriminatory Acts which operate against the Aboriginals. However if some provisions which appear to be discriminatory are designed to protect the Aboriginals I would be opposed to their repeal particularly while the Aboriginals are in settlements in charge of the government. Senator Wilkinson asked why it is that there is a provision which makes it necessary for a person to get a permit to go onto a settlement. The answer is obvious. Without the need for a permit we would have every Tom, Dick and Harry entering settlements poking in here and there, creating disorder and mischief, searching for young women and making a general nuisance of themselves. A person is not permitted to go into a lot of institutions. He cannot go into a hospital at any time of the day or night. Visiting hours are prescribed when a person is permitted to see sick relatives and friends. These institutions must be conducted in an orderly fashion. They cannot be thrown open to the public. After all, a lot of white people are not very desirable characters and if they had an open entree to these settlements it would not be in the best interests of these settlements or those who are living there.

Senator Wilkinson—We should make it so that the Aboriginals have the same sort of rights, as an ordinary person in his home. If they invite you in, you can go in. At present you cannot be invited in.

Senator GAIR—Even so I think that the management of a settlement should be required to have some knowledge of the visitor. I am in favour of the amendment to abolish all discriminatory provisions. The Aboriginals now have the adult franchise. We have lifted the embargo on their drinking. I sometimes wonder whether that was wise, but nevertheless they must have equal rights although, indisputably, for some reason or other, they do not seem to handle their grog as well as they might.

On the question of land rights I point out that land rights are given to naturalised British subjects from almost all countries. There is no prohibition on their owning land. Italians and others who come here permanently enjoy such rights. It would be unjust and unfair to suggest that the Aboriginals, the descendants of the original people of Australia, should not have equal rights. My colleagues and I will support the amendment because we favour the provision of additional money if it can be obtained and if it is properly and judiciously expended in the interests of the Aboriginals. We favour also the elimination of any section of any Act that discriminates against the Aboriginal as a citizen of Australia, but we do not favour the repeal of sections of Acts that are designed obviously for the protection of these people. That is the phase of the case that we have to watch. The amendments ask for the Commonwealth to request the States of Queensland and Western Australia to take immediate legislative action to abolish all discriminatory legislation in both States. Those Acts can be classified in 2 categories. One category is of discriminatory Acts which operate against the Aboriginal and make him a lesser citizen than his white friends. The other is of Acts which appear to be discriminatory but which are there for the protection of the Aboriginal. That is how I classify them.

## 7.26 4 November 1970. Dame Annebelle Rankin's motion.

(*Ibid.*, p. 2067.)

*Dame Annebelle Rankin closed the Debate on State Grants, Aboriginal Advancement Bill, by moving that the amendment calling for the abolition of all discriminatory legislation in Western Australia and Queensland be disregarded.*

I wish to inform the Senate that the Government opposes the amendment which has been moved by Senator Georges on behalf of the Opposition. In opposing the amendment I would like to repeat what the Leader of the Government (Senator Sir Kenneth Anderson) said in his second reading speech. In this amendment the Opposition proposes that the Commonwealth requests the States of Queensland and Western Australia to take immediate legislative action to abolish all discriminatory Acts and regulations in those States. I remind the Senate that the Prime Minister (Mr. Gorton) promised that all legislation which discriminated against Aboriginals whether on a State or Federal basis would be eliminated in the lifetime of this Parliament. I endorse the words of the Leader of the Government when he said:

"This promise, will, of course, be kept but I know that the Senate will share my desire that in keeping it we should to the greatest possible extent co-operate with the States . . ."

I know that the Senate will be interested to know that further talks concerning this very matter will be taking place very shortly. In fact, I think they might take place as early as next week. The Government is carrying out a programme which will assist the Aboriginal people. It is a programme which is sympathetic to their needs. I believe that this programme will equip them to live happily in the community. Because the Prime Minister has promised that this discriminatory legislation will be eliminated I say to you, Sir, and to the Senate, that the Government opposes the amendment moved by the Opposition.

Question put:
"That the amendment (Senator Georges') be agreed to."
The Senate divided.
(The President—Senator Sir Alister McMullin)

Ayes ..... ..... ..... 25
Noes ..... ..... ..... 22
———
Majority ..... 3
———

## 7.27 1970. "A Letter to the Editor."

(*The Koorier, op. cit.*, Vol. 1, No. 14, 1970, p. 7.)

*A black man speaks to all Australian Aborigines, in a newspaper article printed in Melbourne.*

Dear Sir,

Being born under the domination of Western Society, we all realize the toll that we have paid. This domination has various forms and characteristics, one of which is the belief that we are not capable of doing anything worthwhile for ourselves. We should realize that we are working against many disadvantages that have been purposely set in our way. However, we should never allow ourselves to be fooled into believing that obstacles which prevent us from getting better jobs, housing etc., are unrelated to racial superiority. The acceptance of the ideology of inferiority coupled with direct repression has produced and moulded the type of people who are frequently condemned as dirty, lazy and lacking ambition.

In whatever form the scars of racism have affected us in the past we must always try to rid ourselves of the last vestiges of it. To this end we should be critical of ourselves and of our brothers and sisters and try to lead ourselves to fully exposing bad habits which may be due to residual racist ideology, always keeping in mind that the erring brother is still a brother.

Keep up the good work.

WATSON BRIGGS


## 7.28  18 March 1971. Aborigines' communication to the United Nations.

(Commonwealth Hansard, H of R, Question upon notice No. 1654, 18 March 1971.)

*This communnication drew attention to the Aborigines' struggle for land rights.*

This is an urgent plea of several hundred thousand so called "Aborigines" of Australia that the United Nations use its legal and moral powers for the vindication of our rights to the lands which we have traditionally occupied.

We make this plea under Item 55 of the General Assembly, which deals with the elimination of all racial discrimination; for it is only racial discrimination which can explain the refusal of the Government of Australia to grant us, and us alone, our rights.

In support of our plea we call attention to Part II, Article 11 of Convention 107 of the International Labour Conference, to which conference the Government of Australia is a party:

"The right of ownership, collective or individually, of the members of the populations concerned over the lands which these populations traditionally occupied shall be recognised."

And we call further attention to Article 12 of that convention, which provided that if traditional populations are removed without their free consent from their lands, they must be fully compensated.

By Aboriginal law in Australia generally, land was traditionally inalienable. Moreover, the only known time in Australian history when the invading white exploiters made so much as a pretence of negotiating for the purchase of land in Australia from the indigenous people was in March 1835, when one John Batman signed the Batman Treaty with eight Aboriginal Elders for the "purchase" of 100,000 acres of land in the vicinity of Port Phillip, in exchange for smaller quantities of trade goods. Even this supposed "purchase" was never recognised by the governor in Victoria, Governor Bourke, when he stated that only the Crown had power to make treaties or contract for the acquisition of land.

We must emphasize: FROM THE TIME OF THE FIRST SETTLEMENT IN 1788 TO DATE, THE CROWN HAS NEVER USED EVEN ITS CLAIMED POWER TO TAKE OUR LAND, EITHER BY TREATY OR BY PURCHASE. THE CROWN HAS BLATANTLY TAKEN OUR LAND WITHOUT TREATY, WITHOUT PURCHASE AND WITHOUT COMPENSATION OF ANY KIND.

We, the Aborigines of Australia whom the invaders have not yet succeeded in wiping off the face of the earth, are the owners of the land of Australia in equity, in the eyes of any system of civilized law and in justice and yet we have no share in the great mineral, agricultural and pastoral wealth of our country.

We are sent to reservations which are described as Crown Lands, and the Government has complete control over these lands. When we ask for certain lands in our tribal areas, we are told that the Government has leased them, sometimes at the rate of 50 cents (U.S.) per square mile for periods of 99 years, but we never are consulted as to these unlawful leases.

To favour Bauxite miners, the lands of the Yirrkala people on the Gove Peninsula in the Northern Territory have been stolen from them and their special sacred areas desecrated.

The Gurindji people at Wattie Creek demanded remuneration of its claim to 500 square miles of their tribal lands, and also they were promised a meagre 8½ square miles. They in fact have received nothing whatever on the pretext that the Government cannot reclaim the land from those to whom it has given it.

When bauxite was discovered at Weipa on the Western coast of Cape York Peninsula, the Aboriginal people living there were forcibly ousted so that the area could be mined. It was possible for the Government to make land available for the construction of a mining town for whites, but the Aborigines' claims to their tribal lands were ignored.

We could recite case after case, but these three instances are enough to show that the rights of the Aboriginal peoples of Australia have been systematically taken from them.

Wherefore, we demand:

1. That all land occupied by the Aboriginal people of Australia at the present time can be turned over to them including the mineral rights pertaining to such lands.

2. That all Crown land not actually in use be returned to the Aboriginal peoples who originally owned it and who in justice must be recognised as the owners of it today.

3. That just compensation be paid to the Aboriginal peoples of Australia in the sum of 6 billion dollars.

This petition is accompanied by another petition, in which we protest the genocide which the Government of Australia is practicing on us. We show in that petition that compensation in the order of the amount we claim is required if we are to be enabled to survive. We ask that this petition be considered in light of the showing we are making and that that petition be considered with this one.

We are with all respect,

Aborigines Advancement League, 56 Cunningham Street, Northcote 3070, Victoria, Australia.


**7.29 15 September 1971. "The Shaping of a New Aboriginal Policy in South Australia."**

(Commonwealth Hansard, Senate Budget Debate 1971-72, 15 September 1971, pp. 756-759.)

*A statement issued by Mr. Len King, South Australian Minister for Aboriginal Affairs.*

### THE SHAPING OF A NEW ABORIGINAL POLICY
All Governments, both Federal and State, are deeply involved with Aboriginal affairs. There is a Department of Aboriginal Affairs at both

Federal and State level and both a Federal and State Minister of Aboriginal Affairs. Political policies and decisions necessarily affect Aborigines at many points. It will be possible tonight to consider only certain broad principles upon which such policies should rest.

The first and fundamental question to be settled in any discussion of policy as to Aboriginal affairs is the objective or objectives which a policy in relation to the Aborigines should seek to attain. One possible objective is the assimilation of the Aboriginal population into the white community on the basis that there will be no differentiation between black and white in the community. This is an understandable objective and was indeed the objective of all Australian Governments until 1965. It is based upon an attitude towards the Aboriginal people and the culture which is deeply engrained in the outlook of white Australians. The attitude is to regard the Aboriginal people as a primitive and backward people possessed of an inferior culture and traditions. According to this view, Aborigines can never hope to lead a full and satisfactory civilized life until they are severed from their cultural traditions and from ties with their past. They must, it is said, be taught the white man's ways and be made an indistinguishable part of the white community. Only in this way, it is said, can they be regarded as having full equality with the white citizen in a homogenous community.

Understandable as this objective is, it was repudiated in South Australia in 1965 and must, I believe, be consistently and firmly rejected in future. Many wrongs have been done to the Aboriginal people. Initial conquest and deprivation of their lands, was followed by cruelty and in many cases virtual enslavement. This in turn was followed by and indeed at times accompanied by a handout system of charity which had the effect of producing a pauper mentality in many Aborigines. The final wrong would be to attempt to destroy the Aborigine's racial and cultural identity and to turn him into a pseudo-white man. Self respect is easily lost and once lost is difficult to recover. The unhappy Aboriginal history since the white man came to this country has had the effect of undermining and in some cases destroying the self respect of Aboriginal people. All too many of them see themselves as inferior to the white man and incapable of sustained effort and true achievement. Any worthwhile objective of policy in relation to Aboriginal affairs must therefore be consistent with the restoration to the Aboriginal people of their self respect. There is no better means of restoring the self respect of any depressed group than to encourage an authentic sense of pride in that group's heritage and culture. To be proud of one's race and history is to go a long way towards the attainment of self-respect. This is clearly demonstrated in the history of Asian and African nationalism. It is also demonstrated in the history of depressed migrant groups of European settlers, both in the United States and Australia. A most encouraging sign is the development amongst Aborigines of a desire to identify with their own people and to be proud of their race and its culture. A most commonly expressed sentiment amongst Aborigines nowadays, both educated and uneducated is the desire to be with their own people. This desire of educated Aborigines to be with their own people rather than to escape from their environment into the white community, is a most hopeful indication of the rapid recovery of self respect of the Aboriginal people.

In 1965 the Government of South Australia set itself an objective which recognised the importance of the Aborigine's sense of pride in his people and his people's traditions and culture. The Government turned its back upon the objective of assimilation and set itself an objective which is usually described as integration. This recognises the right of the Aboriginal people to live in our community on fully equal terms but retaining, if they so desire, a separate and identifiable Aboriginal heritage and culture. Such an objective has many ramifications. On the reserves, it means the end of any economic pressure on Aborigines to leave the reserves and to work in the white community. It involves the provision of facilities to enable the Aborigines on the reserves to live their own lives in the manner of their own choosing. If they wish to remain on the reserves in tribal situations or conditions, it must be made possible for them to do so. If they wish to live on the reserves under detribalised communal conditions, housing and employment should be provided. If they wish to obtain employment off the reserve but to continue to live on the reserve amongst their own people, this should also be possible. They should, of course, have every opportunity to live in the white community as white men, if that is their desire. It should be possible for the Aborigines in the city and country towns to work in the community but to live in groups with their own centres and opportunities for the preservation of their own culture. They must be given the opportunity to make their own choices. In education, this means that Aboriginal children should, where possible, be taught in their mother tongue. English would follow as a second language. They should be given the fullest opportunity to learn about and understand their own race, culture and traditions, and every effort should be made to ensure that civilised education does not have the effect of educating them away from their own people and traditions. Nevertheless it is inevitable that as the children are educated, many of them will reject tribal conditions and practices and particularly tribal initiation and authority. This will undoubtedly produce social difficulties amongst the tribal Aborigine—and social tensions which will take a long period of time to resolve. . . .

The principal objective of policies in relation to Aborigines should I believe therefore be the integration of the Aboriginal people into the community upon the basis of respect for their culture and traditions and their right to live in their own way and in a way which is different from the way of life of the white community. To this objective should be directed political policies relating to Aboriginal education, housing, employment and, of course, racial discrimination.

This process of shaping satisfactory policies for the Aboriginal people is dependent to a great extent on the development of a sophisticated and articulate aboriginal public opinion, and of aboriginal organisations.

I should now like to glance at the involvement of Aborigines in political activity in South Australia. Four Aboriginal community groups, with exclusive Aboriginal membership, have emerged as stable organisations in recent years and all have to some extent influenced and sought to influence Government policies. They each, therefore, merit a mention in any discussion of the development of Aboriginal organisations. The Council of Aboriginal Women is a well-established body. . . . The Aborigines Progress Association also engages in social welfare work. . . . Other groups of similar character are the Port Lincoln Aboriginal Helpers Association, formed in 1969, and the Whyalla Aboriginal Association, also formed in 1969.

Turning from Associations which voice Aboriginal opinion as to political policies and decisions, I now consider the development of political or semi-political institutions amongst the Aborigines themselves. Of these by far the most significant have been the Aboriginal Reserve Councils. These Councils are functioning on all Aboriginal reserves, except those in the far northern semi-tribal area. The Yalata Lutheran Mission also has a Council. The Councils have now been operating for some 6 or 7 years and it has become the custom to have annual elections, at which nine Councillors are chosen by the residents of the reserve. The problem has been to find candidates for election to the Council. Many do not have the confidence to seek such a position of leadership. Others shrink from the difficulties and unpleasantness associated with public life in any form. Difficult and unpopular decisions must be made. Sometimes these decisions involve relatives, friends and close associates on the reserve and result in unpleasantness an unpopularity. There are too the strong disagreements and controversies which are inseparable from the public debate and decision. The position however is improving and more and more Aborigines are taking the responsibility, . . . The Superintendent's advice is available but in general the Councils conduct their own business and run their own meetings. Successful training courses have been conducted by the Adult Education Department for Aborigines who are interested in taking positions on Councils.

The ultimate objective must be autonomous local government for the reserves. The Councils are indeed assuming greater and greater responsibilities. At the present time the Councils act as a buffer and intermediary between the Superintendent and the residents. The Councils advise the Superintendent about the needs and wishes of the residents. They are concerned with the employment available and the organisation of the work force. They are concerned too with the provision of transport and ambulance services and the general running of the reserve town. Where changes are made by the Superintendent in consultation with the Council, the Council seeks to make the residents understand the reason for the change. The Councils have considerable authority in relation to permits for persons wishing to visit the reserves. They may grant a visiting permit to a person who wishes to visit the reserve for a day or so. They are then responsible for seeing that the conditions of the permit are observed. Where an Aborigine desires to live on the reserve, the Council considers his application and makes a recommendation to the Director of Aboriginal Affairs. The Council also organises sporting and welfare activities. A combined conference of Councillors has been held successfully at Port Augusta.

The Councils are, I think significant political institutions developed by Aborigines for their own self government in local matters. As they gain experience, further powers can be conferred on them until the reserves have all-Aboriginal local Government.

A development which exemplifies both the impact of political decision on the lives of Aborigines and also the involvment of Aborigines in the political process is the Aboriginal Lands Trust. The political decision involved was the recognition by the Aboriginal Lands Trust Act, 1966, of the need for Aboriginal ownership of land and of the need to place in the hands of Aborigines themselves control of their own economic destinies. The Act was a belated recognition of Aboriginal land rights so long and unfairly denied. The policy behind the creation of the Trust was that by degrees Aboriginal reserves, with the consent of the Councils, would be transferred to the Trust to be managed for the benefit of the Aboriginal people as a whole. Other Crown land could be transferred to the Trust or acquired by it. The Trust is a practical and flexible means of rendering possible land rights for Aborigines. The Act confers on the Trust the right to minerals found on the Trust property and provides for the payment of royalties in respect of such mineral discoveries.

From the point of view of Aboriginal involvement in the political process, the central feature of the Act is that all members of the Trust must be Aborigines. Three are appointed by the Government and there is provision for nine further members to be elected by Aboriginal Councils. To the present time, the Aboriginal Councils have not elected members to the Trust but I intend on visiting the reserves to give them every encouragement to do so. The Trust has been operating actively since its formation and has a full-time Manager and a full-time Stenographer/Secretary and a city office. On its formation, the Trust set about the making of a preliminary assessment of the problems involved in the acquisition and development of land resources. . . . I believe that the Trust is the most important single feature of the impact of political policy on the Aborigine and the Aborigine on political policy in South Australia. The Governments, both Commonwealth and State, must give it every encouragement and assistance.

There are some 150,000 Aborigines (including part-Aborigines) in Australia, of whom about 8,000 reside in South Australia. They are gradually becoming more independent and articulate and, in the process, more politically conscious. It is inevitable, and of course desirable, that their organisations will play an increasing part in influencing public opinion in the activities and policies of Governments. It is of course inevitable that specifically Aboriginal organisations will continue to agitate and press for solutions of specifically Aboriginal problems. Sectional organisations concerned with sectional interests and problems have a definite place in the community. Maturity of political development for the Aborigines will not be in sight, however, until the political outlook of Aborigines transcends their purely sectional interests and problems and begins to comprehend the problems and interests of the wider community. It is my hope that the development of specifically Aboriginal organisations with political interests will not have the effect of concentrating Aboriginal political interest and activity in specifically Aboriginal organisations. I look to the day when Aborigines will take their places in the political parties, in general organisations of the community, and will seek and attain political office. The Aborigines' own somewhat rudimentary political institutions, such as Aboriginal Councils, serve an important purpose. They are, however, only a stage in the fuller political development of the Aboriginal people. The ultimate political goal depends upon the wishes of the Aborigines themselves. It is to be hoped that whatever the precise form of the ultimate involvement of the Aborigines in the political community, it will involve a full integration based upon the preservation of the Aborigines distinctive cultural and racial traditions and upon a recognition by the whole community of the contribution which this distinctive tradition has to make to the development of the community as a whole.

In shaping a new Aboriginal policy for the future, we must have full regard for the certainty that an increasing number of Aborigines, particularly young Aborigines, will seek employment in the cities and country towns. The problem of employment is difficult. Many of these Aborigines will lack the education and skills and even the habits of work necessary to obtain and hold regular employment. Future policies must embrace training programmes and programmes for the discovery of avenues of employment. I am convinced that the community generally, and the aborigines in particular, will be served best if these programmes are treated as part of ordinary welfare activities of the community rather than as special Aboriginal services smacking of patronage. Obviously of course the welfare agencies should be equipped to deal with the special problems of Aboriginal people needing welfare assistance.

The movement of Aboriginal people into the cities and towns also necessitates the development of an adequate housing policy. Realism requires recognition of a number of problems. Many of the Aboriginal people who come to urban areas are unaccustomed to life in houses of the type prevailing in those areas. Moreover their traditions are such that they are very ready to accommodate relatives and friends with consequent overcrowding. The problems of house maintenance and relations with the neighbours thereby created are obvious. The reluctance of many Aboriginal people to continue to live in a house where a death has occurred also creates problems.

Future policy therefore must emphasise education and the provision of counselling and welfare services forming part of the general welfare service of the community, but specially equipped to assist in solving the personal and social problems of the Aboriginal people.

**7.30  23 August 1972. No race within a race for Australia.**

(Commonwealth Hansard, Appropriation Bill No. 1 Debate, Senate,
23 August 1972.)

*Dr. Mackay, during a Senate debate, argues that the Aborigines should be
welcomed beside white Australians rather than isolated by an apartheid
system.*

I refer now to another area, small in terms of numbers and money, but
large in terms of human values, namely, the Aborigines—these bewildered,
gentle folk of another civilisation whose land we share. Today, the savage
apostles of race hatred and class division try to fan their problems into
issues calculated to harm our society. What is the truth? Are they brutally
neglected and disregarded? In some places this may still be true, but a
great new concern and practical commitment is abroad. This year the
Government will spend $53m in direct aid to 144,000 Aborigines, which
amounts to about $370 a head, man, woman and child. A family of 5—that
is, with 3 children—have, in addition to the benefits and entitlements of all
Australian citizens, an average expenditure on them of $1,850. Money
is not everything, nor does the Government see it that way. In the Northern
Territory, 75 per cent of Aboriginal children of pre-school age are in such
schools. This is the highest average in the land. Over 90 per cent of
Aboriginal children of primary school age are so enrolled. Special leases
provide land for them on conditions that are peculiarly lenient and sympathetic. Their growth in numbers by natural increase exceeds that of the
white population. Yet at our very doors the apostles of class and race
hatred have stirred up many good people to support a cause which is aimed
at the creation of apartheid and race friction.

The Government is not prepared to see a separate race within a race
developed in Australia, with an embassy from the Aborigines to the
Government of Australia as though they were a foreign power. Like all
other groups within our widening society, we welcome their participation
and their political aspirations as part of a family, not as aliens holding the
nation to ransom. We have a long, long way to go to help these ancient
people into the 21st century. It will not be done in one generation, not
by anyone, but we are doing a very great deal right now. But once again
Labor stands, in most of its expressions, with the apostles of radical and
even violent action to divide and denigrate this nation in our own eyes
and in the esteem of the world.

**7.31  26 October 1972. Racially discriminating legislation.**

(Commonwealth Hansard, H of R, Questions upon Notice No. 6417,
26 October 1972.)

*A question addressed to Mr. Bowen, Minister for Foreign Affairs asks what
has been done to remove discriminating legislation in Australia.*

Racial Discrimination
(Question No. 6417)

Mr. Whitlam asked the Minister for Foreign Affairs, upon notice:

"(1) Did Australia advise the Secretary-General of the United Nations
on 27th October 1971, in the course of the International Year for Action
to Combat Racism and Racial Discrimination that active consideration was
being given by the Commonwealth and State Governments to the removal

of the few remaining elements of legislation which may not be compatible with the provisions of the 1965 International Convention on the Elimination of All Forms of Racial Discrimination.

(2) If so, which elements in the legislation of the Commonwealth or any State were considered at that time to be incompatible with the provisions of the Convention and what action has since been, or is now being, taken in each Parliament to remove those elements."

Mr. N. H. Bowen—The answer to the honourable member's question is as follows:

(1) Yes.

(2) (a) Commonwealth Legislation: The relevant provisions were as follows:

Section 64 of the Migration Act 1958-1966.
Section 423A of the Navigation Act 1912-1970.
Section 4 of the Native Members of the Forces Benefits Act 1957-1968. Section 423A of the Navigation Act was repealed by the Navigation Act 1972. It is proposed to repeal Section 64 of the Migration Act when the next bill to amend the Migration Act is introduced. Legislation is before the Parliament to provide that Australian Aborigines and Torres Strait Islanders, now receiving war compensation and associated benefits under the Native Members of the Forces Benefits Act 1957-1968, will receive these benefits under the Repatriation Act 1920-1972.

(b) State Legislation: The following State Laws were considered to contain provisions that were, or could be regarded as, incompatible with the Convention:

Queensland
    The Aborigines' and Torres Strait Islanders' Affairs Act 1965-1967 and the Regulations thereunder.
Western Australia
    Firearms and Guns Act 1931-1969.
    Gold Buyers Act 1921-1961.
    Liquor Act 1970.
    Mining Act 1904-1970.

In Queensland the Aborigines Act 1971 and the Torres Strait Islanders Act 1971 have been enacted and upon their coming into force will replace the Aborigines' and Torres Strait Islanders' Affairs Act. However, the new legislation does not fully satisfy the requirements of the Convention. In Western Australia the only discriminatory provision in the Firearms and Guns Act was repealed in 1971. I understand that the Western Australian authorities propose to seek the repeal of the discriminatory element in the Gold Buyers Act. In regard to the Liquor Act, since 1st July 1971 there has been no prohibition concerning the consumption of liquor by Aborigines. I am also informed that a new Mining Act is being examined by the Western Australian Parliament and that it does not contain any provisions which are discriminatory on racial grounds.

**7.32  16 May 1973. Plans for an Aboriginal Consultative Council.**

(*The Courier Mail*, Brisbane, Queensland, 16 May 1973, p. 1.)

*A press statement reporting the proposals to give Aborigines the opportunity to participate more fully in making decisions affecting them.*

The Federal Government is considering sweeping new plans for aboriginal representation in Australia.

It plans to set up an Aboriginal Consultative Council, with members elected from the aboriginal and part-aboriginal population.

Federal mapping officials already have drawn maps, on lines suggested by aboriginals themselves, to provide electorates in all mainland States and the Northern Territory. . . .

The council, if formed, would advise the Aboriginal Affairs Minister (Mr. Bryant).

Other proposals under consideration envisage the setting up of special electoral zones and the creation of special electoral rolls for aboriginal and part-aboriginals.

Aboriginal community leaders believe the formation of the Consultative Council could be a step towards the eventual establishment of a "Black Parliament," set up to deal with problems affecting aboriginals and part-aboriginals.

The mainland States and the Northern Territory are understood to have been divided into electoral zones for the formation of the Consultative Council.

About 80 representatives are expected to be selected from 27 divisions— six each in Queensland, the Northern Territory and New South Wales, five in South Australia and four in Victoria.

Tasmania, with no static aboriginal population, would have no representatives.

The Federal Government's aboriginal affairs committee, chaired by Senator J. Keeffe (Qld.) will meet today to consider the technicalities of the proposals and will seek the views of a top Commonwealth electoral officer.

The idea for the council has grown from the National Aboriginals Consultative Committee, which was formed by Mr. Bryant soon after Labor took office. . . .


**7.33 29 May 1973. Responsibility for Aborigines, Federal Cabinet approved Takeover.**

(*The Sydney Morning Herald*, Sydney, 29 May 1973.)

*An article appearing in the press which notes the conclusion of lengthy negotiations.*

CANBERRA, Monday.—Federal Cabinet agreed in principle today to the Commonwealth assuming direct responsibility for Aborigines throughout Australia.

South Australia has already asked the Commonwealth to accept responsibility by July 1 but talks with other States are not so advanced.

The Minister for Aboriginal Affairs, Mr. Bryant, said Cabinet had authorised him today to negotiate with State ministers for the transfer of policy planning and co-ordination functions.

This would be done on the basis of discussions between officers of the Department of Aboriginal Affairs, the Public Service Board and Treasury with appropriate State officers.

Mr. Bryant said members of the National Aboriginal Consultative Committee, acting as representatives of the Aboriginal people, had called on the Premiers of each of the mainland States to transfer responsibility for Aboriginal affairs to the Commonwealth.

The decision fulfilled Labor policy that the Commonwealth assume the ultimate responsibility for Aborigines accorded it by the 1967 national referendum.

# References

### Government and Official Publications

COMMONWEALTH

Historical Records of Australia, Series 1, Vols. I-XXVI, Government Printer, 1917.
Historical Records of New South Wales, Vol. 1, Parts 1-4.

*Parliamentary papers*
The Aboriginals and Half-Castes of Central Australia and North Australia. Report by J. W. Bleakley, 1928, No. 21, 1929.
Aboriginal Welfare. Conference of Commonwealth and State Ministers, Darwin, July 1963, in Vol. 3, 1962-1963.
Report from the Select Committee on Grievances of Yirrkala Aborigines, Arnhem Land Reserve, 1963, in (HofR) No. 311, 1962-1963.
Report from the Select Committee on Voting Rights of Aboriginals, 1961. (HofR 1 and 2) Vol. 2, 1961.
Recommendations by Donald Thomson, Aboriginal Policy, in No. 56, Vol. 3, 1937.

*Parliamentary debates*
Revised Estimates, 7 December 1939, in HofR, 1939-1940.
Questions, Aborigines, 8 April 1964, in HofR, Vol. 41, 1964.
Questions, Black Power, 30 April 1968, in HofR, Vol. 58, 1968.
Ministerial Statement, 9 August 1968, in HofR, Vol. 60, 1968.
Questions, Tourism, 4 March 1969, in HofR, Vol. 62, 1969.
Questions, Sterilisation of Aborigines, 18 September 1969, HofR, Vol. 65, 1969.
Debate on Aborigines, 18 March 1970, in Vol. S43, Senate Debates.
Abschol Summary of Legislation, in Debate on State Grants (Aboriginal Advancement Bill), Vol. S46, p.2052, 1970.
Question upon Notice No. 1654, 18 March 1971, Commonwealth Hansard, HofR, 1971.
Senate Budget Debate 1971-1972, 15 September 1971, Commonwealth Hansard, 1971.
Questions upon Notice No. 6417, 26 October 1972, Commonwealth Hansard, 1972.

*Bulletins*
Preliminary Report on the Aboriginals of the Northern Territory, Dept. of External Affairs, by Professor W. Baldwin Spencer, M.A., C.M.G., Melbourne, Bulletin No. 7, 1913.

NEW SOUTH WALES

*Parliamentary papers*

Select Committee on the Administration of the Aborigine's Protection Board, 1938, Vol. 7, 1938-39-40.

Report and Recommendations of the Public Service Board, N.S.W., No. 13, Vol. 7, 1938-39-40.

QUEENSLAND

*Parliamentary votes and proceedings*

Report from the Select Committee on the Native Police Force, and the Condition of the Aborigines Generally, Vol. 1, 1861.

SOUTH AUSTRALIA

Gazette and Colonial Register, Adelaide, Vol. 1, No. 11, 1857.

Oodnadatta Police Station, Annual Report on Aborigines, N.W. Division, 1943.

*Parliamentary papers*

Progress Report on the Royal Commission on the Aborigines, No. 26, Vol. 2, 1913.

Select Committee of the Legislative Council on the Aborigines Bill, Vol. 2, 1899.

Select Committee of the Legislative Council on Aborigines, No. 165, 1860.

*Statutes*

No. 45, Elizabethae ii Reginae, Aboriginal Affairs Act, 1962.

WESTERN AUSTRALIA

*Parliamentary votes and proceedings*

Royal Commission into the conditions of the Natives, Vol. 1, No. 5, 1905.

Royal Commission on the Condition and Treatment of Aborigines, Vol. 1, 1935, No. 2.

Royal Commission of Inquiry into the Alleged Killing and Burning of Bodies of Aborigines in East Kimberley and into Police Methods when Effecting Arrest, No. 3, 1927.

*Parliamentary debates*

Northern Settlers Protection Bill, Vol. 2, 1892 (14 January).

*Statutes*

No. 23, Geo vi., Native (Citizen Rights) Act, 1944.

UNITED KINGDOM

*House of Commons, Parliamentary Papers.*

Copies of Extracts from Dispatches Relative to the Massacre of Various Aborigines of Australia, in the year 1838, etc., Vol. 43, 1839.

Copies of Extracts from Dispatches of the Governors of the Australian Colonies with the Reports of the Protectors of Aborigines, etc., etc., N.S.W., Vol. 34, 1844.

BOOKS, JOURNALS

Barton, G. B., *History of New South Wales from the Records*, Government Printer, Vol. 1, 1889.

Dampier, William, *A New Voyage Round the World*, N. M. Penzer (ed.), The Argonaut Press, London, 1927.

Ernabella Newsletter, Ernabella Mission, S.A., 1944.

Eyre, Edward John, *Journals of Expeditions into Central Australia*, London, Vol. 1 and 2, 1840.

Hasluck, P. M. C., *Native Welfare in Australia; Speeches and Addresses by the Hon. Paul Hasluck, M.P.*, Perth, 1953.

Howitt, A. W., *On the Organisation of the Australian Tribes, An Anthropological Investigation*; The Transactions of the Royal Society of Victoria, 1889.

Mitchell, Major Thomas L., *Three Expeditions into the Interior of Eastern Australia*; First Edition, London, 1838, Vol. 2.

Mitchell, Lt. Col. Sir T. L., *Journal of an Expedition into the Interior of Tropical Australia*, Longman, Brown, Green, and Longmans, London, 1848.

Parker, Edward Stone, First Periodical Report from the Loddon District, in Edgar Morrison, *Early Days of the Loddon Valley*, 1966.

Sutherland, Alexander, *Victoria and its Metropolis, Past and Present*, McCarron and Bird and Co., Vol. 1, 1888.

Walker, James Backhouse, *The Walker Memorial Volume, Early Tasmania*, Government Printer, 1902.

Wharton, W. J. L. (ed.), *Captain Cook's Journal During the First Voyage Round the World*, London, 1893, Australian Facsimile Editions, No. 188, Adelaide, 1968.


LECTURES

Lang, Gideon, *The Aborigines of Australia in their Original Condition, and in their Relations with the White Man*, Melbourne, 1865.

Maconochie, Captain K. H., *Thoughts on Convict Management and other Subjects Connected with the Australian Penal Colonies*, Hobart Town, 1838.

Parker, Edward Stone, *The Aborigines of Australia*, Melbourne, 1854.


NEWSPAPERS

*The Age*, Melbourne, 1950s, 1967.

*The Argus*, Melbourne, 1846.

*The Courier Mail*, Brisbane, 1973.

*The Bulletin*, Rockhampton, 1865.

*The Koorier*, Melbourne, 1969, 1970.

*The Illustrated Australian News*, Melbourne, 1876, 1884.

*The Illustrated Sydney News and N.S.W. Agriculturist and Grazier*, Sydney, 1880.

*The Illustrated Melbourne Post*, Melbourne, 1864.

*The Leader*, Melbourne, Supplement, 1882.

*The Maryborough Chronicle*, Maryborough, 1865.
*The Queenslander*, Brisbane, 1877, 1880.
*The Sun*, Melbourne, 1965, 1966, 1967.
*The Sydney Morning Herald*, Sydney, 1927, 1973.

# Index

Aborigines, 58; character, 15, 20, 24, 25, 38, 58-62, 70-74; in battle, 87-88, 92; elderly, 170; (and education) 80; (as prisoners) 126; (starved) 112, 113; (on reserves) 145; (given rations) 116; elders, 101; intellect of, 62-63, 66, 69, 70, 119-120; (in N.S.W.) 17, 25; (in Qld) 90; (in Tas.) 39, 40, 42; (in Vic.) 64, 98; as liars, 74, 84; morality of, 49, 50, 59, 65, 70, 71, 91; (in N.T.) 136-137, 155; (in the tribal state) 73, 74, 95; (training in) 144, 145; pride in heritage, 214, 215, 216, 232; in Qld, 78, 85, 90-91; in Tas., 38-39; see also Tribes, Part-Aborigines, Children, Women

Aborigines Advancement League, 208
Aborigines' Advisory Board, (S.A.) 164
Aborigines' Consultative Council, 237-238
Aborigines' Department, (S.A.) 147; (W.A.) 122, 129, 170
Aborigines' Friends Association, 135-136
Aborigines' Land Trust, 234
Aborigines' Progress Association, 233
Aborigines' Protection Board, (N.S.W.) 171, 172, 173, 174, 177-178, 179-180; (W.A.) 108; (Vic.) 95, 98-99, 108
Aborigines' Welfare Board, (N.S.W.) 208
Aboriginal Courts, 222, 223
Aboriginal Reserve Councils, (Qld) 222, (S.A.) 233-234, 235
Aboriginal Tax, 92
Abschol, (Qld) 219-226
Adelaide River (N.T.), 118
Adult Education Council, (S.A.) 234
Africa, Western, 58
African nationalism, 232
Age, The, Melbourne, 205
Agriculture, (Department of) 179, (tropical), 170
Air Force, 182-183
Albert River (Qld), 76
Alcohol, 206, 228; in N.S.W., 95, in N.T.; 114, 115, 116, 137; in Qld, 79, 92; in Vic., 72; in W.A., 108, 123; and legislation, 120-121, and murder, 71; prohibition of, 180, 218-219; and prostitution, 115, 123
Alice Springs (N.T.), 157, 158-159, 160-161; Half-Caste Bungalow, 158-159, 160, 181
Alligator River Reserve (N.T.), 140, 144
Anderson, George, 54-55
Anderson, Sir Kenneth, 229
Angledool Aborigines' Settlement (N.S.W.), 171, 174
Anthropologists, 97, 101, 164; at Sydney University, 133; criticising missions, 162, 166; report, D. Thomson, 175-176; and assimilation 179; and de-tribalisation 196
Amelioration of Aborigines, 40, 42, 90-92, 95
Argus, The, 68
Armit, Inspector, 89
Armit, William, 95
Arnhem Land, 134; reserves, 116, 118, 141, 143, 144, 146, 164, 176, 203-205
Arsenic, 79, 153
Ashburton River (W.A.), 109
Asians, 133; and Aboriginal employment, 137; harbouring, 120-121; and opium, 114, 117, 120-121, 137; and prostitution, and venereal disease, 111, 123, 124, 137; and the pearl shell industry, 123-124; nationalism, 232
Assimilation, 60-61; Commonwealth Government Policy, 187, 195, 196, 197, 201-202, 232; and land rights, 210; and mining operations, 205; in N.S.W., 35, 179; of part-Aborigines, 133-134, 158; and special assistance, 213; in Tas., 42; see also Integration
Australia Felix, 62-63, 71
Australian Agricultural Company, 53
Australian Institute of Aboriginal Studies, 213

Backhouse and Walker, 28, 38, 39
Bark cutting, 86
Barnard, 181
Bass Strait, 27, 38
Bathurst Island Reserve, 118, 143, 144, 158
Batman, John, 230
Bauxite, 204, 205, 231
Beagle Bay (W.A.), 123, 126
Beazley, 205-206
Begging, (N.S.W.) 17; (W.A.) 108

Bell, 83-84
Belyando (Qld), 89
Berry, 99
Bible, The, 61
Big River (N.S.W.), 55, 56
Black Parliament, 237
Black Power, 209, 216
Blankets (distributed), Qld, 78, 82, 84,
    91, 95, 99; (to Native Police) 81;
    S.A., 112; W.A., 108
Bleakley, J. W., 133, 154-166
Blue Mts (N.S.W.), 33
Board of National Education, 70
Boats, 117
Boiling Down Establishment (Qld), 78
Bora (Qld), 89
Botany Bay (N.S.W.), 17, 19, 21, 22, 23
Bourke, Governor Sir Richard, 230
Bowen, N. H., 237
Brain, R. R., 170-176
Brewarrina (N.S.W.), 174
Briggs, Watson, 230
Bringelly, (Qld) 38
Brisbane (Qld), 78, 79, 227
British Government, 32, 34, 35, 45, 49,
    52, 58, 67
Broken Bay (N.S.W.), 20
Broome (W.A.), 123, 126
Brute Species: Aborigines as, 15, 42, 66,
    69, 93, 135
Bryant, 238
Buckland, Sergeant, 150
Bunya Scrub (Qld), 76
Burial: Aboriginal, 131-132
Burton, Justice, 57
Burwan Cks (Vic.), 54

Caffre Frontier, 58, 60
Campbell, Captain, 22
Campbell, J. T., 36, 38
Camps: Aborigines', 87; Alice Springs,
    160-161; Moore River Settlement, 169-
    170; N.S.W., 95; N.T., 144, 145;
    numbers in, 156
Camooweal (Qld), 111
Canada, 131
Cannibalism, 22, 99-100; of part-
    Aborigines, 96
Canoes, 19, 21, 93
Carr, Lieutenant, 81
Cartridge Springs (W.A.), 128
Castlereagh River (Qld), 86
Cattle: spearing, 86; N.S.W., 23, 31, 33;
    N.T., 138; Pt Phillip, 52, 53, 54;
    Qld, 76, 78, 79; W.A., 109, 126, 128,
    130, 136, 150, 154; see also pastoral
    industry
Cape York Peninsula, 94, 231
Carnarvon Municipal Council, 128
Central Australia, 196; and tourism, 217,
    218; missions, 119; cattle stations, 156-
    157

Chaining Aborigines, 107, 124, 125, 127,
    129, 150, 151, 152
Charlotte Waters (N.T.), 120
Charters Towers (Qld), 90
Chief, Headmen, 101, 207; as Police-
    men, 61; in Tas., 39; in Vic., 68, 72
Chief Secretary's Department, 98
Children: Aboriginal, 24, 64-65, 74, 198;
    apprentices, 122, 173, 178; cattle kill-
    ing, 126, 128; census taken, 129;
    chaining, 125, 126; education of, 35,
    69-70, 129-130, 144, 145, 156-157,
    178, 202, 236; murder of, 32, 55, 57,
    151; on missions, 116; and parents,
    73; birth registration, 129; in poverty,
    205, 206, 207-208; part-Aborigines
    (training), 116, 122, 129-130, 144,
    148-149, 157, 160; sexual exploitation,
    95, 115; syphilis, 113, 169
Child Welfare Department, 159, 161,
    202
Chinese, 137, 138; and opium, 120-121,
    137; and part-Aborigines, 141; see
    Pearl shell fishing, Asians
Christian conversion, 59, 61-62, 194; in
    N.S.W., 49, 94; in N.T., 119; in
    Qld, 91; in S.A., 75, 183-184; in Tas.,
    28, 39, 40-44; in Vic., 64-65, 72, 73-
    74; see also Missions
Christmas Creek (Qld), 76
Cinema, censored, 154
Citizenship, 180-181; applications for,
    207; education in, 164, 166, 187; and
    part-Aborigines, 187; and legislation,
    184-185, 202
Civilising attempts, 35, 62, 69, 94, 194;
    Maconochie's theory, 59-62; in N.S.W.,
    34, 49, 51; in Tas., 41, 42; in Vic.,
    74, 95-96, 98
Clark, Dr Jonathon, 54
Clark, Kenneth, 54
Clermont Free Press, 90
Clothing, 111, 112, 183, 184; by Govern-
    ment and employers, 35, 39, 82, 91,
    173, 174; Native Police, 59, 61, 81
Cobham, 88
Cobham, Lieutenant, 53
Coburg Peninsula Flora and Fauna
    Reserve, 204
Colaband River (Vic.), 64
Coley, Captain John, 78-80
Collarenebri (N.S.W.), 171, 172
Collins, Captain, 76
Colonial Government, 85, 86, 89; see
    also N.S.W., British Govt
Colonial Secretary's Office, 51
Colonial Surgeon (W.A.), 80
Colonisation, British, 58
Commonwealth Arbitration Commission,
    205, 206
Commonwealth Capital Fund for Abori-
    gines' Enterprises, 210, 218

Commonwealth Government, 137, 146; Assimilation Policy, 196, 201-202, 209, 211-212, 213; expenditure, 236; Integration Policy, 198; responsibilities and powers, 141, 145, 153, 192, 193, 199, 211, 238-239; rights for land, 209, 211; see also Legislation
Compound, Darwin, 137, 142, 154, 155, 182; Moore River 168-169
Compulsory saving, N.S.W., 172, 178; N.T., 142; Qld, 149, 225; S.A., 149
Compigne, 76, 77
Conference of Commonwealth and State Ministers of Aboriginal Affairs, 1936, 192; 1937, 192, 194; 1947, 192, 195; 1948, 192, 194; 1951, 193; 1963, 201-202; 1968, 211
Convicts, 17, 19, 21, 22, 23, 27, 37, 42, 54, 57, 59, 62
Coochin (Qld), 75
Cook, Captain James, 13, 15, 19, 20
Cookson, Police Magistrate, 174
Cooktown Coorier (Qld), 93, 94
Coombs, Dr H. C., 216-217
Coranderrk Aborigines' Settlement (Vic.), 98-99
Corroborees, 41, 73, 89, 137, 155
Country Party, 212, 213
Creen Creek (Qld), 89
Criminal Courts, 27, 31, 56-57, 220; and cattle killing, 127, 128; evidence, 32-33, 45, 84, 87, 139-140, 152; see also Prisoners.
Crown Lands, 35, 231, 234; commissioners of, 63; and reserves, 145-146; see also Legislation
Cultivation by Aborigines, 35, 49, 64, 66, 69
Cunningham Point (W.A.), 123
Cyanide, 153
Cygnet Bay (W.A.), 123

Dalton, W. E., 135-136
Daly River (N.T.), 114, 140, 143; settlement, 144
Damper, 99
Dampier, William, 13, 15
Danger, H., 53, 54, 56-57
Dareton (N.S.W.), 208-209
Darling Downs (Qld), 79
Darling River (N.S.W.), 208
Darwin, Charles, 46
Darwin (N.T.), 120, 136, 139, 143; compound, 137, 142, 154, 155, 182; Half-caste Home, 154, 182; air force base, 182; see also Palmerston, Northern Territory, Legislation
Davey, J. H., 209
Day, 57
Deaken, 98-99
Depopulation, 69, 84, 96, 153; N.T., 117, 136; Qld, 78, 91, 94; S.A., 115; Tas., 40; and tribal wars, 67-68; Vic., 71-72, 95-96, 100; W.A., 80; see also Population
Derby (W.A.), 126, 128, 129, 131
Dingo scalps, 184
Discrimination; legislation, 228-229, 236-237; see also Legislation, Employment, Education, Wages
Disease, 17, 24, 61, 69, 78, 96, 154; Darwin, 154; legislation, 201; Native State, 164, 165; on settlements, 171-172, 226; smallpox, 24, 72, 96, 100; venereal, (N.S.W.), 95; (N.T.), 115, 154; (S.A.), 111, 113, 146; (Vic.), 65; (W.A.), 123, 169; see also Malnutrition, Leprosy, Health, Hospitals
Dispersal, 77, 93-94; Qld, 46, 76, 77, 89, 90
Divine Law, 74, 100-101
Dogs, 54, 66, 130; scalps, 152, 153, 183
Doomed race, 74, 75, 94, 96, 119, 147, 194
Dormitory: detention in, 168-169, 222; "system", 175
Douglas, Inspector, 151
Drays, attacked, 79
Dredge, Assistant Protector, 49
Dugandan (Qld), 75, 76, 77
Dugong fishery, 96
Durandur (Qld), 78, 79

Education, 187, for apprentices, 123; compulsory, 69, 70, 71, 148, 164, 165; at Darwin, 155; failure of, 66, 90; on government stations, 169-170, 173, 179-180; integration and, 198-199, 235; and malnutrition, 226-227; Maconochie's theory, 59, 60-62; on missions, 119, 161, 162; in N.S.W., 35, 49, 180; in N.T., 144, 213, 235; in Qld, 91, 138-139, 220, 223, 227; and S.A., 200-201; in Tas., 39, 41, 43; in Vic., 67; and vocational training, 80, 144, 145, 148, 149, 165, 202, 217; at university, 227
Employment, 60-61, 91, 96, 103-104, 135-136; in agriculture, 149, 165; access to those in, 201; and assisted Aborigines, (Qld), 225-226; as domestic servants, 114, 116, 121, 154, 165, 227; on farms, 35, 80, 168; on frontiers, 86; killing vermin, 89-90; on missions, 67, 135-136; numbers in, 1944, 191; in pastoral industry, 65, 95, 109-110, 112, 114, 133, 136, 137-138, 153, 166-167, 168, 170, 183, 191, 207; of prisoners, 128-129; in Qld, 82, 92; as seasonal workers, 192, 208; as 112, 117; (N.S.W.), 173, 174; (S.A.), sleeper cutters, 156; regulations, 111, 120-121; (W.A.), 121-124, 153; see also Pearl Shell Fishing, Aborigines and Torres Strait Islanders Affairs Act, Wages

Equality, see Status
Ernabella Mission (S.A.), 183-184
Ernest River (W.A.), 150, 151
Evidence, legal, 22, 33, 45, 84, 87, 152;
    see also Witness
Evolution, Theory of, 46, 60, 74, 94, 96,
    97, 98, 100-101, 195
Execution of Aborigines, 24, 33, 107;
    of Whites, 45, 57
Executive and Judicial Authority, 31;
    Executive Council, 45, 50-51, 57; see
    also Colonial Government
Explorers, 13, 15; Eyre, 66; Kennedy,
    97; Mitchell, 62-63; Tench, 25
Extinction, 175; N.T. and Central Aus-
    tralia, 164; S.A., 119, 147; in Tas., 28;
    see also Doomed, Depopulation
"Extermination", 78, 85, 87-88, 91,
    94, 96-97
Eyre, Edward John, 66


Faithful, W. Pitt, 51, 53
Farms, 33-37; for Aborigines, 35, 49,
    64; employment on, 35, 80, 91, 142,
    165, 170; and missions, 67; see also
    Cultivation
Farrell, Corporal, 33
Fassifern (Qld), 77
Field Island (N.T.), 140
Finch, 53
Fire, 20, 66, 73; Aborigines threatening,
    31, 32
Fire arms, Aborigines use of, 54, 68;
    see also Shooting
First Fleet, 17
Fishing, Aborigines, 22, 23; dugong, 96;
    trepang, 156
Fitzroy River (W.A.), 130
Fleming, John, 56
Flinders Island Aboriginal Settlement,
    27, 40-44; Native Police of, 61; see
    also Tasmania
Flogging, 80; Native Police, 82, 83
Flour, 99, 109; exchanged for part-
    Aboriginals, 116; poisoned, 79, 153;
    prostitution for, 115, 123; see also
    Rations
Flying Doctor Service, 193
Forestry Commission (N.S.W.), 179
Forrest River (W.A.), 151
Franchise, Aboriginal, 197-200; denied,
    180; offered, 187; see also Legislation
Frazer, 88
Frost, 182-183


Gair, Senator, 227-229
Gair, Mrs, 227, 228
Gale, 53
Gambling, 168
Gaols, Broome (W.A.), 128; Carnarvon,
    128; Roebourne, 126, 128; Rottnest,
    106, 109; Wyndham, 128; (N.T.),

Darwin, 140; (N.S.W.), Sydney, 58;
    see also Prisoners
Gardiner, John, 54
Geelong (Vic.), 53, 54, 67
George, His Majesty King, 19
Georgetown (Qld), 89
Georgina River, 112
Giese, Senator, 205
Gifts to Aborigines, 15, 19, 20, 35, 50,
    84; see also Rations, Blankets, Food
Gillen, F. J., 119-121
Gins, 77; see Women
Gipps, Sir George, 45, 49, 50, 52, 56-57
Glenelg, Lord, 45, 49
Glenelg River (Vic.), 68, 71
Gold, 72; prospecting, 94; on Reserves,
    204; see also Mining
Gonorrhoea, 113
Goodall, Sergeant, 33
Goodooga (N.S.W.), 172
Gorman, 53
Gorton, J. G., 189, 229
Goulburn River (Vic.), 53
Gove Peninsula (N.T.), 204, 231
Government Settlement, 219; see Re-
    serves
Grant, 98
Grazing Lands, 45, 63; see also Pastoral
    Industry, Stock
Green, 98
Gregor, 80
Gregory, A. C., 80
Gribble, E. R. B., 149-152
Gribble, J. B., 94-95
Griffith, Sir Samuel, 109
Grose River (N.S.W.), 33, 38
Groote Eylandt, 158
Guide: Aboriginal, 63, 87; see also
    Trackers
Gulf of Carpentaria, 152
Gurindji, 210, 212, 231


Hall's Creek (W.A.), 126, 128
Hardie, 76, 78
Hasluck, Sir Paul, 187, 191-197, 204
Hawkesbury River (N.S.W.), 25, 31, 33,
    38; protection association, 37
Health, Aboriginal, 134, 146, 211, 213,
    216-217; medical care, 24, 154, 155,
    177, 178; in N.S.W., 22, 23, 24, 61,
    171-172; in S.A., 111, 146-147; in
    W.A., 80, 81, 107; see also Malnutri-
    tion, Disease, Hospitals
Henderson, 76
Her Majesty's Gaol, Sydney, 58
Hermannsburg Lutheran Mission (S.A.),
    119, 143, 144, 158, 159, 160, 161, 183
Hobbs 54
Hobby, Lieutenant, 32
Hodgkinson, 32
Holloway, 182

Hospitals, 139, 155; Leper Lazarette (N.T.), 161-162; "lock-up", 139, 146; N.S.W., 171, 177; N.T., 138-139, 154; W.A., 169; see also Health, Disease
House of Commons Parliamentary Papers, 40, 45, 49, 52, 58, 63, 67
Housing, 199, for part-Aborigines, 158-159, 160, 181; and assimilation, 202; in Darwin, 142, 155, 181-182; on N.S.W. government settlements, 172-173, 226; on pastoral properties, 167, 168; S.A., 147; in urban areas, 235; in wurlies, 146-147
Hottentots, 58, 59
Howitt, A. W., 101
Hunter, Governor John, 27, 31
Hunting, Aborigines, 66, 85, 94; in Central and North Australia, 118, 183; and dogs, 54, 130; on pastoral properties, 131, 210; and Native Police, 59; in Qld, 85; in S.A., 112, 113; in Vic., 64-65, 74; in W.A., 107; on reserves, 204
Huts and Keepers, 54, 86

Industrial Mission Homes, 163
Infanticide, 73, 96, 100; of part-Aborigines, 113
*Illustrated Sydney News* and *N.S.W. Agriculturist and Grazier*, 94-95
Integration Policy, 198, 232-233; "integrateds", 215
Intellect, Aborigines', see Aborigines
Interior, the, 36, 62-63, 66; Pt Phillip, 51; Qld, 46
International Labour Organisation, 214, 230
Intrepreters, 71, 127, 139; see also Prisoners
Ipswich (Qld), 76, 79
Irwin River (W.A.), 109

Jackson, Samuel, 54
Jam, 99, 172, 176; see also Rations
Japanese, 123, 141; see also Asians
Jay Creek (N.T.), 160
Jeffcot, Sir John, 39
Jelley, Hon. J., 146, 147, 148
Jesuits, 114, 119; see also Missions
Jolly, 150
Jones, Thomas, 54

Kangaroos, 89-90, 99, 109, 130
Katherine Creek (N.T.), 143
Keck, Henry, 58
Keeffe, Senator J., 218-219, 226-227, 237
Kilcoy Station (Qld), 79
Kilmeister, 55
King Camp (N.T.), 142
King Georges Sound (W.A.), 80
King, Governor Philip, 52
King, Dr Martin Luther, 209

King, Len, 231-235
King Sound (W.A.), 123-124
Kimberleys (W.A.), 170; murders at, 109, 149-152, 152-153; pastoral workers, 166-167; prisoners 129

Labour incentives, 35, 36, 39, 41; see also Wages, Employment
La Grange Bay (W.A.), 123
Lake Woods Aboriginal Settlement, 144
Lamaru Camp (N.T.), 142
Lambe, Henry, 33
Land Grants, 35; see Land Rights, Reserves
Land Rights, 49, 52, 60, 64, 66, 85, 187; Aborigines' Lands Trust, 234-235; discussion, 228; Gurindjis and, 210, 212-214, and I.L.O. Convention, 1957, 214; in S.A., 148, 234; and reserves, 98, 118, 234; in Vic., 64, 100; and United Nations petition, 230-231
Landsdowne Hills (N.S.W.), 22
Land utilisation, by Aborigines, 58, 66
Lang, Gideon, 84-87, 87-88
Language, (tribal), 23, 24, 49, 62, 72, 73; and church services, 119; in schools, 233; English, to be taught, 61-62, 67, 72; interpreters, 71, 127, 139; Aborigines use of, 98; pidgin, 139, 168
Lanne (Lanney) Billy, 28, 216
La Perouse, 19
Larakia Reserve (N.T.), 143
Legislation, and alcohol, 95, 115; and deaths, 131-132; and discrimination, 228-229, 236-237; and reserves, 131; and state and federal responsibility, 192; and opium, 117; and electors, 180; and employment, 121-124; and protection, 107-110, 117; Commonwealth: 137, 140, 145-146, 197, 199, 202, 204, 237; N.S.W., 180-181; N.T., 213; Qld, 189, 219-224, 237; S.A., 110, 113, 120, 148, 200, 201, 234; W.A., 122, 124, 127, 128, 130, 184-185, 237
Leprosy, 213, 216; Lazarette for Lepers, N.T., 161-162
Life after death, 38-39, 73
Liverpool (N.S.W.), 38
Loddon River (Vic.), 63; Aboriginal settlement, 71, 74
Logan River (Vic.), 76, 78
Lumbia, 150

McDonald, Sir Ross, 192
McEntire, 24-25
McEwan, J., 181-182
Maconochie, K. H., R. N., 58-62
Mackenzie, Evan, 79
Mackenzie River (Qld), 89, 90
McPhersons Range (Qld), 76

Macquarie, Governor Lachlan, 27, 33-36, 36-38
Malays, 123, 124, 141
Mallae Reserve (N.T.), 143
Malnutrition, 216-217, at Botany Bay, 17, 22; on government settlements, 171, 225, 226; in N.S.W., 95, 171; prisoners, 126; in S.A., 112; in Tas., 28; in Vic., 65; in W.A., 107
Maningrida (N.T.), 206
Mannassite Reserve (N.T.), 143
Marble Bar (W.A.), 129
Marriage, (tribal), 61, 73, 95, 101, 198; and education, 69, 80; (of part-Aborigines), 141, 158, 163
Massacre of Aborigines, 65, 79, 87, 93; East Kimberleys, 149-152, 152-153; Myall Creek, 45, 53, 55-57; of Whites, 88; see also Murder, Wars
Melbourne (Vic.), 51, 98-99
Memorial, pastoralists, 50-51; Aborigines, 98-99
Methylated spirits, 206, 218
Melville Bay (N.T.), 203
Mildura (Vic.), 208
Military Force, and Aborigines, 27, 31, 32, 34, 36, 37, 45, 51, 53, 59; see also N.S.W. Marine Corps
Miller, 109
Mimicry, 39, 60, 61, 62
Mining, 139, 143; and Asians, 137; and land rights, 234; on reserves, 204, 231; and royalties, 234
Missions, 66, 67, 71, 99, 114, 133, 143, 144, 149-151, 153, 193; abandoned, 119; in Central and North Australia, 119, 162-164; destroying tribal culture, 119, 162, 175; expenditure on, 91, 119; government (assistance), 116, 149, 159, 161, 162-163; (control), 135; and part-Aborigines, 116, 129, 159-160; and population decline, 175; Tas., 27; in S.A., 183-184, 233; (Hermannsburg), 119, 143, 144, 158, 159, 160, 161, 183; (N.T.), 140, 158; (N.S.W.), 53, 94; (Qld), 175; and education, 119, 161, 162
Moola Bulla Aboriginal Settlement, 164, 170
Moograh (Qld), 78
Moore River (W.A.), Aboriginal Settlement, 168-169
Morrill, 85
Morrison, Edgar, 63
Mortality rates, Infant, 187, 216; see also Depopulation
Morton Bay (Qld), 79
Moseley, Commissioner H. D., 166-170
Mount Alexander (Vic.), 64
Mount Franklin (Vic.), 63
Mount Lindsay (Qld), 76
Mudburra Aboriginal Reserve (N.T.), 143

Muggleton, S., 128
Munja Aboriginal Settlement (W.A.), 170
Munro, 64
Murchison (W.A.), 106, 108, 168
Murder of Aborigines, 31, 32, 33, 53-55, 67-68, 77; of Whites, 32, 53, 54, 79, 115; ceasing, 71; see also Massacre, War
Murray River (N.S.W.), 53, 71
Murray Valley, 207, 209
Murrumbidgee River (N.S.W.), 94
Myall Creek massacre, 45, 53, 54-57, 58

National Aboriginal Consultative Committee, 238
National Museum, 97
National reputation, 192
Native animals, 17, 23, 66; and cattle, 130; as food, 81, 99, 130; as vermin, 89
Native Police, 46, 58-60, 61, 70, 88, 89, 92, 93-94; blanket and ration distribution, 81, 82, 83, 84; confrontation, 83, 85, 87, 88, 90; discipline, 76-77, 82, 83, 84, 85; desertions, 75, 82; officers, 77, 89, 97; reserves, 223; Qld Royal Commission, 75-84; secret patrolling, 92, 94, 97; Tas., 42, 61
Native State, 164-165
Neal, Superintendent, 169
Nebo (Qld), 96
Nepean River (N.S.W.), 33, 37, 38
Newcastle Waters (N.T.), 144. Aboriginal Settlement.
New Guinea, 176
New Holland, 15
New South Wales, Aborigines of, 49, 91, 94-95; Aborigines' Protection Board, 177-180; penal settlement, 17, 19-25; Government Settlements, 170-174, 176-177; Government, 34, 37, 50-51, 59, 63; and Qld, 79, 80; mission, 94; see also Legislation, Tribes, Aborigines
New South Wales Marine Corps, 17, 19, 22, 23
Nigger, 109, 110, 112, 128; see Aborigines, Tribes
Ninety Mile Beach (W.A.), 167
Nixon, P. J., 209-211
Noble, Rev. James, 150, 151
Nomadism, 71, 96, 99, 184, 191
Normanton (Normantown), (Qld), 89, 97
Northern Territory, Aborigines of, 114, 136-146, 156-166, 181, 211; award wages, 205, 207; Chinese of, 120-121; housing, 137, 142, 154, 155, 182, 199; and land rights, 209-211; mission, 119, 140, 158, 162-164; part-Aborigines, 141, 156-157, 181-183;

reserves, 116, 118, 141, 143, 144, 145, 146; social welfare, 206; stockmen, 153-154; see also Pastoral Industry, Reserves, Legislation
Northern Territory Aborigines Benefits Trust Fund, 218
Nulla-Nulla cattle station (W.A.), 151

O'Connell, J., 82-84
O'Leary, 150
On the Origin of Species, 46
Oodnadatta (S.A.), 183
Opium Act; and Aborigines, 114, 116, 137, 153; 117; and Chinese, 120-121; and prostitution, 115, 123
Outlaws, Aboriginal, 27, 37
Ovens River (Vic.), 51, 53
Overheu, 150
Oyster Cove (Tas.), 28

Palmer Gold Fields, 94, 114
Palmerston (N.T.), 114, 120; see also Darwin
Palm Island Aboriginal Settlement, 218
Parap (N.T.), 154
Parker, Edward Stone, 46, 49, 63-65, 70-74
Parramatta (N.S.W.), Congress of Natives and School, 35
Parsons, J. L., 115, 117
Part-Aborigines, 28, 73, 95, 135-136, 167; absorption, 159; adoption, 147-148; advancement, 161, 164; assimilation, 148-149; births to be registered, 117; children, 122, 129-130, 144, 148-149, 156-157, 159-160; (killing of), 113, 116; as domestics, 103, 157, 163; education, 133, 141, 156-157, 157-158, 159-160, 160-164, 166; government policy, 157-158; marriage, 141, 158, 163; morality, 135; octoroons, 158, 159, 161, 163; on pastoral properties, 130; population, 133, 156; (increasing), 103, 115; (1944 census), 191; quadroons, 135, 141, 157, 158, 161, 162, 163; segregation of, 159-160, 163, 182; status, 135, 141; wages, 163; see also Employment
Pastoral Industry, 45, 85-87; cattle killing prosecutions, 125, 127-128; capturing labour, 115, 127; of Central Australia, 156-157; educating Aborigines, 130, 156; and employment, 109-110, 133, 136, 137-138, 155-156, 166-167, 183, 191, 207; (part-Aborigines), 156, 167; housing, 138, 167, 168; hunting grounds, 131, 210; licenses, 63, 93; of Qld, 76, 77, 83, 85, 87-88; rations to workers, 103, 138; sexual exploitation, 63, 86, 93, 111, 115, 130, 155, 157, 167; and stock watering, 64, 66, 86, 121, 130; of

W.A., 103, 107-110, 112, 166-168, 170; wages, 112-113, 155-156, 167-168, 191; see also Employment, Northern Territory
Pastoral Properties, 56, 155-156; for Aborigines, 165; Burwan Creeks, 54; Central Australia, 156-157; Myall Creek, 57; sheep, 86; in Vic., 64
Pastoralists, 85, 87-88, 108-109, 110, 127-128, 157
Paternalism, 62, 227, 228
Pearl Shell Fishing Industry, 122, 123, 176, 204
Penal settlements, (N.S.W.), 13, 17; (Qld), 79
Pentecost River (W.A.), 149
Personal hygiene, 59, 207, 208, 217; in housing, 147, 155; in Tas., 41; see also Health
Perth (W.A.), 108, 206
Phillip, Captain Arthur, 17, 19, 20, 21-22, 23, 24, 27
Phrenology, 170
Pidgin English, 139, 168
Piesse, 107-108
Pilbara (W.A.), 167
Pine Creek (N.T.), 115, 117
Piper, 65
Point Danger (Qld), 76
Point McLeay (S.A.), Aboriginal Settlement, 146-147, 148, 149
Point Pierce (S.A.), Aboriginal Settlement, 147, 148
Poisoning, 79, 153
Police, 90, 95, 111-112, 161; and Aborigines Dept S.A., 147, 149; and apprentices, 122; arresting methods, 124, 127, 152-153; and assimilation, 179; corruption, 125-127; and employment, 173, 201; and E. Kimberley massacre, 150-152; magistrates, 126, 128, 129, 130; mounted, 51, 52, 57; native police and, 82, 83; as protectors, 67, 108; and sexual exploitation, 125-127
Political organisations: Aborigines, 233-234, 235, 237-238; Aborigines/Council, 222-223
Pooncarie (N.S.W.), 208
Population, 117, 133, 192, 235; at Angledool Aborigines Settlement, 171, birth rates, 40, 100, at Botany Bay, 21, 23, census, 1944, 191, (Vic.), 71-72, Central and Northern Australia part-Aborigines, 133, 156, 211; decreasing, 69, 103, 153, 175; infant mortality, 216; of Kimberleys, 161; on pastoral properties, 156, 191; of Qld, 78, 85; rates increasing, 198; of S.A., 235
Port Augusta (S.A.), 234
Port Charles (N.T.), 139
Port Curtis (Qld), 75, 83
Port Jackson (N.S.W.), 19, 20, 22, 95
Port Mackay (Qld), 90

Port Macquarie (N.S.W.), 97
Portland, Duke of, 31
*Portland Gazette*, 68
Port Lincoln Aboriginal Helpers Association, 233
Port Phillip (Vic.), 45, 49, 50, 52-53, 68
Powell, 32
Press, the, 80, 153-154, 205, 207, 209
Presbyterian, see Missions
Prison, see Gaols
Prisoners, Aboriginal, 37, 58; arresting of, 152-153; dormitory detention, 222; on government settlements, 169; massacre of, 149-152; Myall Creek confessions, 58; Native Police, 124; New South Wales, 24, 25, 33, 34, 37, 54; and police corruption, 126; and sexual exploitation, 125, 127; white prisoner police, 59; women as, 63; in W.A., 107, 109, 126, 128; children as, 125, 126; see also Chaining, Police
Proclamations to Aborigines, 33-34; of Outlawry, 36
Prostitution, see Sexual exploitation
Protection, Aboriginal, 117, on government settlements, 228, and inter-tribal fighting, 67-68, in N.S.W., 34, 35, 42; in S.A., 111-114; in towns, 227; in Vic., 63-65; in W.A., 110; not required, 191, 194; see also Legislation
Protection, of White settlers, 27, 31, 34, 36, 37-38, 45, 51-52; by Native Police, 75-84, 93; in Tas., 27; in W.A., 103-104, 106-110
Protectorate, The, 45, 49, 100; cost of, 68, 95, E. S. Parker's report, 63-65; "protectorships", 61
Protectors, 117, 149-153; to be married, 112, 138, 157; opium and alcohol, 120; powers of (N.T.), 140, 162; proposed in S.A., 112, 113, 114; in W.A., 110
Public Health Department, 179
Public Instruction, Department of, (N.S.W.), 179; Education Dept, 180

Quadroons and Octoroons, 135, 148, 159; as domestics, 163; in European institutions, 161; and leprosy, 163-164; marriage of, 158; government policy, 163-164; see also Part-Aborigines, Population
Queensland, 85-97; government settlements, 78, 219; legislation, 84, 219-226, 237; Native Police, 85, 88, 89, 90, 93, 97; (Royal Commission), 75-84; pastoralists, 85, 87, 88, 115; see also Legislation, Reserves

Railways, 143; camps, 90, 160, 161
Rankin, Dame Annebelle, 229

Rapid River (S.A.), 114
Rations, 160-161; depots, 91; on government settlements, 144; (N.S.W.), 172, 176-177; (N.T.), 142; (Qld), 227; (W.A.), 108, 169; in Vic., 64, 65, 99; prisoners, 126-127
Referendum, 187; of 1967, 211, 214, 238
Reformatory (N.T.), 140
Regan, Constable, 150
Reincarnation: Aborigines' beliefs, 73; Tas., 38-39
Remuneration, see Wages
Representation for Aborigines, 45, 49; in a Native State, 164; political organisations, 237, 238
Reserves, 45, 91, 92, 96, 203-204; and assimilation, 204-205; to be established, 85, 95, 116, 165, 175-176, 196; (for nomads), 165, 175-176, 196; equipping of, 144, 148; encroached upon, 92, 98, 203; excision of, 203, 204-205; and legislation, (S.A.), 200-201; (Qld), 222-223; (W.A.), 130-131; (Lands Ordinance), 145-146; local government of, (Qld), 222-223; (S.A.), 233, 234; management of, 144, 220, 222, 223, 224, 225; mining on, 204-206; in N.S.W., 177, 178; in N.T., 116, 118, 141, 143, 146, 203-204; in Qld, 95, 218-219, 221-222, 226; in Vic., 100; W.A., 110, 149-152, 168-169, 170; Tribal Reserve Councils, 222-223, 233-234; see also Settlements
Reward for capture of Aborigines, 37
Richardson, 107, 108
Rights, 35, 45, 49; as British subjects, 19, 32, 104, 199; denied, 52, 85; to water, 64, 66, 86, 121, 130; Qld, 82; Vic., 99; see also Land Rights
Robinvale (N.S.W.), 207, 208
Robinson, George Augustus, 27, 28, 40
Rockhampton (Qld), 75, 85, 88
Roebourne (W.A.), 129; gaol, 126, 128
Roper River (N.T., Qld), 118
Ross, Major R., 22
Roth Report, 121-132; deaths and burials, 131; employment, 121-124; Native Police, 124; Part-Aborigines, 129-130; prisoners, 124-129; Reserves, 130; see also West Australia
Royal Commission (governors' directions), 17, 19, 32
Royal Commissions, (Qld) Native Police, 75-84; (S.A.), On Aborigines, 133, 148-149; (W.A.), On the Natives, 1904, 121-132; 1935, 166-170; Into the Kimberley Massacre, and Police methods, 149-153
Runs, 64; Qld, 76; see Pastoralists, Pastoral Industry
Russel, 55

Sacred sites, 203, 210; and tourism, 217-218; and mining, 231
Salvation Army, 159-160, 161
Sandgate (Qld), 75
Save the Children Fund, 208, 209
Schools, 69, 123, 144; on settlements, 169; and integration, 198; in N.T., 181, 182; mission, 119; Parramatta, 35; Tas., 41, 43-44; Vic., 100; see also Education
Sealers, 42
Segregation, 152, 196; and land rights, 210; of nomads, 165, 197; of part-Aborigines, 158, 159-160, 163, 182
Sepoys, Indian, 58
Servants, domestic, 35, 65, 114, 121, 123, 130, 143, 168; whites as, 37, 54; see also Employment
Settlements, Government, 133, 193, employment on, 156; malnutrition on, 169, 171, 225, 226; N.S.W., 171-174, 178-179, 207-208; N.T., 144; Tas., 40-44; Vic., 100, 207; Qld, 218, 225, 227, 228; S.A., 146-147, 148, 149; W.A., 164, 168, 169, 170; see also Reserves
Settlers: White, 32, 34, 35, 36, 64-65, 82; and defence, 36-37, 45, 107-110; see also Pastoralists
Sexual exploitation, 55, 63, 86, 93, 96; and alcohol and opium, 115, 123; and Asians, 111, 123, 124, 137, 138; children, 115; in N.T., 115, 116, 158, 206; and part-Aborigines, 117, 129-130; and pastoralists, 115, 130, 157, 167; and pearl shell fishing, 123; and police, 125, 127; and sterility, 69, 72, 138; see also Women
Shannon, 80
Sheep, speared, 54, 76, 86; and Aboriginal shepherds, 65
Sholl, R. F., 107
Shooting, of Aborigines, 54-57, 79, 87, 151-152; by Native Police, 76-77; see also Massacre, War
Sievwright, Assistant Protector, 49
Singing, 144
Sirius, 23
Slavery, 58, 232; women as, 111; on pastoral stations, 155
Small pox, 24, 72, 96, 100
Smyth-Brough, 95, 97
Social Welfare services, 235; denied, 180; offered, 202, 205, 206
South Australia, 27, 39, 91; assimilation policy, 232; government control and Aboriginal affairs, 148; part-Aborigines, 135-136; police report, 110-114, 114-118, 183; protectorate boundary, 49; protectors, 112-113, 114; Royal Commission, 133, 146-148; self determination, 231-235; see also Employment
South Creek (N.S.W.), 33

Spencer, W. Baldwin, 119, 133, 136-146
Sport, 202; cricket, 91; on reserves, 234
Squatter, 45, 50, 64, 87; see also Pastoralist
Starvation, see Malnutrition
State governments' responsibilities, 192, 193, 194, 238
Stations, government, see Settlements, Reserves
Status, 59, 60; and British law, 19, 32, 104, 193, 199; in N.S.W., 36, 45, 49; equality with Whites, 61, 89, 195, 199; at Pt Phillip, 52, 65; Qld, 90-91; see also part-Aborigines, Assimilation, Legislation, Segregation
Sterilisation, 215
Sterility, 69, 72, 138
Stirling, E. C., 146-148
Stockmen, 55, 59, 63, 125, 127
Stockenstrom, Captain, 61
Strychnine, 79
Strzelecki, Count, 72
Sturts Creek (W.A.), 130
Sun, The, Melbourne, 207, 209
Superstition, 59, 70, 72, 74; see Tribal Beliefs
Swan Hill (Vic.), 207
Sydney Morning Herald, 153-154 57, 79; Harbour, 23; Past and Present, 94-95; native of, 71
Sydney Morning Herald, 153-154
Syphilis, 113, 169

Tabragalba (Qld), 77
Tasmania, 24, 42; Aborigines of, 27-28, 38-39, 40-44; Native Police, 61
Tatz, Colin, 221
Teachers, 49, 144, 145; see Education
Telegraph station, 89
Telemon River (Qld), 76, 77
Tench, Captain Watkin, 24-25
Tennants Creek (N.T.), 112
Teviot Brook (Qld), 76
Thatching, 21, 22
Thomas, Assistant Protector W., 49
Thomas, Donald, 133, 175-176, 207
Thomson, E. Deas, 52, 63
Thorpe, Mounted Constable, 110-114
Tobacco, 99, 137, 176; for work, 128; for prostitution, 115, 123
Torres Strait Islanders, franchaise for, 198, 199; and legislation, 189, 219-224, 237
Tourism, 217-218
Towns, 95, 142-143; White residents, (and Native Police), 92; (and pastoralists), 104, 108; Aborigines excluded from, 90, 91, 92, 116, 117, 130, 142, 154, 178, 183; (part-Aborigines), 130-131; and begging, 108; numbers employed in, 156; and social advancement, 90; and welfare assistance, 202; and prostitution, 206

Trackers, 38, 63, 81, 124, 150, 152-153; interpreters, 127; and prostitution, 125, 127; see also Native Police.

Tribal Beliefs, 27, 34, 41, 45, 72, 74, 85, 94, 101, 195; practices banned, 34; cannibalism, 22, 96, 99-100; childrens rejection of, 233; clans, 94, 95; communication, 73; communistic, 137, 138, 233; corroborees, 41, 73, 89, 137, 155; democracy, 164; detribalisation, 119, 162, 175, 196; and education, 69-70, 80; and family life, 73, 101; and inter-tribal disputes, 45, 64, 67; and kinship, 72; and marriage, 61, 73, 136; and mutual assistance, 94-95; in N.T., 118; preservation of, 232, 235; reincarnation, 38, 39, 73; and religion, 73, 101; sectional interest, 235; superstition, 59, 70, 72, 74; Tas., 40, 41; traditional enemies, 45, 67, 69-70, 71, 89; in Vic., 67-68, 73; see also Tribes

Tribes, 58, 59, 195; adornment, 19, 41, 73; (markings), 20, 41; artefacts, 15; (theft of), 23, 24, 152; confrontation with settlers, 21, 31, 71; (and cattle killing), 125, 126; courage, 20, 54; in Darwin Compound, 155; Federation of, 164; and game killing, 89; language, 23, 24, 49, 62, 72, 73, 119-233; numbers in, 21, 23, 78, 198, 199; physical appearance of, 23, 71, 98, 118; reserves for, 118, 165, 176; retaliation, 23, 38, 40, 42, 52; revenge, 67, 89, 90; segregation of, 165, 175-176, 197; treachery, 23, 38, 66; threats, 31, 76, 78; territory, 64, 71, 131; Vic., 64, 67, 71, 101; Qld, 78; N.T., 116, 117, 139, 142, 203; weapons, 15, 19, 20, 27, 87; (banned), 34-35; see also Aborigines

Umbilijie, 150
Unaipon, David, 165
United Nations; land rights, 230-231; and discriminatory legislation, 236
United States of America, 131, 153, 209, 215, 232
Upper Dawson River (Qld), 88

Van Dieman's Land, 38, 61; see also Tasmania
Victoria, 46, 64-65, 84, 97; expenditure on Aborigines, 91; missions, 67-68, 91; parliamentary deputation, 98-99; Protectorate, 45, 49, 63-65, 68, 95; settlement, 98, 100
Violet Creek (Vic.) 53; see also Port Phillip

Wages, 90; award, 205, 206, 213; in Darwin, 142; and Native Police, 42; in N.S.W., 173-174, 178; of part-Aborigines, 163; on pastoral properties, 112-113, 155-156, 167-168, 191; prisoners, 129; Qld legislation, 224-225; in S.A., 112, 149; trackers, 124; in W.A., 122, 123, 153; see Employment

Walcott Inlet (W.A.), 170
Waldeck, 108
Wallaby, 90
Wallal (W.A.), 167
War, State of, 45, 50, 52; defeat of Whites, 87; on the frontiers, 27, 50, 52, 85-87; guerilla tactics, 46; courage displayed in, 54; in Qld, 83, 85, 93-94; strategy, 87; see also Tribes, Aborigines
Warangesda mission, 94
Wardship (N.T.), 205; wages, 206
Warrants, 76, 83, 124; see also Prisoners
Wattie Creek (N.T.), 210, 231
Wave Hill (N.T.), 210, 212
Weipa (Qld), 231
Wentworth, 217-218
Wesleyan, 67, 80
Wessel Islands, 204
Western Australia, 103, 123-124; deaths and burials, 131; education in, 80, 133; employment in, 105, 121-124, 167-168, 169-170; legislation of, 127, 128, 184-185, 237; Native Police of, 124; Northern region, 131; North-West, 123-124, 126, 130; pastoralists of, 103, 107-110, 112, 164, 166-168, 170; pearl shell fishing, 122-124; reserves, 110, 149-152, 168-169; Royal Commissions, (into Conditions of the Natives, 1904), 121-132; (on Aborigines, 1935), 166-170; (into the Killing and Burning of Bodies of Aborigines in East Kimberley, and into Police Methods when Effecting Arrest, 1928), 149-153
Wheeler, Lieutenant F., 75-78
White, Major, 33
White Australia Policy, 175
Whitlam, E. G., 211-214, 236-237
Whyalla Aborigines Association (S.A.), 233
Witnesses, 125, 127, 128, 150; see also Chaining
Wickham, Captain, 79
Wilkinson, 228
Williams District (W.A.), 108
Wills, 88
Windsor (N.S.W.), 36
Women, Aboriginal, 20, 28, 32, 41, 77, 79; abducted, 63, 89, 93, 111, 113; abandoned, 95; abortion, 138; and Asians, 111, 123, 124, 137, 138; betrothed, 73; chained, 125, 127, 150; child bearing, 69, 72; cotton picking, 69; Council of Aboriginal Women,

233; in Darwin, 155; in Kimberley massacre, 150, 151, 152; on missions, 67; at Myall Creek massacre, 54-55; and part-Aboriginal children, 113, 129, 148; on pastoral properties, 63, 156-157, 168; rations for, 177; starved, 113; as witnesses, 125, 127, 128, 150; see also Sexual Exploitation, Employment

Women, White, 156-157

World War Two, 182, 183, 184; employment during, 183

Wyndham (W.A.), 125, 126, 128, 149, 150, 151, 153

Yaldwyn, 54

Yass (N.S.W.), 52

Yirrkala Reserve (N.T.), 187; land excision, 203; social welfare payments on, 206; see also Land Rights